THE NEW YORK ACADEMY OF SCIENCES

Statement of Purpose

Science is expanding, and with it our vision of the universe. Although this new and constantly changing view may not always give us comfort, it does have the virtue of truth according to our most effective resources for acquiring knowledge. No philosophy, moral outlook, or religion can be inconsistent with the findings of science and hope to endure among educated people.

A few years ago, as part of its charge to bring new scientific information to the public, The New York Academy of Sciences launched a project to help scientists and science writers get their books published for a popular audience. Anyone who has written a book on a complex subject in the sciences has learned that it is not easy to communicate to the lay reader the excitement and enthusiasm of discovery. Science books can become technically obscure, or drift off into superficiality. Finding the balance between scientific exposition and narrative literature is a major challenge, and the goal of this project.

HEINZ R. PAGELS
Executive Director
New York Academy of Sciences

A COMPLETE ILLUSTRATED GUIDE
WRITTEN AND DRAWN. BY

GREGORY S. PAUL

PREDATORY

OF

SIMON AND SCHUSTER
NEW YORK • LONDON • TORONTO • SYDNEY • TOKYO

DINOSAURS
THE WORLD

A NEW YORK ACADEMY OF SCIENCES BOOK

SIMON AND SCHUSTER
Simon & Schuster Building
Rockefeller Center
1230 Avenue of the Americas
New York, New York 10020

10 9 8 7 6 5 4 3 2 1

Library of Congress Cataloging in Publication
Data

Paul, Gregory S.
    Predatory dinosaurs of the world / written and
illustrated by Gregory Paul.
        p.   cm.
    "A New York Academy of Sciences book."
    Bibliography: p.
    Includes index.
    ISBN 0-671-61946-2
    1. Dinosaurs.   2. Predatory animals.   I. Title.
QE862.D5P38   1988   88-23052
567.9'1—dc19   CIP

To my Great-Aunt, Laurel Dewey,
who taught me that Tyrannosaurus
is pronounced ty-ran-no-saurus, not try-an-osaurus,
and many other things about dinosaurs and nature

CONTENTS

PREFACE

This book got its start about seven years ago when Robert Bakker—the progressive dinosaurologist I studied with for many years—suggested that I draw up illustrations of some predatory dinosaur skeletons. About the same time, I started looking into the problem of bird origins, which I believed was tied to dinosaurs. One thing led to another and after a while I realized I had enough material available to put together a book on the dinosaurian meat eaters. So I decided to do something that has never been done before. Most dinosaur books are general books. No one has done a volume tuned to a particular group, examining each species in turn. This is rather odd: There are books on Allied fighter aircraft of World War II, and on waterfowl of North America; why not one on predaceous dinosaurs? Indeed, it is my hope that this will be the first in a series of books on the groups of animals related to dinosaurs—the archosaurs. The herbivorous dinosaurs might make up the next two or three volumes—there are a lot more herbivorous dinosaurs than predatory ones—then one on the dinosaur's ancestors, the primitive thecodonts and crocodilians, another on the flying pterosaurs, and perhaps last the fossil birds.

This is my first book, and in it I have tried to do two things, one having to do with the text, the other with the illustrations. Regarding the first, there have been a few good recent books on dinosaurs, but only a very very few. Most dinosaur books commit the ultimate sin—they are boring. Dinosaurs were *not* boring, and one can only make them so via ignorance. Which brings us to the next point: dinosaur books are usually inaccurate. These twin faults often—not always, but often—result when books are written by nonscientists who, unfamiliar with dinosaurology, refer to previous books on the subject as primary sources—sources that themselves either were written by nonprofessionals that had done the same thing, or were dated and obsolete. Dinosaurology has undergone a complete revolution, and works from the sixties are now more misleading than informative. The consequences of all this have been a repetitive series of books on the subject, parroting ad nauseum what no one who actually works on the creatures believes anymore. New ideas may be explored, but in a superficial manner that denies the reader an understanding of dinosaur biology in its whole. And even some of the books that explore the new dinosaur concepts are marred by sloppy thinking that does more harm to the field than good.

Other problems with dinosaur texts stem from the misuse or

misunderstanding of modern biology. Recent decades have seen an explosion in field biology, the observations of living animals in their wild habitats. The same has occurred in biomechanics, the study of how animals work. A knowledge of modern biology is vital for understanding extinct animals. Sadly, a number of false ideas have become established as truisms in the popular science oriented toward publications and media. Dinosaurology especially seems stuck with some out-of-date ideas: that predators never kill for pleasure, for instance, or that land animals can scavenge for a living, or that big animals cannot run fast and that they overheat in hot climates. The innocent and professional alike often pick up these items, and into their books they go.

As for dinosaur illustrations, there is no way to express how poor is the accuracy and workmanship of most. It is very upsetting, for people are rendering what I think of as Earth history's most wonderful beasts insipidly, and dinosaurs were not insipid. Most notorious of all are "ballon" dinosaur pictures, so called because they most resemble the floats in the Macy's Thanksgiving Day Parade. Again, errors committed by dinosaur artists of decades past are repeated, even emphasized. I have a big advantage here, being a professional paleontologist who can illustrate what I think. Those dinosaurologists who cannot draw often expend much frustration trying to get artists to translate their work into two dimensions. The problem is exacerbated by the professional neglect dinosaur illustrations often receive, as if drawing dinosaurs is somehow less important than studying them. This attitude can be seen in many book reviews which, after a lengthy critique of the text, pass over the illustrations with the comment that they are informative and helpful, or "worth the price of the book." One of my hopes is that this volume will help set a new standard for dinosaur illustrations.

So, I have tried to be different in this work. Certainly the ideas about dinosaurs presented herein are up to date. Many are controversial, and I have made no attempt to present a neutral position—others can do that. I have tried to warn the reader what are matters in dispute. Another thing I have done is admit that there is no good answer to a question, when there is none. All too often readers are given the impression that a paleobiological problem has been solved when it has not. It is my hope that the concept of predatory dinosaur biology detailed in this book forms a logical whole. I asked myself whether what is said here is the sort of thing I would like to see in a book on whales, or aircraft

—things I am interested in but lack professional knowledge of. Of course, some of the concepts could not be defended in detail —that is for technical works. However, much of the information should be useful for the professional. Indeed, a new scheme for classifying and naming predatory dinosaurs is presented. I felt justified in doing this because the traditional system is universally considered obsolete, and a new scheme has yet to replace it. To help both the expert and enthusiast alike, an extensive bibliography is included. By no means is this a definitive work. As time goes on and the field's body of knowledge grows, it will become a good idea to update this volume, so criticisms and notices of omissions will be most appreciated.

Another key aim of this book is to present those who know and love dinosaurs with something they have never had before: skeletal restorations of every predatory dinosaur species for which a restoration can be done. These are very useful to artists, and have been done to a consistent format to make comparing them to one another easier. I hope to do the same for all archosaurs in subsequent volumes. As for the full life restorations, the idea is to use art to translate scientific thoughts and concepts into visual images. Besides, dinosaurs look neat.

This book was made possible by a series of chances. When I first started to consider it seriously, Steven Stanley at the Johns Hopkins Department of Earth and Planetary Sciences suggested I talk to Horace Judson down the hall. He suggested submitting a proposal to the New York Academy of Sciences book project, "The Scientific Prospect," under Heinz Pagels. This I did, and my proposal was accepted. The Academy arranged for an agent, John Brockman, who in turn arranged for a publisher, Simon & Schuster. There Alice Mayhew, Erika Goldman, Ursula Obst, George Hodgman, Veronica Johnson, and others provided excellent editing advice. Many thanks to all these people for their help and patience, and for allowing this book to be very much what I had originally hoped.

As for the science behind this book, first thanks go to Robert Bakker and our years of co-work and discussion when he was at the Department of Earth and Planetary Sciences at Johns Hopkins. Many of his teachings on dinosaurs have found their way into this volume. Many thanks also go to Kenneth Carpenter for his long co-work and exchanges, especially on protobirds, and information on many specimens. Many other people have provided discussion, data, and other assistance and grateful thanks are due them all. Philip Currie of the Tyrrell Museum in Alberta has supplied much hospitality and information on Canadian dinosaurs; Donald Brinkman at the same institution has been helpful, too. Dale Russell at the National Museum of Canada and Chris McGowen of the Royal Ontario Museum have also told me much about their dinosaurs. Very helpful with protobirds were John Ostrom and Bob Allen of Yale, who provided access to and data on the collections under their care. Alick Walker's correspondence on *Archaeopteryx* was always enlightening. Gunter Viohl at the Jura Museum in Bavaria, Herman Jaeger at Berlin's Humboldt Museum für Naturkunde, and Alan Charig and Angela Milner at the British Museum (Natural History) were helpful and hospitable when I was examining the *Archaeopteryx* specimens in their care. Angela Milner also sent information on the theropods in her musuem. Philip Powell at the Oxford University Museum supplied information on megalosaurs and other British theropods; Philippe Taquet in Paris helped out on the French collections. Charles Schaff helped with the protobirds and early dinosaurs in the Harvard collection. Sankar Chatterjee was informative about his new birdlike dinosaur, "Protoavis." On theropods and their footprints, James Farlow, Hartmut Haubold, and Paul Olsen provided help. On early theropods, Edwin Colbert, the dean of dinosaur paleontology, has been helpful, as have Tim Rowe and Alan McCrady. Of much assistance over many years at the United States National Museum, alias the Smithsonian, have been Nicholas Hotton, Michael Brett-Surman, and Arnold Lewis, and more recently Hans-Dieter Sues. Halszka Osmolska and Teresa Maryanska have been hospitable and most informative, especially during my visit to Warsaw in 1981. S. Kurzanov assisted from Moscow on protobirds. Further east, Masahiro Tanimoto in Japan has fed me facts on Asian dinosaurs I could not have obtained otherwise. During a visit to the United States, Dong Zhiming told me many things about Chinese theropods. From the south, José Bonaparte, Fernando Novas, and Andrea Arcucci have sent data on Argentinian dinosaurs. And from down under, Ralph Molnar has supplied information on Australian species. Concerning allosaurs, ceratosaurs, and other big theropods, James Madsen, Wann Langston, and Jeff Pittman have helped. Information on the new Cretaceous theropods and birds of Alabama came from Daniel Womechel and James Lamb. For facts on early birds, Andrei Elzanowski, Peter Houde, and Storrs Olson at the United States National Museum have been vital sources. Guy Leahy's discussions on dinosaur biology have been informative, as have Thomas MacMahon's on animal locomotion and Daniel Costanzo's on the more philosophical aspects of dinosaurology. Lewis Hurxthal provided much fascinating data from his ostrich studies. Questions about dinosaur taxonomy and the Russian literature often ended up in George Olshevsky's mail, and Donald Glut has been helpful too. As for dinosaur art, Stephen and Sylvia Czerkas, Mark Hallett, John Gurchie, and Doug Henderson have been inspiring colleagues. In building the full-size *Dilophosaurus,* Donald Baird, Richard Rush, and Rodger Walshlager were great fun. Many of the illustrations were reproduced at Monotype Composition Company in Baltimore. This is not a complete list, and I apologize to those I have inadvertently left off. To everyone, thank you again.

The above and other paleontologists' works are mentioned throughout the text. Following the premise that what people do is more important than where they do it from, I list their studies in the bibliography rather than citing their places of work.

GREGORY S. PAUL
Baltimore, Maryland
1988

PART ONE
THE LIFE AND EVOLUTION OF PREDATORY DINOSAURS

1

GETTING TO KNOW PREDATORY DINOSAURS

If Dorothy Gale had been swept by the whirlwind to some Mesozoic glade instead of to the Haunted Forest of Oz, she might have observed, "Lions and tigers and bears are one thing, but these predatory dinosaurs are way out of hand!"

The biggest living terrestrial predator, the Siberian tiger, at about a third of a metric ton (300 kg) pales in comparison to the biggest of the meat-eating dinosaurs, which reached 5 to perhaps 20 metric tons—the size of elephants and bigger. But while elephants cannot run, the biggest predatory dinosaurs probably ran as fast as horses, and they hunted herbivores that themselves were as big as or bigger than elephants. There has never been anything like *Allosaurus, Tyrannosaurus,* and their cousins. Of course, not all predatory dinosaurs were giants; the smallest, *Lagosuchus,* was only the size of a weasel.

How would we think and feel about predatory dinosaurs if they were alive today? Humans have long felt antipathy toward carnivores, our competitors for scarce protein. But our feelings are somewhat mollified by the attractive qualities we see in them. For all their size and power, lions remind us of the little creatures that we like to have curl up in our laps and purr as we stroke them. Likewise, noble wolves recall our canine pets. Cats and dogs make good companions because they are intelligent and responsive to our commands, and their supple furry bodies make them pleasing to touch and play with. And, very importantly, they are house-trainable. Their forward-facing eyes remind us of ourselves.

However, even small predaceous dinosaurs would have had no such advantage. None were brainy enough to be companionable or house-trainable; in fact, they would always be a danger to their owners. Their stiff, perhaps feathery bodies were not what one would care to have sleep at the foot of the bed. The reptilian-faced giants that were the big predatory dinosaurs would truly be horrible and terrifying. We might admire their size and power, much as many are fascinated with war and its machines, but we would not like them. Their images in literature and music would be demonic and powerful—monsters to be feared and destroyed, yet emulated at the same time.

As interesting as it is to imagine dinosaurs being alive in modern times, it is just as interesting that, in a sense, predatory dinosaurs really *are* still with us—and in a form we find both familiar and often pleasing—for birds are direct descendants of predatory dinosaurs. And much as predatory dinosaurs were the

1-1
Good times in the Jurassic. A typical predatory dinosaur in size and shape was the 1.5-tonne theropod Allosaurus atrox. *Pack feeding allowed a carcass to be better defended against intruders, and to be finished before it rotted. These animals' bellies are bloated, and the youngsters are shown partly covered in down feathers. Fernlike cycads and umbrella-shaped araucarian conifers make up part of the flora.*

chief land animals of their time, predaceous birds are the main killers of mammals and reptiles in many places.

"Lions and tigers and bears" and the fantasy animals of Oz and science fiction are fun, but, as a paleontologist, I prefer the stranger than fiction animals of the past. Paleontology, the study of fossil organisms, is, to me, a form of time travel. Dinosaur bones and the sediments they are preserved in are relics of past events. One of the fine things about paleo is that all you need is transportation, tents, a few tools, one person who can cook, the proper paleontological training, and there you are traveling back in time 145 million years.

Predatory dinosaurs lived from about 235 to 65 million years ago—give or take a million here and there—during the Mesozoic Era (see the time chart on pages 224-225). The Mesozoic is split into the three periods. About halfway through the first period of the Era—the Triassic, which lasted from 248 to 213 million years before the present (MYBP)—the first dinosaurs showed up, and they had to get along with a number of nondinosaurian predators. By the second period, the Jurassic (213–144 MYBP), predatory dinosaurs had become the sole big killers. The same was true through the third, the Cretaceous Period (144–65 MYBP), which also saw the first flourishing of birds. Dinosaurs were extinguished at the end of the Mesozoic Era, and the following era—the Cenozoic—was the age of mammals. Compared to the briefness of our civilization, the span of predatory dinosaur existence appears vast. But dinosaurs are recent and short-lived compared to the Earth itself, which is celebrating its 4.5 billionth or so birthday.

1-2
The Great One. At 6 to 12 tonnes, Tyrannosaurus rex *combined the size of an African elephant and the speed of a tiger with unprecedented firepower. The* T. rex *is scaled to the size of the largest known specimen; the Siberian tiger and elephant are exceptionally large males at 300 kg and 7.5 tonnes, respectively.*

1-3
The sickle-clawed theropod Velociraptor antirrhopus in a fast run. The 1960s discovery of this obviously agile and birdlike predatory dinosaur helped spur the dinosaur revival we are enjoying today. Like a bird, Velociraptor could tightly fold its forelimbs.

The word *dinosaur* comes from the Greek for "terrible lizard," but despite their name, dinosaurs are not really lizards at all. Rather, they are members of the animal group called archosaurs. Living archosaurs are crocodilians and birds. The extinct flying "reptiles" or pterosaurs, which flew on batlike wings, are also in this bunch. All archosaurs descended from the earliest archosaur group, the rather crocodile-like thecodonts of the Triassic Period. Usually, archosaurs are considered reptiles, but some of us progressive types think they are too different from reptiles to be called that. Hence, the reader will find that I never refer to dinosaurs as reptiles, but as archosaurs.

Predatory dinosaurs came in three basic types—paleodinosaurs, herreravians, and theropods. The first two, which were four-toed, were limited in success. The theropods, which had three toes, were much more numerous and longer lasting; among the better known genera are *Tyrannosaurus, Allosaurus, Coelophysis, Velociraptor,* and *Ornithomimus.* Sporting a birdlike

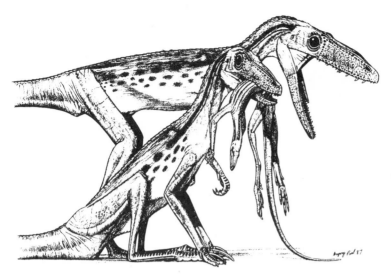

1-4
The little Argentinian paleodino-
saur Lewisuchus admixtus *has*
picked up its yet smaller cousin
Lagosuchus talampayensis. *These*
Middle Triassic predators are
among the very first of the known
dinosaurs. They may already
have been feathered, although a
thin band of armor ran down
their backs.

motif, this great group lasted from the Triassic Period to the end of the Mesozoic. Although they varied much in size and detail, they were all quite uniform and unmistakable in basic design. Their heads were deep and narrow, and while most were toothed predators, a few were beaked herbivores. Their necks were strongly S-curved, and their short trunks were counterbalanced by long tails. They were always bipedal, and had birdlike hind limbs with flexed knees and drumstick shanks. In particular, take note of the birdlike hind foot, with its three load-bearing toes. Small species may have been feathered, big ones scaled, and all were marked by hornlets and ridges on their heads.

The key word here is *birdlike*. If not for the long tail, one might mistake a theropod for a big, toothy, marauding bird in the dark. That theropods are birdlike is logical, since birds are their closest living relatives. Remember that next time you eat a drumstick or scramble some eggs.

Jurassic *Archaeopteryx,* often considered the first bird, is in most regards a theropod dinosaur, albeit a flying one. And some theropods are even more birdlike than *Archaeopteryx.* It is extraordinary that when one looks at a jewel hummingbird, hovering as it sips nectar, one is seeing a true relative of *Tyrannosaurus rex.* It is a wonderful thing, and a superb example of what random genetic mutations guided by selective forces can do.

The relationship between theropods and birds is so close that birds can be considered flying theropods, and theropods can in turn be thought of as early terrestrial birds. This may be true in the formal, literal sense. A good argument can be made that birds should be classified as dinosaurs, just as the flying bats are considered mammals. So if someone points to a sparrow and says, "Oh, what a nice little dinosaur," they are quite in line with the latest thinking.

Dinosaurology is often an exasperating field of study, because so much of the past is buried beyond our reach. I have stood on the sediments of a dinosaur-bearing formation and felt palpable frustration at the knowledge that here and there, just a few yards underground, there are remains of amazing beasts that will not be uncovered by erosion for another thousand years. Since we cannot dig up an entire formation, we must go looking for the telltale scraps that have come to the surface. Usually, it's hot, *very* hot during a dig, and the insects can make it hard to appreciate the beauty of the badlands. Most remains are just bits and pieces, but these can tell us a lot. One claw of a distinctive sickle shape can show us that a certain kind of small killer lived at that place; a tooth can mean a tyrannosaur.

And then there are those spectacular sunsets, with a cool breeze whipping by, that top off the days that something really good turns up. For every once in a while the few pieces of bone lead to a nearly complete skeleton, or to a bone bed thick with dinosaur remains.

Predatory dinosaurs have been found on every continent— even, just recently, some bits in Antarctica. The first properly recognized predatory dinosaur was *Megalosaurus* of Jurassic

1-5
A black swan. All birds are direct descendants of small theropods, and as such are truly flying dinosaurs—even regal birds like this one.

England, published by the Reverend William Buckland in 1824. The fragmentary remains were enough to show only its great size, not its shape. A series of finds from Bavaria in the mid 1800s shed much light on the nature of theropods and birds. Of those small *Compsognathus* was the first complete theropod skeleton to be found, and, as we shall see, the discovery of *Archaeopteryx* was one of the most important in all science.

Things really began to break loose in the 1800s, with the opening of the Western Territories of North America to paleobiologists—most especially Othniel Marsh and Edward Drinker Cope. Engaged in a bitter feud—almost from the beginning of their paleontological careers—they competed in opened multiple quarries in the Late Jurassic Morrison Formation, quarries with wonderful names like Bone Cabin and Freeze Out Hills. From them came good skeletons of big *Allosaurus,* horned *Ceratosaurus,* and small *Ornitholestes*. The finding of these new dinosaur skeletons had two effects. First, dinosaurs became immensely and permanently popular with the American public, which still associates them with the frontier days. Second, the debate on the evolutionary significance of dinosaurs was intensified, with some workers suggesting that dinosaurs were ancestral to birds and warm-blooded.

By the late 1800s and through the 1920s, when the Great Depression and World War II put a damper on things, dinosaurs were being discovered in abundance in other formations in western North America, formations with more fantastic names: Lance, Hell Creek, Two Medicine, Oldman, and others. These were largely Late Cretaceous forms, among them gigantic *Tyrannosaurus,* its somewhat smaller relative *Albertosaurus,* the ostrich-mimicking *Ornithomimus,* and sickle-clawed *Dromaeosaurus*.

In a more exotic locale, Mongolia, the famous American Museum Expeditions of the twenties led by Roy Chapman Andrews found three small Late Cretaceous theropods, ones that would later become important to the question of bird origins: sickle-clawed *Velociraptor* and *Troodon,* and the very bizarre head-crested *Oviraptor*.

By the 1930s, dinosaurology had another problem besides the Depression. Dinosaurs had become so popular with the public that the subject had taken on something of a circus air, and paleontologists shied away from studying the creatures. They became reptilian curiosities, good for drawing crowds into the

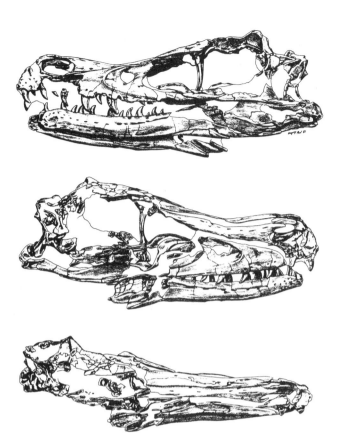

1-6
The skull, as preserved, of the original or type specimen of Velociraptor mongoliensis *AMNH 6515, discovered by the American Museum expeditions to Mongolia in 1922. It is remains like these that tell us about dinosaur anatomy and action.*

museum, but evolutionary dead ends of little theoretical importance. Besides, the number of dinosaur skeletons that can be found and studied is always limited. A comparable amount of work can produce dozens of fossil mammal remains, or tens of thousands of fossil invertebrates. In an era when mathematical studies of large populations are preeminent, this is an important reason why only a few dozen people study dinosaurs full-time.

The beginnings of today's dinosaur renaissance can be traced to the mid-sixties, when John Ostrom's digs in the mid-Cretaceous of Montana found examples of a new species of *Velociraptor*. The remains revealed a strikingly birdlike, agile, and probably warm-blooded dinosaur. Ostrom also reexamined the *Archaeopteryx* specimens, and showed that they were theropods as well as early birds. The controversy surrounding these ideas did much good for dinosaurology; in fact, of the one hundred two species detailed in this book, forty-three were described after 1965 (although some of the latter remains were found before this date). Great gaps are being closed by these new finds. In particular, we finally have good mid/late Jurassic theropods, and know something about how the very first predatory dinosaurs looked.

Indeed, we are just beginning to understand what the dinosaurs really were. The view in vogue only two decades ago—that dinosaurs were slow, sluggish, dull-witted reptilian creatures—is well out of favor now. Otherwise, almost everything is in dispute. Should dinosaurs be considered reptiles, or do they form a new group with birds? Were predatory dinosaurs warm- or cold-blooded, or both? Were the giant tyrannosaurs walkers like elephants, or runners like ostriches? Theories abound, and if you want to get on the evening news, just come up with a new idea on what killed them off.

In this book, I offer very strong views on what dinosaurs were and what they did, and the reader should know that many will disagree with my conclusions. Things probably will settle down eventually; most revolutions gradually taper off into uneasy consensus, at least until the next revolution. But science does, on occasion, get closer to the truth. We do know nowadays that the earth revolves around the sun, not the reverse. Likewise, dinosaur physiology will probably be pinned down someday, and everyone will look back at the eighties and shake their heads at whoever turned out to be wrong. In any case, I am very upset at how little time life gives one to work on the beasts. There is so much to be done, and it is such fun doing it.

Part II of this book is an illustrated catalog of all important predatory dinosaurs known to date. It includes the first published modern skeletal restorations of such basic theropods as *Allosaurus, Albertosaurus,* and *Coelophysis.* But I wish to bring you more than just dry portraits of these animals. When I imagine dinosaurs, it is like watching a documentary on African wildlife. There is a feeling of reality to it, with intricate details, color, dust in the air, and patterns of sunlight. In Part I, I will try to supply you with the information that you need to do the same. The metabolics of dinosaurs are explored in Chapter 7, and how surprisingly fast they may have moved is discussed in Chapter 6. The basics of dinosaur anatomy are to be found in Chapter 4, their footprints are looked over in 5. Chapter 3 examines who lived where and when, and asks some intriguing questions about predatory dinosaur evolution. Who was related to whom is the subject of Chapter 8, while 9 tells how some theropods may have turned into birds. But first, let us begin by examining the features that made predaceous dinosaurs the arch hunters and killers that they were.

2

LIFE-STYLES OF THE BIG AND POWERFUL, AND THE SMALL AND FIERCE TOO

Crouched down in a flat-footed stalk, the *Tyrannosaurus rex* cranes its neck to peer around the sable palm. Yes, the *Triceratops* are still there, up wind, quite unaware of her presence, or of her cohorts as they slowly come up from behind. It's a hot day, but her hollow belly growls—got to fill it up. That one *Triceratops* looks a tad lame, it's a good target.

The *T. rex* is a monster of ten tonnes, her frightful face adorned with hornlets and scales and a red stripe before the eyes. Mottled green and brown camouflage makes her look like a NATO tank lurking in the brush. Suddenly she and her consorts launch themselves into a horse-speed run, panicking the rhino-like, elephant-sized *Triceratops* into a galloping stampede that exposes their vulnerable rear ends to attack—just the way the *T. rex* want it. The tyrannosaur's 5-foot-long jaws and 7-inch teeth rip open a gaping hole in the herbivore's belly, spilling some of its moist guts onto the dusty ground. Satisfied with its work, the *T. rex* slowly trots down to a halt. Another couple of *T. rex* snap at one another in a tiff over who gets the intestines, one asserts themselves and gobbles them down. The theropods can wait to deliver the coup de grace to the prey. Even though it is hobbling away, there is no reason to risk entanglement with its horns. Let its life bleed away. Finally, dazed and wobbly, *Triceratops* slows, its great wound glistening in the sun, and the tyrannosaurs judge that things are safe enough. The pack of titans moves in, yanking, pulling, slicing, and gorging, squabbling over bits—the biggest gets the most. One of the grown-ups leads in the youngsters. Having been hiding in the bush, they now chirp in excitement as they join in the feast.

Not much is left of the *Triceratops,* and its consumers drift off. Some big-eyed sickle-claws, about the size of jackals and of the same inclinations, come up and pick at the carcass. They ignore the flies swarming around the remains. Feathers make them very birdy in looks. So do their jerky, nervous motions; they fear return of the tyrannosaurs. They need not worry; the drowsy *T. rex* are napping as they digest their meal.

Predatory dinosaurs have been gone for 650,000 centuries, but that does not stop us from painting such pictures of how they made a living—how they hunted, how they spent their spare time, their social behavior, reproduction, and the like.[1] We are able to do so by making deductions based on what we know about their structure and on the fossil records. In describing the life-styles of the predatory dinosaurs, I am going to work from a basic assumption that the dinosaurs were fully warm-blooded in the way birds and mammals are. As I explain in Chapter 7, I do not think the alternative physiologies are viable ones.

Let us begin with the one feature that made most predatory dinosaurs what they were—killers—and that is their teeth. (The habits of the toothless predators—ostrich-mimics, oviraptors, and avimimids—are investigated in Part II, page 358). Most typical theropods had long rows of sharp teeth. This tells us that they were predators—for herbivores simply do not have such teeth. The fact that they were predators in turn tells us something less obvious: that theropods enjoyed much more leisure time than do most humans, and spent most of it asleep. This is typical

2-1

Tyrannosaurus rex was far from a mere scavenger; the greatest dino-saurian battles were between packs of this incredibly powerful theropod and the equally huge herbivore, Triceratops horridus. The Triceratops culled out from its companions here is in deadly trouble. Surprised and attacked from the rear, it has not had time to gallop to safety or wheel about and face down its attackers with horns and beak. For the results of the attack, see Figure 2-5.

2-2
A Velociraptor mongoliensis *pair doing what large predators always have been very good at, spending time lazing and sleeping. Hunting takes up only a little of their day, and the bellies of these theropods are still partly full from their last meal.*

of medium sized and big predators—lions and even house cats for that matter spend up to twenty hours a day napping. Predators, especially those that kill big game, go out and kill something, eat it in one quick sitting, and then sleep it off until they are hungry again. As detailed in Appendix A, big predators can go for days or, in the case of giants, even weeks between meals. This is quite unlike herbivores, which must spend long hours nipping at and chewing large quantities of fodder. In fact, sleeping when there is nothing else to do has an important advantage. Bedding down helps keep an animal out of sight and out of trouble. This is especially true for small species and the juveniles of big ones, for big predators are very happy to attack and consume smaller predators.

But whatever amount of time they spent lazing about, predatory dinosaurs were built for those briefer but much more intense and interesting times—when they went off to kill and eat other animals. Killing big animals requires firepower, and in animals such power can only come from muscles. Mammalian carnivores of today have oversized neck muscles which give them tremendous biting power, something our household pets can demonstrate. Feel the neck muscles of a big dog and compare them to your own. Likewise, the heads of most predaceous dinosaurs were packed with powerful jaw-closing muscles (see Figure 4-2, page 90), and their neck muscles were well developed, further increasing the available killing power.

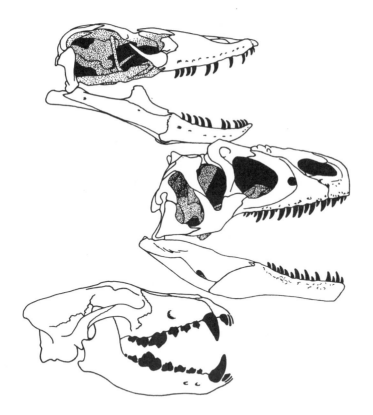

2-3
The long, uniform tooth rows and lightly built skulls of lizards such as the Komodo monitor and the theropod Allosaurus atrox are quite different from the special-ized teeth and solidly constructed skulls of big mammalian carni-vores like the wolf.

An obvious difference between a carnivorous mammal and a theropod is seen in the form and function of the teeth. Predatory dinosaur teeth were not arrayed in the short sets of molars, ca-nines, and incisors seen in modern cats and dogs (Figure 2-3). Dogs' big, sharp, conical canines are used to puncture flesh; ca-nids and hyenas like to grab on to various parts of big prey and pull; weasels and cats deliver precision bites to vulnerable areas such as the base of the skull or the throat, and then use their complex slicing molars to cut up the meat. The predatory dino-saur's long rows of uniform, curved, flattened, serrated blades were very different, more akin to those of the modern predatory lizard. (The closest mammalian analogues were the extinct saber-toothed cats, which, recent research indicates, used a peculiar pinch-and-slash biting action.[2]) The key point is that most pre-daceous dinosaurs were neither grabbers nor precision biters. The long, irregular tooth rows of the theropods were not suitable for precision work, and their bladelike teeth would have tended to slice or cut through the flesh of their prey rather than to hold tight. In fact, the serrations, which were on the keels on the front

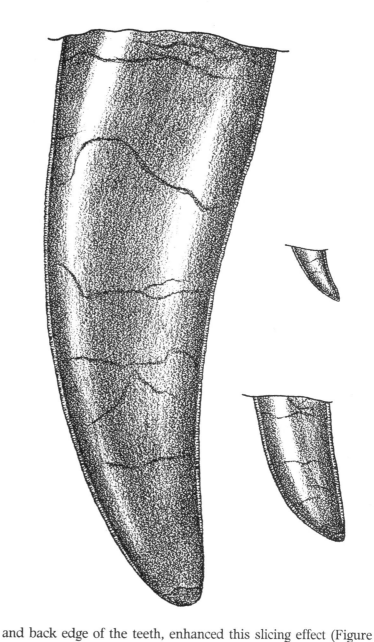

2-4
The crown at natural size of a great mid-row tooth from a 6-tonne Tyrannosaurus rex, *and the same from a 1.5-tonne* Allosaurus atrox *and a 50-kg* Velociraptor antirrhopus. *Such blades were deadly killing tools in the larger species, able to mortally wound animals of elephant size and bigger. Slicing up carcasses and chewing on bones were secondary uses. Note the serrations running down the front and back edges of the tooth, and that the tips are worn off from wear.*

and back edge of the teeth, enhanced this slicing effect (Figure 2-4). A bit of often-repeated nonsense is that these teeth were as sharp-edged and pointed as steak knives. Actually, one can run one's finger hard down the serrations with no adverse effects. But, powered by big jaw and neck muscles, the slicing performance of these tooth rows was potent[3] (see Figure 2-1, and Figure 4-5, page 93). The wounds they inflicted would have bled heavily and readily become infected. Limb muscles could have been sliced, crippling their prey. Or the belly could have been disemboweled—just as the giant Komodo monitors of modern day Indonesia will cut open the bellies of oxen and deer.

The premaxillary teeth in the snout tip of *Tyrannosaurus rex* and its relatives had a somewhat different action. In many theropods these teeth were more D-shaped in cross section than the rest of the teeth, and they tended to cut out a small scoop of flesh (Figure 2-5). In tyrannosaurs the premaxillary teeth were fully D-shaped in cross section, with the flat of the D facing inward (Figure 2-5). Such teeth did not slice; instead, they cut out, like a trowel in dirt, or a cookie cutter. These D-cross-sectioned teeth were themselves arranged in an exceptionally broad, D-shaped, semicircular array at the front of the upper jaw, and were backed by slicing teeth behind them. They would have scooped out a long, deep chunk of flesh, leaving a great, trough-shaped hemorrhaging hole in the hapless victim's side[4] (Figures 2-1 and 2-5)— a diabolically nasty wound, and one rather like those made by some modern sharks.

There were exceptions to this slicing and punching-out way of predation. Some small theropods, such as *Ornitholestes,* had more conical teeth that were built for puncturing and grabbing prey. This suggests they concentrated on picking up small animals, insects, and fish.[5] Of course, the blade-toothed dinosaurs would have picked up small prey also; just as wolves will hunt field mice, bigger theropods might nibble on the larger lizards and mammals they came across. Indeed, the early and most primitive theropods seem to have been well equipped for both small- and big-game hunting, having conical teeth up front and big blades aft.

I am amazed and perplexed at continuing claims that the big theropods were not true predators, but scavengers instead.[6] This unfortunate idea seems to have started in 1917 with Lawrence Lambe's observation that the teeth of big theropods did not show signs of wear near their tips. He thought this meant they fed strictly on soft rotting meat. However, in dinosaurs the teeth were continually and rapidly replaced, like in lizards and crocs, and this kept *most* of the working teeth new and unworn. I say most, because theropod teeth in fact are commonly worn down (see Figure 2-4). A corollary belief is that large theropods were too big and too slow to actively hunt—a rather strange observation since those who argue big theropods were slow usually think that the herbivorous dinosaurs were even slower! In reality, the the-

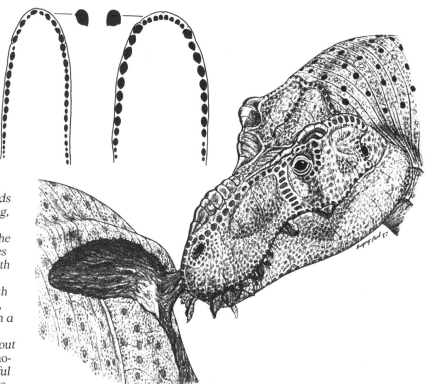

2-5
The tooth rows of most theropods were slicing organs that left long, raking wounds. In Allosaurus atrox (left inset), for instance, the teeth were blades with the edges facing fore and aft, and the tooth rows were fairly straight. In tyrannosaurs the front upper teeth were D-shaped in cross section, and these teeth were arrayed in a broad D-shaped arc, forming a great "cookie cutter" for biting out chunks of flesh. Here, a Tyrannosaurus rex has used the powerful jaw muscles that bulge out of its skull openings to bite out a deep, yard-long chunk from the upper thigh of Triceratops (see Figure 2-1), a crippling, bone-scraping wound that the latter will not survive.

ropod's long, powerful, and very birdlike limbs were built to do the same thing that bird limbs do—run fast. The speed issue is further explored in Chapter 6.

During 1983, Chris McGowen contrasted the lack of good binocular vision (in which the eyes face forward and provide an overlapping image) in theropods with its high development in predatory mammals. But this argument does not mean much. Predatory lizards do fine without forward-facing eyes, and a number of theropods *did* have good binocular vision.

In the optimistic hope of putting the scavenging myth to rest, let me present the facts. *Tyrannosaurus rex* did not have 6- to-8-inch serrated teeth and an arc of D-cross-sectioned teeth set in a massive, powerful skull just to consume rotting carcasses! These were killing tools. In sharp contrast are the weak beaks and feet of vultures and condors—the only true living scavengers. In fact, pure scavengers *must* be soaring flyers, because they alone can rapidly look over and cover the great distances needed to find and reach the occasional carcass.[7] They also have a very good carcass-locating system, because when one vulture starts spiraling down to feed, it can be seen by other vultures for miles around. This is true whether over dense woodlands or open plains. They do all this at almost no energy cost because soaring is close to effortless. A land-bound predator would starve trying to live off what is already dead; they must go out and kill to get enough to eat. In fact, all mammal predators are killers. Even hyenas bring down much or most of their own prey. The idea that animals as big as most theropods were true scavengers is ecologically unfeasible.[8]

Still, most predators do at times feed by scavenging. Cheetahs are an exception, as they are too lightly built to chase other carnivores away from a carcass.[9] Most predaceous dinosaurs were not so disadvantaged and probably did scavenge. This must have been especially true in brontosaur-dominated habitats where their great bodies supplied an abundance of meat for many predators (see Appendix A).

Most theropods used teeth as their main weapons of predation. After all, the long rows of teeth were the largest, highest-powered, and most lethal weapons available. Their arms and the claws of their hands were less effective for inflicting wounds. Instead, they helped position the victim during the attack, or assisted in tearing up the carcass afterward. Note that, being two-legged, dinosaurs could grab on with their arms much more easily than any living four-legged meat eater, which gave them a distinct advantage. The hind legs and toe claws of most theropods were not specialized killing tools either. These were, however, good weapons of *dispute* for fights between species over breeding privileges, hunting territory, and carcasses. Theropods fighting among themselves may have kicked out at their opponents. When at Johns Hopkins, Robert Bakker once pointed out to me that the earlier theropods may have bounced "kangaroo-style" on their stout tails and slashed out with their big clawed feet. This became the subject of my first published dinosaur illustration[10] (Figure 2-6). Most of the more advanced theropods had smaller toe claws and tails, so they must have delivered stun-kicks like modern ostriches do. Theropods probably did not use their teeth as much in disputes, where the risk of delivering or receiving fatal wounds was too great. However, the television nature-show standard that quarreling animals *always* avoid killing one another is another romantic falsehood. Male lions often kill one another in fierce battles over domination of a pride.

Battles between breeding male hippos are also frequently lethal, and even stallions are known to fight to the death. Many a theropod probably lost its life to an opponent of its own species.

As we shall see, the peculiar noasaurs and sickle-clawed protobirds were notable exceptions to the kill-with-the-teeth-and-not-the-feet mode of predation. Their hunting methods are discussed in Part II, page 358.

Another key aspect of how theropods lived is revealed by the trackways that they left behind, and occasionally by the mode of preservation of these tracks. Very often the tracks of individual theropods are not laid out singly, but run parallel to neighboring trackways. John Ostrom's 1972 statistical study of such parallel trackways showed that this could not be coincidence. Some of the group trackways are due to their following shorelines and the like, but as Ostrom showed the majority are attributable to the theropods being organized in packs. Parallel trackways have been discovered for theropods from the smallest up to 2 tonnes or so; group trackways are not known for the most gigantic spe-

2-6
A Ceratosaurus nasicornis *bounces on its heavy tail kangaroo-style to kick out with its big foot claws and intimidate two Allosaurus fragilis. The latter had lighter tails and blunter toe claws.*

cies, but this just may be because such big prints are rare anyway. Pack behavior in large theropods, and small ones too, receives additional support from communal grave sites. Such mass kill sites are difficult and risky to interpret, but some of these may represent packs that were killed by a sudden event.[11] Even big tyrannosaurs have been found together in such quarries and bone beds.[12] It may be that a very important facet of predatory dinosaur behavior is directly preserved in the fossil record.

It is fair to say that some big theropods must have been solitary, like most big cats. This is even more true of the small-bodied, conical-toothed species that led jackal- or small-cat-like lives. But most species probably practiced a sophisticated level of social behavior quite unlike typical reptiles. This is to be expected since herbivorous dinosaur trackways and death sites also show strong evidence of herding,[13] and it would have been vital for the predatory dinosaurs to be able to meet numbers with numbers.

There is possible physical evidence of mass stalking and attacks by theropods on groups of herbivorous dinosaurs. Richard Thulborn and Mary Wade in 1984 described a multitude of running, small theropod and small herbivorous dinosaur trackways laid down at the same time and place in the mid-Cretaceous of Australia. They think these trackways were created when a big theropod moved in and stampeded the small species away from a communal drinking site. But in fact the large "theropod" prints were misidentified, for they are really those of a stubby-toed, blunt-clawed, herbivorous duckbill dinosaur that had walked through the area earlier (the small dinosaurs even stepped into the big one's tracks!). Moreover, predators and herbivores do not peacefully mix in the manner Thulborn and Wade indicate, even if they are equal in size, because the herbivores are too frightened of the predators, who deliberately drive them away from drinking spots. It seems more likely that a pack of theropods attacked the herbivores, which, of course, did their best to escape. But this is not certain, because it cannot be proven that both kinds of small prints did not belong to theropods, or both to herbivorous dinosaurs!

The trackway evidence for pack hunting among big theropods may, as it happens, be better—coincidentally all these examples also come from the middle of the Cretaceous. Philip Currie in 1983 noted that the prints of three medium sized theropods found in Alberta trail those of a herd of iguanodonts (the ancestors of duck-billed dinosaurs) out of the water. In Texas there is a well known pair of trackways that seem to show a big theropod, perhaps an *Acrocanthosaurus,* stalking a giant brontosaur.[14] The predator stepped into the latter's tracks, and changed direction a little at the same time. Roland Bird, who uncovered the tracks circa 1940, believed that the theropod missed a step as it actually bit down upon and was dragged along by the brontosaur, but this point cannot be proven. Less well known is that there are really four or more theropod trails apparently following about a dozen brontosaurs at this same site.[15] A third set of trackways, in this case from Bolivia, seems to tell an even more fantastic story, one that stretches the imagination.[16] Here the trackways of a brontosaur herd are followed by those of *fifty* large theropods! In none of the above examples does the pursuit seem to have broken from a stalk into a full fledged battle; we will never know if they did. We can say that if packs of great theropods did stalk brontosaur herds, then this is yet another point favoring their being active hunters—certainly they could not have been hoping for one of the herbivores to conveniently fall dead for them to scavenge.

How did big theropods go about hunting their prey? So far I have emphasized what we can be pretty certain about, that big theropods were not strict scavengers, that the D-cross-sectioned tooth arcades of some theropods were giant "cookie-cutters," and the like. But there are some things we will never know, because some aspects of behavior are not preserved in the fossil record. We have to make educated guesses. Social theropods may have executed a prehunting "ritual" of signals and displays in order to organize the group for the expedition. Wild canids do this.

Being big-eyed, theropods probably did much of their hunting just before dawn and after sunset. These times can be the best for the hunt, when it is harder for the prey to spot danger, and the midday heat has receded. Nocturnal forays lit by the stars and moon are also likely. As shown in Appendix B, dinosaur herbivore population densities were probably relatively low, like the populations in modern game parks. So theropods would often have to go looking for their prey, rearing up to scan the landscape. Important exceptions would have been during unusual events such as when herds were migrating through an area, when herbivores were nesting in colonies, or when during droughts animals concentrated near water holes and died off in large numbers.

The exact method of approaching the prey depended partly on the habitat, and partly on the prey. Juvenile victims must have been preferred, but adults were common targets too, especially the ill and aged. The tactics also depended upon the design and size of the predatory dinosaur. We are familiar with the way in which supple-bodied cats and dogs grapple with their prey. But the predatory dinosaur's stiff, birdlike trunks and limbs were not meant to be dragged and twirled about by struggling victims. For the big theropods, a simple fall could be catastrophic. The giant, big-clawed brontosaurs and the fast-horned ceratopsians were especially dangerous herbivores. It does a predator no good to kill its victim if it itself is mortally wounded in the process. So, the last thing 8-tonne *Tyrannosaurus rex* wanted to do was play tug with 8-tonne *Triceratops,* and the *Allosaurus amplexus* that held onto a brontosaur was a short-lived *A. amplexus.* Sharks such as the great white are faced with a similar problem. The big-tusked elephant seals that great whites often prey upon are bigger and more agile than the sharks and dangerous to hunt. The sharks are believed to get around these problems by executing a surprise attack from below, and cutting out a bleeding hole that weakens the victim for the final kill.[17] On occasion, hyenas also bite out chunks from their victims and bleed them, and the giant Komodo monitor often slices up its prey and waits for the effects.[18]

Theropods probably tried to surprise brontosaurs and ceratopsians—their aim being to hit as hard as possible, as quickly as possible, and with as little contact with the prey as possible—a hit-and-run attack.[19]

Although the tall, bird-limbed theropods could not crouch and stalk their prey like the supple cats, they could lower their height and visibility by walking on their heels. It happens that there are a surprising number of footprints showing theropods walking this way, and I have seen film of a heron stalking prey in a flat-footed crouch.[20] So, when hunting theropods were closing in on their prey, they may have automatically assumed a flat-footed crouch, much as cats go into their characteristic stalk when the proper stimulus and intent is present. In heavily wooded habitats, theropods might not be spotted until fairly close to their targets, much as big tanks are often able to ambush opponents from behind cover. Elephants are able to walk very quietly, and this was equally true of giant theropods. We can envision predatory and herbivorous dinosaurs trying to hear and smell each other, the predator finally getting close enough to spring up from its crouch for the final dash to reach its victim.

If cover from trees and bushes was lacking, the predators might attempt to panic the herbivores into fleeing and exposing themselves to attack from the rear. The packs of large theropods that made the trackways discussed on page 37 may have been trying to press the herbivores they were trailing into chaotic stampedes. Brontosaurs and ceratopsians that faced down or charged at their tormentors were probably safe from attack; other, lightly armed dinosaurs, such as the big duckbills, could be approached more freely. However, in open woodlands the prey might have spotted a crouching theropod at a considerable distance,[21] and started fleeing well in advance. In an extended chase, the high-volume, long-endurance heart-lung systems and the high metabolic rates of theropods would be advantageous. But even such distance-running carnivores as canids and hyenas give up the chase if it goes on for more than two to four kilometers, and theropods probably did too.

If a pack of medium-sized allosaurs attacked a far bigger brontosaur, then many individuals may have struck the victim in quick succession. When tyrannosaur packs went after a similar-sized ceratopsian, one big bite from the leader was probably enough. The other pack members acted as support, distracting and panicking the victim and his companions. To deliver the wounding strike, a theropod made a high-speed dash at the prey before it could protect itself. The theropod then threw its S-curved neck, propelling its head forward to deliver long, deep slashing wounds or punch out a great chunk of flesh.[22] Bellies and limbs would have been key targets. Necks were, too, but not to the degree as with some modern carnivores. The predator then retreated immediately, leaving the bleeding, festering injury and accompanying shock to weaken the prey. The latter's agony can well be imagined. If enough of the victim's limb muscles were cut through, or if all its guts were spilled out onto the ground, it was totally crippled. If not, a slow death of hours or even a day might follow as life drained from the gaping wounds in the victim's side.

This was sudden, swift, and sophisticated predation, with the predator's firepower delivered as strongly, and yet as safely, as possible. Dinosaurs did not come upon each other, roar away, and then engage in the simplistic, protracted wrestling matches portrayed with dull repetitiveness in film and books.[23] Far from it, for the great size and speed of the participants made meetings between groups of herbivores and theropods fantastic affairs unmatched in the modern world—great tyrannosaurs versus charging horned dinosaurs, one or many dozens of allosaurs massing against a herd of brontosaurs, all followed by a lingering death watch, a wait for a well-earned meal.

The ability of blade-toothed theropods to safely deliver hemorrhaging wounds allowed them to bring down herbivores much bigger than themselves. Modern carnivores usually tangle with prey as big as or smaller than themselves, but by no means is this a hard and fast rule, especially when the predators are organized in a group. In some areas of Africa, Cape buffalo are the most numerous herbivore, and the much smaller lions are skilled at preying on them. Saber-toothed cats, using surprise and slashing attacks, may have been able to kill elephants. Of course humans—able to project everything from knives to nuclear bombs at their prey—are the ultimate big-game hunters. In 1987, Michael Earle showed that predator packs easily bring down victims that weigh as much as all the pack members put together. Social, blade-toothed theropods could do the same; even a ten-pack of coyote-sized *Coelophysis* could bring down a 150-kg prosauropod.

Once the victim was in a bad enough way, the theropods moved in and safely dispatched it. This was a rather crude affair, with the theropods slicing off bolts of meat and the prey still struggling to escape. It may sound disgustingly reptilian, but Cape hunting dogs and hyenas often begin to consume wildebeest and zebra while the prey is still standing. The theropod's communal habits had an important advantage during such proceedings. Microbes of decay compete with big predators for carcasses by producing toxins that poison the meat, and a single tyrannosaur might have trouble eating a large duckbill before it rotted (see Appendix A). Besides, it would have to fight off, or share the feast with, any theropod strangers that came along. A pack of tyrannosaurs, however, could consume the entire duckbill in one sitting, while fending off intruders.

It is too bad that the great flightless predatory birds of South America and the southern United States, the phorusrhacids, died out just a couple of million years ago. If alive today, these large-headed, big-game hunters, similar to theropods in design, might tell us much about how theropods hunted. One wonders if they used their hooked beaks to inflict precise, quick-killing wounds, or to tear out slower-acting ones. There is one living bird that

2-7
Of living birds, the ground-hunting, snake-killing secretary bird of Africa may follow a life-style most like that of some small theropods.

gives us a good idea of how the *small-game* hunting predatory dinosaurs acted: the secretary bird of the African plains (Figure 2-7). Though a powerful flyer, this large, long-legged raptor spends most of its time on the ground, searching for and picking up small reptiles and mammals. Conical-toothed *Compsognathus* and *Ornitholestes* may have pursued such a life.

There are documented cases of modern predators hunting and killing animals that they then made no attempt to consume. Occasionally they dispatch victims for what seems the pleasure of it, or in a frenzy caused by unusual circumstances. Theropods probably did the same on occasion, although it is not likely that bigger, more dangerous herbivores were the victims in such cases.

Aside from hunting, communalism also played a vital role in the manner of predatory dinosaur reproduction. Most reptiles lay their eggs and forget them. A few lizards do exhibit some parental care, and crocodilians show quite sophisticated nesting behavior and parental behavior in the first months of their youngsters' lives. As for dinosaurs, fossil nesting sites that include nest structures, eggs, and juvenile skeletons show that many herbivorous species formed breeding colonies, sometimes enormous ones. It appears that they practiced extended parental care, at least until the juveniles were half grown. In contrast, most crocodilians abandon their young when they are still tiny.

The predatory dinosaurs were much rarer than the herbivores, so it is not surprising that their nesting sites have not been identified yet. Fresh news reports cite a possible *Allosaurus* egg from Utah, a first for theropods. Live birth is also possible,[24] but it is much more likely that these close relatives of birds, with their narrow pelvic canals, laid eggs like many of their herbivorous cousins. Since the pelvic canal of even the biggest predatory dinosaur was rather narrow, it is unlikely that they laid really big eggs. Besides, losses of youngsters to other predators must have been fairly high, so a large number of relatively modest-sized eggs would have been more advantageous. Small dinosaurs could have lain on their eggs to incubate them, but the large ones were too heavy and would have crushed their eggs. Probably instead, large predatory dinosaurs, and small ones too perhaps, built mound nests of vegetation and dirt, relying on the heat of the fermenting plant debris to incubate the eggs (Figure 2-8). The parents would have closely guarded their nests, because small dinosaurs, mammals, and lizards would have been all too happy to dig up the eggs and eat them.

One point of evidence that supposedly supports a more rep-

2-8
An Albertosaurus arctunguis *rests next to the nest mound of dirt and vegetation that contains its eggs. The mound is drawn after those known for some herbivorous dinosaurs; heat from the fermenting vegetation incubated the eggs.*

tilian adult-juvenile relationship among some theropods is the presence of juvenile skeletons in the adult skeletons' bellies. But that may merely be evidence of cannibalism. Mammalian carnivores practice cannibalism on their young—bears, lions, and humans, among others, are reputed to do this (although human cannibalism has recently been disputed). Usually it occurs when the adults are under stress, or when males are trying to eliminate the progeny of other males. Cannibalism sugggests that theropod pairs may have nested apart in order to keep their progeny safe from their own species, although it does not preclude the possibility that packs of predatory dinosaurs may have constructed nesting colonies for mutual protection against other species.

Parental care continued after hatching, for some pack trackways show juveniles and subadults accompanying the adults. Dinosaur youngsters may have been nested and raised by their true parents. Or dinosaur parents may have done what ostriches do: a number of females lay their eggs in the nest of a single, dominant pair. That pair hatches the eggs, and takes the whole set of chicks with them when they leave the nest. After awhile, a number of such pairs bring their broods from as far as thirty kilometers away to meet up with other such families. The adults display to one another, and in the end one pair or trio of adults goes off with the whole creche of chicks, from thirty to a hundred of them! It's an odd system, but it works.

Whether predaceous dinosaurs fed their young, as raptors and mammalian carnivores do, or let the little ones forage for themselves like baby ostriches, or did some of both, is not known. I suspect parental feeding was practiced, because it would have gotten more food to the young and promoted faster growth. As the young got bigger, they would have started picking up small animals on their own.

Just as important as keeping young dinosaurs fed was keeping them from being food for other dinosaurs. *Tyrannosaurus rex* could persuade another big theropod that going after its tiny young would not be worth all the trouble, but littler theropods could dash in and pick off a baby *T. rex* right under its guardian's nose. Small theropod parents could deal with other theropods of like size, but they could not drive away big theropods. Nor could their youngest babies outrun large enemies. Instead, they must have scattered their young into the brush. The grown-ups would then try to lure the big theropod away from the hidden juveniles, returning when the coast was clear.

One thing worth noting is that not all birds take care of their babies. The strange megapode fowl of the Australian region bury their large eggs in huge fermenting mounds of vegetation, and the male goes to inordinate lengths to keep the pile at the right temperature. When the extremely precocious young hatch, they dig their way out of the mound and clumsily fly away, never to associate with their parents again. Megapodes put all their parenting into hatching big "ready to fly" eggs, instead of rearing preflying young. It is conceivable that some theropods did something of the same sort. Traditionally, it has been assumed that the young theropods were out on their own very early, hunting as soon as they hatched from the egg.[25] Such hunting youngsters would have competed with the adults of small species, in effect, acting as separate small "species." However, since, as we have seen, adult theropods very likely cared for and fed their young until they were half or fully grown, other small species could evolve with little or no hindrance from theropodian youths—an important difference in ecological impact.

Many predatory dinosaurs had, or may have had, hornlets, frills, wattles, tall back fins, and bold color patterns on key parts of the body, especially the head and neck. In living animals, these are important visual communication devices. Sometimes communication is between different species as they threaten one another, as when cats raise their hair and dogs pull back their lips in a snarl. Predatory dinosaurs could also bare their teeth, and smaller species may have been able to fluff up feathers. By rearing up, they would have looked more impressive to their opponents. At other times the communication is between members of the same species that are mating, or contending for mates. The horn bosses on theropod heads would have been excellent for butting contests to establish a pecking order within a pack.

It is odd that, in some places, theropod trackways seem to be inordinately numerous relative to those of other dinosaurs, more than the predator/prey ratios of skeletons would indicate.[26] Even low metabolic rate cold-blooded predators cannot make so much of a fauna's population (as we shall see in Chapter 7). One explanation is that the theropods constantly patrolled the shorelines of watercourses—which is where footprints are best made and preserved—looking to pick up things drifting ashore or for herbivores to ambush as they made periodic forays to the shoreline for a drink.

Which brings us to another point, the theropod's long-supposed hydrophobia. The genesis of this sorry idea was a suggestion in the 1800s that the slender-toed theropods were unable to walk on soft muds as well as the broader-footed herbivorous species, so the latter supposedly fled the former by dashing into the water. This idea soon became entrenched in the literature as a full-fledged refusal of theropods to go into water—animals that fought brontosaurs in fear of a swim! It is a belief that never deserved serious consideration, yet was hardly questioned for decades. The reality is that almost any animal will swim well if you throw it into the water. Many wild cats and dogs are quite pleased to swim, and Robert Bakker made the pertinent observation that big ground birds are very good at it too.[27] In fact, the long, slender toes, powerful limbs, and supple tails show that theropods were *better* at mud walking and swimming than the stumpier-footed, stiffer-tailed herbivores.[28] Panicked dinosaurian herbivores probably did splash into the water on occasion, only to find that they then had no escape or defense from their pursuers (Figure 2-9), just as wildebeests that flee into water are invariably dispatched by faster swimming hyenas.[29] Most theropods probably swam with their hind limbs and a sculling action

2-9
Far from trying to escape into water for safety, herbivorous dinosaurs were in dire danger if caught by packs of swimming theropods, as is the case with this Apatosaurus louisae, *surrounded by* Allosaurus atrox.

of the tail. Because the chest was filled with lungs, they swam hip-heavy, with the head held clear of the water. Confirmation of the theropods' swimming ability may come from Walter Coomb's description of what appear to be swimming theropod trackways, in which only the tips of the claws touched bottom and left scratch marks[30] (Figure 2-10). Even better is the Alberta set of trackways (see p. 133) that may show a trio of theropods pursuing some iguanodonts up *out* of the water, the exact opposite of the old the-prey-escaped-into-the-water belief.

Predatory dinosaurs obtained much of the liquids they needed from their victims, and they also slaked their thirst at the water hole and stream bank. The herbivorous dinosaurs had to wait their turn while the predatory ones drank. Lacking cheeks to form a continous suction tube, predatory dinosaurs may have

2-10
The obvious fact that theropods were good swimmers may be confirmed by some trackways that seem to show just the tips of the claws digging into the mud. Dilophosaurus wetherilli is shown leaving such traces.

had to tilt their heads up like birds to get the water down. Dinosaurs probably bathed, the little ones fluttering their feathers like birds, the larger ones ponderously submerging like elephants and snorting water out of their nostrils.

The big naked-skinned species may also have wallowed like rhinos in the mud. Rolling in the dust was probably practiced by all species. Such cosmetic activities are good for suppressing skin parasites, soothing wounds, and screening against solar radiation and were undoubtedly enjoyable even to dinosaurian minds. Scratching the snout and behind the ears, picking at teeth, or nibbling the side of the belly were additional likely grooming practices. Feathered species may have preened their feathers with oils from special glands, like birds do.

Almost all predatory dinosaur fossils come from flat floodplain deposits, deltas, and a few higher basins. This is not because they lived only in such places, but that the sediments that buried and preserved their remains formed only there. Theropods certainly lived in hilly and mountainous terrain, but such high places were subject to erosion, and the remains of animals that lived on them could not be preserved. Just as elephants climb escarpments and steep mountain slopes, so could giant theropods. Small theropods must also have preyed on the little animals living on craggy mountain peaks.

In sum, from the traditional image of sluggish, solitary, scavenging animals afraid to get their feet wet, theropods were active, sociable, and dangerous archpredators.[31]

A HISTORY OF PREDATORY DINOSAUR SUCCESS AND FAILURE, AND OF THEIR AVIAN DESCENDANTS

3-1

*The earliest well-known preda-
tory dinosaur is the theropod* Coelophysis bauri, *which came in
small-skulled "robust" (far left)
and bigger-headed "gracile" (left
center) types. Shown here among
conifers that would one day become part of the famous Petrified
Forest, little* Coelophysis *was a
harbinger of great things to come.*

Predatory dinosaurs were the dominant large predators for some 170 million years, compared to the mammalian predator's 65 million years of mastery. Much is often made of this, perhaps more than should be. After all, modern carnivores are not yet extinct. Even more misleading is the common comparison of dinosaur success with the brief history of homonid evolution. It is not fair to put our one little group of animals up against the full spectrum of dinosaur species. But predatory dinosaurs were successful, and it can be said that their success continues to this very day, for their winged yet otherwise similar avian progeny are the owners of the daylight skies. On the other hand, they failed catastrophically too, for in terms of big terrestrial predators, dinosaurs are nonexistent. That is failure. In the broad sense predatory dinosaurs in the form of the great South American ground birds did manage a resurgence in the fairly recent past, but then these too bit the dust. Why did predatory dinosaurs do so well for so long, and why did they then vanish?

Before we begin to examine the history of predatory dinosaur success and failure, let us familiarize ourselves with the three basic types of predatory dinosaurs: paleodinosaurs, herreravians, and theropods. The first two are not as well known as theropods because they were not very numerous or long lasting.

The Triassic four-toed paleodinosaurs are the earliest predatory dinosaurs, and they are in turn, divided into two general types. The first—indeed, the first of all dinosaurs, and so primitive that they are also labeled protodinosaurs—are the diminutive, so-called "rabbit" lagosuchids and their relatives. These had fairly long, flexible trunks which allowed them to either gallop on all fours like squirrels, or run on two legs like birds. Bigger, but still not modest sized, and more developed were the fully bipedal staurikosaurs. These may represent the group ancestral to both the herbivorous dinosaurs and the predatory herreravians and theropods.

Also four-toed, the herreravians looked like staurikosaurs at first glance, but they were surprisingly birdlike in some ways and, in one case, very big. They may be related to the newly discovered small dinosaur "Protoavis," which may have been a remarkable imitator of birds (see Part II, page 251).

In the previous chapters we discussed the general characteristics of the bipedal, three-toed birdlike theropods, the largest group of predatory dinosaurs, which lasted from the Triassic to the end of the Mesozoic. Theropods also come in two general types: paleotheropods and avetheropods. The first to appear, and the most primitive, were the paleotheropods. Among these are the lightly built coelophysians, which have an unusual kink near the tip of their snout, and the heavier, horned ceratosaurs. More advanced paleotheropods included the unusually robust megalosaurs and the metriacanthosaurs, which were about as typical big theropods as you can get. The second theropod group, which probably descended from the paleotheropods, were the yet more birdlike avetheropods. Again, these can also be split into two basic subdivisions: the grand bunch of allosaurs and two-fingered tyrannosaurs, the fairly big to gigantic meat eaters we are most familiar with; and the most birdy of theropods, the protobirds. These include little, flying *Archaeopteryx,* and an array of modest-sized ground-dwelling forms such as sickle-toe-clawed dromaeosaurs, parrot-beaked oviraptors, ostrich-like ornithomimids, and sharp-snouted troodonts. It is most likely that birds evolved from this particular group of protobirds.

The best place to start looking at predatory dinosaur history is at the beginning, if not before. About 280 million years ago, at the start of the Permian Period, most of the earth's continental pieces were joined together in a single supercontinent. Imagine hiking 10,000 miles from the tip of Siberia to the tip of South America without once wetting your toes in salt water! As counterpoint, the world's deep oceans were joined into a super Pacific covering three quarters of the globe, from which shallow embayments from time to time washed across vast tracts of land. Although many tend to think of the past earth being a hot, steamy jungle, in the Permian Period the earth was locked in an ice age similar to the one we are undergoing now, except that then the great ice sheets bulked largest in the southern hemisphere. Big animals were croc-sized, fin-backed reptiles and amphibians, restricted to a tropical zone banding the equator. By the Late Permian most of the ice was gone, the climate was warmer (although still snowy toward the poles), and a great array of often strange mammal-like predators and herbivores known as therapsids had spread over the supercontinent. These therapsids included the ancestors of true mammals, and they probably had faster metabolic rates than do typical reptiles (note that the therapsid-mammal group has no close relationship to archosaurs). Most therapsid predators were medium-sized, low-slung animals, with big heads and long canine teeth. At the very end of the period the first protoarchosaur, a croclike proterosuchid

3-2
The earliest big-animal communities were made up of amphibians like Eryops *and reptiles like finbacked* Dimetrodon, *the first large land predator, which was very archaic and mammal-like, and the primitive* Araeoscelis, *a pair of which are shown on the tree trunks. These animals are in an Early Permian swamp in what was then equatorial Texas.*

predator, appeared. The harbinger of the great group that would include dinosaurs and birds, it was a very minor component in the world fauna.

With one world continent and a very mild climate, the following period, the Triassic, had a more uniform world fauna than we have at present. At the beginning of this period, modest-sized protoarchosaurs became an important component of the predator fauna. This was despite the fact that they had reptilian metabolisms, and were competing against warmer-blooded therapsids. Soon after, thecodonts proper—the future ancestors of dinosaurs and sometimes big themselves—began to appear. Proterosuchids and the bigger early thecodonts, which looked something like a cross between crocs and big lizards, are sometimes thought of as semiaquatic animals that had strengthened their hind limbs for swimming. But their narrow, blade-toothed skulls indicate they were terrestrial archpredators. Smaller protoarchosaurs and thecodonts could climb well too, using their divergent outer fingers and toes. These thecodonts probably had heightened metabolic rates like those of therapsids. Their main competitors were advanced therapsid predators. In 1983, Michael Benton argued that

3-3
Among the first advanced large predators were the mammal-like therapsids such as wolf-sized, saber-toothed Trochosaurus, *shown here feeding on the herbivorous therapsid* Styracocephalus. *A* Blattoidealestes *looks for scraps. This is a summer scene in the Late Permian of South Africa.*

protoarchosaurs and early thecodonts were not really in competition with one another, but this cannot be so because the two groups were out there squabbling over carcasses and competing for game. This competition seems to have had its effect, for as the Triassic progressed, thecodonts seem to have taken over the big-predator niches, while therapsids declined in size.

Why? What gave archosaurs the edge as large predators at this time, and therapsids the edge as smaller ones? Frankly, I am not sure. Both seem to have had heightened metabolic rates and fur or feather insulation. Some suggest that the archosaurs were better at conserving water and came to dominate the drier highlands.[1] But members of the therapsid-mammal group show no problems in dominating deserts today, and the archosaurs made it in the wet lowlands of the Triassic. Both groups developed more erect limbs at about the same pace, limbs that worked under the body like a bird's or dog's, rather than out to the side as in sprawling lizards. The big thecodonts did develop a special and highly developed form of the fully erect gait that therapsids never did match. *Why* the erect gait may be better than a sprawling one for big active animals has only just been explained. While erect gaits *look* more structurally and energetically efficient, Robert Bakker found that sprawling-limbed lizards running on treadmills are just as energy-thrifty as erect-limbed animals.[2] And as will be explained in Chapter 6, lizards are faster than small hopping dinosaurs. The key to understanding the advantage of an erect gait was offered by David Carrier in 1987. He pointed out that the asymmetrical, sideways body action of running, sprawling-limbed animals directly *inhibits* the operation of the lungs. Hardly able to breathe when moving swiftly, sprawling animals cannot go fast for long. Some lizards stop for brief moments even when running to escape in order to get a breath or two in. Erect-gait animals, tall and with their limbs directly beneath their bodies, flex their trunks in a vertical action that *helps* the lungs work faster. Able to get more oxygen when they run, they can run for much longer.

Perhaps the chief advantage enjoyed by thecodonts centered around their big, slashing attack jaws. These may have made them better big-game hunters, while the more precise cutting teeth of therapsids were more suitable for smaller prey.

A popular misconception is that mammals appeared much later than the first dinosaurs. Actually, protomammals appear the same time as protodinosaurs, at about 235 million years ago in the mid-Triassic, and the two groups shared the rest of the Mesozoic Era. Early dinosaurs were small—down to the size of weasels—which means they were potential competitors for the last therapsids as they rapidly diminished into tiny nocturnal protomammals.

Here arose a great dichotomy that would separate dinosaurs and mammals for the rest of the Mesozoic. Many, but not all, dinosaurs rapidly increased in size—only a few million years into their start one paleodinosaur had reached rhino bulk—and they were daylight-oriented. The mammals stayed small and nocturnal. There was strikingly little overlap in weight between the two groups, for throughout the Mesozoic few dinosaurs and few mammals were in the range between 1 to 5 kg. Again, we ask why. Both probably had high metabolic rates. In fact, the very first dinosaurs, the fully erect lagosuchians, may have already been at the avian level, which is as high as one can get. Some contend that dinosaurs were low-metabolic-rate animals that needed big size to maintain constant temperatures, big bodies being slower to cool and heat than smaller ones. This explanation fails for the obvious reason that many dinosaurs were smaller than the ton or so of body mass required for such temperature constancy, and as will be explained in Chapter 7, big size is advantageous for tropical warm-bloods too.

Limb differences may explain the situation. Even the first dinosaurs had the fully erect, stiff-action limbs of the bird model. Early mammals retained less erect, more supple limbs. The latter did not bar mammals from big size, for many giant reptiles had sprawling limbs. But the dinosaurs' stiff, birdy limbs may have made it difficult for them to deal with the increasing competition from mammals in the rough-terrain world of the small.[3] Meanwhile, the more sprawling-limbed mammals could not make it against the erect-gait dinosaurs among the large. The dinosaurs' ascendancy in big-animal roles was a triumph, but their inability to succeed as small animals may have been their eventual undoing, as we shall see below.

As the Mesozoic progressed, why did mammals not develop fully erect limbs plus high-level warm-bloodedness—some Late Cretaceous herbivorous ungulate mammals did—and start competing with dinosaurs for the small-predator niches? After all, mammals have sophisticated, close-fitting permanent teeth; theropods' were sloppy, replaceable lizard-like arrays. But it may be that finely sculpted mammalian teeth are not superior for predation. In fact, early mammals developed such precisely occluding teeth for chopping up little insects. Big mammalian carnivores did not develop sophisticated teeth *for* predation, they inherited them and had to *modify* them to the task. As a result, mammalian carnivores can deliver precision bites, but these may be no more efficient than the theropods' slashing and cutting methods. Likewise, giant toothless predatory ground birds outcompeted complex-toothed marsupial predators in the South American Tertiary. Lacking any clear-cut advantage over theropods, Mesozoic mammals may never have been able to move into an arena dinosaurs had already mastered.

The reader should be aware that this thesis works only if small dinosaurs were fully warm-blooded. If dinosaurs had had low metabolic rates they would have been in chronic danger from the more energetic, active, and increasingly sophisticated mammalian predators and mammals could eventually have beat out the dinosaurs.

Also mysterious is the failure of most dinosaurs, especially the big ones, to develop brains as big as birds and mammals. Because they were so active and their body temperatures constant, big dinosaurs should have been able to have large brains. In fact, since all dinosaurs were probably warm-blooded, they should have matched most mammals intellectually speaking. One might expect a competition of wits between dinosaurian predator and prey, with the former trying to outwit the latter and vice versa. Predatory dinosaur brains did tend to be larger than those of the herbivores. On the other hand, the South American predatory ground birds were smaller-brained than their mammalian prey, and they seem to have been none the worse for it. In fact, the big birds were much more common than the larger-brained but rare marsupial predators they were up against. Likewise, sharks regularly make meals of bigger-brained sea mammals. The connection between brain size and predation is not at all clear.

But we are getting ahead of the story. We had left off in the Late Triassic with the thecodonts winning out over therapsids in the big predator niches, and dinosaurs coming onto the scene. In 1983, Michael Benton noted that dinosaurs were initially rarer and appeared later in the Late Triassic than usually thought. He therefore believes that the competition with thecodonts was not on the grand scale traditionally thought. I disagree to a certain extent, because good-sized predatory dinosaurs were living

A HISTORY OF PREDATORY
DINOSAUR SUCCESS AND FAILURE,
AND OF THEIR AVIAN DESCENDANTS
55

alongside big thecodonts in some places—in South Africa, for instance, a very large herrerasaur may have been a leading member of the predator guild—and small- to medium-sized thecodonts and predatory dinosaurs lived together for ten million years. So, interactions were going on between thecodonts and dinosaurs of all sizes. But how intense these interactions were is not certain. Thecodonts may have preferred brushy areas where these low-slung creatures could have practiced ambush stalking to best advantage. The more gracile predatory dinosaurs may have opted for longer chases in more open country. Had the thecodonts not failed, these differences might have allowed them and theropods to coexist through the rest of the Mesozoic.

Thecodonts had been hunting an array of big and bizarre reptilian therapsid and thecodont herbivores when the first dinosaurs got their modest start some 235 million years ago in the Landinian Age of the Middle Triassic.[4] The first were the tiny galloping "rabbit" protodinosaurs, such as *Lagosuchus*, which hunted the first protomammals, lizard-like reptiles, and the like. Things evolved astonishingly fast, because only five to ten million years later an array of much larger paleodinosaurs and herrerravians, including *Herrerasaurus*, were setting their sights on the herbivores of the time. The latter included the sometimes rare,

3-4
Thecodonts, including such giants as Saurosuchus galilei, continued to give early dinosaurs like this Herrerasaurus ischigualastensis and its youngsters a difficult time in the Late Triassic. In this scene from the Argentinian Ischigualasto Formation, the carcass is the bizarre plant-eating rynchosaur Scaphonyx; a pair of small Ornithosuchus rusconii thecodonts and the gracile protocroc Trialestes clear the area; the flora is dominated by dicroidium plants.

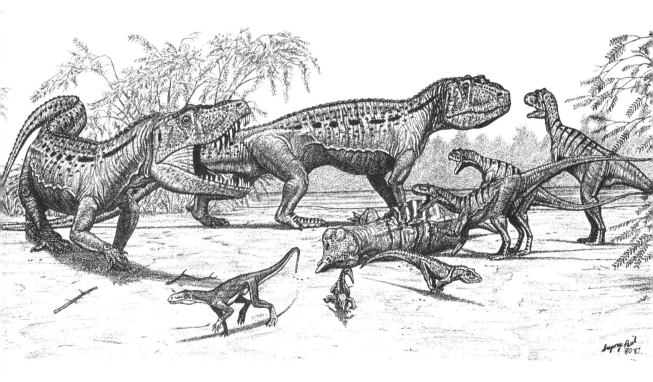

sometimes common, early plant-eating dinosaurs. I was not fully aware when I started this book just how remarkably advanced and birdlike some of these first dinosaurs were. Most notable is the recently discovered, diminutive "Protoavis," which may have flown or been descended from flying ancestors. Nor was I aware that the giant herrerasaur mentioned above had appeared so very soon. Clearly, early dinosaur evolution was startlingly rapid, indeed explosive.

The more advanced paleodinosaurs did an odd thing: they became fully bipedal. Two-leggedness is not the norm; only some herbivorous dinosaurs, kangaroos, a number of small hopping mammals, and hominids walk this way. The reason predatory dinosaurs became bipedal is not at all clear. For a long time we thought that the energy efficiencies of bipedalism and quadrupedalism differed, the first being more efficient at slow speeds and less efficient at larger sizes. But then it was shown that monkeys expend the same calories whether they move on twos or fours. And Michael Fedak and Howard Seerherman proved in 1979 by running bipeds and quadrupeds on the same equipment and rechecking all the previous data that the energy cost is pretty much the same regardless of the kind and number of limbs used.[5] Bipedal *hopping* is somewhat more energy-efficient, at least at moderate speeds, but, as their trackways show, dinosaurs never hopped. And of course, quadrupeds run as fast as bipeds. It has been argued that dinosaur shoulder girdles were immobile and they had to stop using the forelimb to be faster. But as we will see in Chapter 4 (page 108), loosening up the shoulder is a common adaptation that even the first lagosuchid paleodinosaurs had. We cannot even explain dinosaurian bipedalism as a way to free up the arms for nonlocomotory uses, because the arms of early predatory dinosaurs are not especially modified for manipulating objects. Indeed, in the early theropods they could be quite small. The only thing that can be said in the end, is that bipedalism was a serendipitously crucial adaptation for these dinosaurs because it set up their evolution and ultimate survival as birds.

After having begun two-legged walking, paleodinosaurs and herreravians went into terminal decline by the beginning of the Norian Age, perhaps because replacements in the form of gracile, kink-snouted paleotheropods, such as coyote-sized *Coelophysis buari* and larger dilophosaurians, were appearing in abundance. Likewise, the initial radiation of small flying protoavians may have been nipped in the bud by competition from the sophisticated, bat-winged pterosaurs, themselves close dinosaur relatives, which also appeared at this time.

It is surprising how many theropods show up in the Late Triassic just as the Carnian Age ends and the Norian begins, only eight or so million years after the very first protodinosaurs. There are so many that it is hard to tell which one was really the first. The sudden appearance of all these theropods at a time when four-toed predatory dinosaurs were also new and doing well reinforces how remarkably fast the initial evolution of dinosaurs was. These earliest theropods still had herbivorous thecodonts and reptiles, as well as herbivorous dinosaurs, around to prey upon. By the latest Triassic, herbivorous dinosaurs were more abundant, because the old nondinosaurian herbivore fauna had become extinct. The herbivorous dinosaurs were small-headed, long-necked prosauropods and beaked ornithischians. The main predators continued to be early paleotheropods, like *Coelophysis* and *Liliensternus,* who could use their slashing tooth arrays to disable the big prosauropods, and their speed to catch the gracile ornithischians.

It was long believed that the end of the Triassic, about 213 million years ago, saw a widespread extinction of dinosaurs. This was partly because the early Jurassic's dinosaur-bearing formations were mistakenly placed in the Triassic.[6] Instead, however, the Triassic-Jurassic extinction seems to have affected animals *other* than dinosaurs,[7] including, most importantly for the dinosaurs, the last thecodonts. Now a truly fascinating thing happened about this time. At or near the period's boundary, a six-mile-diameter asteroid or comet hit eastern Quebec and left a forty-mile-wide crater. The tremendous explosion may have kicked up a worldwide dust cloud and caused the extinctions (an idea discussed below in relation to another asteroid that may have hit Earth at the end of the Cretaceous, some 150 million years later). What makes this fascinating is the fact that the dinosaurs did not seem to care much, if at all, about this disaster, for herbivorous prosauropods and ornithischians, and *Coelophysis* and its theropod relatives, survived to pursue a flourishing Early Jurassic radiation (Figure 3-6).

Early Jurassic double-head-crested *Dilophosaurus* is the first large theropod we know of. A kink-snouted paleotheropod, it was about the weight of a big bear. Small ceratosaurs, another paleotheropod group, soon showed up too. Prosauropods and ornithischians were still the main prey. Since from the Late

3-5

The best known of the earliest theropods are species of Coelophysis. In this case, C. rhodesiensis *is fighting the heavily armed, early herbivorous dinosaur Plateosaurus carinatus on the dunes of the Forest Sandstone from the South African Early Jurassic. This particular species of* Coelophysis *lived not long after the impact of a giant meteorite with the Earth. In the distance is an oasis that provides food and shelter for these animals.*

Triassic to the Early Cretaceous the continents stayed pretty much in one piece and the climate was mild—and since predators are often wide-ranging animals—the worldwide predatory dinosaur fauna was fairly uniform. *Coelophysis*, in particular, appeared both in the United States and southern Africa. The theropod habitats of this time were on the dry side, from the open forests of the American Chinle Formation to the full desert of the African Forest Sandstone beds. Tall conifers and shorter palmlike cycadiods dominated the plant life, and would continue to do so for another 100 million years.

Our record of theropods deteriorates after the Early Jurassic, and we do not get a really good skeleton until some forty

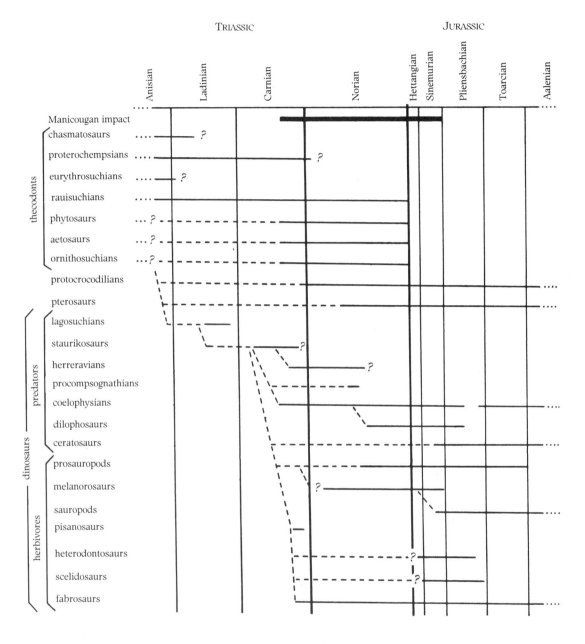

million years later in the Late Jurassic. We do know that elephant-sized brontosaurs were around not very long after the beginning of the Jurassic, in the Sinemurian Age. But something is
out of whack, because I have not been able to find a sure record,
or even a trace, of theropods large enough to hunt brontosaurs
on a regular basis at that particular time. Theropod evolution

This chart shows what happened to the major groups of Late Triassic dinosaurs and other archosaurs when, as indicated by the heavy bar at the top, a giant meteorite hit eastern Quebec. Dinosaurs show little or no disruption. Thecodonts did not make it into the early Jurassic, but they may have already been in a gradual decline.

may well have lagged behind that of the herbivorous dinosaurs, although I cannot think of a good reason why. Among other plant eaters, modest-sized, armored ornithischians were supplementing the swift gracile ones at this time, and there were small- to medium-sized theropods on the scene to hunt them. Small, long-fingered theropods, such as, oasis-and-dune-dwelling *Segisaurus,* started climbing with their divergent inner digits, perhaps the first stage toward bird flight.

About 180 million years ago, in the Middle Jurassic, another giant meteorite impact may have thrown a dust cloud around the world. A short time later we finally find records of big theropods such as rhino-sized *Megalosaurus* and other species of intermediate form and varying sizes in Europe, China, and Argentina. The first certain avetheropod—nose-horned *Proceratosaurus*—is also found here. Toward the end of the Middle Jurassic, in the Oxfordian Age, the record of predaceous dinosaurs improves dramatically and we have theropod faunas that we can really sink our teeth into. Recent Chinese finds have given us the beautiful *Metricanthosaurus* skeletons of the early Late Jurassic. These big to gigantic paleotheropods lived among herbivorous plate-and-spike-bearing stegosaurs and giant brontosaurs.

In the Late Jurassic, it seems that yet *another* huge meteorite crashed into the earth, but again dinosaurs show no ill effects. The continents, still under a mild semiarid climate, were reseparating at that time. As a result, new oceans, such as the narrow Protoatlantic, began to appear, and more provincial faunas began to develop. The advanced ave*theropods* had become pre*eminent,* perhaps because of their more sophisticated, birdlike features. One of these was the air-sac-ventilated lung system which will be described in Chapter 4. *Why* advanced theropods developed such sophisticated lungs, which today are found only in birds, is not clear. Certainly not for flight. Besides, bats fly perfectly well with ordinary lungs. The one clear-cut advantage of the avian lung is its ability to extract oxygen at high altitudes—some birds can fly five miles high.[8] But theropods and even early birds were not specialized for high-altitude flight, so it could not have evolved for this purpose.

So yet another question remains unanswered.

Having seen that some predatory dinosaurs became gigantic, we can ask why. Why, when mammalian land predators never reached such sizes? In the early Tertiary, some of the fast-running mammalian predators such as Wyoming's *Pachyhyaena,* a member of a primitive group of predators called mesonychids, reached bear dimensions. Only 10,000 years ago a 600-kg, short-faced bear, *Arctodus,* lived in North America. Its rather catlike head and long limbs suggest that it was more carnivorous and fleet-footed than living species. Brown and polar bears can reach 800 kg, but the first is mainly herbivorous, and the latter more aquatic than land-dwelling. The biggest of all known mammalian land predators lived in Late Tertiary Africa. This was *Megistotherium,* a primitive creodont which massed perhaps 900 kg, still not in the truly gigantic category. With a head over two feet long, and nearly as broad, it may have hunted elephants by crushing and cutting their lower limb muscles. Then there was *Megalania,* the giant Komodo-like monitor lizard of fairly recent Australia. Some estimates that it was as heavy as two tonnes, as big as most tyrannosaurs, cannot be right because *Megalania* did not reach such dimensions: one tonne is more likely.

These were all big, but not *real* big. Perhaps the question should not be why theropods got so large, but why carnivorous land mammals did not. There have been plenty of elephants, ground sloths, rhino-like titanotheres, true rhinos, and other oversized mammalian herbivores around for giant Tertiary mammalian carnivores to have eaten. Differences in metabolic rates do not offer an explanation, since the biggest predatory lizards were about the same size as the biggest mammalian carnivores. Besides, giant warm-blooded predators should not have any special problems feeding themselves. After all, the giant theropods seem to have done fine (look over the food consumption and population calculations in Appendixes A and B), and orcas and sperm whales are gigantic high-metabolic-rate predators.

On the other hand, predatory dinosaurs never did what some predatory mammals did: return to the sea. And it is in the modern seas that one has to look to find predators both fishy and mammalian as big as dinosaurs. Whales and seals are the descendants of various formerly-land-dwelling, meat-eating mammals. In their new habitat, some mammals have become very large. Killer whales, or orcas, reach the size of *Tyrannosaurus rex,* some seven tonnes. Sperm whales can push fifty tonnes, the size of brontosaurs. No other predator of any land, sea, or time approaches this bulk. However, the conical-toothed orcas and sperm whales feed mainly on such relatively small game as fish, seals, and squid. Even orcas do not make a regular job of killing the giant baleen whales, although some packs do it when in the mood. A recently extinct marine giant that could easily kill the comparatively modest-sized whales of its time was the giant white shark *Carcharodon megalodon,* which weighed perhaps twenty tonnes. This shark dwarfed its close relative, the present-day one-to-two-tonne great white shark, which often attacks big elephant seals. Another mystery is why dinosaurs never returned to the sea, especially since a number of birds, like penguins, have adopted marine ways. Theropods certainly looked like good candidates for conversion, since some species fished, and their tails could have readily been converted into propulsive sculling organs.

Many of the best Jurassic theropods are supplied by Tithonian-Age formations at the end of the period, among them a couple of surprisingly modest-sized species of *Allosaurus* from the sprawling Morrison Formation of the western United States. A gigantic version of *Allosaurus* is also known from rarer remains. For these Morrison predators the menu included an array of titanic brontosaurs, stegosaurs, and various-sized ornithopod ornithiscians. The Morrison was long thought of as a wet, lush, lake-and-swamp-dominated habitat but, in reality, it was sharply dry seasonally, crisscrossed by shallow streams, and topped with open conifer-cycadiod forests.[9] Across the Protoatlantic, two little theropods—*Compsognathus* and the flying protobird *Archaeopteryx*—made a living on a semiarid island archipelago. China, which contained many closed, interior basins quite different from the more spreadout, coastal habitats found elsewhere, had a big allosaur with head crests. Primitive paleotheropods, in the form of *Elephrosaurus* and nose-horned *Ceratosaurus,* were still about at the end of the Jurassic. In fact, teeth suggest that a titanic ceratosaur may have been the primary predator in the sauropod-dominated Tendaguru fauna of eastern Africa.

There are continuing claims of birds more advanced than *Archaeopteryx* in the Late Jurassic,[10] and the discovery of bird-like "Protoavis" in the Triassic has encouraged that belief. However, the finds that seem to support these claims are always either too poorly preserved for certainty, or turn out to be pterosaurs, the flying archosaurs that are so like birds in some parts of their anatomy. The fact that Jurassic advanced bird finds are so far unknown suggests that if such birds existed, they were at best uncommon. If this were so it would be most odd, since one could expect Jurassic birds to have undergone the same fast and dramatic evolution that pterosaurs and bats did. In fact, there is

3-7
The best known Late Jurassic fauna is that of the Morrison Formation of the western United States. In this scene, an Allosaurus atrox naps in the shade while others come down for a drink at a water hole. The latter include the

brontosaurs Camarasaurus supre-
mus, *whip-tailed* Diplodocus car-
negii, *and plated* Stegosaurus
ungulatus. *The small animals include pairs of pterosaurs and turtles, and a crocodilian; conifers
were the main big plants.*

good reason to believe there were no Jurassic members of Aves. Some fine-grained near-shore Jurassic sediments were very effective at trapping and preserving abundances of small flying insects and pterosaurs, especially the Late Jurassic Solnhofen slates of Bavaria. But the only "bird" finds there consist of the six Solnhofen *Archaeopteryx* specimens and a single flight feather that may or may not belong to it. Since birds and a fair number of flight feathers do show up in similar Cretaceous near-shore and lake sediments, it is hard to see how Jurassic birds could have escaped preservation. Even if they were terrestrial rather than shorebirds, they should have flown between the Solnhofen islands and ended up in their lagoons more often than *Archaeopteryx*. Nor do birds show up in the terrestrial Jurassic microfaunas that produce tiny reptiles and mammals, and similar Cretaceous sediments have been producing identifiable bird bits since the 1800s.

What happened immediately after the Jurassic is obscure, for Early Cretaceous theropods are very scarce (much as in the Early Jurassic). However, large allosaurs must have continued to dominate the Northern Hemisphere, because fin-backed *Acrocanthosaurus* and Chinese *Chilantaisaurus* were still in control in the later Early Cretaceous of North America and Eurasia.

3-8
On the Solnhofen islands, small Compsognathus longipes *chases the still littler flying protobird* Archaeopteryx lithographica *among the scrub conifer brush that covered the arid land.*

Strange *Baryonyx* from Barremian times of 120-million-year-old Britain and great sail-backed *Spinosaurus* of later Africa suggest that even these old style, kink-snouted paleotheropods were continuing to make a good go of it. The continental separations became more pronounced, and the resulting isolation may explain how megalosaurs were able to continue to remain dominant in South America. Fantastic among these is the *Carnotaurus* of the Argentinian Albian with its unique brow horns and ultra-deep head. In isolated Australia, big allosaur relatives may have held fort.

In the small-predator roles, things changed much more fundamentally in the Early Cretaceous, for sickle-clawed dromaeosaur protobirds such as wolf-sized *Velociraptor* emerged as the common small- and medium-sized predators in the 110-million-year-old Cloverly Formation of Montana. Other, less birdlike small predators persisted, however. The world herbivore fauna and flora had changed or were changing at this time. Brontosaurs were still out in force, but big, beaked ornithopods had taken over as the primary herbivores. Plate-backed stegosaurs had declined in favor of the tanklike armored ankylosaurs. It has been speculated that these new dinosaurian herbivores helped spark the development of the first bushy, flowering plants.[11] Climate continued to be on the dry side, as in the Cloverly for example, and conifers were the main tall trees. About 100 million years ago, at the end of the Early Cretaceous, there is some evidence that the impact of another giant meteorite wreaked havoc on the world ecology, but dinosaurs persisted in weathering through such disruptions.

A number of Early Cretaceous "bird" finds are based on ambiguous remains. Among these are feathers, some from Australia,[12] many of which are the kind of short contour feathers that many archosaurs may have had covering their bodies. Even the long wing feathers known from this time could have come from flying *Archaeopteryx*-like protobirds. Even so, the sharp increase of feathers in the Early Cretaceous is important, for it suggests that advanced flying birds had finally become abundant, and being better able than the protobirds to fly often and far over water, were shedding many feathers into lakes and lagoons. We have had a tendency in the past to search each possible bird fragment from the Cretaceous for characters found in *modern* bird groups and, when one or two characters were finally found, to identify the remains as belonging to a member of such a group.

Often overlooked was the fact that the remains might not even be avian in the first place. So, protobird theropods were misidentified as owls and pelicans, and the result was an illusory array of birds little different from today's in the Cretaceous. Today, a more critical eye finds a hitherto unsuspected plethora of primitive birds in the late Mesozoic.

While their presence is ambiguous if not nonexistent in the Jurassic, in the Early Cretaceous we do see the first definite signs of fully-developed birds. This is only five to twenty million years after *Archaeopteryx*. Perhaps the earliest are from the earliest Cretaceous of Romania—the flying *Eurolimnornis* and *Palaeocursornis*.[13] Found alongside some *Archaeopteryx*-like remains, *Palaeocursornis* is said to be a ratite, the group of flightless birds that includes present-day ostriches. I have doubts about the ratite claim, but if true then *Palaeocursornis* is the most ancient modern bird, and the oldest flightless one as well. Another indication of a very early bird is a bit of a hind limb from China, around 135 million years in age.[14] Named *Ganius*, it may have been a primitive *Hesperornis*-like diver; certainly, it is not a modern-style shorebird as has been suggested. Soon after lived a bird described this year by Sanz, Bonaparte, and Lacasca in the Las Hoyas Formation of Spain; it looks like the most primitive true bird yet found. Then there is flying, *Ichthyornis*-like *Ambiortus* from the slightly younger Hauterivian-Barremian Age of Mongolia; it was described by Kurochkin in 1985. Finally, another *Hesperornis*-type diver and Canadian wading bird's tracks are found in sediments about thirty million years more recent than *Archaeopteryx*.[15]

The appearance of highly developed birds so soon after *Archaeopteryx*, and the presence of birdlike "Protoavis" way back in the Triassic, cause many to speculate that true birds must have already been evolving much earlier in the Jurassic. This is possible. But as I explained earlier, there is evidence that advanced Jurassic birds did not exist. And besides, I do not understand what the fuss is about. Evolution can be gradual, but it can also move with awesome swiftness. If a suite of newly evolved adaptations is highly advantageous, then strongly favorable selective forces may be able to optimize them very rapidly. The first evolutionary radiation of dinosaurs seems to have had this astonishing quick-burst character. When dinosaurs bit the dust, mammals grew astoundingly in size and diversity of form in only five to ten million years. Especially pertinent to our problem is how the first birds and bats both appear in the fossil record suddenly and fully developed—in neither case are primitive flying grade forms known. Even "Protoavis," with its many flight-related adaptations, appears only a dozen or so million years after the first dinosaurs. That the major flying vertebrate groups always appear fully developed so suddenly is very suspicious. It suggests that flight is so useful that once developed it is rapidly refined. The group's "protoflyers" then quickly lose out to their superior relatives. In the case of birds, we have been lucky to find one of the protoflyers, *Archaeopteryx*. Besides, the distance between *Archaeopteryx* and full birds should not be exaggerated, for it does not take radical and tremendous alterations to make a protobird into a bird.

By the Cretaceous another oddity of theropod evolution has become obvious. None of them could crush and eat bones the way hyenas do. Theropods could chew on bones a little, but even stout-toothed tyrannosaurs were not bone crushers in the class of hyenas. Hyenas consume whole carcasses, bones and all, with their great jaws and teeth. One would like to imagine theropods with super strongly built and powerfully muscled skulls, the backs of their jaws lined with great, flat bone-cracking teeth. These would have been more efficient at consuming dinosaur carcasses than the theropods we know, but none have shown up in the fossil record. By the Cretaceous crocodilians of essentially modern form were the theropods main competitors. Yet crocodilians appear to be less abundant in most Mesozoic deposits than they are later in the mammal-dominated Cenozoic. Not only that, but they tended to be small-bodied: few specimens were as big as American alligators or Nile crocodiles. It is possible that theropods were eating the crocs. Even today, big cats once in a while kill a fairly large crocodilian. A tyrannosaur could have swallowed one whole, and gone into the water after them. Constant attacks could have suppressed croc populations, and favored the smaller, harder to catch species.

There were gigantic crocodilians called phobosuchids in the Late Cretaceous, which reached forty to fifty feet in length. But they too were uncommon. While dozens of good tyrannosaur skulls are known from North America, not a single, fully complete phobosuchid skull has been found. Undoubtedly, tyrannosaurs ate juvenile phobosuchids, and on shore even the adult phobosuchids were not safe. On the other hand, when in the water, the slow-breathing ectothermic croc could drown the high-metabolic theropod by grabbing its foot and dragging it under. Even so, the giant crocs were too rare to ever constitute a serious threat to theropods—in fact, they are missing entirely north of Montana, perhaps because the winters there were too cold for them.[16]

Predators are a major driving force of evolution, for they have an overwhelming impact on the herbivores they prey upon. The speed and grace of gazelles, for example, is solely the result of their need to escape predation. Herbivores have also developed weaponry and armor to deal with predators. Indeed, if not for predators, herbivores would be relatively placid clunkers. Late Cretaceous herbivorous dinosarus were compelled to develop means of defense to an exceptional degree. Duckbills and the rhino-like ceratopsians were fast, ceratopsians were also horned and parrot-beaked, while the tanklike ankylosaurs were armor-plated, spiny, and club-tailed.

The Late Cretaceous is marked by an abundance of theropod- and bird-bearing formations around the world. It is the best record we have got. The continents continued to drift, and exceptionally high seas further divided them so faunas were more provincial and diverse than before, though still not as much as today. In some places, things may have been getting wetter—a point directly contrary to the old idea that once-abundant swamps drained off in the Cretaceous. Flowering trees began to replace conifers. Grasses appeared, but were not important in the Mesozoic. Climate was still on the warm side, but, as will be detailed in Chapter 7, dinosaurs were present in polar regions and may have weathered the long, cool winter nights. In South America the dinosaurs changed less than elsewhere. Brontosaurs lived on, still maintaining a dominant position over the new duckbills. Working on this book has taught me a lesson in how very long some of the primitive kinds of theropods lasted. In particular, the archaic megalosaurs remained dominant in South America until the end of the period. These included not only the giant *Abelisaurus,* but the small sickle-clawed *Noasaurus* as well. Much the same thing would happen in South America during the younger Tertiary, when ground birds and marsupials would fill roles held by more advanced carnivores elsewhere.

Eastern Asia and western North America were connected to each other in the Late Cretaceous, which ended sixty-five million years ago, but were somewhat isolated from neighboring areas. On both sides of the Bering land bridge, there is a series of theropod-bearing formations extending throughout most of the latter half of the Late Cretaceous. Duckbills tended to predominate, especially in North America, and brontosaurs, ankylosaurs, big- and small-horned dinosaurs, and ornithopods were also present or common to varying degrees. The Asian habitats continued to be laid down in a series of dead-end basins deep in the interior of the continent.[17] They seem to have started out as near deserts, and ended up as more savanna-like parklands. In western North America the sediments piled up on the western border of the interior seaway (see Figure 7-4, page 160). The coastlines seem to have been much wetter than further inland, and things appear to have become moister over time[18]—although the latter point is debated. The habitats are often thought to have been heavily wooded, but others believe they were more open. The great and increasingly gigantic tyrannosaurs, *Albertosaurus* and wonderful *Tyrannosaurus rex* itself, dominated. These exceptionally sophisticated theropods partly displaced their advanced allosaur ancestors. Lesser tyrannosaurs and their still smaller relative, *Aublysodon,* may have given such sickle-claws as *Velociraptor* a hard time too. The latter tended to be less abundant, in North America at least, and most species were smaller than before. An array of new flightless protobirds made an appearance, including toothless, plant-eating ones such as surrealistic, parrot-beaked *Oviraptor,* ostrich-mimicking *Ornithomimus,* and the most birdlike of all, *Avimimus.* Swift, sickle-clawed *Troodon* remained toothed and predatory.

Predatory dinosaurs are especially useful for determining intercontinental connections. Herbivores are usually fastidious about what plants they will and will not eat, so the habitat and floral differences between two continents may result in very different herbivore faunas, even if the continents are connected. Since predators are less selective about what they kill, they are less choosy about where they live. A case in point are the dinosaur and mammal faunas of Mongolia and western North America. Most of the herbivorous dinosaurs and mammals differ substantially, so much so that Zofia Kielan-Jaworowska[19] believes the Bering land bridge between Asia and Alaska was intermittent, or was a filtering island barrier. Yet the Mongolian and North American *predators* are very alike. As far as we can tell, the American sickle-claw *Velociraptor langstoni* is very like roughly contemporary *V. mongoliensis.* The same appears to be true of sickle-clawed *Troodon mongoliensis* and Canadian *T. for-*

3-9
The best Late Cretaceous fauna is that of the Judith River Formation of Alberta. Here Tyrannosaurus torosus *is beating a retreat before the beaks of* Chasmosaurus belli *and horn of* Monoclonius apertus. *The duckbills* Hypacrosaurus casuarius *(front) and* Kri-

tosaurus notabilis *(left back) scatter out of its way; an armored* Edmontonia rugosidens *is less concerned. The great pterosaur* Quetzalcoatlus *flaps away in the distance, accompanied by some waterbirds. Hardwoods were making a strong appearance by this time.*

mosus, and of the small tyrannosaur relatives *Aublysodon mirandis* and Chinese *A. huoyanshanensis.* The best similarity is between *Tyrannosaur bataar* of Mongolia and *Tyrannosaurus rex.* These two forms of *Tyrannosaurus* seem to overlap in time, and are so similar that they may have been geographic subspecies of one another. They and the other Mongolian-American theropods suggest the Bering land bridge allowed free exchange between the two continents.[20]

Theropods have things to tell us about the position of India, too. It is generally thought that the subcontinent, which had been attached to east Africa, was drifting toward Asia in the Late Cretaceous, splendidly isolated in the Indian Ocean. If so, then its fauna should have diverged and been very different from the rest of the world's, much as isolated Australia has its own set of peculiar animals. Yet Late Cretaceous India had advanced allosaurs and primitive tyrannosaurs very like those found elsewhere. So India may have been much closer to both Africa and Asia than usually thought.[21] The faunas of Late Cretaceous Europe, Africa, and eastern North America are not very well known. Europe had duckbills, tyrannosaurs, and *Dryptosaurus,* an unusual dinosaur of which little is known. Virtually nothing is known from Australia at this time. In fact, there is a whole class of Mesozoic faunas that we know little of: those on isolated oceanic islands. Strange things happen to animals when they are isolated on small islands. Giant forms become dwarfed, small ones gigantic. Bizarre forms evolve. Flying birds—and proto-birds too, presumably—become flightless. Who knows what peculiar theropods developed on Mesozoic islands, for most have long since eroded away.

We have come to the end of our look at predatory dinosaur communities, and I wish to make a final point about their structure. In modern mammal communities the smaller predators, weasels, small cats, foxes, and the like, are usually more numerous than the big wolves, lions, and so on. Some dinosaur communities were like this. For example, many Late Triassic-Early Jurassic faunas were dominated by the little theropod *Coelophysis,* and jackal- to wolf-sized *Velociraptor* (small by theropod standards) was sometimes the most common predator where it lived. But in most dinosaur communities both skeletons and footprints show that the giants really were dominant, not only in power, but in numbers. In the Morrison, great *Allosaurus* was abundant, and diminutive *Ornitholestes* was rare. In Late Cretaceous North America the remains of tyrannosaurs are twice as numerous as those of small theropods; this is true whether looking at whole skeletons, or at teeth and other bits and pieces. Since the big tyrannosaurs were so much larger, their aggregate mass was many times that of the small theropod population. The same tended to be true of the herbivores. Enormous brontosaurs were the common Morrison plant eaters; horned dinosaurs and duckbills dominated the North American Late Cretaceous. Such worlds, where one would see many big predators and prey, but few smaller ones, are not only alien to our experience, they are biologically extraordinary. Somehow, giant dinosaur herbivores often were able to gain control over and exploit almost all the energy flow in their communities, and only oversized theropods were able to exploit them in their turn.

Returning to the Late Cretaceous, we find that birds did very well. In the interior seaway then covering the plains states and provinces, wingless *Hesperornis* and an array of its relatives were diving with loonlike hind limbs. These birds are intriguing in

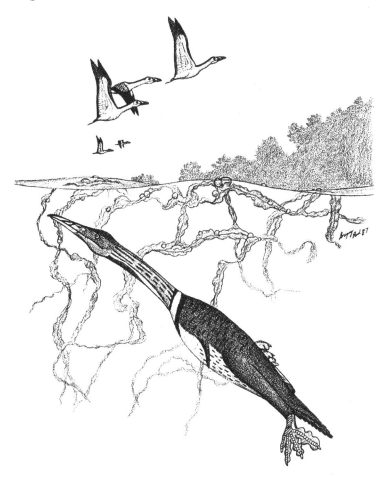

3-10
Two archaic toothed birds inhabited the Niobrara seaway that covered the plains states in the late Cretaceous: little flying Ichthyornis *and big, stub-winged* Hesperornis. *The latter was adapted for swimming like a loon.*

that they are the only "dinosaurs" known to have become fully marine in the Mesozoic. Flying over the interior seaway was little *Ichthyornis*. In the 1950s, this early bird's toothed jaws were claimed to belong to baby sea-going mososaur lizards, something some ornithologists really liked because they preferred their birds to be *birds*. But it has since been reestablished that the ichthyornids did have unserrated, chopping, bladed teeth. The oceanic and shoreline distribution of *Ichthyornis* has long led to suggestions that it was a gull- or tern-like form, but its short wings and big head make it rather more like an auk, and its toothy jaws are quite unlike any modern shorebird's.

Totally unsuspected until recently was a whole group of strange Cretaceous birds, the enantiornithiformes. All seem to be fairly small flying forms, and what little is known already shows great diversity in design and function. Whether they were water-loving or strongly terrestrial, or both, is an open question. In the 1970s, Jose Bonaparte found a small quarry full of them in latest Cretaceous sediments of Argentina. Some of the bones have un-believably contorted and odd shapes, with toe articulations that dwindle to nothing, or arc off to the side. Alas, no complete enantiornithiforme skeletons are yet known. People's eyes are now attuned to these bones and they are showing up all over the world. In fact, many old bird remains once assigned to modern bird groups, or already considered mysterious, are ending up in the enantiornithiformes, so much so that the group is in risk of becoming a convenient Cretaceous dumping ground for bird re-mains that cannot be put elsewhere. We can say that their radia-tion was a substantial one, and apparently occurred toward the close of the Cretaceous when the toothed birds were already in decline.

Paleognathus birds, which today include ostriches and the like, must have been present in the Late Cretaceous, but they have yet to be found there. Neognathus birds are the typical modern birds. There are quite a few of their bones in the North American Late Cretaceous (mainly, but not all, near the very end of the period). Originally these neognathus bones were thought to have belonged to loons, flamingos, rails, shorebirds, and cor-morants, and in one case to *Apatornis*, a supposed *Ichthyornis* relative. In reality, almost all, if not all, really belonged to the shorebird group called charadriiformes, which today includes snipes, plovers, gulls, and ducks. Some of the Cretaceous forms may in fact represent the initial blossoming of ducks, with duck bills, but also with long slender necks and long wading legs. Called presbyornithiforme ducks, they lived alongside *Tyrannosaurus rex,* and later became fantastically abundant in the early Tertiary, in which they form dense bone beds. Other neognathus birds must have been present in the Cretaceous too, and along with paleognathus birds they staged an increasingly diverse Late Cretaceous radiation.

The close of the Cretaceous saw catastrophe. All theropods and protobirds failed to pass this boundary. From what we know, toothed and enantiornithiforme birds did not make it either. In fact, the former may not have made it that far. Only the more modern birds did cross into the Tertiary, though whether they suffered a temporary setback at the time is not known. Many other life forms had trouble at this time as well. The herbivorous dinosaurs bought it, as did some mammals and all pterosaurs. All marine reptiles except the turtles were wiped out. Much other marine life was affected. Plants suffered also. Lizards, turtles, and crocodilians did survive. Again, big questions come up, the most important to us being—what caused predators that had been so successful for 170 million years to vanish?

In one way the answer is obvious. The big predaceous theropods were dependent on the well-being of the herbivores. When big herbivore populations crashed, the big predator populations did too. So the fate of herbivorous dinosaurs is a key question, though not the only one. For even with all herbivorous dinosaurs gone, the small protobird theropods should have been able to survive on the mammals and reptiles that were left over. With their initially larger populations, they could better survive disasters than bigger species. And their faster breeding rates would have allowed them to recover more quickly. Small theropods would have had no competition in the early Tertiary. Indeed, they could have dominated the predator niches up until today, evolving new giant species. They could even have spawned new dinosaurian herbivores. But they did not have the chance.

Actually, dinosaurs seem to have been in trouble well before the end of the Cretaceous.[22] About seven to ten million years before the final event, predatory and herbivorous diversity was high on the western coastline of the interior seaway of North America—not only in numbers of species, but in relative proportions of the population. A large number of horned dinosaurs and duckbills formed a diverse herbivore fauna, and two or more species of big tyrannosaurs were fairly common. Whether the number of species then declined is argued about.[23] It is clear that just before the end, one or two species of *Triceratops* made up 50 to perhaps 90 percent of the coastline's total herbivore populations, and *Tyrannosaurus rex* was the only common predator.[24] This was an unstable situation, for the reduced populations of the other species were in grave danger of extinction. If the few abundant species suffered setbacks, then all the species were in the same dire straits. A big question is whether all areas in the world were experiencing similar situations; we do not have enough data to be sure. We know that diversity increased in Mongolia sometime before the extinction, but it was never very high there anyway, and the modest increase may have been due to the shift away from very arid conditions. We cannot tell what happened in Mongolia as the Cretaceous closed, because the sediments for that time are missing there.

Assuming latest Cretaceous dinosaurs did decline worldwide, what caused this? A good number of explanations have been suggested, many outrageous. In part this is because, like the public in general, many nonpaleontological scientists are, understandably enough, enamored of dinosaurs. So when working on some seemingly unrelated subject they sometimes get the idea that it "explains" the extinction of dinosaurs. They often cannot resist publishing their belief, and the fact that the media picks up almost any new idea and runs with it does not help. The theories that claim the stresses of predation caused herbivorous dinosaurs to lay thinner-shelled eggs, or that the flowering plants poisoned the dinosaurs, are in this class. Changes in climate have often been cited as the cause of the dinosaurs' demise, but dinosaurs' ability to deal with the extremes of the tropics and the polar nights (see Chapter 7) casts doubt on such ideas, especially since the suggested climatic shifts—both warming and cooling trends have been offered—are mild ones. There was nothing approaching an ice age in the Mesozoic. Even when things did change, the dinosaurs had effective means of coping such as moving north or south as required over a few generations, or evolving the ability to deal with the new regimen.

The cause of the dinosaurs' decline may have been more subtle. In 1977, Robert Bakker explored the biological consequences of the slower building of mountains and shrinking of seas that marked the latest Cretaceous. New species often form from part of an existing population when it is cut off in an isolated valley or a continent. No longer breeding with the main population, the new population is free to evolve into its own species. The more such isolated pockets are created, the more quickly new species develop. The opposite happens when isolated highland valleys disappear and isolated continents become connected —species formation slows down. New links between previously separated continents also allow once separated faunas to intermix. This may increase the rate of species extinction, as new competition causes some species to lose out. Such interchanges can also spread diseases to unprotected species, and the ensuing epidemics can drastically reduce their populations. The decimation of Native Americans was an example of such competition and disease—although in this case cultural instead of species differences were the key ingredients. If a species' population is so reduced, it is even more vulnerable to competitive pressures. Especially if a genetic "bottleneck" occurs—that is, the population is reduced to only a dozen or so individuals, making the species' genetic diversity too low for reproductive success.[25] If this happens, the species may survive the initial crisis only to fail to reestablish itself in the long term. If species formation rates decline below the rate of species extinction, and this continues for long enough, then extinction of the entire group is mathematically assured.

All this may have happened to the last dinosaurs. After great activity toward the end of the period, mountain building was quiescent at the very end, and falling seas relinked continental pieces. As for ocean life, there are suggestions that the retreating seaways caused the decline and extinctions of both marine vertebrates and marine invertebrates. Whatever the problem or problems, the whole world fauna seems to have been under increasing stress before the final event.

On the other hand, some other very odd things were going on at the very end of the Cretaceous. Cretaceous sediments do not just blend smoothly into Tertiary beds. Instead, there usually is an alteration of the sediments near and at the boundary, and new types are laid above. The environmental conditions had changed significantly—although the long-term difference was too mild to have caused such heavy extinction by itself. The key is the thin layer at the boundary. It contains abundant heavy metals, especially iridium, and dustlike particles that are the apparent residue of a 10-km-diameter asteroid or comet impacting with the earth.[26] The probable consequences of such a collision, perhaps like that of a full-scale nuclear war, have been made well known to the public.[27] A blanket of high altitude dust would enshroud the earth and block out sunlight, shutting down photosynthesis and plunging world temperatures for months. And this could be just the start of hellish conditions that would last for many decades. Intense air pollution and acid rain could poison animals and plants, while world temperatures might soar after the initial fall.

Some advocates of this theory believe this one event alone could have extinguished the dinosaurs. But there are difficulties. If dinosaur populations were healthy, then it is hard to believe that *every* breeding population of *every* dinosaur species was wiped out by such a short event. One would expect some of the smaller dinosaur species to have made it through with populations large enough to avoid genetic bottlenecks, particularly the opportunistic small theropods, who could have fed on the remains of big species which were gradually dying off from starvation, and then picked up the small animals that survived. After all, since many other small animals did make it through, why not the small dinosaurs?

Polar dinosaurs were another body of potential impact survivors. As detailed in Chapter 7 (pages 157-161), they were already able to weather long periods of winter dark and coolness, so they should not have been overly bothered by a meteoritic winter, especially the polar population that was already going through its winter.[28] The subsequent rise in temperatures would probably be tolerable in the polar summer, and would only serve to drive winter temperatures to more comfortable levels.

Even if the end-of-the-Cretaceous impact was vastly destructive, however, it still does not offer an explanation for the apparent decline of dinosaurs before the event.[29] Davis and company try to get around these problems by postulating a series of cometic bombardments, caused by a disturbance of the cometic Ort cloud that orbits the sun at substellar distances.[30] However, the dinosaurs' seven-to-ten-million-year decline was much longer than the two or so million years a comet bombardment is thought to last. And frankly, this concept still does not explain why every small predatory dinosaur species failed to survive the same catastrophe that other small animals did make it through. In fact, a series of impacts would probably fail to do what it is theoretically supposed to do—further deplete the world fauna after each hit. This is because the first impact would wipe out most of those species vulnerable to impacts, and those left would survive the following impacts as well as they did the first one.

What may really crush the impact hypothesis is something that is becoming increasingly apparent—that as noted previously in this chapter giant meteorites were crashing into the earth all through the Mesozoic (some possible ones are plotted in Figure 10-1, pages 224-25).[31] We have already seen that the best documented of these, the Late Triassic impact, did little or nothing to the world dinosaur population. Although dinosaurs had their ups and downs, at no time during the Mesozoic did the dinosaurs decline to only a handful of species and then recover, as they should have if meteorite impacts affect them so badly. Instead, there was always a diverse array of dinosaur groups and species out in force. This is strong evidence that dinosaurs were highly resistant to the consequences of the biggest meteorite collisions, and that the extinction of dinosaurs just happened to coincide with one of these visits from outer space.

A minority opinion holds that the iridium layer was put down by an intense period of vulcanism at the end of the Cretaceous, and that it was the effects of this planetary upheaval that killed off dinosaurs and other creatures that were already in decline for other reasons.[32] The great Deccan basalts of India were laid down near the end of the Cretaceous, but equally big spasms of vulcanism in the Early Jurassic and Early Cretaceous did not kill off the dinosaurs.

In sum, we do not know what killed off the theropods, their prey, and the primitive birds—while allowing advanced birds to pass through. Perhaps it was a combination of gradual decline due to landscape uniformity, topped off by the impact event or vulcanism. It has not been proven whether or not dinosaurs were still alive at the boundary itself. There have been recent suggestions that dinosaurs survived *beyond* the end of the Cretaceous,[33] but the evidence is ambiguous. Too many basics are simply not known. Did dinosaurs really intermix toward the end, and spread diseases among themselves? Would a meteoritic impact have created a devastating false "winter," or a much milder "fall"? There has not even been an attempt to model what would have happened to the Cretaceous climate after a cosmic hit. One cannot decide what happened when one still does not understand what might have happened. Those who claim that the question has been resolved are jumping the gun. What is needed is far

more data from late Cretaceous and earliest Tertiary deposits around the world. Until then, we will remain in the dark.

One final note: if there had been many species of *really* tiny dinosaurs, mouse- and rat-sized, then it would have been impossible to finish them off; their populations and breeding rates would have been too high. So when nonavian dinosaurs were excluded from the small-animal niches by their mammalian competitors way back in the Triassic, their ultimate doom was sealed.

As for avian "dinosaurs," the birds, primitive paleognathus birds are found early in the Tertiary in both flying and flightless forms. It is important to point out that the recent and living ostrich relatives, the ratites, are not merely a moribund remnant of what once was a diverse assemblage of paleognathus birds. In fact, these big ground birds have been staging a modest radiation. Sometimes it has been in the face of sophisticated equine and bovine competition and carnivore predation, other times on islands isolated from such problems. The ostrich is the largest living "theropod," at 150 kg and 2.4 m tall. Bigger yet was the New Zealand moa *Dinornis,* at a height of 3.6 m and a mass of about 400 kg. The recent elephant bird of Madagascar was shorter but a little heavier at 420 kg. The broad-hipped elephant birds laid what were perhaps the largest of "dinosaurian" eggs, weighing some 12 kg. These eggs were so enormous because the birds lived on a predator-free island where they could safely rear just a few offspring in their lifetime. Moas and elephant birds were still living just a few centuries ago. As for flying paleognathus birds, the pheasant-like tinamous are still holding out in South America.

The early Tertiary saw a flourishing evolution of more advanced neognathus birds, many similar to those of the Late Cretaceous. But the truly great bird radiation was in the latter half of the Tertiary. In addition to the charadriiforme shorebirds and related flamingos, storks, gulls, pelicans, and albatross, there appear penguins, loons, cranes, rails, grebes, hoatzins, cuckoos, a plethora of raptors and owl groups that arose independently from various stocks, plus the chicken-like fowls, pigeons, swifts, hummingbirds, and woodpeckers—to name only a few. Contrary to the general impression that fragile bird bones make rare fossils, there is a fast-growing abundance of Tertiary bird remains.[34]

Many Tertiary neognathe birds, both flying and non, adopted gigantism in the finest dinosaurian tradition. Perhaps the biggest ground bird of all time was ostrich-like *Dromornis* of

3-11
After the dinosaurs disappeared, it took about seven million years for fairly large mammalian predators like Ancalagon *to show up. Here, one emerges from a burrow to help chew on the small crocodilian its partner has caught. A smaller predator,* Criacus, *is on the tree trunk, and the insectivore* Deltotherium *is in the branches.*

Late Tertiary Australia, which massed some 500 kg. Usually it is considered a ratite, but Storrs Olson pointed out that it may not have been. In the early Tertiary, *Diatryma* and its relatives were flightless Northern Hemisphere giants of ostrich dimensions. Though commonly thought to be arch predators, they lacked a truly raptorial hooked beak and therefore may have hunted frogs, small turtles, and the like instead.

The hooked-billed ground phorusrhacid birds of South America and preglacial Antarctica were truly predaceous. Flightless and ranging from medium to ostrich size, they beat out the predatory marsupials and were the dominant meat eaters of that continent's Tertiary. It was recently found that they managed to move north over the new Central American land bridge and into the southern states just before the Ice Age. Whether phorusrhacid birds failed in competition with the big cats and dogs that came up the same land bridge, or whether they were already in trouble, is not certain. What is known is that on two continents, for one extended period of time, big dinosaurian ground predators staged a comeback.

Giant penguins made their homes in the southern oceans of the early to mid-Tertiary. These were more loonlike than modern penguins, and one species was three times the dimensions of the biggest living species. Bigger yet was the largest of the plotopterids, the penguin-like pelican relatives of the mid-Tertiary North Pacific. These super penguins and plotopterids are the largest

3-12
Hooked-beaked running birds like eight-foot-tall Phorusrhacus *carried on the fine tradition of big dinosaurian arch predation until only a few million years ago in South America and the southern United States.*

known ocean "dinosaurs." Their demise may have been at the hands of newly evolving seals.

Even some owls, isolated on late Tertiary islands, grew to exceptional size and reduced their flight abilities. As for fully flying birds, a number of giants populated the Tertiary. Much of this period saw great and bizarre pelican relatives, the pseudodontorns, the biggest of which had wingspans approaching 6 m. Albatross-like in their slender wings, they had big jaws lined with small pseudo teeth. The albatrosses themselves are Late Tertiary giants with wings up to 3.7 m across. Bustards, condors, marabou, storks, and the larger swans are also oversized living flyers with 10-to-18-kg weights and 3.5-to-4.0-m spans. Biggest of all "theropodian" flyers were the teratornes of the Americas, the last of which were still in existence until only about 10,000 years ago.

3-13
The ostrich, the largest and fastest living "dinosaur," and the recently extinct moa Dinornis, *the tallest of birds, drawn to the same scale. The life-styles of these two herbivorous ratites are (or were) very like those of the ostrich-mimic theropods.*

The early form *Argentavis* had about a 7.6-m wingspan and 100-to-120-kg mass. Only the greatest pterosaur—11-m wingspan and similar in weight to *Quetzalcoatlus*—was bigger. Teratornes were long pictured as condor-style scavengers. Although their wings were condor-like, their bills were albatross-like. This has led to suggestions that they were small-game hunters. But perhaps a freshwater shoreline existence of hunting frogs and fish is closer to the mark.

At the other end of things is the bee hummingbird of Cuba, at 57 mm in length and 1.6 g. In a sense it is the smallest known "dinosaur," being one hundred times smaller than *Lagosuchus*. A hummingbird lays the smallest known dinosaurian egg—a third of a gram. The smallest living predaceous bird, the white-fronted falconet of Borneo, is five times smaller than *Lagosuchus* at 35 g.

The most advanced and abundant, and the last appearing of land birds are the little passerines, the crows, robins, sparrows, and myriads of other songbirds we see outside our windows. First appearing in the latest Oligocene and early Miocene, about twenty-five million years ago, the living species number some 5000. With fossils included the total must be much higher, and far in excess of any other archosaur group. So in a sense, songbirds are the most successful dinosaur to date, although the predatory raptors, especially, are experiencing intense stress these days. The next 100 million years and beyond will see many more fantastic things—if we humans only find a way not to interfere with the health and development of the world ava fauna.

3-14
Predators drive much of the evolution of herbivores. Pronghorn antelope are so gracile and swift because of their need to escape fast predators, such as this North American cheetah of a few tens of thousands of years ago.

4

THE NUTS AND BOLTS OF PREDATORY DINOSAUR ANATOMY AND ACTION

I have been drawing dinosaurs since before I can remember. And, through the years, they have remained for me far and away the most satisfying, though frustrating, subject of all. Even as a teenager I knew something was wrong as I drew them, but I did not know what to do about it. All the books said that dinosaurs were reptiles. I was familiar with what crocs and lizards look like, with their sprawling limbs, and slender, rather formless limb muscles, but theropods do not look like them. They look like erect, vertical-limbed birds instead. Even the renowned dinosaur artist Charles R. Knight[1] compromised on this contradiction. He gave theropods erect, birdlike hind limbs, but he draped them in slender, lizard-like muscles. When in the early seventies I read in a little blurb in *Smithsonian* magazine that Robert Bakker believed dinosaurs really were bird and mammal analogues, it all finally made sense. Theropod limbs not only *looked* birdlike, they *were* birdlike. It turns out that birds got their limbs directly from theropods. So when drawing theropods, *think birds*. But don't go too far. Predatory dinosaurs, especially the earlier paleodinosaurs, had a number of adaptations of their own. And the big species, at least, were coated in a veneer of reptilian scales and hornlets.

The bipedal and birdlike design of theropods has been understood since the 1860s, when the complete skeleton of little *Compsognathus* was uncovered in the Solnhofen slates of Bavaria. The first good *Allosaurus* skeletons found in the 1880s confirmed that the big ones were built in much the same way. However, the details of theropod anatomy and function were poorly known until the dinosaur "renaissance" of recent years. Still, many dinosaur restorations, whether illustrations or models, are so bad that they make me cringe. Sometimes the skeleton will not even fit within the fleshy bounds of the restoration. There is no excuse for such nonsense—yet it is encouraged by the common opinion that we can never restore dinosaurs more than approximately. Of course there is some truth to this, but the result has been a casual, anything-goes attitude toward restoring dinosaurs, an attitude that has grievously injured the field. The reality is that we can put together a very accurate picture of those theropods for which good skulls and skeletons are known. Indeed, a rough consensus is emerging on how to restore theropods among those who pursue the business in a serious manner.[2] The paleodinosaurs have always been less well-known, and only lately have discoveries revealed the basics of their anatomy.

The best place to start looking at predacious dinosaur anatomy is at the business end of things, the head and neck. Predatory dinosaur heads are very interesting because they are both advanced in being birdlike, and still "primitive" in certain reptilian ways, such as their long rows of uniform lizard-like teeth (see Figure 2-3, page 30). This is quite unlike the herbivorous ornithischian dinosaurs, whose beaked, solidly constructed skulls and spoon-crowned teeth are far more altered from the typical reptilian pattern. It is also unlike the carnivorous mammals of the time, with their extremely modified skulls and complex teeth.

Narrowness and depth are the most obvious birdlike features of predatory dinosaur heads. This is a basic archosaurian adaptation, that contrasts with the broad, shallow heads of lizards and crocs. Most predacious dinosaur heads were made up of a "box and a triangle." The back of the skull—its cheek region—consisted of a flat-topped and flat-sided box. The skull narrowed in front of the cheeks, at the orbit, into the more triangular-shaped snout—triangular because the snout became shallower and less broad going forward, and because the top of the snout was not as wide as the lower, tooth-bearing edges.

Another avian feature of predatory dinosaur heads is the lightness of their build, especially in the earlier species and in the protobirds. The skull has many large openings, including a large opening before the eyes called the preorbital opening. These improved the weight of the skull to strengthen efficiency by removing bone from where it was not needed and placing it where it was. The openings also improved the workings of the head's jaw-closing muscles. There is debate about how they did this—either they enlarged the area available for attachment or they gave the muscles more room to expand, or both.

Predatory dinosaur skulls may have been kinetic, a feature shared by both lizards and birds. This means that various skull bones were loosely articulated and were moveable relative to one another. (Mammals are just the opposite—the skull bones lock tightly together, and the only moving joint is the jaw's, as can be seen in Figure 2-3, page 30.) To a certain extent, kineticism accomplishes similar things in birds and lizards. However, the anatomical adaptations for kineticism are not the same in the two groups. It is especially difficult to prove which parts of theropod skulls, if any, were kinetic. Bone articulations that look loose

4-1
It was the way in which such predatory dinosaurs as four-tonne Metriacanthosaurus shangyouensis *were put together that allowed them to launch daring attacks on animals twice as large, such as ten-tonne brontosaur* Mamenchisaurus hochuanensis. *In this scene, one of the metriacanthosaurs has diverted a brontosaur's attention while another has sneaked in to deliver a slicing wound to the victim's thigh. A couple of pterosaurs fly by in the upper left; ginkgos, tree ferns, and conifers are in the background.*

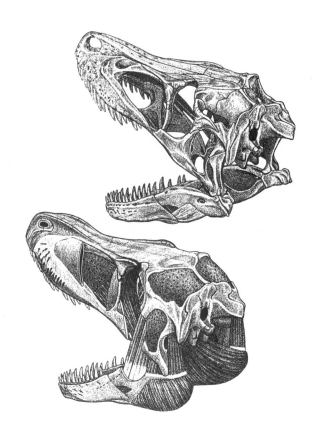

*The skull and its jaw muscles,
hornlets, etc., of Velociraptor antirrhopus; all predatory dinosaur
skulls were built to the same basic
plan. It is likely that nasal sinuses
filled the depression outside of the
preorbital opening. These have
been partly cut away to show how
the jaw-closing anterior pterygoideus muscle may have anchored
on a sheet in the preorbital opening, and to the top of the mouth
roof bones. From there it ran
down via an opening in the roof of
the mouth and anchored in the
large opening on the inside of the
lower jaw. (Some muscle surfaces,
bones, and tissue have been cut
away to show interior muscles
and other features. These include
the temporal muscles which fill
the openings behind the eye
socket and join the anterior pterygoideus in the lower jaw's interior
opening. The dashed line shows
where some of these muscles ran
forward into the hollow lower
jaw.) Perhaps the biggest head
muscle was the jaw-closing posterior pterygoideus, wrapping
around the rear of the lower jaw.
The ear gear is set ahead of the
modest jaw-opening muscles, the
depressor mandibulae, at the
back of the skull.*

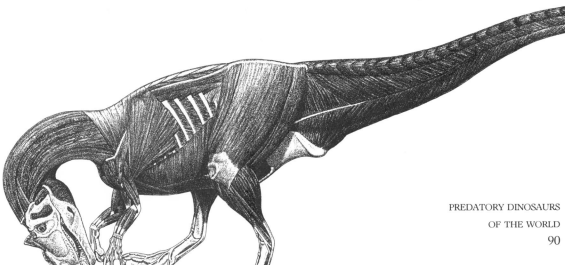

and mobile, and many of them do in predatory dinosaurs, may have been immobile in life. How a kinetic system may have worked also depends on the detailed muscles that operated it, and such anatomical minutiae are hard to restore in fossil animals.

In 1986, Robert Bakker suggested that the theropod skull was just loosely built, and could "give" a lot as big chunks of meat were swallowed. In this simple system, the cheeks and the tooth-bearing jawbones met the skull roof along what is in effect a skull-long hinge joint. At the same time, the tips of the lower jaw could pivot upon one another. Figure 4-5 shows how all this looseness would allow the jaws to bow outward. In addition, there may have been a hinge in the skull roof that allowed the snout to be depressed or lifted relative to the rest of the skull. Birds and lizards can do this, but whether this feature really existed in predatory dinosaurs, and how it might have worked, is much less certain.[3]

One extra head joint is known to have existed in the advanced avetheropod's lower jaw. In primitive predatory dinosaurs the big tooth-bearing bone, the dentary, was braced at its back end. The bracing came from a long upper prong or process of what was the main component of the rear of the jaw, the surangular. In avetheropods, this brace was missing, and Philip Gingerich and Robert Bakker point out that a joint had formed at the mandible's mid length, near its lower edge (Figure 4-5). In the front half of the jaw, lying inside the dentary, was a bone called the splenial; the angular helped to make up the back portion of the jaw. The front tip of the angular formed a loosely articulated hinge joint with the central groove of the splenial.[4] Such a "double-jointed" jaw would have been able to bow outward even further, increasing the size of things that could be bolted down (Figure 4-5). It is also possible, but less certain, that the joint had a vertical action as well that added impetus to its speed and force as it closed, greatly enhancing the jaw's power. In fact, it is interesting that two groups of herbivorous avetheropods, the ostrich-mimics and the oviraptors, lost the double-jointed jaw because they no longer needed it. The first toothed birds did retain the hinge joint, but in many modern birds it is altered. The bones are bound tightly together, but they are so thin that the jaws can still bow outward.

The main jaw joint itself was not a simple hinge. Instead, the lower jaw's cup-shaped joint surfaces were elongated fore and aft

4-3

The musculature of Allosaurus fragilis *USNM 4734; all theropod muscles followed much the same pattern. In the neck the powerful head-lifting muscles over-shadowed the weaker underside set. Trunk muscles were light. The big flat muscle on the side of the rib cage that inserts upon the upper arm is the latissimus dorsi. The muscles of the forearm were bunched around the elbow; they operated the spindly fingers via long tendons. The tail was more muscled than the trunk. Note that the contour of the big leg-pulling caudofemoralis can be seen under the tail-base muscles. The thigh was broad, and the calf muscles formed a great drumstick that operated the long toes via tendons.*

4-4

The skulls of the archaic toothed bird Hesperornis *(below) and the living loon (which share similar diving life-styles) show that the bird skull is even lighter than that of theropods. Struts behind the orbits are gone, and the premaxilla makes up almost the entire upper jaw. Compared to predatory dinosaurs the skeleton of the living big ground bird* Rhea *almost lacks a tail, the neck is longer and more supple, the arms are wings or their remnants, and the leg's femur is shorter, among other things.*

so that the lower jaw could slide back and forth relative to the skull (Figure 4-5).

Teeth were critical to most predatory dinosaurs, and in most they were latterly flattened, backward-curving, serrated blades (see Figure 2-4, page 31). In a minority of species, some or all of the teeth were more conical and serrations were reduced. In some, they were missing altogether. The upper teeth were almost always larger and more bladelike than the lower set, and the lower teeth never had the D-shaped cross section found in the upper teeth of some theropods. As we shall see, these differences between upper and lower teeth have important implications for how they worked. The teeth were always set in deep sockets— an important caution being that the teeth *sometimes* slipped partway out of their sockets after death and therefore look longer today than they did in life. The teeth were constantly replaced, so the tooth row was perpetually rejuvenated and kept sharp. Predatory dinosaur teeth did not intermesh tightly; the lowers slipped inside the uppers when the jaws closed. It is sometimes difficult to get the upper and lower jaws to match up. This is often due in part to preservational distortion, but sometimes it may have been that way in life. Even bird beaks do not always close tightly together. This is alright, since the lack of tightly meshing teeth frees dinosaur-bird systems of the need for close-fitting parts to work in the first place. However, such maladjustments might explain why the occasional theropod tooth shows extreme wear, although most show only a little at the tip. Broken teeth, fractured by the action of teeth on bone, are fairly common, and must have been painful!

Chris McGowen has cautioned strongly about restoring the muscles of extinct organisms.[5] The places to which muscles attach are sometimes marked by a scar on the bone, and we paleontologists often use these scars to map muscle paths. But McGowen found that in birds the muscles and the bone scars they are supposed to attach to often change position relative to one another. And, of course, the more different an extinct animal is from living forms, the more difficult it is to figure out its mus-

4-5
Slicing and swallowing in predaceous dinosaurs. In Allosaurus atrox and many other theropod species the jaw joint allowed the lower jaw to slide back and forth relative to the upper, and the large upper teeth were more bladed than the smaller, more conical lowers. A schematic drawing (lower left) shows how the lower teeth pinched out a fold of flesh, while the uppers were pulled back by head and neck muscles to do the most slicing and cutting. For easier swallowing, some of the skull and jaw bones were loosely attached (indicated by heavy lines in upper left and in the front views) so that the jaws could bow outward (front views).

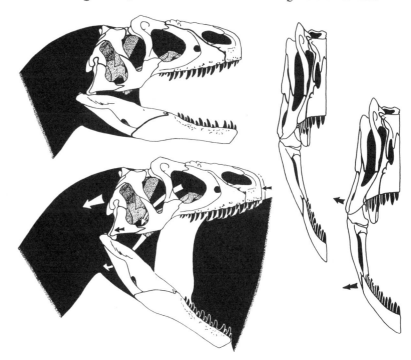

cles. In fact, there are many questions and details we will never know about dinosaur muscles, and my muscle restorations look more precise than they really are. But there is much we can still do. Some muscle scars are consistent and easily identified—such as the big "fourth" process on the back of the femur upon which attaches the large, tail-based caudofemoralis muscle. Other important muscles tend to follow similar anchor and insertion patterns from group to group (muscle anchors are toward the center of the animal, their insertions are closer to the extremities), so we can get a very good idea of what the profiles of many major muscles—the ones that do much of the work—were like in dinosaurs. In terms of restoring life appearances, this means that the basic contours of most of the body and limbs can be recaptured quite reliably.[6]

One important set of muscles, and one that is often ignored, is the anterior pterygoideus muscle complex of the head[7] (see Figure 4-2). Missing in lizards, birds, and mammals, the jaw-closing anterior pterygoideus is found in primitive reptiles and crocs as well as predatory dinosaurs where it fills up much of the snout. From there it runs down and back through a opening in the roof of the mouth into the inner opening of the lower jaw. The anterior pterygoideus probably bulged gently out of the big preorbital opening. In 1987, Lawrence Witmer argued that in dinosaurs the preorbital opening contained pneumatic sinuses, rather than muscles. I find it unlikely that dinosaurs had such large sinuses, much larger than in birds. Witmer points out that crocs do not have a preorbital opening for the anterior pterygoideus to bulge out of, but this probably serves to make the skull heavier for swimming underwater (likewise, the opening behind the orbit is nearly closed in crocs). I believe that the big preorbital openings developed to improve the function of the very large and powerful jaw-closing anterior pterygoideus muscles, whose great length greatly increased the velocity at which the mouth closed.

Working in conjunction with the pterygoideus were the temporalis, which filled up the big cheek "box" of the skull. Anchored around the inner rim of the upper temporal opening, on top of the back of the skull and other points close by, these muscles are found in all vertebrates, and they are the ones you can feel working above your ears as you close your jaws. The openings behind the orbit eyes, the postorbital openings, developed to improve the function of these muscles, and the muscles bulged gently out of these openings. The temporalis group passed downward and inserted in the mandible's inner opening. Some of the temporalis ran forward into the hollow front half of the jaw, where they may have helped operate the extra jaw joint in those species that had one.

Probably the most powerful predatory dinosaur jaw-closer was the pterygoideus posterior. This arose from the bones of the roof of the mouth, then looped around the mandible to its rear outside surface. A very large muscle, it formed a great bulge about the rear of the jaw, one that dinosaur artists should take note of (see Figure 4-2).

The combined power of these muscles was tremendous, indeed fantastic in the big species. Big crocs produce perhaps 3000 pounds of force when they bite. Most predatory dinosaurs had relatively more powerful jaw musculature, and many were bigger-headed than crocs to boot—so you get an idea of the forces involved. The bigger meat-eating dinosaurs, above one or two tons, could have swallowed an average-sized human being whole. Single-gulp meals always went down head first to prevent choking. Predaceous dinosaurs lacked cheek muscles; the jaw joint was an open hinge, and the jaw muscles were long-fibered, so they could open their mouths very wide, like cats and dogs, perhaps to sixty or seventy degrees at the maximum.

Figures 4-4 and 4-6 show how the predatory dinosaur neck was, with a few notable exceptions, S-curved like in birds, though not to as extreme a degree. In most animals, lizards, mammals, etc., the neck is fairly straight. Even in the first predatory dinosaurs the articulating surfaces of the neck vertebrae were strongly beveled wedges that naturally articulated in a vertical, swanlike S curve. In 1983, Tarsitano claimed that theropod necks were really straight; however, the extent of the beveling in most theropod necks not only rules this out as a possibility but in some species was so strong that it is questionable whether they could ever fully straighten out their necks at all! This does not mean the neck was stiff. The auxiliary articulations of the neck vertebrae above the main spools—the zygapophysis—were large, so the vertebrae remained in contact with one another as the neck went through a wide range of motion. The occipital condyle-axis/atlas joint, which connected the head to the neck, was also a highly mobile ball-and-socket joint. The head was not carried in the same line as the swan neck, however, but was held at a fairly sharp angle to it—again, rather like a bird's, but not so extreme.

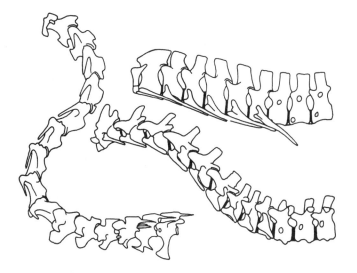

4-6
In thecodonts like Euparkeria *(upper right) the neck is fairly straight. But in such predatory dinosaurs as* Velociraptor *(lower right) the vertebrae are beveled to follow a strong S curve. This is even more developed in birds—a loon is shown (left). Notice that in these archosaurs the first neck vertebra is small; the cartilagenous intervertebral discs are indicated in black.*

A very distinctive feature of archosaurs, including the predatory dinosaurs, was the long overlapping neck ribs (Figure 4-6). These ribs slid past each other, and gave the neck both suppleness and strength.

The most prominent neck muscles were those that ran from the shoulder region and inserted on the back of the braincase (Figure 4-3). In many species, especially the bigger ones, the combination of the S curve and great muscle masses, supported by tall vertebral spines and a broad transverse crest atop the back face of the braincase, resulted in "bulldog" necks.

Now that we have a better picture of how typical flesh-eating dinosaurs' heads and necks were put together, we can figure out in more detail how they bit their victims. The S-curved neck was oriented toward vertical action, as was the deep, narrow skull. These long-limbed bipeds were tall animals that struck out and down at their victims, a very different system than that of low-slung lizards, who use their laterally flexible bodies and necks to strike sideways. Robert Bakker showed that since the lower teeth were smaller, more conical, and less curved than the upper ones, they dug into and pinched out a fold of flesh while the bigger upper blades did the actual slicing and cutting[8] (see Figure 4-5). This means that the skull had to slide backward relative to the mandibles. The sliding jaw joint allowed such a motion, and the powerful down-and-backward-running fibers of the pterygoideus muscles helped accomplish it. So did the high-powered neck muscles, which first helped drive the jaws forward into the prey, then pulled the upper jaw down and back to further lengthen and deepen the wound. Violently shaking the head back and forth would increase the damage.

With the exception of the posterior pterygoideus that loops around the underside of the mandible, the major jaw-working muscles were pretty much inside the skull (see Figure 4-2). So, unlike mammals, but like reptiles and birds, theropods did not have many external facial or other outer skull muscles apart from thin bands of lip muscles, the eyelid muscles, and the depressor mandibulae at the back of the head. The latter helped open the jaws (see Figure 4-2), something gravity alone cannot do as quickly because of the jaw-closing muscles. As for the lip bands, these were like those of lizards, and were supplied with blood vessels and nerves via numerous small openings (foramina).[9] These lips could be lifted to bare the teeth in a threatening gesture, or lowered to help cover the teeth when the mouth was closed. Restorations that show theropods with naked croclike teeth are very much in error. But the tips of the teeth may have sometimes been exposed like some house cats'—especially in the long-toothed forms like *Dilophosaurus, Tyrannosaurus rex,* and young *Albertosaurus libratus.* The soft elastic skin that stretched between the backs of the upper and lower jaws and covered the jaw muscles was a related feature. Completely folded when the jaws were closed, it stretched out to a large sheet when they opened.

The fact that dinosaurs have few facial muscles is a boon to artists. It means that the living head looked very much like the skull, with most of the struts obvious and the internal muscles bulging out a bit between them. Take a look at a big lizard's head and you will see the same thing. This makes dinosaur reconstruction a nirvanic exercise compared to that of doing fossil mammals, where whole layers of facial muscles have to be reconstructed with the vague hope that the finished product has something to do with reality—would one be able to take a dog's skull and come up with Lassie? But despite this wonderful advantage, dinoartists again and again manage to get the basic head shape wrong. And what a shame it is to miss the graceful curves of the *Albertosaurus libratus* snout, or to shape the head of *Tyrannosaurus rex* more like a box than the ingeniously intricate object it really was!

The roofs or palates of theropod mouths were a little like

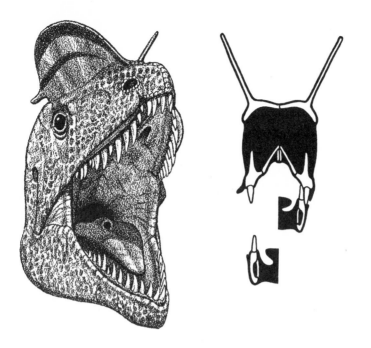

cathedrals, being highly vaulted in transverse cross section. This advanced feature is unlike the flat-topped mouths of most reptiles. The soft tissues pretty much followed the contours of the supporting bones, so we know what the roof of the mouth looked like as the jaws gaped open, as shown in Figure 4-7. Important openings were the paired internal nostrils, which in most forms entered the mouth a little forward of its mid length. However, at least some of the advanced theropods may have had soft secondary palates, rather like the hard secondary palates of crocodilians and mammals. Secondary palates entube the external nostrils so that they exit at the back of the mouth. Both vaulted and secondary palates give air room to pass over the food as their owners work it in their mouths. In birds, the opening of the throat trachea can be seen at the base of the tongue when the mouth is opened, and this may have been true of theropods as well. The predatory dinosaurs' big snout must have held very large olfactory organs, and the contours of theropod braincases show that their brain's olfactory lobes were usually large too. Hence, they could smell quite well, though not as well as such mammalian specialists as dogs.

On page 94 of this chapter I discussed my disagreement with Lawrence Witmer's belief that the preorbital opening contained sinuses. What is more likely is that the shallow depression *around* the preorbital opening was filled with sinuses, as shown in Figure 4-2. The one or two small openings in the depression ahead of the big preorbital opening probably channeled air tubes from the head's inner sinuses to its outer preorbital set. These same sinuses probably covered the jaw muscle that filled the preorbital opening, and like them bulged gently outward.

Long, slender hyoid or throat bones have been found with theropods. They probably supported tongues that were fairly large but rather stiff, like a lizard's. Stiff tongues served the purpose, for predators gulp their food and have no need to carefully and precisely manipulate bolts of meat in their mouths. Herbivores, in contrast, use more supple tongues to properly position each wad of fodder for chewing.

The large eye sockets of most theropods show that they had big eyes. In smaller species the eyeball often filled the entire orbit. In larger species the eye did not fill the eye socket. Instead, it invariably was set high in the orbit. We know this because in some theropods the lower half of the orbit is closed off by a bony process. We can sometimes tell exactly how big the eye was by the bony rings found in many species, which were nearly the same diameter as the eyeballs they contained. Birds still have eye rings, though oddly enough the bigger theropods seem not to have them. However, the size of the *exposed* eyes are often exaggerated in dinosaur restorations. Much of the eyeball was covered by the eyelids, and even an ostrich's great eyes do not look that enormous. Also, as theropods got larger, eye size increased less rapidly. So while *Tyrannosaurus rex* had very big eyes, they did not appear so in its four-foot-long head. Theropod irises were probably large, as they are in birds and reptiles. This means that the eye whites were pushed toward the periphery of the eyeball and were always covered by the eyelids.

Large dinosaur irises allowed more pupil dilation, which helps increase the light-gathering ability of an eye. Slit pupils can further increase dilation over round pupils, and various theropod species may have had either kind. Most reptiles have a high density of retinal cones for superb, high-resolution, color eyesight during the day; birds even more so. It is most probable that the big-eyed dinosaurs, being in between the two groups, did too. Indeed, their ability to see objects in fine detail was most likely well above ours. To improve night vision, it is likely that dinosaur retinas had numerous low-light sensitive rods, and catlike reflective screens behind the retina. Most reptiles and birds do. If you shone a flashlight into a theropod's eyes, they would probably have glowed red, green, or yellow.

Dinosaurs, like reptiles and birds, were so visually oriented, their olfactory and auditory senses playing a secondary role, because they tended to be creatures of the day. This all started because the ancestral reptiles had to sun themselves to operate, so they tended to bed down at night. Early, warm-blooded mammals on the other hand were largely nocturnal; hence, they developed uniquely sophisticated and sensitive smell and hearing organs for living in the dark. Mammalian eyesight is therefore relatively less important, and humans and other primates are unusual among mammals in our well-developed color vision.

The majority of predaceous dinosaur eyes faced sideways; their forward-looking binocular vision was very limited. However, in tyrannosaurs and many protobirds the upper temporal bars behind the eye sockets became much broader than the preorbital bones in front of the same. This tilted the eyes forward, giving the eyes a good deal of overlapping, depth-perceiving forward vision.

Predatory dinosaur ears were set at the back of the skull, high up between the jaw-opening muscle and the jaw-supporting quadrate bone (see Figure 4-2). The eardrum was set in a shallow pit, as there was no external ear like those of mammals. Part of the quadrate's back face was sculpted to support the ear channel's front surface. The details of this arrangement vary from group to group. For example, in allosaur-tyrannosaurs the backside of the quadrate is flat and the ear opening pointed directly sideways. In archaeopterygians and dromaeosaurs the auditory surface of the quadrate was a forwardly directed funnel, and the ear pointed that way.

Brain size in predatory dinosaurs ranged from the high reptilian to the low avian.[10] The former was true of the paleodinosaurs and bigger theropods, which tended to have more brains than big herbivorous dinosaurs. The smaller theropods were especially large-brained for dinosaurs. Even early, primitive *Coelophysis* had a brain relatively as big as that of the more birdlike *Archaeopteryx*. The advanced protobirds had the biggest brains of all, equal to ostriches and the like. Comparing brain size is somewhat difficult, for in a series of animals of similar anatomy the size of the brain does not increase as fast as overall size. In predatory dinosaurs, the big ones especially, the braincase was a modest part of the skull, which served more as a support for various muscles than as the brain's housing. The actual size of the brain in the small-brained species is difficult to estimate, because like in living reptiles the brain did not fill the entire brain cavity. Only as brains got larger did they come to fill out the entire space. Dinosaur brains tended to be rather simple, and braincase structure shows that the various sensory lobes—optic, olfactory, and auditory—made up much of the volume. So predatory dinosaurs were not as bright as their modern mammalian counterparts. But one should not underestimate their intelligence. Reptiles do surprisingly well in a number of aptitude tests, and the bird-brained theropods were quite smart. One does wonder what kind of thoughts the dinosaurs thought—I often wonder the same about my bigger-brained, predaceous cat.

My skeletal restorations show the necks in the "neutral" S curve that the vertebrae naturally followed. When walking and running, however, the dinosaurs often pulled their necks back into an even stronger, head-high S curve that lightened the load on the muscles, improved the view, and helped shift these biped's center of weight further aft and closer to the hind limbs (see Figure 6-4, page 142).

Along with the neck, the rest of the predatory dinosaur's spinal column was distinctly birdlike. This is manifest in a demarcation of four distinct sections—neck, trunk, hip, and tail. Although this may seem an obvious point, in many reptiles the vertebrae are not so demarcated and are fairly alike (see Figure 4-6, page 96). While the swan-curved neck of theropods has long been recognized, the gentle upward arch formed by the moderately beveled trunk vertebrae has been less so—for only the first couple of trunk vertebrae curved up into the neck. Indeed, almost all archosaurs are like this, the one exception, ironically enough, being birds which all have straight backs. This also differs from the straight or down-slung backs of many reptiles and mammals.

Usually, the vertebrae's large, spool-shaped bodies, the centra, are separated from each other by cartilage discs. It is important to take these into account, for if the vertebrae were put together without these spacers then the column would be too short by 10 percent or so. Sometimes articulated backbones were preserved like this, because the cartilage discs dried up after death and pulled the vertebrae tightly together. The cartilage discs were elastic, and the early galloping lagosuchians still had fairly flexible trunks like the thecodonts'. But the other bipedal predaceous dinosaurs' vertebral spines were often interconnected by partly ossified ligaments, and they had much smaller zygapophysis on the back trunk vertebrae. Both features restricted the mobility of the trunk, especially the back half of it, yet another adaptation found in birds. Indeed, the back vertebrae of some birds are fused together.

The hip, attached to the spinal column by two sacral vertebrae in paleodinosaurs, also becomes more firmly placed in theropods by four to six such hip vertebrae. So, although the front of the trunk was fairly flexible, drawings showing theropods bending their backs sharply over a victim are incorrect.[11] These rigid backs and hips were very unlike the supple bodies of such modern predators as cats and dogs—and they are hard to explain. They could not have been simply for weight support, as they were a feature of even the small, early theropods. Nor were they more efficient, since birds have been found to have as much bone mass in their bodies as mammals. We can, however, now see why the theropod neck was so very flexible: it made up for the stiffness of the body.

There was a third and final arch in predatory dinosaur vertebral columns. The tail base vertebrae were beveled, so they too formed a short, gentle, upward arch. The tail vertebrae's zygapophysis were oriented more toward the vertical than the horizontal; hence, tail motion was freer up and down than sideways. The amount of vertical flexibility was good, but restorations showing theropod tails undulating in serpentine curves go too far.

The consistency in the number of vertebrae in theropods is a surprising thing. In most species there are ten neck, thirteen trunk, and five hip vertebrae.[12] Usually, reptiles, dinosaurs, and birds are much more variable; although most mammals have seven neck vertebrae. Why the vertebral counts of most theropods were so synchronized is not known. It could have been a genetic quirk, a random fixation that stayed in place as long as it did no harm. In some protobirds the last trunk vertebra did start turning into a support for the hip, giving them twelve trunk and six hip vertebrae.

The bipedal predatory dinosaur's spinal column was cantilevered over the hind limbs. Because support started at the hips, each vertebra going forward had less to support than the one behind it. Consequently, there was a tendency, though not an absolute one, for the trunk and neck vertebrae to decrease in size going forward, whereas in quadrupedal animals the shoulder vertebrae are often the largest. Of course the tail bones also dwindle in size going back toward the tip. The neck and tail were dynamic balance beams, but not critical ones; ostriches balance on two feet without the benefit of tails, and people do fine without tails or long necks.

The vertebral spines over the trunk and hips of allosaurs and tyrannosaurs were not very tall, showing that taller ones were not needed in bipeds of their size. On the other hand, ceratosaurs, metriacanthosaurs, acrocanthosaurs, and spinosaurs developed increasingly tall neck, trunk, and tail spines that projected well above the large ilial bone of the hip. As these were taller than needed for simple support, their hosts must have been true finbacks (albeit modest ones in the case of ceratosaurs and metriacanthosaurs). The fin was very prominent in acrocanthosaurs, and so tall in spinosaurs that it formed a great "sail." There would have been no purpose in having muscles on the spines, since the spines were spaced too closely together for them to move much. The fin's functions were probably multiple, having most likely evolved for display, especially in the breeding season. The sails may also have become important as cooling radiators, like elephant ears.

The forward trunk ribs of paleodinosaurs and theropods were backswept, sometimes sharply so, a typically archosaurian feature still found in crocs and birds. It is quite obvious in articulated dinosaur specimens. Yet dinosaurs are usually restored with vertical front ribs, as though they were mammals. This mistake leads to other errors: the shoulder girdle is swung further forward than it really was, because the rib heads are angled relative to the body's main axis and swung too far outward, and the chest is overbloated. In reality the chest was always deep rather than broad in predatory dinosaurs. The mid-trunk *was* broader, in part because these ribs are more vertical than those behind. In summary, the dinosaur rib cage was short and deep, very much of the avian mold. Note that in early theropods the first trunk rib was bowed forward, the second was straight in side view, and the rest are bowed backward. In advanced theropods, all the ribs were usually bowed backward.

In slender-necked species, some of the more superficial side muscles of the neck may have been narrow enough to expose the internal neck muscles. In bigger species, these would be entirely covered over (compare the muscle studies of smaller and larger species in Part II). The powerful side neck muscles must have formed a prominent and attractive contour over the weaker throat set, something like in horses.

One group of muscles whose external profile is almost impossible to figure out is the ventral throat muscles. They ran from the side of the skull and back of the jaws down to the base of the shoulder girdle. Some artists restore theropods with deep throat muscles like crocs. This is possible, but I prefer to give these narrow-headed creatures a more modest set, like those of mammalian carnivores. Such throat muscles would have bulged out when whole animals or big chunks of meat were swallowed.

Since predatory dinosaur rib cages were rigid boxes, the trunk musculature was rather light, like in birds. The most powerful were those muscles that ran astride the vertebral spines, in the trough formed by the vertebrae's winglike transverse processes. The upper portions of the spines were more lightly muscled—ligaments held these together. It is quite possible that the ends of the trunk spines formed a knobby profile line in some species, especially the tall, spined ones. Ilio-costalis muscles may have continued the profile of the hip's ilial blade onto the trunk. Behind the hips, the tail muscles were probably confined to the limits of the vertebral processes. The exception is the powerful tail-based hind limb retractor, the great caudofemoralis, that arose from the side of the tail (see Figure 4-3). As each side's caudofemoralis muscles contracted and pulled their respective

4-8
In thecodonts (Euparkeria, upper left), the lungs were of the normal dead-end type, large bags operated by long front ribs. In early theropods (Coelophysis, lower left), air sacs (stippled) may have been beginning to appear on the sides of the belly. In protobird theropods (Velociraptor, upper right) and birds (duck, lower right), short front ribs mean that the lungs were smaller, and that large air sacs on the sides of the belly were ventilated by long belly ribs. The upper rib cage is shown in the last three subjects to show the rib-vertebra articulations.

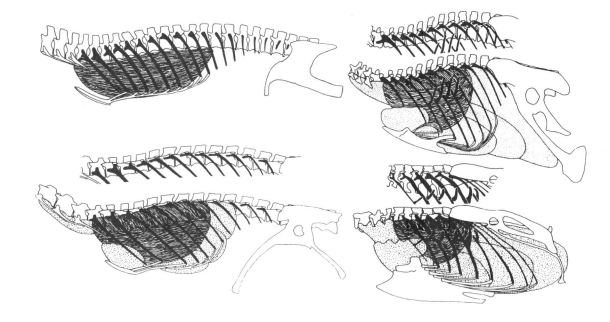

leg backward, they would also have pulled on and swung the tail from side to side with each step.

It is possible that predatory dinosaurs stored fat when prey was especially abundant—perhaps up to 15 percent or so of their lean mass. Much more than this, however, is unlikely because of the need to stay light in weight and fleet of foot. Indeed, theropods probably looked lean, sleek, and a little bony, like big dogs and cats. "Plump" theropod drawings are certainly wrong.[13] What fat they had may have been concentrated around the base of the tail. The fatless tails I usually draw can be taken to show the animals in the lean season.

What can we tell about what was inside predatory dinosaur rib cages? In most animals the lungs are large dead-end bags which are ventilated by motions of the long front ribs. Dinosaur belly ribs are much shorter (Figure 4-8). The paleodinosaurs and basal theropods were like this; in fact, the first trunk rib was a little longer than the next. Birds are very different, having much smaller, stiffer lungs set high up in the rib cage.[14] The frontmost trunk ribs are short and no longer do much to ventilate the lungs. Instead, the lungs are connected to air sacs that line the sides of the abdomen. The belly ribs are long and inflate and deflate these air sacs. The air sacs in turn act as bellows to ventilate the lungs. The system is set up so that air flows through the lungs in one direction only, and it is always fresh. "Dead," oxygen-depleted air is not pushed back and forth with each breath; instead, it is completely exhaled each time. A look at complete avetheropod rib cages shows they were avian in design. The front ribs were short, too short to have ventilated large normal lungs. The belly ribs were long, and this can be explained only if they were ventilating large abdominal air sacs that in turn fed unidirectional-air flow lungs.

Such advanced respiratory systems must have been accompanied by high-performance circulatory systems. The aim would have been to get the oxygen where it was needed as fast as it was needed. Not only that, but high blood pressures were needed to get blood up to the brain carried atop the S-curved neck. High pressure/high speed blood flow requires a sophisticated four-chambered heart of the type found in birds and mammals. In fact, even crocodilians have hearts much like this, and so it was probably a basic archosaurian adaptation. The large heart was set low in the chest, just above the sternum and behind the armpits (Figure 4-9).

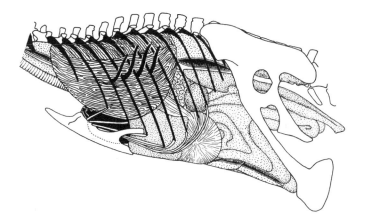

Gut cavity of the theropod Veloci-raptor; all the predaceous dinosaurs were much like this. Most of the air sacs that lined the sides of the trunk (see Figure 4-8) have been cut away. The heart (in black) is just above the sternum. The liver was just behind the heart, the kidneys lay tucked up under the vertebrae, and the digestive tract and reproductive organs filled the belly, ran through the pelvic canal, and exited above the ischium—they did not fill in between the lower hip elements.

To understand the predatory dinosaur's appearance, we must remember how predators live and function. Meat is easy to break down and digest, so predators have short, uncomplicated digestive tracts (Figure 4-9). Predators gorge at a carcass, then fast until they are hungry again. The stomach is highly distendable so it can hold big meals. In accordance with this the abdominal "ribs," or more correctly gastralia, of predatory dinosaurs were poorly ossified, multijointed, and very flexible. So hungry theropods on the hunt should be drawn with hollow cat- or dog-like bellies. In some of the big mounted skeletons, the abdominal ribs are mounted to form a distended belly, which would be true only after feeding on a kill. A satiated theropod must have waddled away from its meal!

The hardest thing to figure out about extinct animals is the position of the shoulder girdle (Figure 4-10), because it hangs independently of the vertebrae column, unlike the hips, which are tightly fixed. Well-articulated specimens can help out, but even here some displacement of the forelimb might have occurred. The shoulder girdle usually attached to the second long trunk rib via a short and often cartilagenous sternal rib, so when the anterior ribs are properly swept back, we are better able to work out its positioning. In general, it seems that the anterior edge of the shoulder girdle was set just below the juncture of the neck and trunk vertebrae in big theropods. In smaller theropods it was set further back by a vertebrae or so, the effect making the neck longer. In birds, the coracoid, the bone below the shoulder joint, is very long. This sets the shoulder joint high on the chest, and makes the shoulder blade horizontal. The protobird theropods were also built this way. But most theropods had more normal, short coracoids, so the shoulder joint was set low and the shoulder blade was much more vertical.

Not much is known of the chest or sternal plates in theropods. The few that have been discovered are usually small, although a few protobird theropods had big, birdlike sternums. Elizabeth Nicholls and Anthony Russell showed in 1985 that an extra sternal process, little and slender, is attached to the back of the sternum; in protobirds and birds this becomes fused to the sternal plates. The clavicles of most theropods are as poorly known as the sternals. Some theropods and birds lack clavicles entirely, or they may be small, separate, and paired like in *Segisaurus*. In some protobirds and most birds, they are quite the opposite, having enlarged and fused together into a kind of "wishbone" furcula (Figure 4-10). In 1984, Richard Thulborn ar-

4-10
In such early theropods as Coelophysis *(upper left), the shoulder girdle was fairly normal, with a short coracoid below the shoulder joint and a large, vertical shoulder blade. In protobirds like Archaeopteryx (upper right section, left figure) and* Velociraptor *(lower left), things became more birdlike, with a long, slender shoulder blade and a very large coracoid. There were two patterns. In* Archaeopteryx *and flying birds (upper right), the coracoid is sharply reflexed relative to the shoulder blade, and the fused clavicles (cl) and acrocoracoid process (ac) are large. In* Velociraptor *and flightless birds (bottom right), the coracoid does not point back as much, and the clavicles and acrocoracoid are often reduced or missing. Note that* Velociraptor *had big sternal plates, like those of birds. The arrows point to the basic orientation of the shoulder joint.*

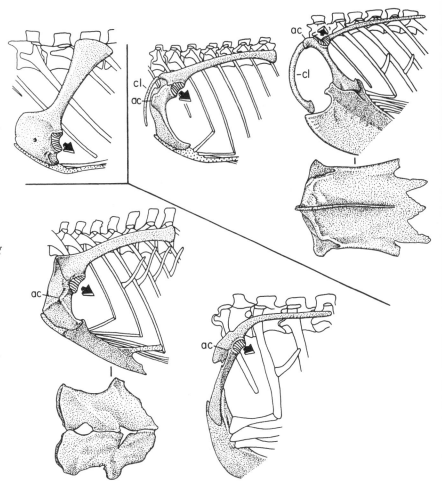

gued a good case for allosaurs and tyrannosaurs having slender furculas, but since no such furcula has been found in place, I am not convinced. Especially since displaced and cojoined abdominal ribs can look very much like a furcula.

Nicholls and Russell made the novel argument that theropods had highly mobile shoulder blades, like those of the peculiar chameleon lizards and many mammals.[15] While it is quite true that quadrupedal dinosaurs were like this,[16] most protobirds were not—their big birdlike furculas and coracoids tightly interlocked and attached in some cases, to big sternal plates. In most theropods the coracoid may have been able to glide back and forth to some degree in the sternal groove—but probably less than in quadrupedal species, and not enough for artists to notice.

In quadrupedal dinosaurs, including the early predatory protodinosaurs, the shoulder joint faced downward. The forelimb could then work in a nearly vertical plane beneath the body.[17] As the bipedal predatory dinosaurs needed the forelimbs for other purposes—ones that required them to reach further out and in front of the body—their shoulder joint faced more outward (see Figure 4-10 and Figure 9-6, page 217). In many predaceous dinosaurs the elbow's twin, bulbous joints for the lower arm bones were equal in size, making it the simple kind of hinge

4-11
The forelimb of the early theropod Coelophysis (left) worked much like those of most animals: the elbow was a simple hinge and the wrist a many-boned, up-and-down flexible joint. In Velociraptor antirrhopus (right), the outer half of the elbow's joint was enlarged like in birds (upper right), and the wrist had become a large pulley. This caused the arm to automatically fold itself up when tucked in. The elbows of some primitive dinosaurs related to herrerasaurs (upper left) seem to have a crude version of this system.

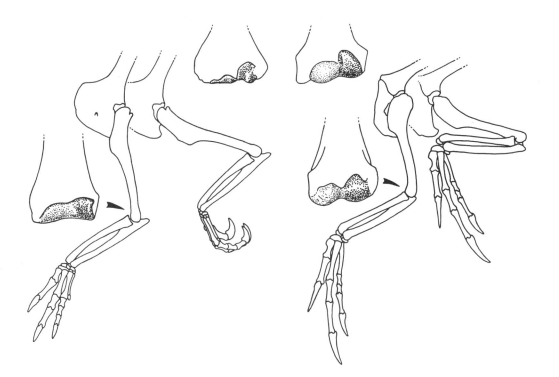

108

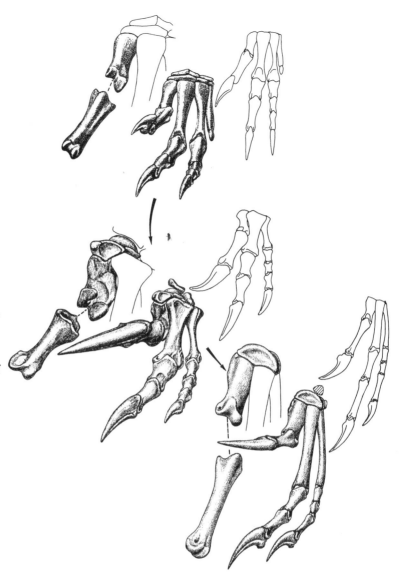

4-12
In predatory dinosaur hands, such as primitive Coelophysis rhodesiensis *(top), big* Allosaurus fragilis *(center), and birdlike* Velociraptor antirrhopus *(lower right), the joint at the base of the thumb was twisted so that the thumb rotated inward as the fingers extended (shaded drawings; outlines show the hands with fingers flattened out). This made for a powerful weapon (for what happens to this joint in birds, see Figure 9-7, page 220). Theropod hands also became more birdlike, going from four short to three long fingers, and developing a pulley-like wrist joint. The last is partly developed in* Allosaurus, *fully so in* Coelophysis.

it is in most animals. The wrist bones were also most flexible in an up-and-down direction, like our wrists. In many protobirds, however, the elbow's outer joint bulb was enlarged, and one of the wrist bones became a large, semicircular pulley upon which the hand could pivot through a large sideways arc. Next time you eat chicken wings, notice that birds still have this kind of "push-pull" elbow-wrist system, which is what folds the forelimb up so neatly (Figure 4-11). Protobirds such as *Archaeopteryx* and *Velociraptor* could fold their arms this way, although not as well as birds. The early herrerasaurs may also have had a less developed version of this system.

Paleodinosaur and theropod fingers were supple so they could flex far back and grasp tightly. The most interesting finger was the thumb. It was the stoutest, and had a base joint that twisted inward. As Figure 4-12 shows, this forced the thumb to turn inward and away from the other digits as it extended forward from the palm.[18] The thumb was big-clawed too, so this divergent organ made for a nasty weapon. In birds the thumb remains divergent, but it is reduced and supports the specialized "alula" feathers that act as an extra aerodynamic control surface, the purpose of which is explained on pages 219-220 in Chapter 9.

One of the more prominent forelimb muscles is the lattisimus dorsi, which arises from the side of the rib cage and inserts on the back of the humerus, about opposite the lower end of that upper arm bone's deltoid crest. This muscle formed a prominent contour at the armpit. The humerus head and deltoid crest must have been prominent also, even when fleshed out. The fingers were rather like bird feet, being slender and knobby-jointed, not heavily muscled or padded like ours. They were operated via long tendons by muscles bunched around the elbow. The back of the ulna bone was unmuscled just below the elbow, however, just like the back of our forearms.

The old way of restoring theropods was with their bodies reared in an upright human-like pose. But such a body posture is unusual even for bipeds, and a few artists dissented by showing them horizontal-backed like ground birds or kangaroos. Newman's 1970 restudy of *Tyrannosaurus* made this the generally accepted standard. But the *real* reason theropods moved with level spinal columns is still not widely understood. It is that muscles operate best when they are not stretched more than 1.3 times their length during a working cycle. In theropods, important hind limb retractors were anchored on the base of the ischium, the back one of the two lower hip bones (Figure 4-14). When the hips were horizontal, these muscles were set behind the hind limb, and could pull back on the femur while staying within their stretch limits. When the hips tilted up, the ischial retractors were then *between* the hind limbs. Not only would they end up being badly overstretched if they tried to work from this position, but they would not even be able to pull back on the femur.

The theropod hip socket confirms this arrangement. The hip joint was fully articulated together only as long as the femur remained perpendicular to the hips, or forward of that. As the

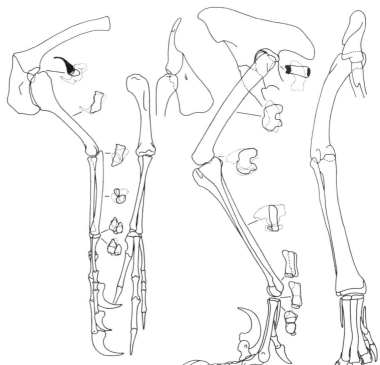

4-13
How the arms and legs were put together in Velociraptor antirrhopus. *The details show how each joint articulated, and the cross sections of the long bones at midshaft. The arm joints were flexible and could move through wide arcs. Leg posture was much more limited to fore and aft action, and the knee was always flexed.*

body reared up and the femur retracted well behind perpendicular, then the femoral head lost its complete articulation with the hip joint's posterior articulating surface. A theropod or paleodinosaur that reared to scan the landscape or intimidate a foe was alright only as long as it stood still or moved slowly. Moving fast with a reared body would be injurious. The exact horizontal positioning of the theropod body when in normal motion is uncertain. Some think it was fully horizontal, while others think it was tilted up twenty or so degrees.[19] Actually, we cannot reconstruct muscle stretch patterns precisely enough to tell, and posture may have varied among and within species, or even within individuals from time to time.

The hips and hind limbs were the most birdlike features of theropods. The hip's big, platelike ilia bones were long, deep rectangular structures. In paleodinosaurs, they were shorter and less avian. The hip socket was especially birdlike, in that it was deep and cylindrical, with a broad posterior joint surface for the head of the femur. The femur and tibia were strong bones, unlike the slender fibula, which was fixed tightly to the tibia not only at

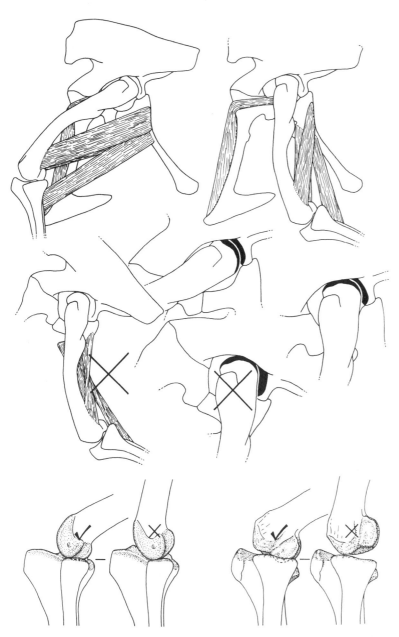

Hip and knee action. The muscles based on the broad apron of the ischium could pull the femur back only when the hip was close to horizontal and the femur moved no further back than perpendicular to the hip (top row). If the body reared up (left center), then the muscles would be badly overshortened as the femur swung back. Likewise, the head of the femur remained in proper articulation with the back of the hip socket (both indicated in black) when the hip was horizontal (center right row). Tilting the hips up leaves the hip socket out of joint with the femoral head. In birds (lower left) the knee is permanently flexed because the outer condyle of the femur is a thin guiding wedge that runs between the heads of the tibia and fibula. If the knee is straightened (far left), then the condyle-wedge is no longer in its groove and the knee is easily twisted. Remarkably, the knee of gigantic Tyrannosaurus rex (lower right) is built in exactly the same way.

both ends, but also a third of the way down its shaft via a special flange of the tibia. Predatory dinosaur knees and ankles were rather simple hinge joints. A very avian detail was an upward projection of the major ankle bone, the astragalus, that ran up the front face of the tibia (see Figures 8-5 and 8-8, pages 182 and 189).

Most birdlike of all was the theropod foot. Narrow and compressed, it was in practical terms three-toed, with toes two, three, and four bearing most of the load (Figure 4-15). The outer digit was reduced to a splint at the ankle, yet it was almost always present and strong. It may have been mobile and flipped backward to act as an extra lever between the achilles tendon and the foot. The exception is *Avimimus,* in which the splint is fused to the other foot bones. This may be the precursor to the avian condition, in which the outer toe is completely lost. The inner or first toe was even more interesting because its cannon bone no longer reached all the way up to the ankle. In birds that still have this toe (the big ground birds and some others do not) it is fully reversed and points backward. In articulated theropod specimens, it seems less reversed. But, oddly enough, some theropod footprints show the toe fully reversed. This discrepancy has been little noticed and is unexplained. Perhaps this toe was loose and could rotate forward and backward in theropods. In the paleodinosaurs and herreravians, the inner toe is still complete and unreversed, hence the foot has four complete toes and is not so birdlike (Figure 4-15).

Mammal and *adult* bird joints have highly finished or ossified bone surfaces covered by a thin veneer of cartilage. Dinosaur joint bone surfaces are rugose and pitted, showing they were capped by thick cartilage joint surfaces. You can see cartilage joints of this type next time you have poultry for dinner. Birds become fully grown in size before their joints are fully ossified—that is, before their bone structure is completely mature. Because

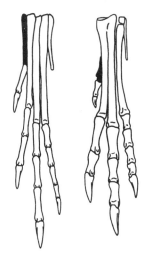

4-15
The two basic foot types in predatory dinosaurs and birds. On the left, a Lagosuchus *foot shows the four toes found in paleodinosaurs and herreravians. On the right, the three-toed foot of early* Coelophysis *typifies those of all theropods and birds. Both feet are lefts. The paleodinosaur-herreravian foot is four-toed because the inner (first) toe is complete—with its cannon bone (in black) reaching all the way to the ankle—and because the inner toe faces the same direction as the others. In theropods and birds the inner toe's cannon bone is shortened and no longer reachs the ankle, and the toe is twisted (reversed) relative to the others, so it is considered three-toed. In a few advanced theropods and some birds the inner toe is lost completely. In both types of feet the three central toes (two, three, and four) usually bear the load, while the outer toe (five) is reduced to a cannon bone splint; the latter is lost in birds.*

it wastes money to feed fowl after they have reached their maximum weight, slaughter houses do them in at this stage. When examining the knee of your meal, notice that the cartilage articular surfaces are very precisely sculpted. Adult bird knees look just the same, but the cartilage has turned into bone. Crocodilians also have complex cartilagenous limb joints, but they retain them into full adulthood. Theropods followed much the same pattern of development.

Predatory dinosaur hind limbs were running legs that worked like those of birds. Because the hip socket, knee, and ankle were cylinders that worked only fore and aft, and the shank bones were locked together, the limb was "stiff." It could not rotate much about its long axis, and its action was always close to vertical. It could not splay outward, despite drawings that show otherwise.[20] Recently, *Archaeopteryx* was accused of having a more lizard-like sprawling gait, in part because the hip socket is closed off to a degree on the inside.[21] Actually, a number of bird hip sockets are partly closed, and it is even a little so in the protobird *Velociraptor antirrhopus*. Overall, the hip joint of *Archaeopteryx* is of the erect theropod-avian type, and it worked that way. The theropod femur and knee were bowed out a little, especially as they swung forward and had to clear the belly. The ankle is also bowed a little, in its case inward. Such bowed-knee, knock-ankled limbs can be seen in birds, in horses, and in antelope. Fossil footprints confirm that predatory dinosaur feet paced along a narrow-gauge trail or trackway—the faster the gait, the narrower the trackway tended to be. Trackways also show that theropods were sometimes a little pigeon-toed, rarely did the feet splay outwards instead. Some have attributed this to a ducklike waddle. Theropods probably did waddle a little, but these long-limbed, narrow-hipped animals moved smoothly, more like the big ground birds than like fat-hipped ducks. Most of the pigeon-toing was inherent to the foot itself.

That predatory dinosaur limbs acted much as described above has been known for some time. More controversial has been the *fore and aft* workings of their limbs. Part of the confusion stems from a misunderstanding of how the femur works in birds. Photos, film, and X-ray film of birds running slowly on trackways or treadmills show the femur nearly horizontal and moving only a little.[22] In mammals the femur is more vertical and swings through a strong propulsive arc. Since theropod hip joints are birdlike, not mammalian, it seemed that their femora might

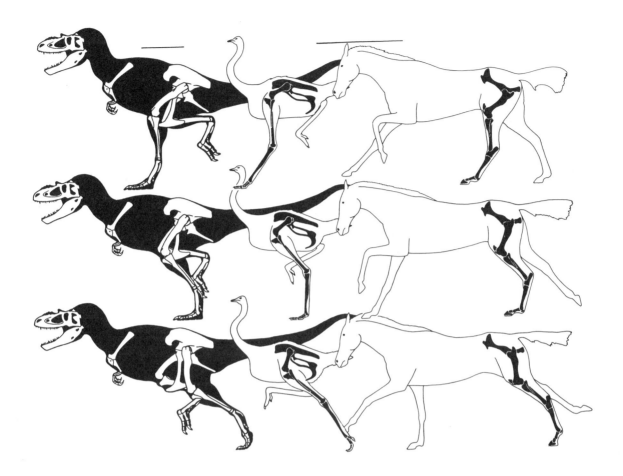

4-16
Hind-limb action in a fast-running ostrich, horse, and Alberto-saurus libratus. Left limbs are shown contacting the ground (top row), at midstroke (center row), and pushing off (bottom row). Note that in all, the hind limbs are more alike than they are different, with long shanks and feet and flexed knees and ankles, and that the hind-limb action is very alike. In particular, the femur moves through an extensive arc, ending at about vertical. The scale bars, one for the dinosaur and another for the bird and horse, equal 1 meter.

be horizontal and immobile too. But when looking at photos and films of ostriches running full tilt over the African flats—their wings held over their backs and exposing their knees to view—I saw, to my great surprise and delight, that the thighs were pumping back and forth much like those of horses and antelope[23] (Figure 4-16). We have already seen that the muscles and joint surfaces of predaceous dinosaur hips allowed the femur to swing through such a wide arc, from about sixty degrees forward of perpendicular to the hips to a little past perpendicular to the hips (see Figure 4-14).

Bird femora move so little at slow speeds because these tail-less bipeds need to keep their knees as far forward as possible in order to hold their limbs under their body's center of gravity. The femur is so short that its non-use makes little difference at slow speeds. At high speeds the balance problem is not critical, while wasting a limb segment would be. Long-tailed theropods did not have the same balance problem, and the femora are so long that they must have been in full use at all speeds.

The time-honored misunderstanding of predatory dinosaur limb action is exacerbated by such gigantic species as *Tyrannosaurus rex.* Animals of great dimensions are supposed to need straight-jointed, columnar limbs to support their bulk. After all, elephants do. Smaller theropods might have more flexed, running knees and ankles, but sometimes even they are portrayed otherwise.

The first thing to note about theropod limbs and their joints is that they are all *very* alike, regardless of size. From the giant tyrannosaurs to the swift, small ostrich-mimics, the similarity is especially striking (see Figure 6-4, page 142). A basic engineering rule is that structures that are built the same way, function the same way. So, whatever the giant species were doing with their limbs, the small ones were doing too! All theropod femora were more or less curve-shafted, yet so strong is the belief that big animals *must* have straight femora that it has been said that *T. rex* was this way, when it most certainly was not (look at the skeletons in Figure 6-4, page 142, and in Part II, page 341).

The next point is that predatory dinosaur knees were built the same as those of birds. This is a wonderful thing for dinosaurologists, because we can directly observe bird knees in action. Figure 4-14 shows that in the theropod-bird knee the two femoral condyles are unequal in size. The inner one is a large roller surface and bears most of the load. The outer condyle is only a thin rectangular wedge, yet it performs a vital function. This condyle runs in a groove between the head of the tibia and the fibula. In doing so, it braces the knee and keeps it from twisting about its long axis. The critical point is that this works only when the knee is flexed. If it is straightened, the condyle is pulled out of the groove and the knee is vulnerable to complete dislocation. This cannot be allowed to happen, so ligaments prevent the knee from straightening and keep it flexed at all times. This must have been as true of *T. rex* as it is of chickens. The predatory dinosaur ankle was straighter than the knee, although not completely so. So predaceous dinosaurs of all sizes walked around on flexed limbs like those of ostriches and antelope, not on columnar limbs like those of elephants. As we shall see in Chapter 6, this has important implications for predatory dinosaur speed.

Predatory dinosaur feet were digitigrade, meaning that the

ankle was well clear of the ground and the foot rested on the flats of the toes like those of birds. Cats and dogs are like this too. Humans and bears are plantigrade, walking on their heels, while horses and antelope are unguligrade toe-tip walkers. It is probably impossible for bipeds to be fully unguligrade, since this does not give them a long enough foot-to-ground contact to balance upon. Ostriches come closest, having only the front halves of their toes touch the ground. No theropod was like this, even though some prints made by running theropods seem to show it. These individuals put so much weight on their toe tips that the rest of the toes did not leave impressions.[24] On the other extreme, some trackways show theropods walking on the flats of their heels, in effect as plantigrades.[25]

When the foot lifted off the ground, the toes drooped, like the toes of big running ground birds. Newman suggested that theropod toes clenched.[26] But this sort of thing is common to *perching* birds, whose toes are automatically clenched by a modified tendon when they squat down on a branch—and as a side effect when a leg is lifted. Dinosaurs were not specialized perchers, so their legs did not work like this.

It is tempting to think that since predatory dinosaurs were not true birds, nor ungulates, that their limbs should work in a different and unique way. Yet for all the differences between them, bird and ungulate limbs follow strikingly similar motions, because they share the same basic adaptations, adaptations that force their legs to work the same way. Most critical among these is a permanently flexed knee. More supple-limbed carnivorous mammals can straighten their knees, so their limbs actually do operate differently. Permanently flex-kneed predatory dinosaur limbs must have worked in the fast-running bird and ungulate pattern (see Figure 4-16).

All in all, theropod limb action was stiff and stereotyped. Femoral action was extensive, with the knee always flexed and the femur never retracting past vertical. The ankle was also flexed, and the feet flat-toed, but usually not flat-heeled. There were modest differences between theropods in limb design, but it is doubtful that these altered the basic action much. Big-animal limbs do move through a shorter arc, about sixty degrees, than those of small species. Otherwise, the limbs of *T. rex* and small *Coelophysis* probably worked pretty much the same way.

So I find myself in sharp disagreement with Samuel Tarsitano's 1983 *T. rex* hind-limb restoration in which the leg is pushing off cat-style, the femur sloping back forty-five degrees, and the knee straight. This is an anatomical impossibility for theropods. The limp, clenching foot and straight knees of Newman's walking *T. rex* [26] are well off the mark too.

Trackways tell us another important thing about our subjects' limbs. There are literally thousands of predatory dinosaur trackways that show two or more steps, and they always, *always,* show that theropods strode like humans and most birds. They never hopped like some birds and kangaroos. In 1977, Michael Raath claimed that a single pair of side-by-side prints implied that *Coelophysis rhodesiensis* hopped. These prints are instead either from a standing animal, or from two similar-sized individuals that left their prints next to one another. A partial exception to the striding rule may be found in the very early lagosuchids which, since they were still partly quadrupedal, may have galloped in a squirrel-like bound, using each set of limbs in parallel. Some crocodilians do this very thing, making them look like reptilian squirrels—a very amusing sight.

When standing still, a theropod's center of gravity was just before the hip socket. So their feet were just below that point, under the front end of the hips. The knee would have been well-flexed; the ankles less so. One of the more persistent errors is to show theropods, whether standing or running, with ankles more sharply angled than the knee.

As I cautioned earlier, the birdlike theropods do not possess all the qualities of birds. This is especially true of the theropod pubis, which differs from that of protobirds and birds in that it is long, vertical, and projects down from the hips, while the protobird and bird pubis is swung backward. In fact, no other animal has anything quite like the great theropod pubis, which in many cases ended with a big expansion, or "boot." What the elongated pubis did is something of a mystery. The muscles the pubis and its boot anchored helped hold the hind limbs close to the body, but other erect-gait animals do not have these muscles. Some suggest the big boot was a rocker that the animals rested upon. Certainly this was true as far as it goes, and the end of the pubis must have been bare of any feathers and calloused, as Bakker shows. [27] But again, *why* such a rocker developed is still unexplained. Other big beasts, some of the large theropods among them, do without them; some small theropods that hardly needed so much support have them. One wonders further why

Theropod hips were complex structures, deep and narrow in cross section (for the rest of the leg musculature, see Figure 4-3). Muscles and guts did not run between the long, downward-projecting lower hip elements (pubis forward, ischium aft); only a sheet of connective tissue (c) did so. Nor did muscles run from the ends of the lower hip bones directly out to the legs. The reclining Allosaurus fragilis *grooming an itch shows what the hips looked like from below; note the callouses underlying the ends of the lower hip bones.*

the long pubis points so far forward in the early theropods, when this would seem to reduce the room for the belly.

Along with perplexing the functional anatomist, the deep, narrow hips of predatory dinosaurs have long confused artists. Artists usually render this area amorphously, with the surrounding flesh following no particular pattern. Or, they show the long pubes and ischia projecting sharply out from the surrounding flesh. Probably neither is correct. Except for the lagosuchians, the lower pubes and ischia of most predatory dinosaur's were elongated into rods. Because they were so narrow and joined along their mid length, there were no guts within them. Nor were there muscles. Instead, a deep yet thin sheet of connective tissue formed a tension brace (Figure 4-17). Tension sheets work best when they follow a gentle arc, so the connective tissue's lower

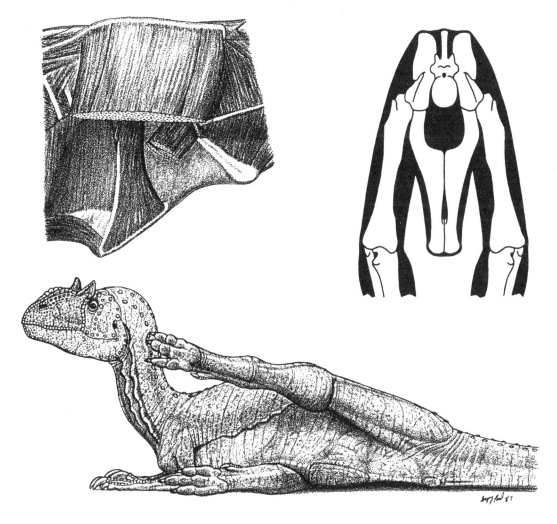

edge probably curved up from the tips of the pubis and ischium. The hollow belly was before the hips. In back, the lower tail muscles ran below the tail base down to the ischium's tip. The elongated lower end of the ischium helped support the tension sheets and muscles fore and aft, but the ischium was otherwise unmuscled. Limb retractors were restricted to its broad upper apron. If these had anchored on the ischial rod, they would have been badly overstretched during limb motion (see Figure 4-14). All this means that the lower ischium and pubis were both free of the thigh. The predatory dinosaur hip with its prominent pubes and ischia was a distinctive looking, "bony," functional structure. In the protobird theropods the lower hip was further modified—the ischial rod was reshortened and the pubis sometimes pointed backward—but otherwise its basic structure was the same.

As long ago as 1923, the famed paleontologist Alfred Romer noted that the dinosaur's birdlike hips bore large, birdlike thigh muscles. The theropod thigh was very broad in side view, running from the front edge of the ilium to the back end. It was rather triangular as it tapered down to the knee. Transversely, it was flattened, to work along with equally flattened hips. Since the belly was hollow and deep, there should have been a fold between the thigh and body—quite unlike birds, whose short thigh is virtually buried in the side of the broad belly. The most superficial muscles of the thigh complex, the anterior and posterior iliotibialis and the hamstrings at the back, formed subtle vertical contours that can be seen in the life restorations. The avian feet were lightly muscled, and were operated via long tendons by a drumstick of shank muscles bunched around the knee.[28] By far the most prominent of these was the great gastrocnemius muscle. Anchored on the knee's large and bird-style tibial crest, it pulled the Achilles tendon. Lacking a heel tuber to insert upon, the Achilles tendon ran in back of the ankle and continued behind the cannon bones down to the toes. The ankle was knobby, and the joint's gap could be seen as it can in birds. Indeed, we can say with full confidence that the whole of theropod limb musculature was little different from a bird's. Thus, you can garner a basic understanding of theropod design by dissecting a chicken or turkey leg.

In 1972, Dale Russell argued that the thigh muscles of the ostrich-mimic ornithomimid theropods were arranged in more fore-and-aft directions than they are in ostriches. He concluded that ornithomimids could not maneuver as well as the big birds, a theory that would be applicable to most theropods since they share fairly similar limbs. Russell erred in his muscle diagrams, however, especially in showing the big tail-based caudofemoralis going all the way down to the knee end of the femur when it really attaches at midshaft. Hence, his conclusions are premature at best. Besides, the dinosaurs may have been able to use their tail's mass to help turn tightly, rather like cats do, but unlike birds, which, of course, have no tails.

One thing we can restore with an exceptional degree of confidence are the soles of theropod feet, because fossil footprints record rows of birdlike pads, one under each joint. More pads were under the heel.

Paleodinosaurs were somewhat less avian. The ilium was shorter, so the thigh muscles were narrower in side view. In particular the anterior tibialis was more slender. The knee crest was smaller and the feet less birdlike, so the shank drumstick may have been less developed.

Theropods were like their avian descendants in having unusually hollow bones. Even *Tyrannosaurus rex* had thinner-walled bones than other animals of its bulk. Yet predatory dinosaurs tended to be more strongly built than the herbivorous dinosaurs. Theropod bone tissue itself appears to have been denser than in other dinosaurs,[29] so the strength of their bones overall would have been higher despite the thinner walls. Theropod hip joints were also deeper and better braced, and the rest of their hind-limb joints fit together more tightly. This strength is not surprising because predators must be able to withstand the impact of tussling with their prey on a regular basis. As for the prey's requirements, escaping the predator's clutches in the first place is better than outfighting it, so escape performance over body strength is stressed in their makeup. This can be seen in the cheetah and gazelle. When a running cheetah trips and takes a tumble, it shakes off its dizziness and walks away. When the cheetah catches the running gazelle, just tripping the prey into a fall can break its limbs.[30]

The final aspect of dinosaur anatomy is their integument, or body covering. Generally, it has been assumed that they all had scales like reptiles. This has been hard to confirm or deny, because until recently no skin traces had been found with theropod skeletons. This was rather odd, because in a number of cases herbivorous dinosaur skin impressions (not the real skin, just impressions of it) have been found in the same sediments. Just recently, however, a tiny impression of skin was found on the tail of a tyrannosaur, one that had been collected some time ago.[31] The skin is not well preserved, but it shows quite small, flat, and nonoverlapping scales in a mosaic pattern. These are more like the nonbony scales of crocodilians and Gila monsters than the overlapping scales of lizards. The scales are so small that they are not visible at more than a few feet. Even more interesting and informative are the large patches of skin found with the new *Carnotaurus* skeleton.[32] These also have small nonoverlapping scales. In addition, there are widely spaced rows of larger, sub-conical scales. Other large theropods may have had the same. Such mosaic skins are also typical of the large herbivorous dinosaurs, most especially the duckbills. And since uninsulated skin is normal in both cold- and warm-blooded big animals, it is highly probable that all big theropods had scaly coverings.[33]

Scales are often important as visual cues and display devices; the bigger scales served this purpose in *Carnotaurus*. Some predaceous dinosaurs may have had flatter large display scales, similar to those found on the horned dinosaurs. Large head scales could have been specially patterned around the nostrils, or along various bones and edges. Other possibilities include fowl-like head combs and head and throat wattles, or long skin folds and midline frills atop the back. The last two features are found in duckbill dinosaurs. Skin folds might have served the important purpose of allowing throat and belly skins to stretch as their owners gorged themselves on great bolts of meat. We can hope that new finds will tell us more about such special features.

What the skin of small predatory dinosaurs was like is a much more difficult and controversial question. There are no positively identified skin (naked or scaly) or insulation (feathers or fur) impressions known for any small predatory dinosaur, except of course the spectacular feather impressions of *Archaeopteryx*. But as a protobird, *Archaeopteryx* provides ambiguous evidence about other species. There is a Triassic trackway that seems to show a resting theropod with long upper arm feathers,[34] but this is by no means proven, and it could be a "Protoavis"-like protobird anyway. Feather impressions are known from Cretaceous sediments, but not from the Triassic or most of the Jurassic. This might be used as an argument against early feathered dinosaurs, but then again, the Triassic "Protoavis" appear birdlike enough to be good candidates for feathers. In fact,

Sankar Chatterjee believes that "Protoavis" has quill nodes on the upper arm and hand for supporting feathers. I have seen them and, although the point is a debatable one, he may be right. Since the big theropods were naked-skinned, many assert that small ones must have been also. But this does not by any means follow. Just because many big mammals—elephants, rhinos, hippos, humans, and pigs among them—lack much in the way of hair does not mean this is true for all mammals. It is also contended, often with much heat, that until insulation is found on dinosaurs it should be assumed they did not have it. The lack of feathers in the one *Compsognathus* specimen from the same sediments as feathered *Archaeopteryx* has been considered especially telling in this regard. I believe this is negative evidence—an absence of data—of the worst kind. Only one of six *Archaeopteryx* specimens show the soft body contour feathers we are looking for in other dinosaurs, and *Compsognathus* may have had even softer, less preservable feathers. It can just as well be argued that, lacking any examples of small theropod scales, we must not assume they were scaly. But while we should *assume* neither scales nor feathers, all theropods are so extremely similar in design to *Archaeopteryx* that I find it difficult to believe that the small ones would not have had feathers. Ultimately, it may depend on whether or not they were warm-blooded. It is widely accepted that the big-brained small theropods were endothermic (see Chapter 7); if this were so, then they would probably have needed insulation to keep their body temperature constant.[35] Indeed, fairly high metabolic rates and insulation may have appeared in the dinosaur's thecodont ancestors.

What it all comes down to is that, at this time, and despite what I know are the traditionalist's strong sentiments, it is every bit as speculative and no more legitimate to portray small dinosaurs in naked skin as it is to show them insulated. Eventually, enough impressions of small dinosaur integument will be found to settle things.[36] Until then, I always draw my small theropods feathered. For those who think I should do some naked for a more "balanced" view, plenty of others have and are doing that.

If feathers did insulate small predatory dinosaurs, there is room for much variation in their form. In living flightless birds the feathers have usually degenerated into simple furlike structures. Some argue that the ground-dwelling predatory dinosaurs should have had such feathers, and this is quite possible.[37] Others believe the first feathers evolved as the broad contour type from increasingly modified scales—contour feathers cover the bodies of living flying birds. If so, and if they first appeared in early archosaurs, then dinosaurs might have had them.[38] Broad contour feathers are better insulators against cold and heat than are furlike structures, so they would have been advantageous even for nonflying dinosaurs. The furry feathers of flightless birds may be a juvenile characteristic that they assumed along with the other immature traits that mark them from flying birds.

Whether dinosaur feathers were distributed uniformly over the entire body, or in distinct tracts like birds, is of course unknown. It is possible that some small predatory dinosaurs bore feather head crests or long winglike display feathers on their arms. Tails too could have sprouted long feathers like those of *Archaeopteryx*. These would be employable not only as startling display surfaces, but also as aerodynamic rudders and brakes during high-speed runs. Juveniles may have been insulated in down that was subsequently shed, to be replaced by an adult feather coat or to expose the scales of big species. Feathers wear out and need to be replaced, and since most predatory dinosaurs did not need a full suit of flight feathers, they probably shed fairly continually, perhaps faster as the warm season approached. Whether feathered dinosaurs would have preened themselves with oil from glands is yet another unknown. One should feel free to draw or sculpt small predatory archosaurs in regular feathers, furlike feathers, scales, or any and all of these. At this time they are all plausible.

Both big and small dinosaurs were scaly in certain ways. Snouts were probably always more or less scaly—much as bird snouts are always beaked, not feathered. Having the snout bare had the advantage of keeping blood off the feathers during feeding. The hands and feet were certainly unfeathered, like the feet of birds, and rows of large scales very likely followed the upper surfaces of the cannon bones, fingers, and toes. Finger and toe pads were probably roughly calloused skin instead of scales.

Horns, beaks, claws, and armor finish off our survey of theropod anatomy. All theropod heads had distinctive arrays of bony bosses, ridges, and even horn cores on the skull, which were often further enlarged by horn sheaths made of keratin. Artists often neglect these very interesting features. The artist's options for covering them include horn ridges, horn lots, and big scales. Common among theropods were nasal ridges, either along the midline or paired along the edges. The top of the preorbital bone

4-18
The head of Allosaurus fragilis *shows off to good advantage the horn ridges and orbital hornlets that often adorned predatory dinosaur heads. Some primitive multituberculate mammals voice their objections to the great predator's presence.*

often sported bosses or hornlets above and before the eyes, while some species' postorbitals also bore little bosses above and behind the eyes. A number of protobird theropods were at least partly beaked, some were completely toothless. Again, the beaks were markedly extended by keratin coverings. Beak keratin grows continually, so the beaks renewed themselves as their cutting edge was worn down. The bony cores of claws support keratin sheaths too—in fact, fingernails are keratin modifications of claws. Like fingernails and beaks, the claw horn renewed itself as its tip was abraded. Toe claw tips were blunted by wear on the ground, especially the shorter more hooflike ones of advanced species. Hand claws and sickle-toe claws were much sharper weapons. Imagine *Velociraptor* or a giant *Allosaurus* sharpening its claws on a tree, like a strange Mesozoic version of a cat.

The first paleodinosaurs, like little *Lewisuchus,* and a row of small, bony, platelike scutes running atop their vertebral spines. Only one theropod is known to have had such "armor"—*Ceratosaurus,* with its series of smaller, more irregular scutes. These were enhanced by keratin, so *Ceratosaurus* is one theropod that really did have the serrated back we often see in dinosaur restorations. No other theropod is yet known to have had these, although soft frills are possible. There were suspicions that *Tyrannosaurus rex* had armor scutes, but these have proven to belong to armored ankylosaur dinosaurs. Personally, I am glad, for I think tyrannosaurs look more sophisticated, aesthetically speaking, without them.

The last thing affecting dinosaurian looks is their coloration, a most frustrating area since this is the least knowable, and hence least important, aspect of dinosaur appearance. Yet the most frequent question the paleontologist hears is, "How did you know what color it was?" In view of the fact that no dinosaur pigmentation has ever been found, any color scheme is possible, though speculative. However, there *are* some basic guidelines. Since big living reptiles, birds, and mammals are never gaily colored like many small reptiles and birds, one can assume that subdued colors were true of the big predatory dinosaurs also, which to human sensibilities gives them a dignified air appropriate to their dimensions and power. They could, however, have been boldly *patterned* like tigers, giraffes, and zebras. Bright, even iridescent color patches may have adorned critical visual points, like snouts, necks, head crests, vertebral fins, wattles, tail sides, and the like. As Robert Bakker postulates, even the insides of the lips may have flashed a bright pink as they were lifted up to uncover the teeth, and the roof of the mouth was probably a pinkish white.[39] Many color schemes may have been specific to breeding males in season. As for the small species, some may have been brilliantly colored and patterned. Baby animals tend to be better camouflaged than their parents, often with spots. Since dinosaurs had excellent color vision, some suggest that they were green-tinged to improve their camouflage qualities. But then, even earth-tinted mammals hide themselves well from color-sensitive human eyes. Besides, the bigger color-seeing reptiles and birds are dun-colored. As for dinosaur eyes, anything from solid black to the brightest reds and blues is possible and probable.

All in all, predatory dinosaurs were graceful if often horrible birdlike beasts, with deep heads and S-curved necks, that walked on flexed, tri-toed (in theropods) hind limbs. We can confidently say that traditional restorations have things backward: it was their bodies that were lean, and their thighs and calves that were powerfully muscled. They were adorned with scales and perhaps feathers, and finished off with eye-catching hornlets and some-times crests. They must have made a wonderful sight.

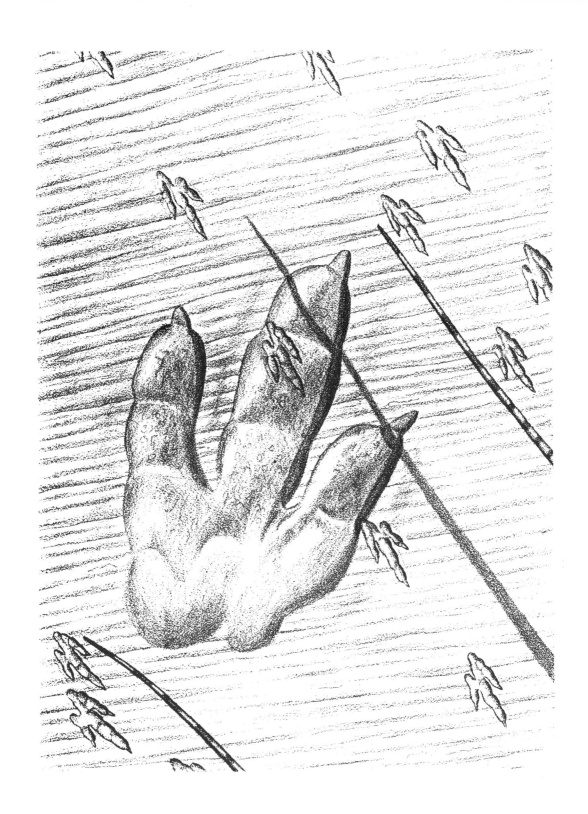

5

A QUICK LOOK AT PREDATORY DINOSAUR FOOTPRINTS

While skeletal remains are our prime source of information about dinosaurs, also vital are the footprints they left behind. Fossil footprints are strangely evocative, because they directly capture the movements of once-living beings. They are the closest thing to dinosaur "motion pictures" that we have.

We have far more predaceous dinosaur prints than skeletons, thousands upon thousands of them in fact (Figure 5-1). They are so common that they are widely available on the private market—which is not always the best thing for science. Many a patio or wall has theropod tracks on it. Better than single prints are entire trackways, which record a series of walking or running steps (Figure 5-2). Most prints are found as parts of such series. The majority of prints were formed on mud or sand flats alongside streams, lakes, and coastlines. The prints were laid when the ground was soft enough to absorb them. Then the mud or sand hardened, and sometimes dried. Occasionally, air-blown sand filled in the prints and preserved them. At other times the sediments from a flood did so. It is interesting but frustrating that the conditions best for preserving prints were often not good for saving bones; some formations will have abundant prints and few skeletal remains, others the opposite. Even in those formations that do include both good print and good skeletal remains it is often difficult to match them up. This state of affairs makes it hard to determine exactly what made the prints. The exception is when one kind of dinosaur is known to make up most of a formation's fauna, one kind of print is most numerous in the formation, and the print type matches the design of the former's foot bones. This happens in the Morrison Formation. *Allosaurus atrox* is easily the most common big predator there, and since the sharp-clawed, three-toed trackways that are present fit *A. atrox*, they very probably belong to it.[1]

Despite such success stories, it is often hard to identify whether a print belongs to a predatory dinosaur, or to something else altogether. This is most true of the early paleodinosaurs, whose four-toed feet are very like those of some herbivorous dinosaurs, especially the prosauropod. While prosauropods were at least partly quadrupedal, most paleodinosaurs were fully bipedal, so if hand impressions show up, the prints are probably not a predator's. The theropod's three-toed feet can be mixed-up with those of the herbivorous ornithopods. It has been thought that the latter's toes are more splayed-out than the former's, but this is a questionable assumption. Things become easier as size

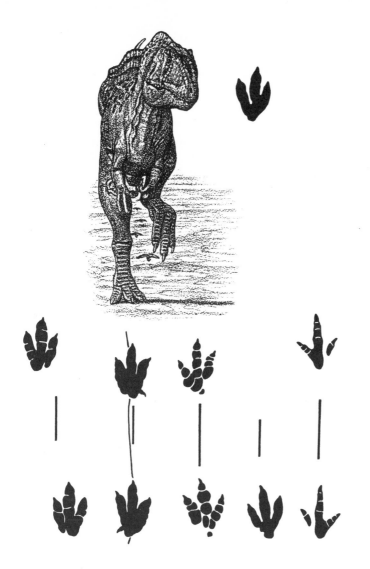

5-2
Some trackways of medium-sized theropods. From left to right, the first two are Eubrontes giganteus *and* Gigandipus caudatus *from the Early Jurassic Newark super- group of eastern North America; note that the latter has left a rare tail-drag mark and fully reversed inner toe prints. Next is a me- dium-sized theropod trackway from the Jurassic-Cretaceous Sousa Formation of Brazil. The next set was probably made by a young* Acrocanthosaurus atoken- sis *from the mid-Cretaceous Glen Rose Formation of Texas. Last are prints possibly attributable to Or- nithomimus brevitertius *from the Horseshoe Canyon Formation of Late Cretaceous Alberta. Scale bars, on the trackway centerlines, are 300 mm. Note that in most cases the pace lengths are much the same, the result of cruising walk speeds. The exception is the long-pace* Acrocanthosaurus *set, which was made by an individual (shown in inset) running about 25 mph.*

goes up. This is true because big theropod toes are built much like the smaller ones; they are just stouter. Hence, big and small theropod prints should share much the same basic form. It is hard to be sure because really big theropod prints have, oddly enough, not been positively identified. Big ornithopod feet are quite different from those of the small ornithopods, for their toe bones are hypershortened and the pads beneath them coalesced into one pad under each toe. The claws are also shorter and broader, although the short claws of really big allosaurs and tyrannosaurs might not show up well either. Many gigantic ornithopod prints have been found, and have, on occasion, been mistaken for theropods.

Making it yet more difficult to identify and name footprints is the different form that each print takes as the same foot makes them. Obviously, as the nature of the footing, the muds and sands, changes, and the speeds, angles, and forces of the foot change, the shape of the print will vary. Prints are not, therefore, simple molds of a foot, but record the complex interaction between the appendage and the ground. This means that very different-looking prints can come from the same individual. Making things worse is that not all prints are the actual impressions made at the surface. Many are really "ghost" prints, left in the layers of sediments directly below the print surface. The deeper these ghost prints are, the less distinct and true is their shape. Not only that, but as animals grow, the prints they leave can change in shape as well as size and look like they come from different-sized species. Careful statistical work has to be applied to large sample sizes to sort these factors out. One thing that must be used very carefully to identify prints is the stride length, since this is mainly a function of the track maker's speed.

An extreme case of mistaken identity stems from the newly recognized heel-walking theropod prints. Some have been mistaken by ardent creationists as human footprints, and as evidence that people lived alongside dinosaurs![2] When I first learned of these prints I could not imagine why any theropod in its right mind would walk crouched down this way, it seemed so awkward. Certainly, it was not a normal walk. It could be that the crouching walk was a stalking posture for their surprise attack technique (see page 38 in Chapter 2). This may not be a full explanation, however, since many of the flat-footed prints were made on tidal flats on which the theropods could not have found cover to crouch behind.

Fossil prints are usually given generic and species names separate from those given to skeletons. However, these are labels only, and unlike skeletal-based names are not accepted as real taxa. This is because the prints may have been made by a species already known from its skeleton, and because it is difficult to prove that a given type of print was made by a given type of dinosaur. Even if a type of print is shown to belong to a named skeletal species, the print name remains valid. A large array of predatory dinosaur prints have been named—too many to review here. Many of these names are certainly redundant, having been

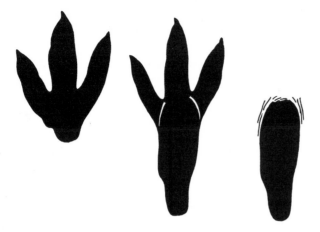

5-3
Right prints based on a Texas theropod, perhaps Acrocantho-saurus atokensis, *showing how the same foot can make a normal digitigrade print on the left, the rarer plantigrade version in the center, and on the right a poorly preserved plantigrade impression. The last, in which the lightly pressed toes do not show up and only the deep heel print is left, are the kind mistaken by some creationists for biblical "human prints."*

given to trackways that look different solely because of the way they were made. Not only that, but the prints do not show nearly the variation that the skeletons of theropods show.

To a fair extent the appearance of predatory dinosaur trackways follows the evolution of the skeletons. The best known of early theropod trackway faunas is that of the Late Triassic-earliest Jurassic found in the Newark and Hartford Basins of New Jersey and Connecticut. The prints found there were the first dinosaur remains described in this country, although they were first thought to belong to birds.[3] They range from intermediate in size to fairly large. Alas, hardly any skeletal remains come from these strata.[4] This is too bad because some of the theropod prints seem surprisingly advanced for the time.

Until very recently, it was thought that the Late Jurassic Morrison Formation produced many skeletons, but few prints. Actually, whole fields of prints have been sitting out there in plain view all the time, but they went hardly noticed until recently.[5] While theropod prints may make up the bulk of the Newark-Hartford trackways, they make up only a small percentage of the Morrison prints, just as they make up a small fraction of the Morrison skeletal fauna.

The most familiar of Cretaceous footprint faunas are the Texas sites from the middle of the period. Their initial exploration was recounted by Roland Bird in 1985. Laid down on coastal mudflats, theropod prints again seem to outnumber the herbivore's, which were mainly brontosaurs. (One reason that theropods may make more prints in some locales is discussed on page 44 of Chapter 2). Created at about the same time, but quite different in character, are the iguanodont dinosaur dominated trackway faunas of Alberta. Here theropod trails are in the minority, as in the Morrison.

Things that predatory dinosaur prints tell us about their maker's anatomy and function are discussed throughout this book. Prints have been dismissed by some as useless for understanding dinosaur biology, while others have gone overboard in drawing conclusions from them. In reality, they are direct records of dinosaur behavior that, when carefully interpreted, reveal much about those who left them behind.

Trackways let us picture a vast mudflat, blindingly hot, with distant trees on one horizon, a lake or sea shimmering on the other, and clouds boiling up in a blue sky heavy with moisture. Across the flats, striding like ostriches but bearing big rapacious heads, walk a sextet of two-tonne theropods. A few body lengths behind them range four dozen of their fellow pack members. All are related via blood or mating. Their open mouths pant in the discomforting heat. Except for the occasional squeak of a youngster they are silent, but one can hear the squish-plop of their many feet treading through the soft mud. The object of their attention is ahead of them, a herd of multi-story tall brontosaurs making their way across the flats. The pack leaders are looking the nervous vegetarian giants over, scouting for an ill juvenile, or an adult that is showing too many signs of old age. For, you see, the theropods are hungry.

Gregory Paul

6

PREDATORY DINOSAUR SPEED

All living big predators are fairly fast: it helps to be able to catch what one wants to eat! The birdlike limbs of small predatory dinosaurs have led most dinosaurologists to conclude that they were good runners. But a funny thing happens when many look at the big species. The long-accepted image of *Tyrannosaurus rex* was of a sluggish, lumbering giant that fought its prey in a slow-motion walk.[1] Some still believe it was too slow to catch prey, and was therefore restricted to scavenging.[2]

Such views are certainly not correct. All theropods, including the most gigantic, could run about as fast as horses and ostriches. This may strike you as heretical and impossible; after all, every one knows that big animals cannot run fast—the stress loads will break their bones. Elephants cannot run, and if big mammals cannot run, surely no overgrown reptile could either.

But think about giant machines for a minute: 400-tonne jets fly almost as fast as sound, 500,000-tonne supertankers plow through storms, and giant earth-moving machines rip up coal seams. Think about the largest wooden sailing ships—these organic artifacts produced 3000 hp to drive 3000-tonne hulls at 14 knots. An animal is also a machine, like a truck or a ship, except that instead of being made up of metal and powered by a diesel engine, it is constructed of bones and powered by muscle. Pound for pound, bone equals mild steel in bending and compressive resistance—it can resist about 3000 kg per square centimeter in compression. Bone fractures more easily than mild steel, but unlike steel can preempt much microfracturing if given enough time to heal.

Considering the high-quality materials animals are made of, it is difficult to understand why their speed would have to be so low at just a few tonnes. Actually, living examples prove the contrary. White rhinos weighing 3.5 tonnes can achieve a full gallop, and there are reports of rhinos outsprinting horses with riders.[3] Why then do 3-tonne Indian elephants not run? Perhaps for the same reasons humans and tortoises cannot run fast: because they don't need to. This brings us to another point. Over the last 10,000 to 1,000,000 years, most of a wonderful and strange array of giant mammals disappeared, perhaps at the hand of humans. The living fauna of big animals is too impoverished to be a good test of large-animal speed. It is also possible that extinct species could have done things modern ones can't.

The theory that big animals cannot be fast is yet another one of those entrenched but unsubstantiated truisms that we keep

6-1
All predatory dinosaurs had running legs, speedy, ostrich-like, and graceful Ornithomimus brevitertius *especially so.*

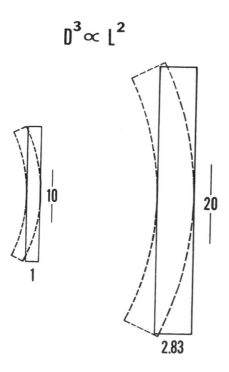

$$D^3 \propto L^2$$

10

20

1

2.83

6-2
In elastically similar structures, resistance to bending is kept constant as size goes up by increasing diameter (D) relative to length (L). So when length is doubled, the diameter should increase nearly three-fold. This allometric solution may be the one used by animals.

stumbling over in this book. Although it is repeated ad infinitum, there never has been a work that has rigorously proved the idea. Instead, the theory that has been most successful at estimating how animals should scale their proportions as size changes indicates just the opposite. Called Elastic Similarity, it predicts that as animals of similar design get bigger, they should get faster. Thomas McMahon's theory[4] starts with the observation that animals are elastic structures that bend under stress. As objects become bigger, they can maintain a constant resistance to bending by becoming shorter and stouter (Figure 6-2). If they do so, then body design can be kept the same regardless of size. This means that big animals can have the same high-speed design as small animals. Furthermore, as the limbs become stouter, their muscles become more powerful, so the stride length increases. Because the stride length increases more rapidly than the stride frequency, speed goes up. This is why the kangaroo can outrun the tiny kangaroo rat, even though they are about equally well built for speed. Bigger animals are also more energy-efficient than smaller forms. On the other hand, the greater inertial mass of big animals reduces their ability to accelerate and turn fast.

Of course, as with most things, the situation is more complicated than it appears. The lower limb sections may become shorter relative to the upper segments as size goes up in order to keep the muscles stretching the proper amounts. But this is a small change and should not affect speed much. Indeed, field observation has so far failed to prove that the ungulates with shorter lower limbs are slower than the others.[5] Ultimately, there are limits to the size of everything. As height increases, the base of the structure becomes overstressed regardless of how it's built, and deformation occurs. This is why really big objects from asteroid size on up collapse under their own weight into a spherical shape. The stress problem does not seem, however, to be critical for animal-sized machines.

So while the old standard equates big size with slow speed, modern theories suggest otherwise. But just because it may be possible for big animals to be fast, does not mean that they were; nonetheless, there are ways to get a better idea of how things were in this case. To estimate speed in extinct animals, we need to compare their design to those of living animals whose speed we can observe and measure. It is also useful to measure their proportions to see if they change as size changes in accordance with elastically similar principles, and to study their trackways.

Trackways are important because, potentially, they offer a direct way of measuring the speed of the animal that made them. This is fairly easy to do because the size of the track maker can be estimated by the size of the footprint, and this can be combined with the length of the stride to get a rough estimate of the speed.[6] However, this sort of data must be used very carefully. If a large group of trackways of a single species all show walking animals, this means nothing more than that all those animals were walking at that time. It does not in any way mean they were incapable of a fast run. In fact, most animals, like humans, take most of their steps in a walk. Running is usually resorted to only in an occasional flight or chase. The fact that even fossil *mammal* trackways were almost never made by running individuals[7] is very telling.

Although the vast majority of theropod trackways show walking individuals, some do show runners. In 1981, James Farlow described a set of trackways from Early Cretaceous Texas that show a number of 400-to-700-kg theropods running at moderate 12 to 25 mph speeds. There is no a priori reason to believe that this represents their top speed. Richard Thulborn and Mary Wade believe that their set of stampeding small bipedal dinosaur trackways do show their top speed, about 25 mph.[8] Their conclusion is questionable because it is not known if the small dinosaurs had run far enough to work up to their top speed. Besides, animals do not always run at their top speed when crowded in a stampeding group. It is when a predator is chasing an isolated individual that it has singled out for attack that the highest speeds tend to be reached.

This is what makes a set of Early Jurassic footprints from Arizona especially intriguing.[9] Made by a small theropod or ornithopod, the prints indicate that a 10-kg bipedal dinosaur was running very fast, with a stride approaching 4 m and a speed of about 40 mph, the speed of greyhounds and racehorses (Figure 6-3). And why not? Theropods were built like birds, and so should have run about as well too. This trackway is a real headache for those who want even the small, gracile dinosaurs to be slower thàn birds and mammals—enough to inspire convoluted attempts to explain it away as the traces of an incredibly long-limbed theropod.[10]

What about big theropods? All their footprints show a walking gait. The Halsteads point to a Glen Rose trackway as proof that this was their top speed.[11] They reason that since the theropod was following a brontosaur, it must have been going as fast as it could. However, the theropod appears to have weighed about 2 tonnes, the brontosaur 20. That the lone theropod had serious plans to attack an animal ten times its size is not likely.

So trackways show that small- and medium-sized theropods could run, and that the smaller ones could probably run very fast. It cannot be proven that large theropods were slow by their trackways, because, as I've explained, this would be another case of unfair use of negative evidence. Someday the prints of a 5-tonne theropod running at high speed may be found and settle the issue once and for all. Until and unless that happens, we must turn to the design and stressing of the theropod skeleton for evidence of their speed.

It is rather disconcerting how much we still do not know about animal locomotion. Actually, this is not as surprising as it sounds. Even the workings of human-built machines are in many ways poorly understood.[12] Over the years, elaborate theories have been constructed arguing that slender-limbed animals with long, graceful feet and shanks should be more efficient and outrun heavy-bodied, stumpy-limbed animals.[13] This makes a lot of sense, and to a degree is true, but in many ways it is not. For example, experiments and observations have shown that energy consumption, the arcs that limbs travel through with each stride, and the frequencies of those strides are pretty much the same regardless of limb design.[14] This came as a great surprise to biologists, and has not been explained. Chris McGowen found that tying weights to his lower limbs degraded running performance,[15] but this does not tell us much because these were dead weights. Adding dead weight to an aircraft likewise degrades its performance, but adding weight in the form of bigger wings or engines may improve things. Muscles produce power that elastic bones store and return, and the effect of their distribution along a limb is a subtle and not well understood one.

Recently, one biologist ran assorted lizards from the same region under the same conditions and timed them. The fat, short-limbed ones ran just as fast as the slender, long-limbed species! What really adds insult to injury is something that has been known for a long time but rarely discussed—that lizards, stout and light ones alike, can outrun such advanced and very gracile hopping desert rodents as the kangaroo rat.

Well, one may think, these are small animals. Limb design must have more effect on large animals. But exactly why having gracile limbs would not increase the speed of kangaroo rats, while it would for kangaroos, has not been explained. Besides, there are the bears. With their short, flat feet, short lower limbs, and fairly straight joints, they have all the hallmarks of real clunkers. But bears do not cooperate with theory. They can achieve a full, fast gallop, and have been reported to outsprint

6-3
An exceptional trackway that shows a small bipedal dinosaur, either a theropod or an ornithischian, running about 40 mph. Some have tried to make the dinosaur into a walker by giving it absurdly hyper-long limbs and tiny toes, but no such animal ever existed. Scale bar equals 0.5 meter.

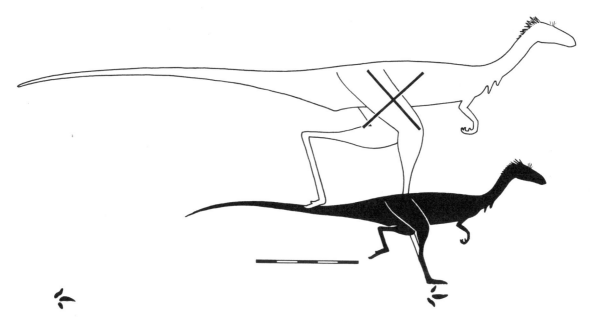

horses and elk for short distances. And as we already noted, it has not been possible to demonstrate that the big, less gracile ungulates are statistically slower than the small, slender forms.[16]

Certain aspects of dinosaur morphology have been cited as evidence for their slowness. Prime among these are their cartilagenous limb joints. Dinosaurs were like crocodilians in that their joints did not ossify after they matured. Their joints were allegedly too primitive and susceptible to damage to allow a fast run. But fully grown immature birds and crocodilians run on their cartilagenous joints with no complaint. Far from hindering speed, cartilage is an excellent, elastic, energy-absorbing material with superb lubricative qualities that spreads the stress at the limb joint over a large area. Big adult orangutans, for instance, survive frighteningly long falls because they have unusually flexible, cartilagenous joints. Another argument for theropod slowness has been their lack of certain details of limb anatomy found in fast mammals. This is simply a case of mammal chauvinism. That this is not so is proven by fast birds, which lack the very same mammal attributes that theropods lack. There is usually more than one way of doing things. Along this line, Nicholas Hotton suggested that the highly cylindrical hind-limb joints of dinosaurs were built more for the gentle stresses of walking than the tougher ones of running on irregular ground.[17] But as we saw in Chapter 4, fast birds have dinosaur-style cylindrical limb joints that work the same way. Even ungulates, among the fastest of mammals, have the most cylindrical limb joints found among mammals. Then there are the rearward facing ankle processes that give the shank muscles better leverage. These too differ in mammals and dinosaurs. In the former the calcaneal tuber, your heel bone, is very prominent. Theropods, and birds too, lack this tuber, and some think it means they were slower. Not so, instead they have a hypotarsus projecting just below the ankle. Although smaller than the calcaneal tuber it does the job just as well.

There is one key adaptation that does separate animals that can only walk (at least one limb is in contact with the ground at all times) from those that are capable of running (with a suspended phase in which no feet contact the ground)—the flexible ankle. In elephants and tortoises the ankles are made up of flat immobile elements, so the foot cannot push the body into a ballistic suspended phase. You can get an idea of what this is like by trying to run on your heels alone. All large animals that have flexible ankles can run, without exceptions. The theropod ankle is very birdlike and has a highly mobile cylindrical joint. This is true at all sizes—the ankle of tyrannosaurs is nearly identical to those of the small ostrich-mimics. The only reason giant theropods would have had such ankles is to run on them.

The next question is, how fast could theropods go? Humans run on flexible ankles, but rather slowly. Trying to estimate precisely the running abilities of fossil tetrapods by grading their limb design is difficult, because there is so much spread between running performance and design in modern animals. Occasionally some of us who work on animal locomotion will nod our heads and admit that, when you get down to it, "if an animal looks fast, it's fast." Anyone can look at ostrich or dog skeletons and see runners; elephants are obvious sluggards. This leads to the following, very reliable observations. Slow animals are slow not necessarily because they are big, but because they have extreme adaptations for being slow, such as stiff ankles, and extremely stumpy feet. If, on the other hand, the animal in question has long limbs with big powerful thigh and calf muscles, long energy-storing spring tendons, flexed spring-action knees and ankles, nonrotatable shank bones that equal at least two thirds of the femur's length, reduced lower fibulas, large high-leverage crests in the knee and another in the ankle (the hypotarsus), and long, narrow, three-toed, lightly padded, digitigrade feet, then it can run very well. No living animal that has such limbs cannot.

The ostrich is one animal that has such limbs, and of course it is a superb runner. So do theropods, which are themselves ostrich-like in most respects of their design. This fact has long been recognized to be true of the smaller theropods, especially the "ostrich-mimic" ornithomimids. It is less often noticed but equally true not only of the small tyrannosaurs, but of *Tyrannosaurus rex* and the other big theropods as well.

The ostrich-mimics and tyrannosaurs show this in a remarkable way. In Figure 6-4, ostrich-mimics and tyrannosaurs of increasing size are compared at the same scale. Because they lived in different ways, they differ in the head, neck, and forelimb. But, from 150 kg to 6 or more tonnes they maintain essentially the same birdlike form in the trunk, tail, and most especially the hind limbs. The hip's ilial bone is big, long and rectangular. The femur is robust and curved—even more in *T. rex* than in ostrich-mimics!—and as explained in Chapter 4, the knee joints were always highly flexed. Fibulas are substantially reduced at the lower end. The foot is long and very compressed, with the upper

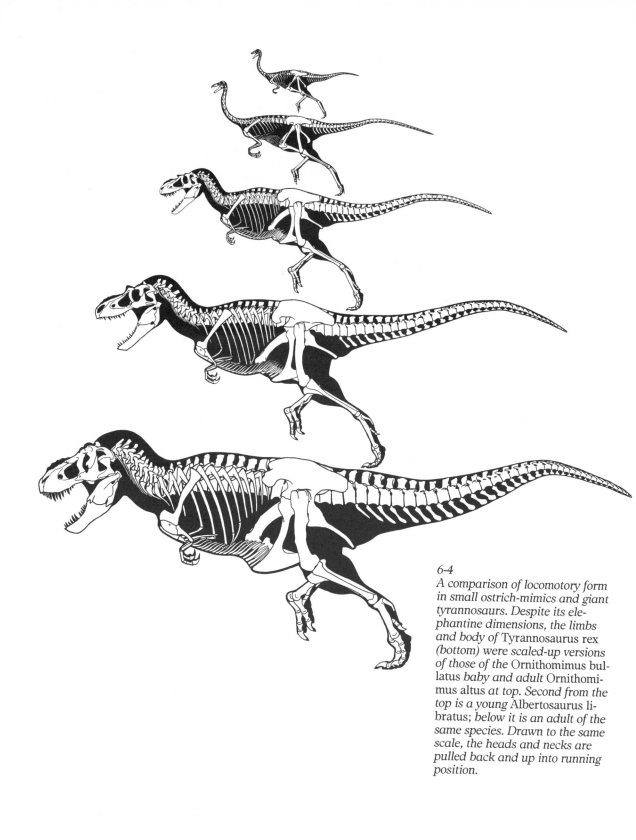

6-4
A comparison of locomotory form in small ostrich-mimics and giant tyrannosaurs. Despite its elephantine dimensions, the limbs and body of Tyrannosaurus rex (bottom) were scaled-up versions of those of the Ornithomimus bullatus *baby and adult* Ornithomimus altus *at top. Second from the top is a young* Albertosaurus libratus; *below it is an adult of the same species. Drawn to the same scale, the heads and necks are pulled back and up into running position.*

half of the central metatarsal almost pinched out of existence. Indeed, the constancy of design in the ostrich-mimics and tyrannosaurs is extraordinary. Only the proportions and a few details change: tyrannosaurs retain a small inner toe and slightly less reduced fibula in the shank, while shank and foot become relatively shorter in the bigger species. The latter is a consequence of elastic similarity and should not affect performance much; it does not in ungulates. Even with these minor differences, no other animal group shows so unchanging a design over this size range. The retention of a flexed knee in *Tyrannosaurus rex* is a really astonishing adaptation; it is as highly flexed as those of gazelles, horses, and ostriches!

Notably, there is nothing of the elephant in the big tyrannosaurs. The tyrannosaurs do not have the heavily padded, stiff-ankled, short feet of elephants, nor their short, weakly muscled shanks and columnar knees (see Figure 6-5). Traditionalists wishing to keep *T. rex* slow have tried to find *some* sort of slow feature in it. Some say that its femur was straight, which it was not. Others point to the "short" lower limb bones, but the shank and foot are as long, relative to the femur, as are a racehorse's. Theropod limbs are not exact copies of those of birds or of any other tetrapod, but the limbs of the biggest tyrannosaurs are the same as those of the small, swift ostrich-mimics. This is powerful evidence of their speed, for the engineering principle that tells us that "machines that are built the same, work the same" shows us that the tyrannosaurs with limbs like ostrich-mimics ran as well as ostrich-mimics. After all, why be built like a fast runner if you are not one?

Were the limbs of the big tyrannosaurs strong enough to run fast on? There is a way to test this. The plot in Figure 6-6 shows that fast-running living bipeds such as jeroboas and kangaroos have stouter, stronger femurs than do slow-running humans. The more robust femora may be necessary to absorb the stresses of longer ballistic suspended phases. Not surprisingly, the ostrich-mimics and tyrannosaurs have stout femora designed to absorb the stresses of high speeds like those of fast mammals. This is very good evidence that they ran fast.

The predictions of elastic similarity provide another means of testing the leg strength and power of theropods. Remember that in animals of similar design the bending resistance of the limbs can also be kept similar as size increases. To understand how this works, consider an animal of a given weight, that has

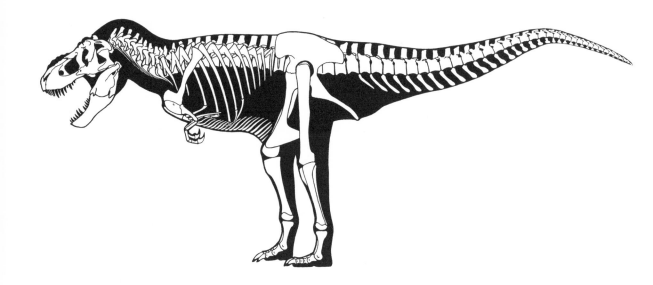

limbs of a certain thickness. If the dimensions of the animal are doubled and all the relative proportions remain the same (isometric), the mass is cubed and will increase eightfold. But the cross-sectional area of the limbs is only squared and increases just four times. The limbs become more easily bent in isometric animals. But we know animals are not isometric; they are allometric and change proportions as they change size. As you can see in Figures 6-4 and 6-5, bending resistance is kept constant—i.e., elastically similar—by increasing the diameter and decreasing the length of the bones relative to the cube of the mass. The proportions should change according to certain values, or exponents. Because the muscles must also increase in diameter in order to power the stouter bones, stride length also increases with size. So speed can remain constant, or even edge up, as size increases.

If ostrich-mimics and tyrannosaurs were keeping their legs strong and powerful enough for high speeds at all sizes, then their limbs should become more robust as they get bigger. The plots in Figure 6-6 prove that this is exactly what happens in these theropods. They were elastically similar animals that maintained the same bending resistance from *Ornithomimus* to *Tyrannosaurus rex*. This also means something else. Ornithomimids have always been considered very gracile animals. In

6-5
What Tyrannosaurus rex *would have looked like if it had been the slow, elephantine animal some think it was. The limbs would have been vertical, the lower elements greatly shortened, and the areas and processes for muscle attachments reduced. The vertebral column would have been lighter, too. To see T. rex as the powerfully built, spring-limbed runner that it really was, see Figure 6-4; in the two drawings the legs were drawn to the same length relative to body size.*

maintaining elastic similarity with ornithomimids, the big tyrannosaurs are, in effect, maintaining the same degree of *gracility* relative to their mass. So, while they are robust in absolute measure, they remain gracile in relative terms.

The results are conclusive. The ostrich-mimics and tyrannosaurs of all sizes were equally well designed, stressed, and powered for running fast. *T. rex*, far from being a lumbering bipedal version of the elephant, was probably about as swift as an ostrich.

Just exactly how swift was swift? In hard, precise measure, this is a real can of worms; for just how fast living animals run is not well known. Racetrack records show that thoroughbreds can run the quarter mile at 43 mph, three quarters of a mile at 40. Greyhounds can make over 34 mph. But how fast wild animals are is disputed, simply because it is so hard to determine speed away from a measured trackway. Some authorities credit cheetahs with 70-mph sprints, others with only 40 to 50. Ostriches

6-6
A log-log plot comparing the robustness of the femur in hopping mammals (solid squares), humans (open squares with a diagonal), and ornithomimids-tyrannosaurs (solid circles). Observe that the theropods, including Tyrannosaurus rex, are like the fast-hopping mammals in having much stouter thigh bones than slow humans. Also, the slope of 1.28 followed by ornithomimid-tyrannosaur femora shows that they increased in robustness in accordance with elastic similarity (the walls of the limb bones also became thicker with size, further increasing strength).

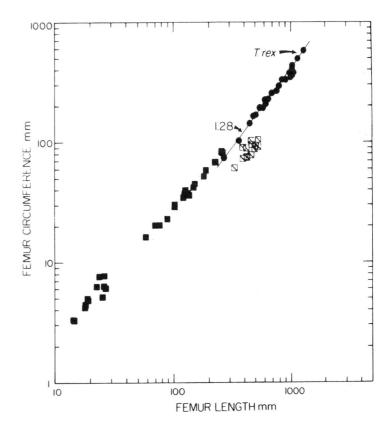

are said to run between 30 and 50 mph. Pronghorn antelope and gazelles are often credited with 60-mph records, but in a comprehensive study of African ungulate speeds, McNeil Alexander and his crew could not get any of the antelope to go faster than 30 mph.[18] Since thoroughbreds are specially bred for speed, Alexander argued that they may be as fast as any other animal. Considering the positive size-speed implications of elastic similarity, it is by no means impossible that *T. rex* could reach 45 mph.[19] Then again, 35 may have been the big tyrannosaur's and ornithomimid's best, but I suspect about 40 is most likely. Certainly 30 mph, the speed rhinos often run at, was the very minimum.

I have concentrated on the ostrich-mimics and tyrannosaurs because they are among the most gracile and the most similar-limbed of the theropods; only the birdlike troodonts and avimimids were as gracile. All theropods share the birdlike limb design, and although there are differences in their joint anatomy, especially between early and more advanced theropods, these are minor and did not affect their speed. All theropods could run well. It is tempting to think of ornithomimids, tyrannosaurs, troodonts, and avimimids as theropodian racehorses, the fastest of their breed. This may well be correct. Then again, we have seen how fat lizards keep up with gracile ones, so estimating comparative theropod speeds is a tricky proposition.

6-7
Tyrannosaurus rex may have been about as fast as a racehorse; it certainly was the fastest animal for its size that we know of.

Theropods did not develop their speed on their own. They inherited it from their early predatory dinosaur ancestors. Indeed, the protodinosaur lagosuchid's name means rabbit lizard, a reference to their very long hind limbs. The thecodontian ancestors of dinosaurs could gallop well themselves. Protodinosaurs and paleodinosaurs retained four toes, but the innermost of these was already shortened. The main modification theropods made was to further reduce this inner toe, resulting in the classic narrow bird foot.

Now we can look again at the question of why, if tyrannosaurs were so fast, are elephants so slow? Since there are no giant fast mammalian predators, elephants do not have to be fast. They can always give a predator a good fight. This is unlike the situation of small animals, which must always be able to flee from bigger animals or be armored for protection, like slow tortoises. Big theropods, in contrast, had to avoid fighting their equally big prey. This meant that they had to be fast in order to make a quick escape after delivering the initial wound. The horned ceratopsids responded by becoming fast and dangerous themselves, while the duckbills acquired both speed and agility. These changes in the prey required yet more speed in the tyrannosaurs so they could catch and wound them safely. The Mesozoic Era saw a predator-prey speed and size race that has not been matched in the mammalian world.

7

WARM OR COOL PREDATORY DINOSAURS?

For most of this century, dinosaurs were accepted as "good reptiles," with low, lizard-like metabolic rates. There was a lot of circular reasoning involved in this. Some books said dinosaurs were "cold-blooded" because they were reptiles, then said they were reptiles because they were cold-blooded! But these days the metabolic systems or physiologies of dinosaurs are a point of great contention.[1]

It is difficult enough to measure the metabolic rates of living animals, much less ones that have been dead for sixty-five-plus million years. In fact, some paleontologists and physiologists believe that attempts to estimate the physiologies of fossil animals are futile. They would rather we limit our efforts to more "do-able" things such as phylogenetics and functional anatomy. I compare these people to Comte, the philosopher who in 1835 argued that we would never be able to tell what stars are made of because we cannot directly sample them. As it happened, astronomers were just then developing the techniques to indirectly "sample" stars by their light spectra. Most of what we do in paleontology is also via indirect observation. I note in Chapter 8 how uncertain dinosaurian relationships may always be, for we can no more watch how dinosaurs evolve into new species than we can read a dinosaur's blood pressure or take its temperature. In fact, we may be able to do a better job understanding dinosaur physiology than their relationships. Much as astronomers sample stars by long distance, we can get estimates of dinosaurs' physiologies via paleontological time travel.

The difference between estimation and direct proof of dinosaurian physiologies is an important one. We cannot have the latter. By the same token, we cannot directly *prove* that recently extinct mammals such as the saber-toothed cat, or even our human ancestors, were physiologically similar to ourselves. But the possibility that they were different is so remote that it can be dismissed without a second thought. Dinosaurs are quite different. They are not the kinds of reptiles, birds, or mammals alive today, so their physiology is not known a priori. And just because the reptilian model is the traditional one does not mean the burden of proof lies on the other models. Therefore, the best way to study theropod physiology is to start with an open mind. The problem should be considered on the same basis as is most science—as a matter of probabilities. Therefore, we will look at many lines of evidence, and at the end see which physiology best

7-1
The skeletons of predatory dinosaurs of all sizes show that they were gracile, agile, active animals, and this implies that they were very energetic, which we can see as 2.5-tonne Albertosaurus libratus *tackles galloping* Monoclonius albertensis *in a cattail marsh.*

149

fits the bill. Eventually, dinosaurologists will probably have enough evidence for a solid consensus to emerge.

This is true because we have a firm foundation upon which to base our studies—the physiologies of living animals. They are well understood, and becoming more so. Therefore, when we look at extinct animals we really can get a good idea of what was going on. This is the opposite of the dinosaur-extinction problem, in which even the basics are murky at best.

So, in order to start our physiological discussion we have to understand what we are talking about, and that is fairly complicated. Most animals, including amphibians and reptiles, are "cold-blooded." They have low metabolic rates that at any given size are about seven to ten times less those of "warm-blooded" mammals and birds. I say "at any given size" because as animals of similar physiology get larger, their metabolic rates decline relative to each unit of mass. So a 1000-kg eland has a metabolic rate only 5.6 times greater than a 100-kg wildebeest (see Appendix A). Having low metabolic rates, reptiles are dependent on the environment for most of their body heat. Hence, they are called ectotherms. However, reptiles are not at the *mercy* of the environment; instead, they *exploit* it. Most reptiles operate best at high body temperatures, from 80° to 100-plus°F (so the label cold-blooded is a partial misnomer). They get there by sunning themselves, and can raise their body temperatures well above that of cool air. Of course, this method only goes so far. There has to be enough sunlight available, it does not work at night, and the air cannot be too cold. Because reptile body temperatures fluctuate, they are heterotherms, or ectothermic heterotherms in sum.

It is important that body temperatures fluctuate less in bigger reptiles. This is because their very bulk effectively insulates them against heat loss and gain. The effect is modest in the big monitor lizards and crocs, but in theory giant ectotherms could have fairly constant temperatures.[2] This is called bulk homeothermy. Another idea suggests that as reptiles get bigger, their metabolic rates converge with those of big mammals.[3] If true, an elephant-sized reptile would have a metabolic rate about as high as an elephant's. Since with a metabolic rate this high the reptile is no longer dependent on the sun to keep warm, this is known as bulk endothermy. Remember the meanings of *bulk homeothermy* and *bulk endothermy,* because these are the two modern models for big, reptile-like dinosaur physiologies. Both envision large dinosaurs as continuously active animals. This is a key point, for the recent debate on dinosaur energetics has caused the old concept of dinosaurs as sluggish lower vertebrates to be universally rejected.

Birds and mammals keep their body temperatures both high (95° to 105°F) and constant. They do so by eating prodigious quantities of food and "burning" or metabolizing the energy it contains. Sophisticated, automatic thermoregulatory controls (sweating, panting, and shivering, among them) keep things on track. Hence, birds and mammals, called endothermic homeotherms, are much less dependent on the environment than reptiles. In particular, they can get by without sun bathing (though some humans seem strangely unaware of this). Some primitive mammals have intermediate metabolic systems. Monotremes (the platypus and the spiny anteater) and the tenrec (a relative of shrews), for instance, have a reptile-like metabolic rate when warm or resting, and body temperatures of about 85°F. But they keep their body temperature constant, and when cold or active they assume a high mammalian metabolic rate.

There is a possible difference in the way birds and mammals thermoregulate that may warrant attention. Both groups shiver to keep warm when they are really cold. When temperatures are cool, many mammals use what is called nonshivering thermogenesis to help keep body temperatures up. This heat is produced by special "brown" fat cells. For a long time it was believed that birds did not have brown fat or use nonshivering thermogenesis. Recent studies indicate that they do,[4] but perhaps not to the same extent as mammals.

A good way to start on theropod metabolics is to stand back and take a good look at one of their skeletons. Then look at some other dinosaur skeletons. This tells us a lot of things. First, dinosaurs are all pretty much the same. Every one is an erect, long-limbed animal. Being so alike structurally, it is reasonable to expect them to be physiologically similar too. Some argue that the anatomically diverse dinosaurs should have diverse physiologies, like mammals. But dinosaurs are not as diverse as mammals in anatomy. No dinosaurs were like the sprawling, lower-metabolic-rate "tenrecs" or "spiny anteaters" in shape. Instead, dinosaurs show about the same amount of structural diversity seen in elephants, ungulates, carnivores, kangaroos, and humans put together, and all of these erect, long-legged mammals share high metabolic rates. A variation on this theme notes that since dinosaurs were a unique group, they should be expected to have a unique physiology, different from either reptiles or birds and mammals. This is quite possible, but birds and mammals, as separate and as different as they are, evolved remarkably similar physiologies. Dinosaurs may have done the same.

The principle of uniformity of design and physiology is most true of predatory dinosaurs, since all are birdlike bipeds. This brings us to a critical point about theropods, that they *are* so very birdlike. Feathered, flying *Archaeopteryx* is the first "bird," and all agree it was endothermic. The theropod *Velociraptor* is nearly identical to the early bird, and may be its descendant. I find it inconceivable that *Velociraptor* had a different physiology from *Archaeopteryx*. To take things further, the early theropod *Coelophysis* and gigantic *Tyrannosaurus* also share an essentially birdlike design. I know of no good reason why either should have a sharply different physiology. This is even more true in view of the fact that *all the big theropods evolved from the smaller ones.* If the small ones were endothermic as most dinosaurologists now believe, it is hard to believe that the large species lost, again and again, the fast metabolisms their ancestors had. The bipedal paleodinosaurs and herbivorous dinosaurs also have an avian build; they too should have a birdlike physiology. Even the big quadrupedal dinosaurs are descendants of small, birdlike species, so *they* should have an avian physiology. There are archosaurs that were not birdlike, and that probably did have intermediate, tenrec-like physiologies. These were the dinosaurs' ancestors, the early thecodonts. Some contend that theropods' closest physiological models are the big monitor lizards. Yet even the world's biggest lizard, the Komodo monitor, is built nothing like *Tyrannosaurus rex* or *Ornitholestes*. That such dissimilar forms share like physiologies is hardly credible.

John Ostrom's and Robert Bakker's important variant of this argument points out that all living animals with fully erect gaits —all birds and most mammals—are high-metabolic-rate homeotherms.[5] There are absolutely no exceptions. All dinosaurs were fully erect, so they should should have been endothermic homeotherms. There are semisprawling mammals that have high metabolic rates, but this only means you need not be fully erect to be endothermic—it does not imply the reverse. Theoretical animals that combine erect gait and reptilian metabolics have been constructed, but whether they would work in reality is another matter. Aside from the empirical evidence that no living animal does so, there is hard evidence that they could not work.

It has already been explained in Chapter 3 (page 53) that only an erect gait allows the animal to breathe rapidly during a run. Obviously, high-metabolic-rate animals need a lot of oxygen when exercising. Another reason may have to do with blood pressure. Lung-breathing ectotherms have three-chambered, lower-pressured hearts that cannot pump blood upward, so they are low-slung animals that carry their head and brain at heart level. The high metabolic rates of endotherms mean that they have to pump large quantities of oxygen and nutrient-carrying blood very rapidly through the body. This requires a complex, four-chambered heart that can maintain high blood pressures. Such pressures can pump blood upward, so endotherms can adopt a tall posture with the head carried high.[6] The swan-necked predatory dinosaurs fit this bill.

Other details of theropod design also fit the endothermic model. The highly vaulted roofs of their mouths, or the secondary palates, allowed theropods to breathe while they ate—an important thing for fast-breathing endotherms! The large lungs in the early forms and increasingly sophisticated avian systems of others were a good way to get lots of oxygen into a fast-running metabolic system. Some other aspects of anatomy are much less informative, such as the finbacks of some predatory dinosaurs. These could be solar heaters for ectotherms, or heat radiators for endotherms: we cannot tell.

It is interesting that bulk endothermy also explains the erect gait, nasal passages, and lungs of *big* theropods. After all, big-bulk endotherms are supposed to have the same metabolic rates as big mammals. But this does *not* explain these adaptations in small predatory dinosaurs, since they would have low lizard-like metabolisms. Again, the uniformity of theropod design places constraints on theoretical models even more so when one considers that all groups of *big*-bodied theropods evolved from *smaller* species. If, as most believe, small theropods were endotherms, why would all the big ones have gone back to reptilian ways, time and time again? This is a serious question that those favoring non-avian-mammalian big-theropod physiologies have tended to skirt.

It is probable that big brains require a constant flow of warm blood to work; otherwise important thoughts will disappear when the metabolic rate goes down. So the large brains of such "protobird" theropods as dromaeosaurs, troodonts, and ostrich-mimics are widely accepted as evidence that they did have high metabolic rates, at least at the tenrec level. The other small theropods had brains as big as that of *Archaeopteryx,* which we are confident was endothermic. On the other hand, the relatively small brains of other theropods are often considered to be the best evidence for lower metabolic rates.[7] But a careful examination of the issue shows that things are not as simple as they appear. Since endotherms have to gather ten times as much food as ectotherms, they are alleged to need bigger brains in order to cope with the intellectual strains of being so active. This theory works fine for small animals. The problem is that *big*-bulk homeotherms and bulk endotherms are both supposed to have fairly constant body temperatures too. This constancy is supposed to make them active, like big endotherms. The bulk endotherms are also projected to eat about as much as big endothermic homeotherms. If, therefore, dinosaurs were bulk endotherms or bulk homeotherms, then the small ones should have small brains and the bigger, more active ones big brains. However, exactly the opposite is true! This means that all the modern theories of big-animal metabolics fail to explain the small brains of large theropods. This indicates that high activity does not require great intellect after all. The real question is why big theropods did not evolve big brains when their possible physiologies show they could have.

The brain-size issue also hits hard at bulk endothermy for theropods in another way. Bulk endothermy postulates that small dinosaurs had slow metabolisms, and that the metabolic rates of big species converged with those of big endotherms. This is simply not so, since the relatively big-brained small theropods almost certainly had faster metabolisms than reptiles of equal size. This means that the size-induced convergence in metabolic rates could not have occurred, and that there is no place for bulk endothermy in theropod metabolics.

Going to ever smaller detail in our look at dinosaur anatomy and physiology, we turn to bone histology—the internal fine structure of bones as revealed by cutting out thin sections and looking at them under a microscope. This ties into another critical factor, growth rates. This is really an old line of work, for as far back as the 1800s it was noted that the insides of dinosaur bones were structured like those of birds and mammals, and quite different from those of reptiles. There has been a lot of debate about the similarities and differences between endothermic and reptilian bones, from which a consensus seems to have emerged. Armand Ricqles and Robin Reid show that most endotherms over 10 kg have well-developed "fibrolamellar" bone, while ectotherms do not.[8] The development of extensive fibrolamellar bone appears to stem from a high rate of growth. We often despair over how fast our children grow. But humans really mature achingly slowly for mammals, perhaps because of our need for a long social education. Horses and ostriches reach adult size in only a year or so. On the other hand, crocodilians and giant tortoises take decades. Speed of growth is also size-related: usually, the bigger the creature, the slower it develops. And at any given size, most endotherms grow an order of magnitude more rapidly than ectotherms. So while elephants[9] and whales take about two or three decades to grow up, similarly gigantic ectotherms would take a couple of centuries or more to do the same.

The critical point is that fast growth requires a fast intake of food, and, in wild juveniles, fast food intake requires greater activity. In small youngsters, only heightened metabolic rates can drive such activity, rates at least at the tenrec level. Because of this, only endotherms grow rapidly and develop substantial fibrolamellar bone in the wild. No known ectotherm can do this. As you might suspect by now, dinosaur bone almost always has well-developed fibrolamellar bone, firm evidence that they grew rapidly in the avian-mammalian manner. This seems to be confirmed by another aspect of bone histology, growth rings. Formed each year as winter or the dry season slows growth, these are common in reptiles, even the tropical ones. Some temperate and polar birds and mammals have similar rings in their long bones, but as far as I know such rings are entirely absent in living tropical ones. It is hard to tell if the birds' rings are real growth marks, and it has been found that more than one forms each year.[10] In any case, such "growth" rings occur in only a few big theropods. When they do show up they are rather low in number. They are not the many dozens of very thin bands crowded into the bones' outer layers that should be expected if these were long-maturing ectotherms. Considering that each ring forms at least once a year, if not more rapidly we deduce that their owners were growing to large sizes in only a few years. So small theropods matured in about a year, and were old in a few. The giants were adults in a decade or two, and reached perhaps sixty or so years in age. Speculations that big theropods lived for centuries are not supported by the data.

That dinosaur growth rings are so rare both in occurrence

and in number implies that dinosaur metabolisms were fast. That
they appear at all suggests dinosaurs differ in some modest way
from tropical mammals and birds. As noted above, birds seem to
employ nonshivering thermogenesis less than mammals. Perhaps
this form of heat production was less developed in dinosaurs,
enough so that it occasionally affected growth. This is a very
tentative idea, and the whole issue needs a lot more work.

In 1979, Johnston found that theropod teeth had rings in
their inner dentine like those of crocodilians, so he thought that
they should be ectothermic.[11] On the other hand, these growth
rings may have something to do with the constant tooth replace-
ment practiced by theropods and crocodilians. Because the latter
two groups' teeth differ so much from the mammalian permanent
adult teeth, they do not offer a clear test of physiology.[12]

We can tell that dinosaurs continued to grow as adults, albeit
slowly, because their cartilage limb joints never ossified. This is
often cited as a reptilian feature, but elephants never seem to
completely stop growing either.[13]

There is another and more subtle problem with either bulk
endothermy or bulk homeothermy for big theropods that took
care of their young. Being sluggish at night, and having to bask

in the morning, the small juveniles would have had trouble keeping up with their big, more-constant-temperature parents. Not only that, but the young of most fully parental animals *must* grow rapidly, otherwise it would be decades before the youngsters would be big enough to be fledged. Crocodilians get around this problem by abandoning their slow-growing young when they are still tiny.

The main argument for bulk homeothermy in big theropods is a twofold one: first, many dinosaurs are large; second, it is much more energy-efficient than true endothermic homeothermy while it supplies much the same temperature constancy. To claim that energy efficiency is paramount to biological systems is to make a big assumption. It may at least partly stem from a misunderstanding of energy efficiency versus energy consumption. One can sometimes *increase* energy efficiency by increasing consumption. For example, each citizen of a developed society consumes far more energy than their recent ancestors did. But this energy goes into producing even more fantastic amounts of material goods. As for organisms, they are always competing with one another for the available energy. It is a lot like a race, and the organism that uses more energy to get more energy faster than the others may win out. If you were entering the Indianapolis 500, would you go with an economy car, or a gas-guzzling racer? So a high-metabolic-rate endotherm may consume more energy than the ectotherm, but it may get proportionately more energy in return for its expenditure. This presents a complicated, subtle problem that ecologists are still grappling with.

Bulk homeothermy may not be good at maintaining a constant temperature under adverse conditions. Sophisticated mathematical models show that big dinosaurs living in warm sunny environments should have stable temperatures. But what about the rainy monsoon season when series of storms move in? Ones with cool breezes and rain? Each storm could last for days, and the monsoon for months. Evaporation is a powerful coolant, especially in a breeze. Hence, even big low-metabolic-rate dinosaurs would suffer a drastic temperature drop. And there would be no sunlight to heat them up. Notably, no one advocating ectothermic dinosaurs has constructed a model to test this problem. Of course, endotherms have little trouble keeping warm in such conditions.

A more serious cooling problem is revealed by a fantastic and recent revelation—polar theropods! We think of dinosaurs

as denizens of warm tropical and semitropical environs, and most of those we know of were. But dinosaur remains, including small and large theropods, have been showing up in Middle and Late Cretaceous deposits that were then close to the poles.[14] As shown in Figure 7-4, the Late Cretaceous North Pole may have then been close to what is now Prince Edward Island. Dinosaurs lived in northernmost Alaska and the northwest Yukon on what was then the Cretaceous coastline, only ten or so degrees south of the pole. Dinosaurs may have also lived on the northern Canadian land even closer to the pole, though no remains have been found there yet. In the mid-Cretaceous, the South Pole was very close to southeastern Australia, and so were dinosaurs.

The Cretaceous poles were not at all as nasty as they are today. Rich forests with small crocodilians and turtles grew around the poles, and tundra was apparently unknown.[15] Still, the polar winter sun set for days or months on end, depriving ectotherms of their heater. Temperatures became cool, at the least, with occasional light freezes and snowfalls.[16] Just how cool the Cretaceous polar winters were is an increasing subject of dispute, for some believe temperatures were startlingly low, enough for hard freezes—river and coastal ice, and even highland glaciers.[17] This was not a problem for the crocs and turtles, or small dinosaurs if they were ectothermic. By seeking shelter in bottom muds or dens, they could hibernate through the winter dark, just as alligators used to live through the sharp winters of southern Virginia until they were hunted out. But if the large arctic dinosaurs were bulk homeotherms, they were in a tough spot. Their temperatures declining as the sun daily sank ever lower and disappeared, and too big to den in for the winter, they could not hibernate exposed to a winter full of chilling, breezy rains and wet snow storms. After all, wind-chill factors and evaporation could have driven their body temperatures to below freezing, a lethal situation even if the milder climatic scenarios are accepted.[18]

Confirmation that really big ectotherms could not tolerate such conditions comes from the giant phobosuchid crocodilians of the Late Cretaceous. Relatively common in the southern United States, they become rare in Wyoming and Montana, and are absent from Alberta up to the arctic. All these formations were well-watered and had plenty of big rivers for the giant crocs. The phobosuchids were too big to hibernate, however, and it may have been that the winter climate of Montana and Wyoming was

7-3

Three extremes in dinosaurian thermoregulation. Even though most dinosaurs lived in balmy climes, monsoons could bring in months of cool, breezy rains (top). If dinosaurs like this Megalosaurus tanneri *wading through a flood did not have high metabolic rates, then they would have become chilled and sluggish. Coldest of all were polar dinosaurs such as this tyrannosaur (center) in the moonglow of a Cretaceous North Alaskan winter midnight. It has broken through the ice glaze of a river for a drink; a light snowfall is at its feet. At the other end of the temperature range (bottom), tropical climates became toughest in a hot drought. Big warm-blooded animals can use their bulk to keep their temperature within reasonable bounds; small ones must retreat to the shade and pant.*

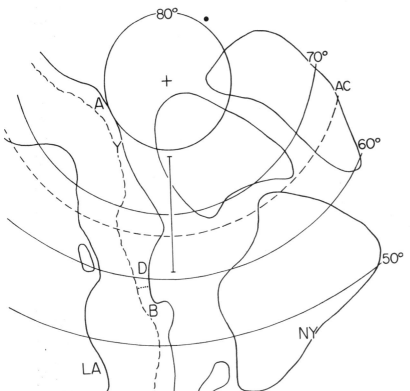

7-4
North America as it was in the very late Cretaceous. The north paleopole (marked by a cross; position of the present North Pole marked by a solid circle) may have been as far south as what is now Prince Patrick Island, and dinosaurs lived on the nearby Alaskan (A) and Yukon (Y) coastlines. To get away from the winter dark, these dinosaurs would have had to migrate all the way south along the interior coastal floodplain (bordered on the west by highlands indicated via irregular lines) to the Montana-Wyoming border (B). AC is the paleoarctic circle; D marks the famous dinosaur beds of Alberta; LA and NY indicate the future sites of Los Angeles and New York; the vertical bar equals 2000 km.

just able to support them. The Montana-Wyoming border was then at about 55°N, and the sun would be up for about five hours and rise eleven degrees above the horizon at winter solstice. Further north, it was apparently too cold and sunless to keep really big ectotherms going.[19]

If so, then big ectothermic polar dinosaurs may have had only one choice: to migrate south. In 1980, Nicholas Hotton built a grand theory of vast herds of sun-following dinosaurs pushing toward medium latitudes in the fall, then returning to the poles each spring. Ironically, this will not work for low-metabolic-rate animals. Imagine a 2.5-tonne theropod standing on the north slope of Alaska, or in southern Mid-Cretaceous Australia. Getting out measuring string and a globe, and taking into account detours around obstacles and the like, it turns out that our dinosaur would have to make a yearly roundtrip of 9000 or more km to reach latitude 55° (see Figure 7-4). That is equal to a walk from New York to Los Angeles and back! As a standard ectotherm, the 2.5-tonne theropod would have a metabolic rate of about

1,900,000 kcal/year (Appendix A). It would cost the same theropod about 11,000,000 kcal to walk 9000 km a year, many times its yearly ectothermic energy budget. Large, low-metabolic-rate polar theropods would have been in a bind. Unable to tolerate the polar winter, it does not look like they had enough energy to follow Mark Twain's advice that if you do not like the weather, move.[20]

Of course the whole problem disappears if dinosaurs had high metabolic rates. With energetics ten times as great, they *could* have migrated such long distances; a few humans have walked cross country. Or they could have weathered the polar winter. At first it seems that bulk endothermy would work as well for polar theropods as would an avian-mammalian system. After all, the big ones would have high metabolic rates, and small species could hibernate. But this does not really work, because the low-metabolic-rate juveniles of big-bulk endotherms would be unable to keep up with their parents during the migration because of their lack of energy. Nor could they hibernate, because the social dinosaur's young has to stay with the active adults.[21] In the end, only avian-mammalian physiologies offer a full explanation of polar theropods.

I strongly suspect that polar theropods did not migrate very far. After all, no living terrestrial animal wanders anywhere near the distances involved. Even arctic caribou and polar bears move only 2500 km each year. Today, caribou and musk oxen stick it out through vicious arctic winters, and the wolves and foxes that feed on them remain too. Surely the herbivorous endothermic dinosaurs could tolerate the much milder Cretaceous winters as well, if not better. And if the herbivorous dinosaurs stayed, the predatory species would have been there to prey on them. It is even possible, though perhaps not necessary, that big polar dinosaurs sported a winter coat of feather insulation. So we can envision a tyrannosaur under the arctic night, the moon low on the horizon and the ghostly aurora borealis overhead; its breath condenses in the cool damp air, its shuffling feet disturb the melting snow that has dusted the landscape. For those of us who live in high northern latitudes the image of winter dinosaurs is appealing, for it puts them in the crisp, late fall conditions we are familiar and comfortable with.

Quite different from the coolness of rainstorms and polar nights is the problem of big, *overheated* theropods in sunny dry seasons. As animals increase in size, their surface area per kilogram gets smaller. The metabolic rate per kilogram declines too, but not as fast as the skin area. In effect, it is the very bulk of large animals that insulates them. Alas, this fact is misunderstood by most. They believe that since big animals are less able to dump excess heat through their skins, that they have a hard time keeping cool when the environment is hot. To avoid this quandary, it is argued that big dinosaurs *had* to have had low metabolic rates. This is another fallacious yet persistent truism, which has been disproved by modern physiologists such as Knut Schmidt-Nielsen and C. Richard Taylor. That this false theory has endured seems most strange when one realizes that *all* of the biggest living tropical animals (elephants and rhinos) have fast mammalian metabolisms, and there used to be far more giant mammals in the tropics than there are today.

The crux of the matter is this. Assume that the total environmental heat load (from the sun, air, sky, and landscape) is fairly high, but still low enough for the animal to radiate heat out into the environment (around 95°–100°F). No study has ever shown that giants really will overheat under such conditions. In fact, the higher the normal body temperature of an animal, the better. This is because the air temperature must be even higher before it can start flowing into the animal. The heating problem is reduced if plenty of water is available for the animal to drink and use for evaporative cooling.

Things really get tough *when the total external heat flux is so high that more heat flows into the animal than can flow out, and water is not available for evaporative cooling.* These are the classic conditions of a tropical drought. Water holes dry up and clear skies let daytime temperatures reach 100° to 120°F or more. In this case, animals are desperate to keep the heat out, for there is no way they can get rid of the heat already inside them. The best way to do this is to be big, to let sheer bulk insulate against the in-flowing warmth. Not only that, but the abundant mass stores the heat building up inside without raising the body temperature as fast. So, little antelopes overheat in a few minutes, and must seek the cooling shade of the brush. Big antelopes and elephants heat up much more slowly, and they can remain more in the open as their body temperatures gradually rise to such fantastic heights as 115°F. The reason that this method works is because the big animals get a daily break from the heat. Unwanted heat is radiated into the cool night sky, and the bulk insulators are ready to start the cycle over again next morning.

This is a really fascinating thing, for these animals are no longer truly homeothermic. They are hypertherms, letting their body temperature rise to cope with extreme heat and drought. Brains are kept cool by "counter-current" heat exchange systems in the blood vessels. So, far from being a barrier to high metabolic rates, the large size of many theropods may have been an adaptation for being endothermic in hot, seasonally dry climates.

So, we now see that a key argument for a theropodian physiology of the reptilian type, the large size of many species, works just as well if they were full endotherms. This means that the suggestion by Hotton and others that dinosaurs tended to be big for bulk endothermy [22] is neutralized. Besides, as explained in Chapter 3, theropods had a hard time being really small because of their stiff-action limb design.

There is yet another body-size-related factor that supposedly favors theropod ectothermy. As certain therapsids evolved into mammals, they went through a "size squeeze"—i.e., the first mammals were quite small, the size of shrews and mice. Likewise, the first birds, such as *Archaeopteryx,* were exceptionally small. There are arguments that full-blown mammalian-avian endothermy can evolve only during such size squeezes. [23] Dinosaurs, being large, supposedly do not fit this criterion. This is a rickety anti-endothermy argument. We do not *really* know if animals have to go through a size squeeze to become full endotherms; it is only a theory. Even worse, early dinosaurs *did* go through such a size squeeze. Protodinosaurs such as predatory *Lagosuchus* were tiny fellows, smaller than the first birds.

Aside from big size, how did theropods keep cool and satisfy their thirst when things were hot? Smaller species could have used their air-sac systems and rapid panting as internal evaporative cooling ventilators. Living birds do this. When small animals pant, they breathe at the resonant frequency of their rib cage to minimize the energy used. [24] The resonant frequency of big-animal chests is too low for rapid panting, so they cannot use internal cooling. But with their bulk, they did not need it as badly. The few species with finbacks could have used them for cooling, as long as the temperatures were not too high. Regardless of their size, the body fluids of the predatory dinosaurs' victims would satisfy much of their water needs, and as predators they could always drive other dinosaurs away from water holes and get the most of what was available.

Robert Bakker has recently come up with another way to

measure extinct animal metabolic rates—fossil trackways,[25] of which there are many thousands made by a wide variety of species. It is fairly simple to estimate the speed at which a trackway was made (see page 137, Chapter 6). It turns out that early amphibians and primitive reptiles "cruised" at a slow but constant speed. All but a few trackways show them walking only a couple of miles per hour. This is quite different from fossil mammal herbivores, which typically cruised much faster. Faster yet were mammalian carnivores, which paced along at 3 to 6 mph. What is happening here is fairly straightforward. Because the mammals have to consume more food to keep up with their voracious metabolisms, they have to cover more territory to find it. So they move faster. It is all part of the race to expend more energy in order to get even more energy. As you might expect, dinosaur trackways show that they cruised fast—some 2 to 4 mph for the herbivores, even faster for the predators. This can only mean that they had a hunger of endothermic proportions. As always, this applies to theropods of all sizes, so bulk endothermy could only explain part of the phenomenon.

Another difference betwen low- and high-metabolic-rate animals is that the first tend to evolve more slowly than the latter. This is at least partly because low-metabolic-rate animals live longer and reproduce themselves more slowly, so they have less chances for changing. At first glance it might seem that theropods evolved slowly; *Tyrannosaurus rex* does not seem all that different from *Metricanthosaurus* of ninety million years before. Likewise, some modern shorebirds do not look very different from what was around in the Cretaceous. But this is looking at the wrong end of things, after they had become stable. At their start, predatory dinosaurs evolved dashingly fast, from primitive lagosuchids to surprisingly birdlike, and sometimes very big, herrerasaurs, "Protoavis," and *Coelophysis* in only five to ten million years. This suggests that even at their very beginnings dinosaurs were at least as metabolically active as tenrecs and monotremes.

The last aspect of theropod physiology we will look at is one explicitly applicable to predators. This is the biomass ratios of predators and their prey (Figure 7-5). It was long ago realized that predatory dinosaur skeletons were being found at a far lower rate than those of herbivorous species. I have walked the sediments of the Lance Formation and seen a number of *Triceratops* skeletons, but no *Tyrannosaurus rex*. On the Morrison, I have come across many a brontosaur bone, but nary an *Allosaurus*.

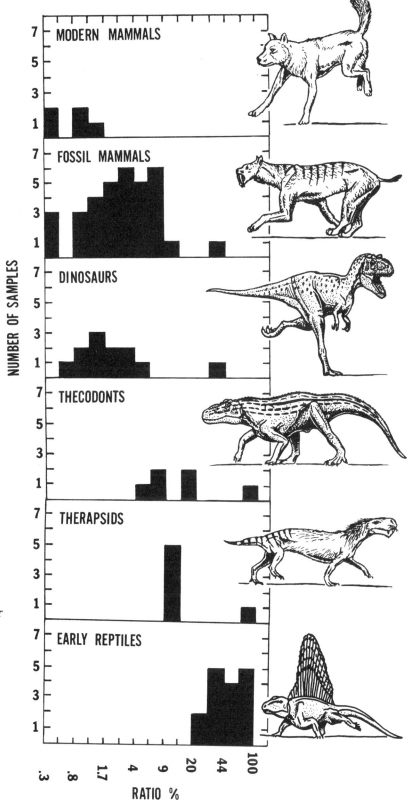

7-5
Predator/prey ratios in various animal communities. The ratio is the percent of predator biomass relative to the herbivores. In the archaic ectothermic finback communities, there was a predator for every two or so prey animals. Among mammal-like therapsids and the thecodonts, the ratio was more like one in five. In mammal populations, especially extinct ones, and dinosaurs, herbivores outnumbered their consumers by twenty or more to one, except in the rare predator traps.

NUMBER OF SAMPLES

MODERN MAMMALS

FOSSIL MAMMALS

DINOSAURS

THECODONTS

THERAPSIDS

EARLY REPTILES

RATIO %

This is attributable to a simple and obvious fact: any given tonnage, or biomass, of herbivores can never support as large a tonnage of predators over an extended period. What is not so obvious is that the exact ratio of predator to prey should depend on the predator's metabolic rate. Ectothermic predators eat only a seventh to a tenth as much as endotherms of similar size, so a given biomass of herbivores can support more predatory ectotherms than predatory endotherms. In quantitative terms, ectothermic spider and insect communities have "predator/prey ratios" of 50 percent or more. In sharp contrast, mammalian predators such as shrews, weasels, wolves, and the big African carnivores make up only a few percent of the herbivore's biomass.

Robert Bakker realized that this may offer a way to measure the metabolic rates of extinct animals. He surveyed a wide array of fossil communities. Sure enough, such primitive reptile predators as the fin-backed dimorphodonts had biomasses 25 to 65 percent those of the reptiles and amphibians they fed upon. In fossil mammal populations, predator/prey ratios clustered around a scant 5 percent.[26] This has long been known in a general way. Predatory finback reptiles are a dime a dozen in many collections, while good mammalian carnivores are the prize centerpieces of a museum's fossils. There are exceptions to this. So-called predator traps, such as the saber-tooth cat- and wolf-rich La Brea Tar Pits, have preferentially enticed, killed, and preserved enormous numbers of mammalian predators. But these are isolated cases, easily identifiable in the record. Normal fossil endothermic predator/prey ratios are much smaller, some ten times less, than those of ectothermic predators.

The group ancestral to dinosaurs, the predatory thecodonts, have intermediate predator/prey ratios of 4 to 20 percent. This is right in line with the tenrec-like metabolic rates that their intermediate morphology indicates. As for the birdlike theropods, Bakker and others found that in a dozen faunas they make up 0.7 to 6 percent of the herbivore biomass, just like the fossil mammal carnivores. Again there are exceptions. The predator-packed Cleveland-Lloyd, Ghost Ranch, and Chitake quarries are obvious predator kill sites. But overall the evidence is conclusive that predatory dinosaur populations are structured like those of fossil mammals, and are very different from those of lower-metabolic-rate vertebrate fossils. Bulk endothermy could explain the low predator/prey ratios of big theropods, but not the equally low ratios of small *Velociraptor*. Predator/prey ratios offer firm evidence that theropods had mammal-like metabolic systems.

This argument has not been accepted by the "biomass" of dinosaurologists, however. Some skeptics say that since we do not fully understand how animals get preserved in the fossil record, we cannot yet trust the reliability of what predator/prey ratios tell us. This sounds wise and prudent, but if it were really true we would have been seeing chaos. The P/P ratios of the various communities would fluctuate widely and show no particular pattern. But as we just saw, this is not the case. With few exceptions, the archaic sprawling reptiles show just the sort of high ratios we would expect them to have, the intermediate-design mammal-like reptiles and thecodonts exhibit the intermediate ratios that best fit them, and erect-legged dinosaurs and mammals share the lowest figures. This is just too much consistency to be mere coincidence—P/P ratios must be reflections of physiology.

Another, more specific criticism suggests that theropods may not have preserved as well as herbivorous dinosaurs. If so, then the predators would appear to be rarer than they really were. But in fact, it has just been found that the *opposite* is true. As I explained in Chapter 4, predatory dinosaur bones are denser than those of herbivorous dinosaurs of equal size. This probably made theropod bones more resistant to rot, and more likely to be incorporated into the fossil record, than those of other dinosaurs. Not only that, but Philip Currie finds that when exposed today by erosion, theropod bones disintegrate much more slowly than the herbivore bones.[27] It is difficult, perhaps impossible, to tell exactly how much this alters the preservation rates of predatory dinosaurs vis-à-vis the herbivores. But it does mean that the dinosaur predator/prey ratios we find are probably higher than the true values, perhaps by as much as half or more.

This may help explain another perplexing thing about predator/prey ratios. In modern mammal communities, P/P ratios are extremely low, only 0.2 to 1.5 percent. Because dinosaur P/P ratios are consistently higher, it has been argued that the dinosaurian predators had a higher metabolic rate than modern carnivores.[28] This sounds fair enough, except that fossil mammal P/P ratios are also higher than today's, running from 1.5 to 9 percent! Part of the problem is that the number of predator remains found at a given fossil locale is so low that fluctuations around the true value are to be expected. Another part of the problem stems from the fact that modern communities are not unspoiled. Interference and competition from man has suppressed the numbers and species of predators. Even in big game parks, poachers often compete with the carnivores, and they are not counted in the predator/prey ratios! Past mammal communities often had many more species of really big, powerful predators than to today's, able to kill more of the population's herbivores. Perhaps most importantly, mammal carnivores also have the relatively denser bones found in theropods. So they too may be more numerous in the fossil record than they really were. Hence, in both dinosaur and extinct mammal faunas the original P/P ratios may have been closer to, but still higher than, the modern range.

In 1980, Halszka Osmolska pointed to two Late Cretaceous Mongolian dinosaur faunas as exceptions to the rule of low predator/prey ratios. No statistics have been published, but it seems that skeletons of *Tyrannosaurus bataar* are unseemingly common relative to the herbivores of the Nemegt Formation of Mongolia. This is no isolated predator trap—we are talking about a whole formation. In the Barun Goyot Formation, immediately below the Nemegt, the sickle-clawed theropods are also unusually abundant. But since there is a consensus that the big-brained and very birdlike sickle-claws were high-metabolic-rate animals, the abundance of the sickle-claws suggests that there was a very strong bias favoring the preservation of theropods in Mongolia. In fact, a suspiciously large portion of the Nemegt's tyrannosaurs seem to be juveniles (see Part II, pages 342-43). It is possible that this was a tyrannosaurian nesting ground, where the high juvenile mortality natural to wild animals resulted in an excess of tyrannosaur remains.

Another attack on P/P ratios comes from Walter Auffenberg's classic 1981 study of the giant Komodo monitor lizard. Auffenberg found that the monitors make up only a fraction of a percent of the total fauna, much as dinosaurs and mammals. Some take this to mean that big ectotherms have metabolic rates similar to those of large-sized endotherms. If true, this would confirm the idea of bulk endothermy. But Auffenberg's field observations show that Komodo monitors eat only a small fraction of the amount that similar-sized mammalian carnivores consume. In fact, all big reptiles—crocs, pythons, and tortoises—consume the same relatively low amounts of food as do small reptiles. This is not surprising. It has long been documented that the relative metabolic rates of animals decline with size in a consistent manner. This is probably related to elastic similarity, the way animals scale their body proportions to resist stress loads as size changes (see pages 136-37, Chapter 6).

Cross-sectional areas of the body scale to mass .75, and since metabolic rates must flow over these cross-sectional areas, physiologically similar animals should then scale their energetics to this exponent. This applies to endotherms and ectotherms alike, so their metabolic rates should never converge. The very basis of the bulk endothermy concept is contradicted by the living reptiles that are supposed to practice it.

Alternately, the Komodo monitor's low P/P ratio has been taken as evidence that the dinosaur's equally low P/P ratios are as compatible with a slow lizard-like metabolism as with a fast one. But a closer look shows that the Komodo monitor's scarcity really tells us little about its physiology, for three reasons. First, much as the big mammalian carnivores have declined under human pressure, Komodo monitors have had to share their islands with humans for many millennia. Almost certainly this has been to their detriment. Indeed, they have been considered a borderline endangered species. Secondly, it is questionable whether these big lizards are as effective at hunting mammals as are big canids and cats. So their populations may be low anyway. Lastly, Auffenberg makes a big mistake in not taking into account the many packs of feral dogs that fight with the monitors over carcasses. Since the dogs eat much of the available dead meat, they hopelessly contaminate the P/P ratio, and cloud the meaning of the Komodo's portion of it. Not only that, but the dog packs, which came in with humans, may contribute to suppressing the Komodo monitors themselves, especially by harassing the youngsters.

All in all, predatory dinosaurs fit the birdlike physiological model very well. Endothermic homeothermy is fully in line with their body and limb design, bone histology and the fast growth it implies, parental care, fast walking speeds, predator/prey ratios, and polar populations. It even explains the great size of the "bulk-insulating" species on the one hand, and the dinosaur's initial size squeeze on the other. It is a very straightforward situation, and an obvious one since dinosaurs *are* built like mammals and birds. One possible difference is that dinosaurs may have had less nonshivering thermogenesis-producing brown fat than do birds and mammals, or none at all. As explained above, this may have led to the occasional formation of growth rings. Only the small brains of big theropods are not explained by high metabolic rates, but the reptilian metabolics do not solve that issue either.

In contrast, the idea that theropods were either bulk homeotherms or bulk endotherms is fraught with flaws and implausibilities. Both concepts are hypothetical, and the latter is at odds with what we know about living reptile physiology. Indeed, bulk endothermy is virtually disproved by the big brains of small theropods. By taking a negative stance, one can take each argument for theropodian endothermy of the avian-mammalian style in isolation and find problems with it. One can get dinosaurs to fit, with difficulty, into a few points of the reptilian models. Big low-metabolic-rate theropods would have fairly constant body temperatures under normal conditions, and their fast growth does not demand the very highest metabolisms. But when one ties to fit the *entirety* of what is known about theropodian anatomy and ecology into the reptilian box, it takes inordinate pushing and shoving. Even then many things, such as their birdlike limbs and the existence of polar theropods, still hang out.

So it is safe to say that predatory dinosaurs of all sizes were almost certainly full endothermic homeotherms. This still leaves some questions unresolved. In particular, metabolic rates vary considerably even among fully endothermic mammals and birds, so I do not know of a way to tell which kind of system dinosaurs had. Resting marsupials such as kangaroos and the large predatory thylacine wolves expend about 30 percent less energy than most mammals of like size. However, their daily *active* metabolic rates are similar. Perhaps advanced thecodonts and protodinosaurs were marsupial-like, and the rest of the dinosaurs more energetic. On another extreme are passerine ("song") birds, whose unusually high body temperatures are stoked by voracious metabolic rates. It can be doubted that any dinosaurs were like this. After all, many flying birds and all the big ground birds have more normal physiologies.

As for how dinosaur endothermy is doing in the scientific marketplace, informal polls indicate that more paleontologists believe that all dinosaurs were endothermic than that all were ectothermic. Most think they were a mixture. After an initial burst of enthusiasm for dinosaur endothermy in the first half of the seventies, things tailed off for awhile. This was partly due to some badly presented arguments for warm-blooded dinosaurs.[29] The paleontologists arguing for the concept were not happy, and those against took this to mean that dinosaur endothermy was more of a crowd-pleaser—it was very popular with the public—than a solid idea. The belief by a number of dinosaurologists that the burden of proof lies with the new and "radical" theory has also hindered an objective appraisal of the problem. But as data has accumulated, it looks like it is gradually grinding down the concept of dinosaurs as scaled-up reptiles. The greatest impact, it seems, comes from the evidence for high growth rates. Indeed, this has helped inspire Dale Russell, for many years one of the strongest advocates of ectothermic dinosaurs, to begin looking more favorably upon their being warm-blooded.[30]

8

THE GENEALOGY AND NOMENCLATURE OF PREDATORY DINOSAURS AND BIRDS

The study of how predatory dinosaurs were related to one another, their phylogenetics, is an area of much action these days. This is different from most of this century, a period in which theropods were thought to form two separate and rather simple dead-end groups that left no living descendants. It is now clear that theropod evolution was much more complex, and includes the origin of birds. Once a plausible phylogenetic arrangement is worked out, then the groups need to be named. Naming such groups and species is taxonomy; formally arranging them in ordered groups is systematics. All this may sound dry and dull, but I've never found it so. After all, many people love trivia games and crossword puzzles, and figuring out how to identify, arrange, and name once-living things is much more challenging. I tend to be like the hobbit who wants everything "set out fair and square, with no contradictions." This is a futile desire. The sands of phylogeny and taxonomy are always shifting beneath the dinosaurologist's feet, and always will.

There are two basic ways to explore phylogenetic relationships. One is based on molecular studies of the genetic material contained in soft tissues. There are various ways to conduct these studies; one of the more recent methods—considered by many the best available way of determining animal relationship—is a process called DNA-DNA hybridization.[1] Birds and their crocodilian relatives can be studied molecularly, but of course since we have no soft tissues of dinosaurs, they cannot be. This is an important drawback, as I shall explain below. On the other hand, there are those that do not have much confidence in molecular phylogenetics; it is a deeply complex issue that will take time to resolve.

The other basic way of looking at phylogeny is the old standby, structural comparison, in which one looks for similarities and differences, called characters or features, between the designs of species, or their morphology. The more similarities and fewer differences, the closer the relationship may be. But there is more than one way for two animals to become similar. The first, of course, is to develop from the same stock. A second way is by developing similar adaptations independently, under similar selective pressures. This is called convergence when it happens among distantly related animals, parallelism if two closely related taxa do it. Take the cat, the dog, and the thylacine. The thylacine, or Tasmanian "wolf," looks a lot like a dog. In fact, the shape of its skull is remarkably doglike. But the details of the

8-1
A sickle-clawed Velociraptor antirrhopus *leaps in display against another of its species.* Velociraptor *was one of the most birdlike of theropods; indeed, its ancestors may have been flyers. As such, the sickle-claws are an important link between dinosaurs and birds.*

skeleton and soft tissues show that thylacines are really marsupials, like kangaroos. Thylacines and canids look so alike because they hunt in similar ways, and they have converged. Cats, on the other hand, are close dog relatives, but they do not look as doglike as thylacines because their body form evolved for a different, stealthier method of hunting. Such a change in form away from a common pattern is called divergence. Then there are reversals, in which species evolve adaptations that look like ones earlier members of the group had lost.

Convergence, parallelism, divergence, and reversals can really confuse the phylogenetic investigator. The modern way to sort out these problems is based on cladistic principles. A clade is a group of animals that share a common ancestor. Such a group is called monophyletic. A group of animals that has multiple ancestors is polyphyletic, and is not a true phylogenetic clade. Of course, all this is relative—ultimately, every living thing shares a 3.6-plus-billion-year-old single cell as the first great-grandparent many times over.

Cladistics is a recently developed methodology, with its adherents and detractors, and many disagreements over how it should be practiced. I follow a pragmatic approach, one that falls back on common sense when all else fails. To construct a cladistic "family tree," a cladogram, one starts with an outgroup—this is the group or species of primitive forms that the species being looked at will be compared to. The reader is cautioned that the terms *primitive* and *advanced* are often loaded terms in lay use, with primitive considered inferior to advanced. In phylogenetic use, they do not carry the same connotation. Primitive or archaic is the initial or basal condition, advanced is the subsequent or derived condition. Advanced *may* be more sophisticated and effective than primitive, or it may simply be different. Lizards, for example, are more "primitive" than mammals; but lizards have been increasingly successful over the last hundred million years, showing they are effective animals well adapted to the conditions they live in.

Having a basal outgroup, one then looks for shared-derived characters among the rest of the groups under investigation. Shared-derived characters are simply those that differ from the outgroup's and are shared by two or more species. Quality is important as well as quantity, for the more complex an adaptation, the less likely it is to have developed more than once. After tabulating the shared-derived characters, the possibilities of convergence and parallelism are assessed. There is no simple formula for this, and a good deal of judgment is involved. Bias in the characters chosen and the tremendous gaps in our knowledge make things worse. Indeed, some recent studies have come up with bizarre and misleading results becasue they looked at too few characters. So, the more data the better. Yet the greater the number of species and characters looked at, the less the human mind is able to take it all in and weigh the various factors. Even computers are strained when assessing a modest number of characters and taxa. Some of us paleontologists delight in accumulating and assessing vast numbers of characters and trying to sort them out into a logical family tree. Detailing all this minutiae would take up much of the book, so only the telling highlights are explored here.

The problem with cladistics, and all anatomically based phylogenics, is that they are often contradicted by DNA-DNA hybridization studies. This suggests that even the best cladograms may be grossly in error. Then again, it is possible that the DNA-DNA studies are wrong or misleading. If the subjects are long extinct, like dinosaurs, there is no way to compare the two methods. What we can say is that cladograms map character patterns, not necessarily true relationships. But there are many cases where we can show that the potential relationship, even an ancestor-descendant one, has a high probability of being real. This is most true when a series of very similar species is found in a sequence of sediments lying directly one atop another, and the species show a consistent trend of change. However, such straight "lineages" are the exception. Mostly we are dealing with complex branching patterns or mainstreams of ancestry and descent. The main cladistic relationship is the sister clade or group. These are two clades which are neither ancestors nor descendants of each other, but which share a common ancestor.

Along with figuring out the relationships of animals, one has to label them and their groups. Sad to say, dinosaur taxonomy has been near chaos, with every one doing pretty much their own thing. This laissez-faire attitude has led to a state where the single genus *Megalosaurus* contains an array of very dissimilar forms, while extremely similar *Tarbosaurus bataar* and *Tyrannosaurus rex* are placed in different genera. Even worse, dinosaur taxonomy has been executed in isolation from the modern biological world. This violates a basic foundation of paleobiological sciences, the principle of uniformitarianism. Simply put, past systems are roughly similar to modern ones, and as far as possible should be categorized according to equivalent criteria. Only then can we compare fossil and living species in a truly meaningful way.

But this is easier said than done. The basic unit of all taxonomy and systematics is the species. When one reads about *Tyrannosaurus* and *Brontosaurus,* one is not dealing with species, like lions or African elephants. Instead, these are genera, a group of animal species. For example, the lion is in the genus *Panthera.* Species of *Panthera* include the lion *Panthera leo,* the tiger *P. Tigris,* and the leopard *P. pardus,* among others. So saying *Tyrannosaurus* is much like saying "the big cats." This is all right for certain purposes, but usually we want to be more specific. Then full species names are used. These always include both the generic and species titles, such as *Tyrannosaurus rex,* or *T. rex* for short. Much as genera are populations of species, families are populations of genera, orders are populations of families, and then come classes, phyla, and at the top of the hierarchial pyramid, kingdoms. These groups can be further subdivided, for example, into superorders, suborders, and infraorders. This system of classification is the Linnaen system, started by Carolus Linnaeus (Carl von Linné) in the 1700s.

Living species are identified on a basis that is simple in concept, but often complicated in application. A species is a population of animals that is reproductively isolated from other animal groups. Take the lion and tiger, which live in the same Indian forests. Despite their close similarity and relationships, they do not normally interbreed. If interbreeding does occur, the progeny is a hybrid, a sometimes sterile oddity that will not contribute to the regular breeding populations of either species.

Some species are easy to identify. The moose, for example, is obviously not going to interbreed with anything else. Other cases are much more difficult. Many bird species are almost identical to related species, but they do not interbreed. There may be even more difference between the sexes of a given species than between two different species. For example, the skeleton of the big, robust male lion differs more from a female lion's than the latter does from the skeleton of a female tiger. Or, there can be great geographic variation. The south Alaskan brown bear, a subspecies of *Ursus arctos,* is enormous, heavy-set, and small-clawed. The grizzly, the American subspecies of *U. arctos* that lives outside of southern Alaska, is a good deal smaller, scrawnier, and has long claws.

So the modern concept of a species is based on breeding dynamics, not on the morphology of animals—which means that species are real, natural systems. Moreover, many of the morphological features that biologists use to help identify living species are contained in the soft tissues—for instance, color, feather, or fur patterns, the superficial display devices that animals often use to identify members of their own and other species. It is through these devices that they avoid sex with the wrong kind. Things are difficult, for paleontologists trying to identify extinct species because they do not have access to such information.

Higher level systematics differs from the species work in that it depends almost wholly on morphological divergence. This divergence is made up of two components, phylogenetic and gradistic. Only related species can be put together in a given taxa. As related taxonomic groups evolve from one another the degree, or grade, of morphological difference between them is used to further separate them. But unlike the true separation of species, the boundaries of genera, families, etc., are arbitrary ones, set by humans. For instance, the big-cat genus *Panthera* excludes cougars and house cats. There is no a priori reason for doing this— they are close relatives. But most catologists think there are enough differences to put house cats in another genus, *Felis.* It is much as meterologists arbitrarily set the boundaries between differing cloud types—there is no precise moment when a little cumulus cloud becomes a great cumulonimbus. Stellar astronomers, who can choose precise surface temperatures to classify stars, have an easier task. But higher taxa are by no means entirely artificial. Just as the cumulonimbus thunderhead is different from the fluffy cumulus cloud, the family Tyrannosauridae really is different from the Allosauridae. In the case of genera, the rule of thumb is to separate when there is one significant functional difference present. As morphological and functional differences accumulate, then families, orders, and so on are split off.

A good system contains as much information as it can while remaining simple enough to grasp in a single good look. Only the evolutionary high points, the major nodes of functional and phylogenetic divergence, should be formally recognized. In attempting to classify extinct animals, it is tempting for paleontologists to designate as many phylogenetic clades as possible, but this results in bewildering arrays of mega, hypo, and micro orders and families. If this tendency is followed to its logical conclusion, every two genera would be in a separate systematic group. To avoid such unmanageable proliferation, only the normal sub-rankings listed above should be used. These are all that are needed. Besides, the uncertainty inherent in the phylogenetics of long-extinct groups also works against unduly complex rankings.

At the other extreme, a few workers, such as Jacques Gauthier in his 1986 study of theropod-bird relationships, hold forth that a taxonomic system should be based solely on phylogeny. In this system grade is avoided, so there are no classes, families, or the like; each name merely designates a major phylogenetic splitting point. Supposedly this is less arbitrary than the Linnaen system. But this is really true only if every two species are given a name, something we just saw is not workable. If instead reasonable judgments are made as to what splitting points will be named, then the system is really as arbitrary as any other. Even then, phylogeny-only classification systems are hard to understand because they lack equivalent rankings to guide one by. Most importantly, as we more traditional (at least in this area) workers like to say, "grade is as important as clade." So grade should and can be formally recognized in classification, as outlined above.

Finally, there is a procedure to be followed when uniting taxa. Basically, the first named title has priority. For example, *Tyrannosaurus* was named by Osborn in 1905, *Tarbosaurus* by Maleev in 1955. So when these are united, *Tarbosaurus* is "sunk." This means that some fine names, often the more properly descriptive or better known ones, are lost. But it is important to prevent wholesale chaos. There are exceptions, such as when a not fully proper name is so well established that changing it would result in undue confusion.

Having looked at how to relate and name animals, it is time to start a predatory dinosaur cladogram. The very primitive diapsid reptiles are chosen as the outgroup. Generally, diapsids have two temporal openings in the skull behind the orbit, or eye socket (Figure 8-2); other reptiles have only the upper one of these, or neither. Lizards, crocodilians, and birds are living diapsids. A key feature further uniting some diapsids is yet another opening in front of the orbit. Diapsids with this preorbital opening are classified as archosaurs, among which are birds and crocodil-

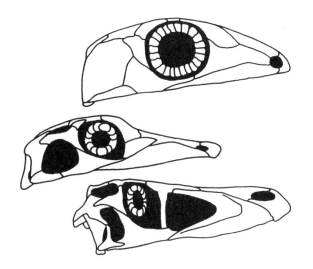

8-2
Diapsid skull openings. In the earliest reptiles (top) the skull's surface was almost unbroken, the only large opening being the orbit with its bony eye ring. In early diapsids, such as the reptile Youngina (center), two new openings appear behind the orbits. Archosaurian diapsids, such as Velociraptor (bottom), have yet a third opening in front of the orbits, often set inside a shallow fossa. These extra openings increased the effectiveness of the jaw muscles they supported, while lightening the construction of the skull.

ians. Actually, living birds and crocodilians have little or no preorbital opening left, but their earliest forms did. Lizards and their ancestors never had a preorbital opening and are not archosaurs.

Among extinct animals, thecodonts, pterosaurs, and dinosaurs had a preorbital opening, and with crocs and birds form the Archosauria. Most of these also share more erect gaits, and a bird-type bone histology that, as explained in Chapter 7 (pages 151-56), suggests they had faster growth rates and heightened metabolisms. The higher level systematics of these archosaurs, and the dinosaurs they include, is in a great state of flux. The traditional way of classifying dinosaurs is no longer preeminent and in fact is so obsolete that it is misleading to perpetuate it. For this reason, in this book I have gone ahead and offered a new reorganization of predatory dinosaur taxonomy and systematics, even though the phylogenetic conclusions it is based upon are not yet firm. I do so because some working scheme is needed, and because I doubt that the phylogenetics will solidify soon enough to produce a better arrangement before this book is published.

Dinosaurs have traditionally been classified as two separate orders of the subclass Archosauria, in the class Reptilia. But dinosaurs are radically different from all living reptiles. As we have seen, structurally and physiologically they are more like birds. It makes no more sense to put *Tyrannosaurus* and *Triceratops* in the same group as turtles and lizards than it does to put

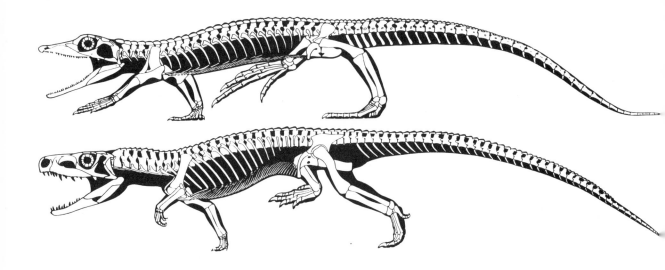

8-3
The very archaic diapsid Youngina capensis *(top) of the Permian and the famous Early Triassic* Euparkeria capensis *(bottom). Lizards, thecodonts, crocodilians, dinosaurs, and birds are descendants of such simple creatures as the former. In turn, the latter is the sort of small, generalized thecodont from which arose dinosaurs, birds, pterosaurs, and crocodilians. (Drawings are not to scale.)*

birds in the Reptilia. Starting with Robert Bakker and Peter Galton in 1974, this has led a number of scholars to suggest that dinosaurs and birds be united in a class of their own. Probably it is best simply to raise the Archosauria to class rank, and include in it thecodonts, crocodilians, pterosaurs, dinosaurs, and birds. Some have criticized the use of the archosaur's high growth and metabolic rates to define this group. But the classes Aves and Mammalia have long been defined, in part, by their warm-blooded nature. Besides, the archosaur's distinctive bone histology is itself a hard, morphological character that can be directly measured. The whole idea of taking crocodilians and dinosaurs out of reptiles and putting them together with birds has met considerable resistance. But if archosaurs are given a new class, then there is no justification for keeping their very similar avian descendants in another class. Whatever happens, at least dinosaurs and their relatives are no longer either "lower" vertebrates or reptiles, they are archosaurs, equal to mammals in status.

As archosaurs evolved, they developed many derived adaptations, among which were increasingly erect gaits. This occurred in two very different ways. In some thecodonts the upper hip bone, the platelike ilium, and its hip socket rotated out and downward so the socket supported the femur from above[2] (Figure 8-4). In ornithosuchid thecodonts, protocrocodilians, pterosaurs, dinosaurs, and birds the ilium stayed vertical, and the hip socket became a deep, internally open cylinder into which fitted a cylindrical, in-turned head of the femur. These two ways of bringing the limbs closer under the body are so different that they obviously evolved independently.[3]

Ankle design has been thought to divide archosaurs into simple groups. In dinosaurs and birds, both of the upper ankle bones, the astragalus and calcaneum, are fixed immobile to the shank bones. This makes the ankle an uncomplicated *mesotarsal* hinge (Figure 8-5). Many thecodonts and most crocodilians have a much more complex *crurotarsal* ankle, in which the astragalus is fixed to the shank, but the calcaneum rotates along with the foot. The calcaneum also has a large heel tuber to which the Achilles tendon attaches, just like the one in your foot. There are three subtypes of archosaurian crurotarsal ankle in which the peg-and-socket articulation between the astragalus and calcaneum switch positions, or are absent. The last main ankle type is the primitive thecodont's intermediate kind, in which the calca-

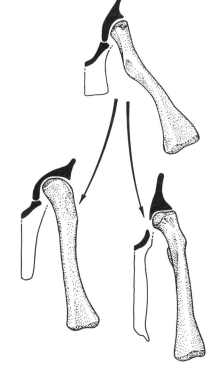

8-4
In such early archosaurs as Euparkeria (top), the femur was held semi-erect in a shallow, sideways-oriented hip socket. More advanced archosaurs evolved two very different ways of walking on more vertical, erect hind limbs. In most thecodonts, such as Saurosuchus (left), the hip socket grew out over the head of the femur. In dinosaurs and birds, the head of the femur bent inward to fit into a deep, vertical hip socket, as in Herrerasaurus (right).

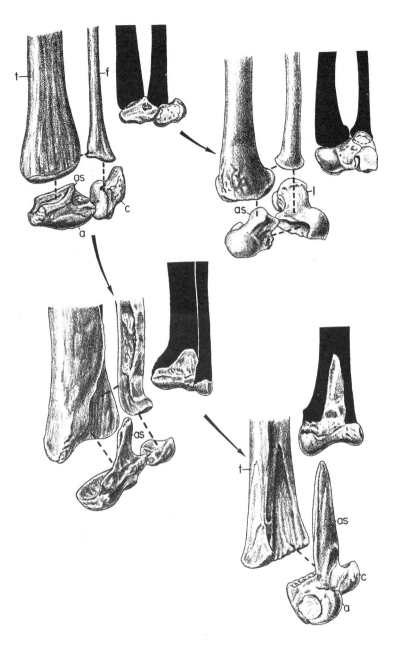

8-5
Archosaurs developed a number of distinctive ankle types (left ankles are shown here blown apart, then articulated in the insets). In primitive thecodonts like Chanaresuchus (upper left), the astragalus (a) and calcaneum (c) were rather simple. Some advanced thecodonts and crocodilians (a modern croc is on the upper right) have complex ankles in which the calcaneum was highly mobile and developed a long lever (l). Dinosaurs such as Allosaurus (center left) went the opposite way; the calcaneum became small and bound tightly to the astragalus, and the latter grew a tall ascending process (as) that fit tightly to the tibia (t; f is fibula). Such birds as the moa (lower right) have taken this system to further extremes. The arrows used in some of the figures in this chapter indicate general trends, not detailed relationships.

neum is only partly mobile with the foot, and lacks a well developed heel tuber. Often, archosaurs are divided so as to follow the differing peg-and-socket types, with dino-avian mesotarsal ankles descending from the appropriate crurotarsal types. That evolution followed this path is extremely unlikely, because developing the simple mesotarsal ankle from the complex crurotarsal kind requires a drastic alteration of function—one with no apparent gain in performance. It is much more likely that the fully mesotarsal ankle developed from the unsophisticated intermediate ankle of primitive thecodonts.

It appears that two main archosaur sister groups, with fundamentally different types of hips and ankles, evolved in the Middle and Late Triassic. The main thecodont group had the overhanging hip sockets and crurotarsal ankles. The one that concerns us is the dinosaur-bird clade, with its perforated cylindrical hip sockets and usually mesotarsal ankles. Other features that mark this group are the small size of the early members, the enlarged shoulder crest on the upper arm bone (humerus), and a big-clawed thumb that points inward when it is extended. The last is a potent defensive weapon, and even birds retain it in modified form as the alula feather on the wing's leading edge (see Figure 9-7, page 220). The initial members of this group are the small ornithosuchians. Rather bizarre-headed animals, they independently developed a unique crurotarsal ankle with the peg in the calcaneum. Ornithosuchians were still flat-footed plantigrades, unlike the members of the dino-bird clade which carried their ankles well clear of the ground.

The various dinosaur groups share some additional features that ornithosuchids lack. One is the loosening up and loss of the full collarbone (clavicle-interclavicle) brace. This frees up the shoulder girdle so it can rotate and increase the step length of the forelimb. Another is an even deeper hip socket and a fully erect hind limb.

8-6

As bizarre as Late Jurassic Riojasuchus tenuisceps *was, this ornithosuchid thecodont may have been a relative of early protodinosaurs. So too may have been the flying pterosaur* Rhamphorynchus muensteri; *it and its brethren mimicked birds in many ways, and differed sharply in others. (Drawings are not to scale.)*

Dinosaurs and birds were long thought to have evolved as three or more separate groups from differing thecodonts, and were usually split into two hip types, the differences centering around the pubis, which projects below the hips. The "reptile-hipped" Saurischia, including the herbivorous prosauropods and brontosaurs along with the predatory theropods, had vertical pubes, while the "bird-hipped" herbivorous Ornithischia were those dinosaurs that had backward-pointing pubes. This theory started coming unglued in 1974 when John Ostrom showed that birds were most like theropods, and Robert Bakker and Peter Galton pointed out that as a whole, dinosaurs are united by a number of key characters. Today a consensus among a number, but not all, of dinosaurologists supports this view, myself among them.[4]

Among the more important of these key dino-bird characters is the strongly S-curved neck for down and forward plunges of the head. Other dino-bird unifying features include enlarged preorbital depressions, slender bones in the roof of the mouth, fully erect arms with more downward-facing shoulder joints, deeply cylindrical hip joints, larger knee crests, inner shank bones (tibias) that back a tall process of the ankle's astragalus, transversely compressed cannon bones, and an outer toe that is always reduced. This suite of characters is a solid one, and it clearly separates dinosaurs and birds from all other four-limbed vertebrates, or tetrapods. It is possible that different groups evolved these traits independently, but the fact is that there is no good evidence that they did so. Just the opposite. The evidence strongly indicates that these traits form a true monophyletic clade.

That this is so has wonderful systematic implications. Way back in 1841, Sir Richard Owen placed what few dinosaurs were then known in a new order, Dinosauria. This has long been held to be an obsolete concept, but it is now apparent that Owen was right after all. Dinosaurs should be reunited in a revived Dinosauria grouping and raised to the rank of subclass or infraclass[5] —just which subrank depends on the interrelationships of other archosaurs that do not concern us here. Some still want to keep the lagosuchians and other archaic "protodinosaurs" in the thecodonts, both because of their primitive build and the possibility that they evolved their dinosaur features independently. I completely disagree, since they have all the key dinosaurian adaptations.

Alan Charig noted back in 1976 that if dinosaurs are monophyletic, then Saurischia and Ornithischia are no longer equivalent clades. Saurischians are just those dinosaurs that happen to retain relatively primitive hips, and ornithischians are just one of many groups that evolved "bird hips." Bakker has gone ahead and abandoned the Saurischia.[6] So have I, and I use four new dinosaur groups, which I consider superorders. First is the Paleodinosauria, including early, four-toed predatory forms as described at the beginning of Chapter 3, and in Part II, page 239. The protodinosaur lagosuchians and the more advanced staurikosaurs are also members. Exactly how the paleodinosaurs are related to the other dinosaurs is not clear. Because the paleodinosaurs are so archaic, and because their unspecialized nature makes them suitable ancestors for the other superorders, they are given a superorder of their own.

The next new superorder is the predatory Herreravia, typified by big *Herrerasaurus* and detailed in Part II, pages 247-51. The birdlike "Protoavis" remains may belong in this group. The herreravians are still thecodont-like with their short ilia and four-toed feet, but they developed birdlike lower hips and upper arms. This is a small group for superorder status, but because herreravians probably developed their birdlike specializations on their own, and because they may have arisen from paleodinosaurs independently from theropods (there is no way of telling for sure at this time), they are best given such a high-level separation.

Another big dinosaur superorder is the herbivorous Phytodinosauria, just coined by Bakker in 1986. Not the subject of this volume, this group includes the paleodinosaur-like prosauropods, the great brontosaurs, and the bird-hipped, beaked segnosaur-ornithischians (Figure 8-7). Among other things, this monophyletic clade is typified by blunt, "spoon"-crowned teeth suitable for cropping plants.

The final superorder is the great Theropoda—the birdlike and usually predaceous theropods and their bird descendants—the prime subject of this volume. This is a very distinctive archosaur clade, marked by three-toed bird-feet in which the inner cannon bone does not reach up to the ankle (see Figure 4-15). Theropods also have ilia that are long and subrectangular, hands with four or less fingers that are no longer good for walking, rigid rib cages, and very large knee crests. And there are ten neck vertebrae, generally thirteen in the trunk, and usually five in the hip. Theropods are scrutinized in Part II, on pages 253-403.

The three advanced dinosaur groups are coincidentally symmetrical in that each independently developed bird-hipped forms. However, the exact nature of these hips differs. In protobirds and birds the projection of the ilium that supports the pubis is tilted backward along with the pubis. In herrerasaurs and the segnosaur-ornithischians, only the pubis points backward. This is important because it has been thought that the recently discovered segnosaurs were some sort of theropod, but their hips are quite different from even the most birdlike of theropod hips (see pages 353-363 in Part II).[7]

Now we can take a closer look at the three predatory dinosaur superorders in turn. Figure 10-1, on pages 224-25, is a cladogram of most of the genera of these superorders. The first Paleodinosauria are the galloping "rabbit" forms, the odd-footed lagerpetids (their fourth toe is the longest), which are an early

8-7
A few early herbivorous dinosaurs: the prosauropod Plateosaurus carinatus *(top) and the early ornithischians* Heterodontosaurus tucki *(center) and* Scelidosaurus harrisoni *(bottom). As you can see, all dinosaurs share many anatomical similarities. Unlike theropods, many herbivorous dinosaurs were quadrupedal, and they retained four complete toes. (Drawings are not to scale.)*

side branch of the normal-footed lagosuchids. The two-legged staurikosaurs form a clade above the lagosuchians because they have the longer kind of pubes found in all other dinosaurs; hence, split into two orders: the very primitive Lagosuchia and the Staurikosauria.

Exactly how these Paleodinosaurs are interrelated to the herreravians, herbivorous dinosaurs, and theropods is not clear. We can say that herreravians are, in spite of their early appearance, a sophisticated predatory side group. Herrerasaurs themselves had hourglass-shaped vertebral bodies that were later mimicked by allosaurs, and big pubic boots like those of the advanced theropods. Very importantly, herreravians also show some shoulder and hip features that imitate birds to a surprising degree.

This brings us to the very big problem recently posed by Triassic "Protoavis." This little animal is amazingly birdlike in much of its morphology, even more so than *Archaeopteryx* and most other protobird theropods. Some of the points cited as evidence of bird affinity do not mean much: the wishbone furcula (cojoined collarbones) is also seen in a thecodont and some theropods, and the absence of *back* teeth in "Protoavis" is not like the early bird's lack of *front* teeth. Besides, some theropods also lost their teeth. But most of the avian-type details have not reached the press yet, and cannot be so easily dismissed. Taken at face value, these characters imply that birds arose directly from Triassic predatory dinosaurs. This is a big problem because better evidence discussed elsewhere indicates that birds evolved much later, from advanced theropods in the Jurassic. But although it is too soon to tell what is going on, there is a way out of this bind. It starts with the fact that Jurassic *Archaeopteryx* and the Cretaceous protobird theropods have their own birdlike characters that "Protoavis" does not, such as more birdlike ankles with the tall ascending projection of the astragalus. The protobird *Avimimus* in particular is more birdy than "Protoavis" in most, but not all, regards. Perhaps most importantly, "Protoavis" seems to have retained four complete toes. This would mean it is not a true theropod, but a herreravian instead. That "Protoavis" and the Jurassic-Cretaceous protobirds each have birdlike characters that the other lacks can only mean that the evolution of birdlike dinosaurs occurred at least twice. That is not really too surprising; after all, even the earliest predatory dinosaurs were already very birdy.

The issue is: which group actually evolved into birds, and

which was a dead end? My very tentative solution is based on the fact that, as explained in Chapter 3, bird fossils are suspiciously absent in the Jurassic. If Triassic "Protoavis" was a true bird ancestor, then where were all the Jurassic birds? My answer is that there may have been none. "Protoavis" could be a logical, albeit extreme, development of the already very birdlike herrerasaurs and therefore a member of the Herreravia—one that took to climbing and leaping, and that may have started to fly. For reasons that are unclear, the evolution of these bird-mimics was then aborted. But the reader must realize that this is not proven. There is a remote possibility that "Protoavis," and perhaps herrerasaurs too, are the true bird ancestors. *Archaeopteryx* and other birdlike theropods would then be mere sidelines, or even bird-mimics that had nothing to do with true bird evolution. It is possible that theropod groups and birds are not monophyletic as I argue, but arose independently from paleodinosaur stock. There is a myriad of plausible alternatives, all of which invoke massive convergence and parallelism. One may well doubt whether we will ever resolve the problem, since we will always be limited by relatively fragmentary data, especially since we cannot get a helping hand from DNA-DNA hybridization. But there is the hope that some of the patterns I see emerging just now may point the way to a satisfactory solution.

Having looked at paleodinosaurs and herreravians, we now turn to the biggest predatory dinosaur superorder, Theropoda. As the theropods evolved, they tended to become increasingly birdlike. But this is a large and complex group that exhibited much parallelism, some important reversals, and specializations of its own. It has become clear that the old way of dividing theropods into two simple groups is useless. In the old arrangement, the Coelurosauria held the small, hollow-boned species, starting with Triassic, kink-snouted *Coelophysis* and ending with the Late Cretaceous ostrich-mimics, and the Carnosauria incorporated the big-bodied, big-headed, heavy-boned forms. This started with *Dilophosaurus,* which also had a kinked snout, and *Megalosaurus,* both of the Jurassic, and finished up in the Cretaceous with tyrannosaurs. This division was meaningless, for large size and stoutness of build and bones is just the sort of thing that many groups tend to develop on their own. In 1984, Jacques Gauthier and Kevin Padian tried to revive and revise these old terms to fit the new phylogenetics, but the process of adapting them involves so much distortion that there is little point in doing

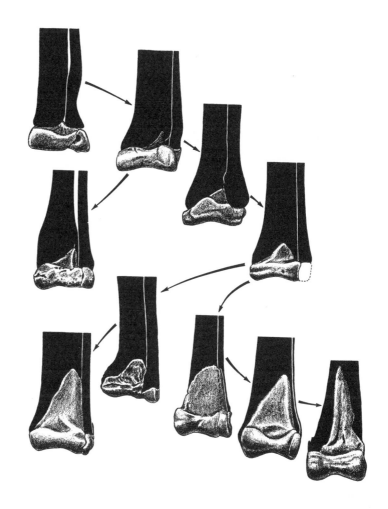

so. At best, carnosaur and coelurosaur are informal terms for big and small theropods; it is better just to say big and small. A modern assessment of theropods finds that Theropoda contain two orders: the archaic Paleotheropoda and the more advanced, more birdlike Avetheropoda, which includes the direct ancestors of birds. The two theropod orders are especially satisfying because they each show about the same anatomical diversity as is found in the two ungulate orders, the Perissodactlya (odd-toed horses and rhinos) and Artiodactyla (even-toed pigs, deer, and cattle), and both are marked by differing ankle and foot details (Figures 8-8, 8-9).

The most primitive paleotheropod is small *Procompsognathus,* which retains an archaic broad pubis. The least advanced

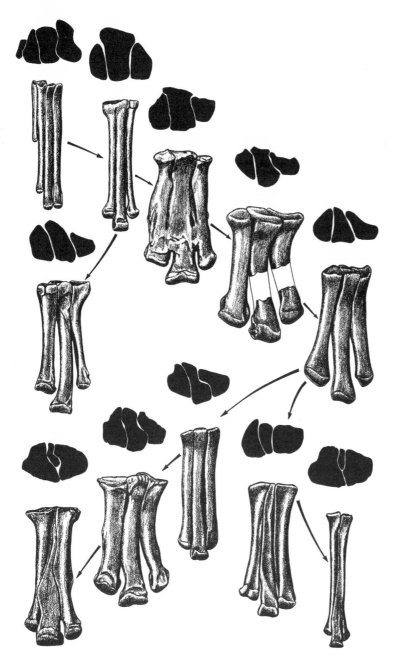

of the narrow-hipped theropods are the coelophysids. These include small coelophysians as well as larger dilophosaurs. Coelophysids are an example of a bewildering combination of primitive and derived characters. Quite primitive in most regards, dilophosaurs had only four hip vertebrae. Yet the group's unique kinked

190

articulation between the premaxillary and maxilla bones in the snout, the many co-ossified bones, and the unique double head crests, are advanced. Dilophosaurs were even more like advanced theropods in some other ways, and had a unique and sophisticated suspensorium (the complex of cheek bones that support the lower jaw). All this can be sorted out satisfactorily. The kinked snouts, crests, and peculiar jaw supports show that coelophysids were an increasingly aberrant side branch that left no descendants. This means they paralleled other advanced theropods and birds in such details as extensive bone ossification and increasingly narrow cannon bones (Figure 8-9). Crests, peculiar jaw supports, and narrow cannon bones show that dilophosaurs are the most advanced of the bunch, so their reduced hips must be a secondary reversal to a more primitive condition. It may be that the extraordinarily aberrant *Baryonyx* and *Spinosaurus* are extremely specialized developments of the dilophosaur branch; their deeply kinked snout and other similarities certainly suggest so.

In 1986, Robert Bakker made the ceratosaurs, famous for their nasal horn, the first of a major, more advanced group of theropods, the Neotheropoda.[8] This is because he thinks they have the double-jointed lower jaws (see Chapter 4, page 96). However, having looked over the best existing skull, I do not think they did. Instead, ceratosaurs were very primitive theropods because they retained a very coelophysian-like anatomy. They are a bit more advanced than coelophysians in having more slender shoulder blades, longer ilia, bigger outer processes near the femoral head, and somewhat taller ankle processes.

The next more derived group is the intertheropods, which are good-sized theropods with features that place them between the basal and the advanced theropods. This group includes the heavily built megalosaurs and the normally built eustreptospondylians and metriacanthosaurs. These advanced paleotheropods are more derived than the coelophysians and ceratosaurs because of their still more slender shoulder blades, larger outer femoral process, vertical pubes with growing boots, and narrower central cannon bone (see figure 8-9). The short-forearmed megalosaurs are rather strange theropods, especially the South American abelisaurs and noasaurs. This shows that they had left the mainstream of theropod evolution. Small *Noasaurus* paralleled some protobirds by developing a special killing claw on the second toe. *Megalosaurus* is also unusual in that it has broad pubes, like

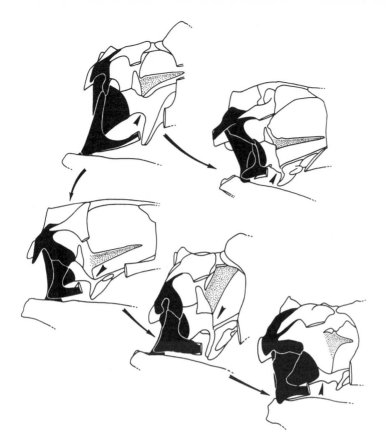

8-10

In primitive theropods like Ceratosaurus *(upper left) the bar con-
necting the front and back ends of
the pterygoid (short arrow) was
broad, the two outer bones in the
suspensorium (in black) were
slender, and the anterior process
of the braincase (stippled) were
rodlike. Advanced protobird theropods such as* Velociraptor antirrhopus *(right) retained the
slender outer suspensorium bones
and braincase process, but the in-
trapterygoid connection had become a slender rod. The slender
pterygoid rod is also true of* Ornitholestes, Allosaurus, *and tyrannosaurs (lower row). However, in
this clade the suspensorium elements became robust, and started
to close off the opening behind the
orbit. Also, allosaurs and tyrannosaurs share an unusual platelike braincase process that
contacts the skull roof.*

early dinosaurs. This once led me to believe that it was the most archaic of theropods,[9] and Peter Galton and James ("Dinosaur") Jensen to conclude that megalosaurs and some other big theropods evolved completely separately from small theropods. But megalosaurs share too many characters with other theropods for this to be true. I now believe the broad hips are a secondary reversal to the old condition. Eustreptospondylians and metriacanthosaurs are a bit more advanced than megalosaurs in the above listed characters, and less aberrant. Theropods like these may have been the ancestors of more advanced theropods. *Metriacanthosaurus* is especially important in helping us ascertain the evolutionary sequence, because this well-preserved form has a large, expanded pubic tip, or boot, and the shorter anterior trunk ribs that go with the start of an avian lung system.

We now come to avetheropods.[10] These are very birdlike dinosaurs, even for theropods, having many avian adaptations. For example, the lower jaw is hinged at its midlength, and many birds retain this in a modified form. At the back of the roof of the mouth the pterygoid bone has a reduced connection between its two main sections; this would become a hinge in many birds (Figure 8-10). The front trunk ribs are short and slender, and the back ones are long in order to operate abdominal air sacs (see Figure 4-8, page 104). The shoulder blade is very narrow, also a birdlike feature, as are the big inner wrist bone and three-fingered hand (see Figure 4-12, page 109, and Figure 9-7, page 220). The pubic boot is very large, and the outer process of the femoral head is very tall. Figure 8-8 shows that the ankle has another very avian adaptation, a tall ascending process of the astragalus.[11] Finally, the upper part of the central cannon bone is narrower than in paleotheropods (Figure 8-9). The progressive narrowing of the central cannon bone in theropods is sometimes portrayed as either strongly compressed at its upper end, or not compressed at all. Actually it is the *degree* of narrowing that is very important.

The small Late Jurassic compsognathids and coelurids are the most primitive definite avetheropods, although the first is barely in the order. Beyond these there are two main avetheropod clades. One is the classic allosaur-tyrannosaur group, which also includes the small ornitholestians and aublysodonts. These are advanced relative to other theropods because they have robust suspensoriums (Figure 8-10). Another distinctive character is a central cannon bone that is L-shaped at the upper end. A subtle character, it is important because it is consistent regardless of how reduced this bone becomes, and because it distinguishes the allosaur-tyrannosaur group from other avetheropods in which this element is always straight at its upper end (see Figure 8-9).

Although tyrannosaurs and their aublysodont relatives share some qualities with the sickle-clawed dromaeosaurs discussed below,[12] they are really united with allosaurs above the ornitholestians. Allosaurs and tyrannosaurs share unusual plate-like processes that project forward from the braincase and run up to the skull roof (Figure 8-10), and a more flexible extra joint in the lower jaw. Aublysodonts and tyrannosaurs share even more similarities with each other: D-cross-sectioned front teeth followed by bigger blades behind, small premaxillas in the tip of the snout, deep maxillas behind them, extremely slender shoulder blades, big pubic boots—and most notable of all—atrophied arms and hands. Allosaurs have some minor specializations that tyrannosaurs lack, and this made me think at first that they were sister groups with a common Jurassic ancestor. But Cretaceous allosaurs became increasingly tyrannosaur-like, so it really looks like advanced Cretaceous allosaurs directly spawned the aublysodont-tyrannosaurs. Sankar Chatterjee disagrees, contending that differing peg-and-socket articulations in the allosaurs and tyrannosaurs show they directly and independently evolved from different thecodonts.[13] But the theropods' "pegs and sockets" are just interlocking bumps, not at all like the thecodonts' systems. Otherwise, the dinosaurs' mesotarsal ankles are extremely alike, and completely different from the thecodonts' crurotarsal ones (see Figure 8-6). The same is true of the rest of these animals.

The allosaur-tyrannosaur clade is a sister group to the other major avetheropod clade, the "true" protobirds and birds. Protobirds are less advanced than the allosaur-tyrannosaurs in their retention of slender cheek bones, strong intermandibular joints, and straight-ended central cannon bones. But protobirds have many avian features not found in most other dinosaurs, although as mentioned earlier some may have been mimicked by earlier "Protoavis" and its relatives. Perhaps the first protobird is famous *Archaeopteryx,* often considered the original bird. This little animal's very large arms bore fully aerodynamic feathered wings. However, these are not as genealogically important as the birdlike skeletal details of *Archaeopteryx* and other protobird theropods. These details include an enlarged braincase, triangular frontal bones over the eye socket which give the large eyes binocular vision, a reduced quadratojugal bone just above the jaw joint, low-set upper cheek bars, and reduced lower braincase elements. Neck ribs are short, and the neck vertebrae's articulations are becoming saddle-shaped. Especially birdlike are the arms. A big furcula formed as the paired collarbones fused together. The very large coracoid, which helps form part of the shoulder joint, has a big acrocoracoid projection (see Figure 4-9, page 109) and is tilted back relative to the very slender shoulder blade. Because the shoulder joint sets so high, the shoulder blade is horizontal. The long and slender hand's thumb bone is very short, and the central digit is the most robust. Also very birdlike is the hip. The pubis and its base are tilted way back, and the iliac blade is parallelogram-shaped. Because the tail is reduced, the femur's projection for anchoring the tail muscle, the fourth trochanter, is very small.

John Ostrom's demonstration that birds are flying dinosaurs[14] was partly inspired by his work on the unexpectedly birdlike sickle-claws. Although Ostrom did not examine what kind of theropod *Archaeopteryx* was, it turns out that the sickle-clawed dromaeosaurs are by far its closest relatives.[15] Not only do they have all the above bird characters—including backward-tilted coracoids and pubes—but they share many additional features with *Archaeopteryx*. Some are subtle yet striking details, such as a diamond-shaped bone on the back of the braincase just above the opening for the spinal cord, and an identical scalloped articulation between the pubis and ilium. Overall, the hips are uniquely similar. The tails are alike in the short, blocky chevron bones running under their bases, while in the cheeks the quadrotojugal bone has a peculiar inverted-T shape. *Archaeopteryx* even has an early version of the short, hyperextendable second toe like the one the sickle-claws are so noted for.

I have listed so many of the characters shared by archaeopterygians, dromaesaurs, and other protobird theropods—but by no means all of them—to make a point. As long ago as 1868, Thomas Huxley noted the close similarities between *Compsognathus,* some herbivorous dinosaurs, and *Archaeopteryx.* He suggested that birds arose from dinosaurs. This idea was considered respectable until Gerhard Heilmann's classic study of 1926. In this exhaustive and wide-ranging work, Heilmann came within one sentence of concluding that small predatory dinosaurs were protobirds. But he argued that birds could not have descended from theropods because he thought the latter lacked collarbones (see Figure 4-9, page 109), which most animals and birds have. It was a fatal mistake, for Henry Osborn had described the collarbones of the theropod *Oviraptor* just two years before! Apparently unaware of this, Heilmann turned to the only available alternative, the generalized species of thecodonts. Of course some thecodonts must be the ancestors of birds, because they are ancestral to all other archosaurs. But no thecodont has a suite of birdlike adaptations that other archosaurs lack. Occasional claims that one has been found continue to be made, but subsequent investigations always show that the "bird" adaptations are typical to small archosaurs, or do not exist.[16] In some cases the "thecodont" cited has turned out to be something else altogether.

Most predatory thecodonts had splayed-out, grasping outer fingers and toes, and long forelimbs. This made them good climbers. Theropods are quintessential ground runners, often with short forelimbs. Many contend that birds must have learned flight by gliding from tree to tree, so climbing thecodonts, not running theropods, must be their ancestors. Unfortunately, even some of those who do favor a theropod origin for birds try to solve the problem by having birds learn to fly from the ground up. Starting as insect-chasing leapers. These ground-based theories are a mistake, for as I will explain in Chapter 9, pages 211-213, the arguments are badly flawed. Bird flight probably developed as protobirds leaped from branch to branch. There is no reason to dismiss the theropods in this scenario because small advanced theropods were good climbers. Their long arms and long, big-clawed fingers show that they were. Not only that, but *Archaeopteryx* itself climbed in the theropod manner, using *inwardly* grasping thumbs and first toes that were completely unlike the thecodonts' divergent *outer* digits. The two groups began climbing in totally different ways with ornithosuchids and early dinosaurs. They turned their thumbs into a divergent weapon, and lost the grasping outer digits. As a result, climbing performance was reduced. Such short-handed theropods as *Coelophysis* were especially poor climbers. But more advanced small avetheropods and protobirds relengthened their hands. These used thumbs and more divergent inner toes to perform the same climbing functions that thecodonts had used their outer sets for.

Despite its weakness, the thecodont hypothesis of bird origins remained the accepted one for almost a half a century. I suspect one reason was a prejudice, a difficulty in believing that the spectacular but "dead-end" dinosaurs could have been the ancestors of robins and hummingbirds. The scarcity of good dinosaur science in the middle of this century hardly helped. Circumstances finally changed in the early seventies. John Ostrom compared theropods and birds, and in 1972 Alick Walker found that early crocodilians share a number of features with birds. That crocs would be the closest living relatives of birds seems odd, though less so when we realize that the early protocrocodilians were small gracile animals. And they do share some structural things with birds—mainly the way the braincase articulates with some of the surrounding bones. However, crocodilians—even the earliest ones—have features that disqualify them as bird relatives. Among these are hyper-elongated wrist bones, so long that they perform as auxiliary upper hand bones. This does not bar a sister group relationship with birds, but closer examination of their shared-derived characters shows that they were developed in parallel, not inherited from a common ancestor. Even Walker now prefers a theropod ancestry for birds.[17]

Some continue to argue that thecodonts or protocrocodilians

are the closest relatives to birds.[18] Yet *Archaeopteryx* not only has all the basic theropodian adaptations, it is exquisitely and astonishingly similar to dromaeosaurs—so much so that they should be in the same *family*. Theories of crocodilian or thecodontian origins for birds have little chance under these circumstances. Indeed, Alan Feduccia has become skeptical about the arboreal-thecodont concept he long advocated, and the general feeling at the 1984 *Archaeopteryx* conference in Eichstatt was that the theropod concept was the best one.[19] So while birds have often been called "glorified reptiles," it clearly is better to think of them as "glorified dinosaurs."

Another odd and surprising thing is that the dromaeosaurs seem to be *more* advanced and birdlike than *Archaeopteryx*. This is because they have a number of basic avian adaptations that earlier *Archaeopteryx* does not, including a more birdlike quadratojugal bone in the cheek, more hip vertebrae, very short nonoverlapping neck ribs, shorter trunks, auxiliary hooked processes on the side of the rib cage, and even more birdlike femoral heads and hip sockets. *Archaeopteryx* is closer to *flying* birds in its big forelimbs, with more backwardly angled coracoids and a big wishbone furcula. But this does not mean dromaeosaurs are less birdlike in these characters; instead, they are similar to *flightless* birds, especially the archaic ratites (ostriches and the like). Dromaeosaurs just may be secondarily flightless Cretaceous descendants of the earlier, flying archaeopterygians. This would explain why dromaeosaurs had big breastplates, a classic and advanced flight adaptation (see Figure 4-10, page 107).

A wide variety of bird groups of all degrees of advancement have seen members lose flight in favor of an earth-bound existence. Following the loonlike, toothy hesperornithiforme divers of the Cretaceous, there have been ostriches and their relatives, penguins, auks, the great predatory phorusrhacids of South America, flightless rails, ibises, parrots, even flightless geese, ducks, and so on. This seems to have happened with protobirds too. So, as a mainstream of flying protobirds evolved in the Late Jurassic and early Cretaceous, they may have spawned a series of ever more advanced protobird theropods that separately lost the ability to fly. The first full birds appear very early in the Cretaceous, and the split of the flightless protobirds from flying protobird stock should have happened before that time—perhaps in a rapid burst at the Jurassic-Cretaceous boundary.

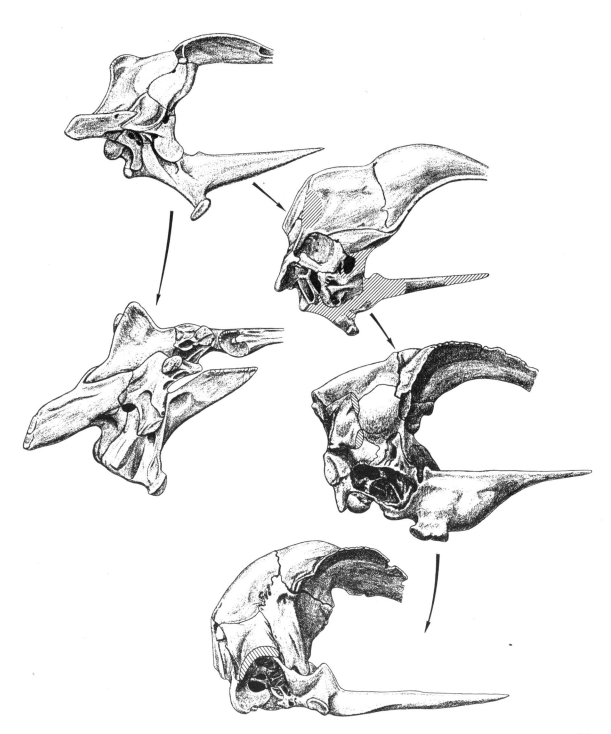

Next in line above the dromaeosaurs are the bizarre oviraptors. These parrot-beaked beasts are very similar to archaeopterygians and dromaeosaurs in the neck, shoulder girdle, hand, and the hip's ilium and ischium. They are more like birds than prior protobirds in the roof of the mouth, and in their very pneumatic skull bones. The ostrich-mimic ornithomimids also may belong in the protobird clade. Their braincases are quite birdlike, and they have the middle ear set in a shallow depression of the braincase. The roof of the mouth is rather avian in structure. At one time I thought ostrich-mimics were close relatives to tyrannosaurs, because the tails and legs in the advanced species of both are extremely alike. But early ostrich-mimics are not nearly so tyrannosaur-like. Even those who share characters differ in some subtle but key ways—for example, an L-shaped versus a straight central cannon bone. This is a classic case of parallelism in fast theropods. It is more likely, though still tenuous, that oviraptors and ornithomimids share a common, secondarily flightless ancestor.

Exceptionally birdlike in the braincase, middle ear, roof of the mouth, and hind legs are the sickle-clawed troodonts (see Figure 8-11). Usually these are considered close relatives of dromaeosaurs, and as protobirds they are. But troodonts are too advanced to be really close dromaeosaur relatives. That hyperextendable second toes are present in archaeopterygians, dromaeosaurs, and troodonts suggests that the mainstream of flying protobirds had them. Their predaceous and grounded offshoots retained them, while the nonpredatory oviraptors and ostrich-mimics did not. Last among protobirds are the terrifically birdlike avimimids—their head is basically that of a bird, and the upper hand is fused into a single unit also just like a bird's. Among the evidence indicating that Cretaceous protobirds were secondarily flightless, the avimimid's tightly folding arms and fused wrist and hand bones must be considered some of the most telling.

I am the first to admit that there are problems with this scenario of secondarily flightless protobirds. The worst is that in some ways some protobirds are less birdlike than archaeopterygians and dromaeosaurs. In particular, oviraptors, ostrich-mimics, troodonts, and avimimids seem to have normal and vertical pubes like most theropods. Perhaps this is a reversal, for unlike birds, proper protobirds still had good tails and pubes that were behind the guts instead of on either side of them. If they reen-

199

larged their tails, they no longer needed the belly under the hips for balance, so it might have been swung forward again along with the supporting pubes.

There may have been fewer cases of secondary flight loss in the protobird clade than I suspect. Instead, the nonflying protobirds may have experienced massive parallelism with the main body of flying protobirds. Another possibility is that flying protobirds continued as their own clade, competing with the true birds (including, possibly, "Protoavis") and spilling off flightless forms during the Cretaceous.

A vital point about bird origin is that the increasingly avian design of *Archaeopteryx* and cretaceous protobirds makes them, in the whole, the best potential ancestors of birds, much better than protobirds. So much so that this is the view accepted throughout this book.

A good thing about the predatory dinosaur phylogenetic tree outlined here is that it is in pretty good agreement with time. One has to be careful in using time as a check for phylogenetic trees. For one thing, it is possible for primitive group members to survive long after the more advanced ones have died out. Nonetheless, the protodinosaur lagosuchians are the first known dinosaurs, and the archaic paleodinosaurs and "Protoavis" are restricted to the Carnian and early Norian of the Triassic. The most primitive theropods appear at about this time, and are abundant until the Early Jurassic. The more advanced paleotheropods, the intertheropods, show up in the middle of the Jurassic, as do the first avetheropods. Protobirds appear in the Late Jurassic, with the most primitive member of the clade soon followed by more advanced protobirds and full birds in the Early Cretaceous. Highly derived tyrannosaurs appear as their advanced allosaur ancestors decline, later in the Cretaceous. Likewise, advanced birds do not appear until the later Cretaceous.

I have stressed that the phylogeny outlined here is not carved in stone, and is subject to change. However, I do firmly believe that dinosaurs and birds are monophyletic. I am also certain that the kink-snouted coelophysians and dilophosaurs formed a clade, with the also-kink-snouted and very strange spinosaurs as a possible tag-on. I am also convinced that the ornitholestian-allosaur-tyrannosaur clade is true. *Archaeopteryx* must have been an extremely close relative of dromaeosaurs. And I believe that some of the most birdlike theropods were secondarily flightless.

All the various predatory dinosaur suborders, families, and so on are detailed in Part II. There has been a recent tendency to split up closely related theropod groups into separate infraorders. For example, the dromaeosaurs, oviraptors, and ostrich-mimics have each been given an infraorder of their own.[20] I feel this is unduly complex, and that these theropods are better classified as families within a united suborder.

Ironically, it is in some ways easier to work with extinct genera and higher-level taxa than with extinct species. This is because both living and fossil higher-level taxa are identified on the basis of morphological differences. The problems in identifying fossil species are obvious. We cannot observe their breeding patterns, and we cannot look at their soft display structures. And even if soft tissues were available, they are more useful for sorting out living genera, than for species indentification. There is no full solution to these problems. In fact, extinct species, based on morphological differences and not breeding dynamics, cannot be considered true species. But uniformitarianism demands we do the best we can.

It is helpful, if not essential, to look at modern taxa because we can apply to fossils the values of skeletal variation usually found within a number of well-established species, genera, families, and so on. For extinct species attempts must be made to take into account individual, sexual, and geographic variation, but using modern vertebrates as benchmarks gives us a reasonably firm basis on which to measure fossil taxa.

What do modern taxa tell us? First, that many genera have a large number of species in them. We have already seen how *Panthera* is a multispecies genus. *Canis* and *Gazella* contain about a dozen species each. Another thing is that morphological variation is very high in many multispecies genera (figure 8-12). This is seen in *Canis* species, which range from the big robust Siberian timber wolf to the much smaller, delicate, and long-snouted Simien jackal. Fossil and living species of *Ursus* are quite variable.[21] Among other genera, *Varanus* lizards, *Bovis*, *Gazella*, *Anas* (various ducks), and even *Homo* show similar degrees of variation. Admittedly, not all living genera have been arranged to show as much variation as these, and this shows that modern biologists are still having their problems with consistency. But we need to start somewhere.

How do predatory dinosaur genera and species compare to modern ones? It is all too obvious that many major dinosaur

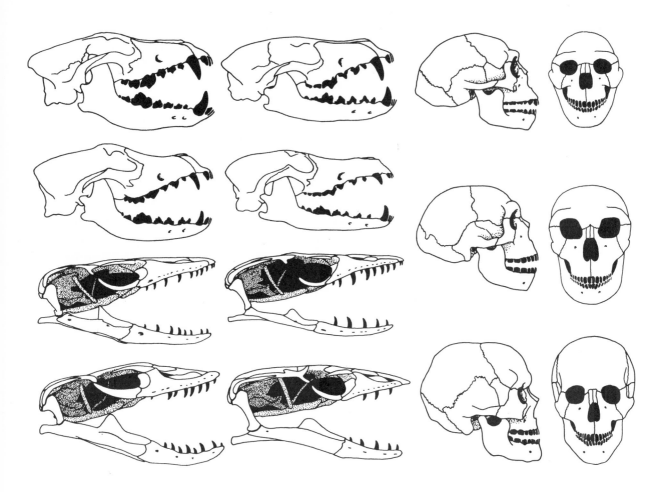

genera have only one or two species. *Coelophysis, Syntarsus, Struthiomimus, Gallimimus, Daspletosaurus, Tarbosaurus,* and *Tyrannosaurus* traditionally have a single species each. This sounds very suspicious. True, dealing with fossils we should not expect to find all of a genera's species, but there is strong evidence that the genera have been "oversplit."

This is confirmed by the similarities between some of these genera. An excellent case is *Tyrannosaurus rex* and *Tarbosaurus bataar*. These predators are very alike. If found in the same sediments they would probably be confused as the same species. They certainly show much less difference than seen between jackals and wolves, or lions and leopards. Likewise, *Coelophysis bauri* and *Syntarsus rhodesiensis* are no different from one an-

8-12
Morphological variation can be very substantial in modern genera, such as Canis *(upper left group),* Varanus *(lower left group), and even* Homo *(on right, from top to bottom,* H. erectus, H. neanderthalis, H. sapiens*).*

other than species of many modern genera. All the advanced ostrich-mimics are so alike it is often hard to tell them apart.

This means that dinosaurologists have often used generic titles to distinguish what are really species. Indeed, this has been the usual methodology. It is always enticing to name a whole new genus, but it is too far out of line with modern biology to be tolerable. Therefore, many dinosaur genera should be united. There is no way to justify keeping *Tarbosaurus* separate from *Tyrannosaurus*. *Syntarsus* and *Coelophysis* are very probably the same. All advanced ostrich-mimics belong in one genus. I do not believe it is useful—I'd say it's downright misleading—to perpetuate obsolete names, even when they are long-established and familiar to the public. So, I have not hesitated to unite taxa when appropriate, although this will be argued over and new data will change things yet again.

Not all dinosaurs are oversplit. *Megalosaurus* should be cut down to two or three species. Another good case of "lumping" is the Morrison *Allosaurus,* which has three species though it's usually considered to consist of one. The point is to try to be consistent.

As noted above, sexual differences can be confused with species differences. Sorting out these and other species problems properly requires large numbers of samples. If enough specimens are available, the quantitative variations between them can be compared statistically. This is not possible with most theropods. There are only half a dozen or so *Tyrannosaurus rex* skeletons, for example. The biggest samples available are of *Coelophysis bauri* and *C. rhodesiensis*. Both have been found in quarries containing dozens or hundreds of specimens. It has been determined that there are two proportional types of each. The question is whether these are sexes or species. That the two types have been found together at what are apparently mass-kill sites has been taken to mean that they are the two sexes of a single population. Sex ratios do not have to be equal; single males can possess whole harems, for instance. On the other hand, it is also possible for two very similar species of the same genus to coexist in the same area. Indian lion and tiger skeletons are so alike that paleontologists find it very difficult to separate them. There are some things that commonly distinguish sexual from species differences. Sexual variations are usually size-related.[22] Hence, male lions are extreme, robust, and big-toothed forms of the smaller female model, while female emus are stouter and larger than the males. When two types are similar in size, it is species differences that are often the cause.

Another factor involved in determining taxa—genera and species especially—is time. Generally, the closer in time, the more likely one taxa is involved. Species of recently living high-metabolic-rate animals typically last about 1.0 to 3.0 million years, and this seems to hold for dinosaurs. Cold-blooded species, with their longer generation turnovers, last longer. Genera of either type can last much longer, but not indefinitely. Yet morphology must have the final say on fossil species and genus identification. If two thoroughly known animals look so similar that they are one genus or species, then this should be recognized taxonomically regardless of the time displacement.

That is more or less the extent of our review of predatory dinosaur phylogeny and systematics. But we are not really finished, for birds are the last and continuing expression of theropod evolution. Fully evolved birds can be told from protobirds such as *Archaeopteryx* by a set of very distinctive adaptations. One of these is the splitting apart of the lower hip elements along the body midline, so the belly is slung *between* these bones. The hip socket's antitrochanter and the femoral head have a very extensive articulation. Skulls are reduced in that the bar behind the eye socket and in the upper cheek are both lost, as is most of the snout's maxilla bone and the preorbital opening it contains (see Figure 4-4, page 92). In the skull the quadrate, which supports the lower jaw, can also push forward on the lower cheek and roof of the mouth to elevate the beak. The articulations between the vertebrae have adopted a complex saddle-like shape, for better mobility. And of course the tail is reduced to a stub.

This brings us to the problem of what to do about classifying birds. By taking them down from their own class and uniting them with other archosaurs, we have already offended many ornithologists. This is a serious problem, and dinosaurologists and ornithologists may come to loggerheads over the issue. If it becomes accepted that theropods were warm-blooded, that they were the ancestors of birds, and, most importantly, that small ones were feathered, then ornithologists *may* come to accept the placement of birds in the Archosauria. That birds fly does not mean that they deserve their own subclass. After all, bats do not get their own subclass. Birds are not only direct descendants of theropods, they are little different in much of their morphology. However, birds should not be put in the Theropoda, just as bats

8-13
Most birdlike of all theropods in gross anatomy were the well-named ostrich-mimics, such as this flock of adult Ornithomimus bullatus *walking their chicks. They are also the hardest to place, genealogically, of the major theropod groups. The hills of the Nemegt are to the southwest.*

don't belong in the Insectivoria they arose from. This is especially true since the Herreravia may have produced their own version of "birds" via "Protoavis." A good case could be made for making Aves a fifth dinosaur superorder, equal to the Theropoda. After all, the strong parallelism with birds shown by some predatory dinosaurs proves that birds are a repeated variation on the dinosaur theme, not a radical new group. The problem with this logic is that ornithologists may not agree to birds being "reduced" from their present status of a class, equal to the Mammalia, all the way down to a subgroup of dinosaurs. So in the end we may settle on a subclass rank, equal to the Dinosauria.

Here we come to the difficulty of where to draw the line between the Theropoda and Aves. The potential confusion lies not so much with true birds, but with protobirds such as *Archaeopteryx,* dromaeosaurs, ostrich-mimics, and the like. (Again, we assume that "Protoavis" was an early bird-mimic, not a true protobird.) *Archaeopteryx* is often considered the first member of Aves, mainly because it has that hallmark of birds—feathers. But feathers are a poor taxonomic character, as many other archosaurs could have had them. Asserting that unless it is *proven*

that theropods had feathers we can assume they did not, is reliance on negative evidence of the worst sort. Besides, we can do better, for we can pick and choose which characters best define taxa. Indeed, we must rely on characters we can be sure that certain animals had and certain others did not, especially when defining major rankings.

In this view, we know that *Archaeopteryx,* with its hyperenlarged winged forelimbs, had an aerodynamic capability that shorter-forelimbed theropods did not—regardless of their possible arm feathers. So birds can be defined as that clade which has developed a certain level of flight. This is a perfectly reasonable arrangement. That certain protobirds and birds later lost their aerodynamic abilities does not harm the concept, any more than the crocodilian's loss of the preorbital opening affects their archosaurian status. But this bird definition is far from perfect. For one thing, *Archaeopteryx* and certain theropods are so alike that they should be placed in the same family. Also, some protobirds may be secondarily terrestrial descendants of archaeopterygians. This definition would include such protobirds as dromaeosaurs and ostrich-mimics that have long been thought of as theropods. Should *Velociraptor* be classified along with hummingbirds?

One way out of this is to limit Aves to birds proper. In this case, *Archaeopteryx* is formally a theropod. This too can be criticized, for it leaves those taxa that are probably at the base of the bird clade out of the Aves. But theropods as a whole are part of the bird clade in as much as they have many of the key adaptations that mark living birds. So they could just as well be placed in Aves. In 1975, Richard Thulborn did just this, making *Tyrannosaurus rex* and *Coelophysis* birds. Although this sounds outrageous, it is a fully sound idea. It just depends on how one defines the limits. At the other extreme, Gauthier wants to exclude the toothed birds *Hesperornis* and *Ichthyornis* from Aves, in the hope of achieving future stability.[23] But these are true birds, with all the adaptations that mark living forms. Nor are ornithologists likely to accept such a critical exclusion. As for myself, since most theropods are usually excluded from Aves, I feel it is all right to exclude protobirds too, even a flying one like *Archaeopteryx,* and I prefer to restrict Aves to true birds, including the toothy ones. One advantage is that Aves is then a morphologically uniform group, and protobirds are left in the group that matches their anatomical grade.

Turning to the Aves proper, it seems that the tiny flying bird discovered in Spain by Sanz, Bonaparte, and Lacasca is the most primitive found yet—among flying species only *Archaeopteryx* is more achaic. The head and hand are missing, and some of the apparently primitive features may be due to its being a youngster with many unfused bones. It is the tail that is most interesting, for while it has a short set of fused vertebrae at its end as in modern birds, it is still longer than in any other bird.

Next in line are small, flying *Ambiortus* and *Ichthyornis*.[24] These share similar and distinctive shoulder blades, and are alike in other features such as the retention of big protobird deltoid crests in the forearm. They may, or may not, be close relatives. Their primitive nature is shown by the rather protobird-like skull with toothed jaws of *Ichthyornis,* and the supple-clawed fingers of *Ambiortus* (the skull is not known in the latter, nor the hand in the first).

Also showing toothy jaws and a protobird-like skull, but very different in body form, are the loonlike diving hesperornithiformes.[25] The retention of primitive characters does not prove that all these toothed, or odontornithians, birds are truly close relatives. On the other hand, odontornithians are so primitive that they are far removed from all other birds.

The peculiar details of the mysterious and bizarre enantiornithian birds of the Cretaceous suggest they were a sister group to the normal and toothless neornithian birds—or perhaps to the odontornithians. Whether enantiornithians had teeth is uncertain. What especially concerns us is Larry Martin's misplacement of *Archaeopteryx* in with the enantiornithians.[26] He supposed that they share aberrant braincases, shoulder girdles, and other features. But none of these actually exist in *Archaeopteryx,* and most are not found in enantornithians either. It cannot be overemphasized that *Archaeopteryx* is a very theropodian and generalized protobird—one that shares no special characters with any particular bird group.

Some cannon bones that have been identified by some as enantiornithian are good examples of the problems that sometimes arise in telling theropods from birds. A small, strange set of fused cannon bones was found in the North American Hell Creek Formation of the latest Cretaceous. It proved to be much the same as others found in Argentina. A colleague and I named them *Avisaurus archibaldi* Brett-Surman and Paul, 1984, and applied a set of usually reliable criteria to them. These criteria indicated that *Avisaurus* was fully theropodian, and rather primitive at that. So we put it in the Theropoda. But some day this set of *Avisaurus* cannon bones may prove us wrong by showing up on the leg of an enantiornithian bird!

All modern birds, from ostriches to sparrows, are neornithes. These differ in a number of respects from enantiornithians, and are more advanced than odontornithes. Neornithes come in two basic types, paleognathus and neognathus. The first includes the ostriches, emus, and other big ratites, plus the pheasant-like tinamous of South America. These have vaguely protobird-like, unsophisticated mouth roofs, are still somewhat protobird-like in the hips, and are especially protobird-like in their ankles. Whether paleognathus birds are a natural group, or are in part or all descendants of advanced birds that have reverted to the primitive condition, is a matter of much controversy. The first view seems to be winning out. The second neornithian group is the neognathus birds, the fully advanced birds that make up all but a handful of the living species. With their sophisticated, hinge-jointed palates, there is little doubt that they form a monophyletic clade. However, in trying to sort out relationships within the neognathes, the 8700 or so living species and many more extinct ones pose a daunting taxonomic challenge that will take decades to work out. Many of the major bird groups have not been studied with modern techniques, and the vastness of the available data combined with the many gaps in the fossil record is overwhelming.

We have a much better understanding of how predatory dinosaurs and birds evolved and were related to each other than we did just a few years ago. There is very little doubt that birds are the descendants of these dinosaurs. Big questions remain, however, many of which may be impossible to resolve. And more will arise as new species are found and old ones are reconsidered. Because we know more about predatory dinosaur phylogeny, we are able to construct more realistic classifications. But will a consensus emerge and dinosaur systematics restabilize? I really do not know, but I have hopes.

9

THE BEGINNINGS OF BIRD FLIGHT: FROM THE GROUND UP OR THE TREES UP?

Some small dinosaurs found that there were advantages in not being earthbound, and to them we owe the gift of birds.[1] Just when and how this started is not clear; flight may have happened more than once, with only one of the groups of flying predatory dinosaurs ultimately making it as birds. The first attempt may have been made by the Triassic herrerasaurs in the form of "Protoavis." As explained earlier, it is possible that these Triassic forms were an early, dead-end experiment in flight.

The more successful attempt may have started with the long-fingered small avetheropods of the Jurassic, which could climb better than the earlier, shorter-fingered theropods. And understand that these predators' strong bones and joints made them well suited for the tumbles and falls that leaping in the trees leads to. Bushes were a place both to escape to and to chase prey into—cats use bushes in this way. Theropod climbing was both bipedal and quadrupedal, and leaps also started with a two-legged push-off, and ended with an all-hands-and-feet landing. Some avetheropods got better at this by evolving longer, stronger forelimbs with larger, more recurved claws, and longer, more reversed inner toes. In effect, they returned to a more quadrupedal way of doing things. Just this sort of arboreality is practiced by the young of the living hoatzin, a strange bird of South America whose juveniles have theropod-like claws on two supple fingers, a reversion to the old pattern.[2] With these, they scramble semiquadrupedally about the branches of trees.

Some theropod species may have been predominantly arboreal, and under pressures to further enhance their leaping abilities. While working on bird origins, Robert Bakker and I concluded that *Archaeopteryx* was just such a climber. This is a key issue, for to understand the beginnings of bird flight we must understand what the protobirds were up to. *Archaeopteryx*'s inner toe, the hallux, is not as well-developed as those of modern perching birds, but we should not expect it to already be at the songbird level. What is more telling is that the hallux was a larger, more backward-pointing, and better grasping toe than in any other theropod. In 1984, Derik Yalden showed that *Archaeopteryx*'s sharp-tipped claws, the hand claws especially, are most like those of modern climbing animals. The strength of the forelimbs is also vital because they are longer and more powerful than the hind limbs. Such extreme forelimb dominance cannot be explained as display organs or insect traps, but only if they had become the protobird's main locomotory organs. The long,

slender fingers are useless for walking. Hence climbing, flying, and swimming are the potential locomotory uses. At the same time, *Archaeopteryx* is really not as well built for running as is often thought, since the hips and knee crest are smaller than in any other theropod. But the short iliac blade behind the hip socket and the small knee crest, and the slender leg muscles they supported, are rather like those of leaping tree frogs and monkeys. The leaping and climbing abilities of *Archaeopteryx* cannot be used as absolute proof of arboreality in all Jurassic proto-

9-1
The habitat of the first "bird," Archaeopteryx lithographica, *was not woodlands, but arid, brush-covered sea islands. Here a pair display to each other, and another pair fly by, as flocks of pterosaurs return from fishing expeditions.*

birds, because *Archaeopteryx* could be an exception that evolved from running protobirds.

Here we come to a very interesting subject, and must digress from the main thesis for awhile. At various times it has been argued that birds learned to fly from the ground up, not the trees down. John Ostrom revived this idea in 1974 with his vision of protobirds as insect snatchers, using long arm feathers to ensnare flying insects. Ostrom has since abandoned this idea as untenable, but it did inspire much needed debate on the subject. Caple and company took the insect idea and modified it so that protobirds were using their jaws to catch flying insects.[3] Of course this would have required ground-to-air leaping. Caple and colleagues constructed an aerodynamic model showing how increasingly long arm, hand, and tail feathers improve the range and accuracy of anti-insect leaps.

Alas, the whole idea of leaping insectivorous ground animals is a near certain chimera. No such animal is alive today, and for

9-2
Like many small theropods, Ornitholestes hermanni climbed well with its hooked claws, long fingers, and supple toes. It was in the trees that bird flight began.

9-3
The first "bird," Archaeopteryx lithographica, *was very well built for climbing, with very long, strong arms, big hooked claws, and grasping feet.*

good reason. Insects are small food items, and even a small warm-blooded protobird would need to eat some 100 to 200 half-gram-size insects a day (see Appendix A for how this is calculated). Most small animals have daily foraging ranges of only 1.0 to 4.0 kilometers. Anything beyond that stretches their energy budgets too much. Even a slow-running protobird would cover this foraging range in less than half an hour, far too little time to catch the multitudes of insects it needed. Not only that, but the very idea that protobirds, which were just learning to fly, could make a living by catching high-performance flying insects is too much to swallow. It would be like trying to shoot down Spitfires with a 1908 Wright Flyer. Only specialized, fast-flying birds—those that can cover large volumes of airspace rapidly, outrun and outmaneuver their targets, and do it at low cost since flying consumes much less energy per distance traveled—are successful aerial insectivores. So restorations that show protobirds chas-

Archaeopteryx lithographica
*HMN 1880, shown in flight profile,
cuts a strikingly aerodynamic figure. The smaller figure shows the
wings and tail feathers folded for
swimming. The inset shows that
the hand (center) and foot (right)
claws of* Archaeopteryx *are in-
triguingly similar to the toe claws
with which fish-eating bats (left)
snatch up their meals (bony cores
are in white; the horny sheaths,
preserved in* Archaeopteryx *specimens, are black). This protobird
may have both fished and
climbed with its claws. The leaping strength and agility of* A. lithographica *HMN 1880 is well
illustrated in the muscle study;
note the great pectoralis muscle
on the chest. The flight and muscle studies are to the same scale.*

ing dragonflies and the like, and there have been a great many of
late, are in gross error.

Protobirds the size of *Archaeopteryx* were too large for full-
time insectivory anyway; most insect-eating mammals and birds
are a good deal smaller. So what were protobirds eating? Here
we need to look more closely at *Archaeopteryx.* We have already
seen how the conical teeth of some small theropods were suitable
for fishing. In fact, the very conical, unserrated, and big-rooted
teeth of *Archaeopteryx* are most like those of marine crocodilians, whales, and the toothed diving bird *Hesperornis.* Not only
that, but the hooked and laterally flattened claws, especially
those of the hands, are strikingly like the toe claws of fish-eating
bats (Figure 9-4). So *Archaeopteryx* does seem well-adapted for
going after small aquatic organisms.[4] It may have swum well too.
With wings half folded, and the tail feathers slipped together like

the long tails of the strange swimming anhinga birds, the power-fully muscled wings could have propelled it along like baby hoat-zin or the little water ouzal of mountain streams. *Archaeopteryx* even lived on an island chain, and its remains are found only in lagoons—small animal fossil sites have yet to turn up archaeop-terygian remains on land. Fish eating and arboreality may seem inconsistent, but many cats are both good climbers and good fishers. And again there is the hoatzin, which when juvenile will drop from the stream-loving trees it dwells in into the water to escape danger. Things that seem odd are sometimes valid none the less. Fish eating also helps explain something else, the fact that most of the Cretaceous birds found so far come from watery habitats, and that birds seem to be rare in land faunas, at least until the Late Cretaceous.

Now we can return to the main thesis. Even though we can put protobirds in the trees, we still cannot easily explain how they came to fly. Arboreal gliders are common, but it never has been explained exactly how one can switch from gliding to flap-ping flight. It seems that the first stages of primitive flapping can actually decrease the length of a glide. Ulla Norberg, in 1985, tried to show how short, low-frequency flaps might be able to get around this problem, to be followed by full flapping later. How-ever, just as no living animal leaps after insects for a living, no living bird, bat, or other creature "glide-flaps" the way Norberg suggests. Other scholars believe this does not happen because it cannot work.

Which brings us to the core of the problem. Aerodynamics is a tricky science, especially when applied to live flying ma-chines. The aerodynamics of relatively simple aircraft are often difficult to understand. The problems only multiply when looking at creatures whose intricate airfoils change shape with each mo-tion. Little work has been done in the area, which is not surpris-ing since it is a nightmare observing and measuring flying animals; the resulting calculations can fry a computer. Nor is there much money around to spend on such things, since the practical applications of bird flight are not obvious. I do not believe that we truly understand organic flight; certainly, every-one working on the problem disagrees with everyone else. So, although the morphological and ecological evidence makes it clear that bird flight did originate in the trees, the aerodynamic uncertainties currently make it almost impossible to decide on exactly how this occurred.

Until recently, some have argued, exacerbating the problem, that birds started flying either by leaping *up* from the ground, or by gliding *down* from trees or cliffs. This up and down dichotomy is unfortunate because it may be unnecessary, and because it stifles consideration of alternatives.

One possible alternative melds arboreality with *horizontal* leaping. In this concept the gliding stage is skipped and birds learn to fly directly via interbranch leaps—some leaps being downward, others up, and some level, so in total the average is horizontal. We know that arboreal leaping is a viable life-style, because there are thousands of living branch-leapers. As for climbing theropods, they were uniquely preadapted for wings and tails of the *avian* kind. They were bipeds with short trunks and stiff-action vertical hind limbs that could not splay out to the side and support a flying squirrel or bat type of interlimb membrane. The only places available to develop airfoils were on the tail and forelimbs. The ability to better orient the body and limbs into the best position for landing on branches would have been very valuable, since misses could result in injurious or fatal falls. Indeed, tree-leaping primates of about this size suffer substantial mortality from such mishaps.

If the work of Caple et al. on leaping aerodynamics is correct, then they inadvertently explained much of how *interbranch* leaps of climbing protobirds could be developed into full-powered avian flight. They believe that just a slight lengthening of forelimb and tail feathers would give theropod-protobirds greatly improved roll and pitch control. They thought this would help bring the mouth closer to insects—but it would have been just as good at helping swing the hind feet closer to a branch. The motions of the arms as they maneuvered the developing winglets also mimicked the flaps of power flight. As the feet gripped the branch, the hands would continue to help by grabbing on too.

Further enlargement of the airfoils and of the forelimb muscles to better control them not only increased control, but started to lengthen the leaps by turning them into glides. As the wings and their power sources continued to enlarge, the protobirds started to power-fly. Now they could not only leap further, but they could start landing higher than where they took off—a tremendous advance in arboreal rapid transit. In this sense, powered flight probably developed from the *trees up*, not the ground up. Some more of this and you have full size, high-powered wings, of the stage at which we find *Archaeopteryx*.

THE BEGINNINGS OF BIRD FLIGHT:
FROM THE GROUND UP
OR THE TREES UP?

215

But there are problems with this idea too. The worst is that powered flight is most efficient at moderate speeds, much less so at slow speeds. Since interbranch leaps are rather slow, developing powered flight at this stage could be difficult. Interbranch glides are faster, well within the range for efficient flapping flight. Perhaps it was a combination of developing controls for leaping and landings plus the speed of gliding that contains the answer, but I wouldn't be surprised if somone came up with an aerodynamic criticism of this scenario as well.

Actually, much of this theorizing may be redundant. It is possible that theropods had developed long arm display feathers well before they tried anything aerodynamic with them, as the supposed Triassic feather prints mentioned in Chapter 4 may indicate. In this case, small theropods were preadapted for flight,

9-5

Log-log plots comparing wing area and humerus circumference relative to body mass in modern flying birds and Archaeopteryx lithographica *(solid circles indicate the three main specimens, left to right, JM 2257, HMN 1880, and BMNH 37001). The protobird was as big-winged and strong-armed as are birds. In wing area, A.* lithographica *was closest to crows and gulls (corvids and larids), and much bigger winged than ducks (anatids). Notice that the wings of* Archaeopteryx lithographica *became larger relative to body mass with maturity.*

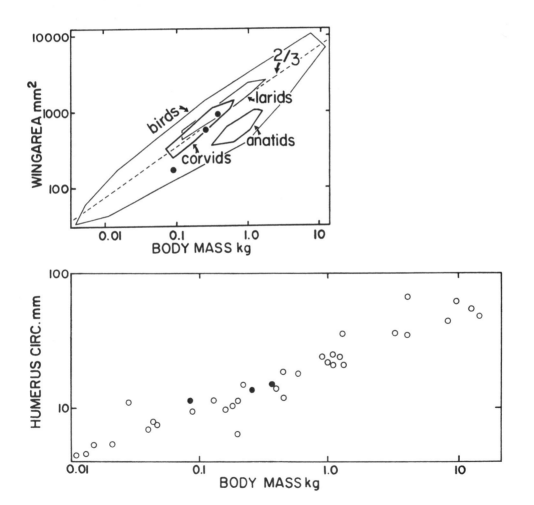

and we would not need to explain the intitial evolution of wing feathers in aerodynamic terms.[5]

How well *Archaeopteryx* flew—and when good, powered flight was first achieved—is a bone of much contention. I am sure that *Archaeopteryx* was a good power-flyer, not just a glider as often thought. It was certainly not the sort of fine-tuned flyer modern birds are, but it is hardly likely that it could have developed all the anatomical refinements of high-performance flight *before* it could power-fly. It would make more sense that the basics of powered flight would have been achieved before flight was refined. In *Archaeopteryx* the wing feathers are fully aerodynamic, being the asymmetrical winglike airfoils found in modern flying birds.[6] In a flight posture, *Archaeopteryx* looks reasonably streamlined and aerodynamic (see Figure 9-4). Figure 9-5 shows that the wing's surface/total weight ratio was well within the flying bird range, about equal to a crow's. The wing bones are also as strong as flying birds. The big furcula, created

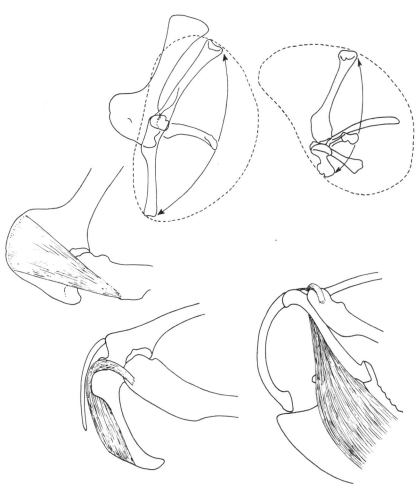

9-6

The possible motions of the humerus (dotted lines) in theropods like Coelophysis *(upper left) are close to those of* Archaeopteryx. *This is enough like a bird's (upper right) to allow the arm to flap for flight (arrowed lines). Birds (lower right) have a sophisticated supracoracoideus muscle system in which the muscle loops around a pulley formed by the acrocoracoid to help elevate the wing. This is very unusual, since in most animals such as* Coelophysis *(left) the supracoracoideus pulls down on the humerus. In* Archaeopteryx lithographica *(lower left) the system was partly developed.*

by fusing the clavicles into one unit, helped lock together and immobilize the shoulder girdle. This is disadvantageous in most animals, who need as much arm reach as they can get. But it is a classically avian way of strengthening the shoulder for flight. And not just flight, but powered flight, since flying squirrels and other gliding mammals do have furculas. Although *Archaeopteryx*'s theropod-like shoulder joint is not specifically adapted for flight, I have found that the upper arm of even early theropods such as *Coelophysis* can be manipulated in the basic flapping pattern of powered flight (Figure 9-6; such experiments cannot be done with *Archaeopteryx* itself since all the bones are still set in the original slabs).

All that is needed now is enough power. *Archaeopteryx* lacks the great keeled breastplate of modern flying birds. But a key part of this structure's function is to support a specialized wing-elevating supracoracoideus muscle. Storrs Olson and Alan Feduccia explained in 1979 that the main flight-power source of birds, the wing-depressing pectoralis, is supported up front by the furcula. The great size of *Archaeopteryx*'s furcula must have evolved for this task. The rest of its enlarged wing depressors could have been spread out over the chest, like in bats. If the pectoralis made up 10 to 15 percent of the total body mass, it would be enough for flight.

Archaeopteryx had only the beginnings of the supracoracoideus wing-elevating system (see Figure 9-6). Modern birds have trouble with climbing flight if the wing-elevating supracoracoideus muscle is disabled, but this is probably because they have become dependent upon this specialized system. Bats do fine without it. Good wing elevation could have been achieved by the well-developed upper shoulder muscles in *Archaeopteryx*.

So *Archaeopteryx* could probably have taken off from level ground, either with a push from the hind limbs or a short run. It could then climb to cruising height, and if it had enough long-endurance red fibers in its flight muscles, flap along for long distances. If the flight muscles were mainly short-burst white fibers, like a chicken's, then short-term climb and speed performance would be enhanced at the expense of endurance. Upturning the long tail and sweeping the wings forward as airbrakes, it could make bipedal ground landings. But its flight was still on the crude side. The deep, keeled body and very long tail surface made for good stability, but countered quick rolls and turns. *Archaeopteryx* still had well-developing, grasping hands, so most branch landings were probably sloppy quadrupedal affairs in which the hands helped ensure a good hold, and the robust theropod body build minimized injuries. In sum, *Archaeopteryx* was probably a competent but unrefined flyer, much like a Wright Flyer of 1908. It could get from here to there and little else. But even such basic mobility must have been very useful.

The issue of when true avian powered flight began is complicated by the Triassic "Protoavis" remains, which may in part have represented a creature able to achieve a clumsy sort of flight. If so, then the way protoavians developed flight probably followed much the same climbing course as outlined above.

Regardless of whether protoavians or archaeopterygians are the first avian flyers, what course did bird flight take afterward? One change was in the folding of the arms and the wing feathers. In *Archaeopteryx* the arms themselves could not fold as tightly as bird wings do. But the wing feathers were not attached tightly to the arm bones and they may have folded back along the arm. This would have kept them out of the way when climbing, or when the arms snatched after prey. To improve flight, early birds anchored the wing feathers firmly to the forelimb bones, and the arm became more tightly foldable in compensation. Another major adaptation was, of course, the big, keeled breastplate. As mentioned above, its main purpose was and is to anchor an enlarged supracoracoideus wing-elevating muscle. This muscle loops around the special acrocoracoid process in front of the shoulder joint to pull on the humerus from above (see Figure 9-6), and greatly improves birds' rate of climb.

Caple and company cite the problem of switching from the early quadrupedal branch landings to the modern bipedal method as one of the most serious problems faced by early birds. I disagree, because this is a logical and rather easily achieved consequence of the improvement of bird flight. It is also one of the last such refinements, as shown by Early Cretaceous *Ambiortus*.[7] This bird has the highly developed shoulder girdle and keeled sternum of modern flying birds, and it looks like it is close to being an adept enough flyer to branch-land on two legs. Yet *Ambiortus* still has clawed fingers, so it may have often grabbed branches with all fours. It would have been advantageous at this stage for birds to better overall flight performance by fusing the clawed fingers into the flattened, unclawed, and streamlined structure of modern birds. To do so, alula feathers developed on the thumb (Figure 9-7). Held a little above the wing, they acted

THE BEGINNINGS OF BIRD FLIGHT:
FROM THE GROUND UP
OR THE TREES UP?

219

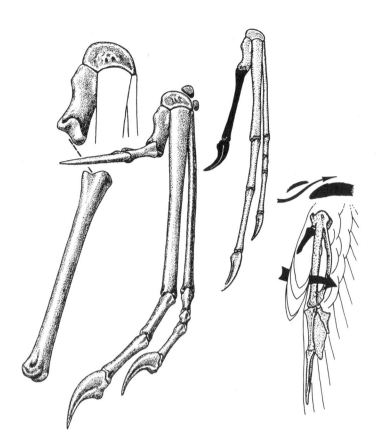

9-7
In Archaeopteryx lithographica *the thumb was still a clawed, inwardly divergent weapon (also see Figure 4-12). In birds the thumb remains divergent, but it is modified to support the special alula feathers. These act as leading-edge slots to control the flow of the air (black arrows) over the wing at slow speeds.*

as a leading-edge "wing slot" to reduce the landing speed. This allowed surer, more precise bipedal landings, and eliminated the need for wing claws.

Once the hand was so modified, birds had all the modern flight refinements. Nowadays, various birds fly as high as Everest, cruise at 50 mph, soar over ocean waves for tens of thousands of miles, and dominate the daylight skies. It all may have started with a little predatory dinosaur, a mutant with longer fingers than its parents', longing for a lizard that had just scampered into a bush.

PART TWO
THE CATALOG
OF
PREDATORY
DINOSAURS

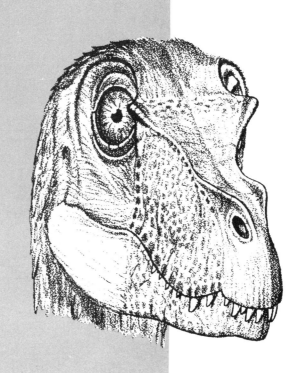

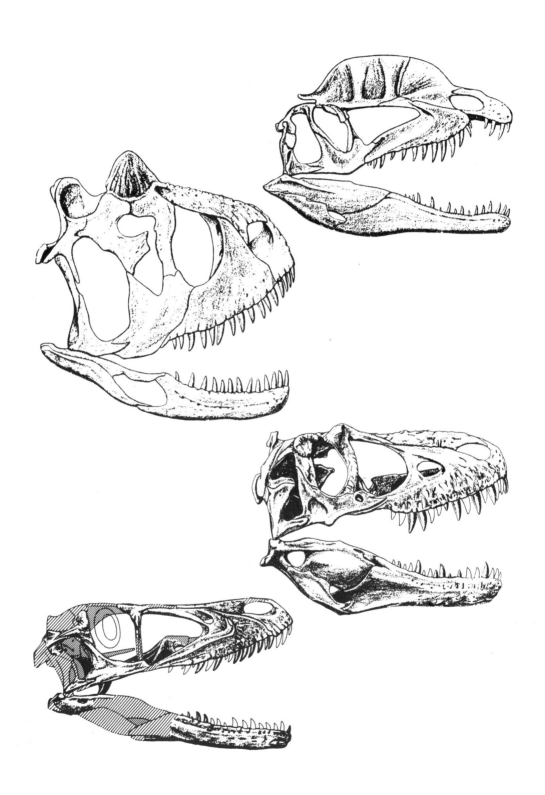

10

AN EXPLANATION OF THE CATALOG

Part II is the meat and potatoes of this book—a group-by-group, species-by-species catalog of the world's predatory dinosaurs. But it is by no means an exhaustive account of every predatory dinosaur species that has ever been named. I have omitted those species whose designation is based on inconsequential material that cannot be properly identified, or those determined by remains that really belong to another, earlier named species.

The seventy genera and 102 species that do get full treatment in this catalog are those that I am fairly confident are real. In some cases the remains are fragmentary, but since they are found isolated in formations that otherwise lack fossils of their type, they are worth noting. At best, the species is based upon a good specimen, called a type (more properly, holotype), the remains of a single individual which are used to exemplify that species' skeleton. Alas, it is all too rare that the type is a beautifully complete skeleton, one clearly distinctive from all previously identified remains. More often the type is a paltry collection of bones. In such cases, better secondary type (paratype) specimens may show the species' full character. So, horrifically complex situations can arise, in which the species' validity or the correctness of the name is not clear. This can have us paleontologists hitting our heads against the proverbial wall, wondering why we did not go into something simpler—like nuclear particle physics.

A number of dinosaur species are based on nothing more than isolated teeth. This is not as bad as it sounds, for it is becoming increasingly likely that each species of predatory dinosaur had teeth unique to itself. But unless skeletal remains have been found that tell us more about the animal, such tooth-based species are not included in this text.

Each group and species is considered in rough phylogenetic order (according to its evolutionary development), so the species tend to get progressively more "advanced" as one reads on. The phylogenetic relationships and age of most genera examined in this catalog are detailed in Figure 10-1. In the chart, species become younger going to the right, and more "advanced" going down and, sometimes, right. All the relationships are tenuous to lesser or greater degrees; I have indicated when they are especially so by a question mark.

OVERLEAF
10-1
A time and phylogenetic chart. Almost all the theropod genera discussed in Part II are plotted here; the heavy bars show the known time span of the genera. In general, taxa become more advanced progressing from top to bottom, and from left to right. The approximate ages in millions of years of each stage are along the bottom; possible times of some giant meteoritic impacts are plotted at top.

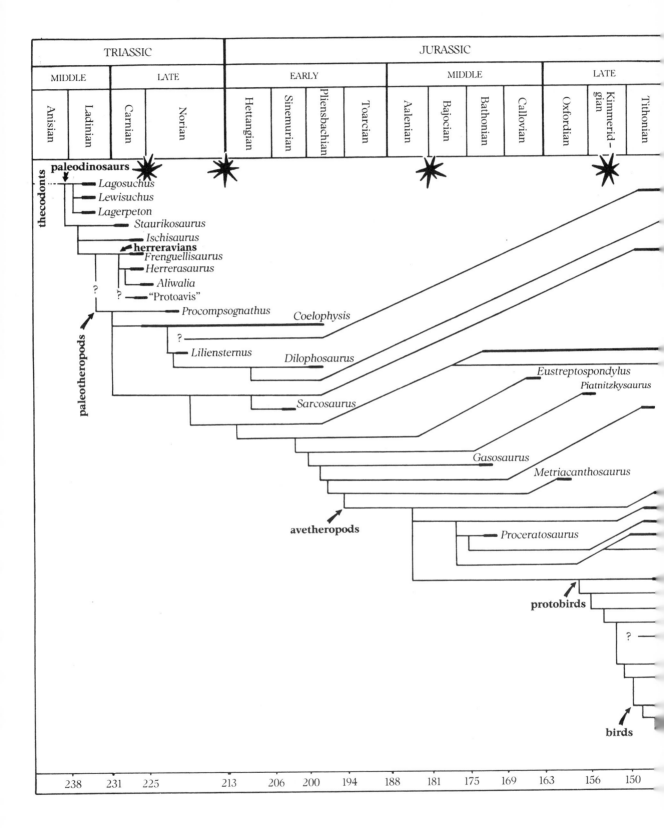

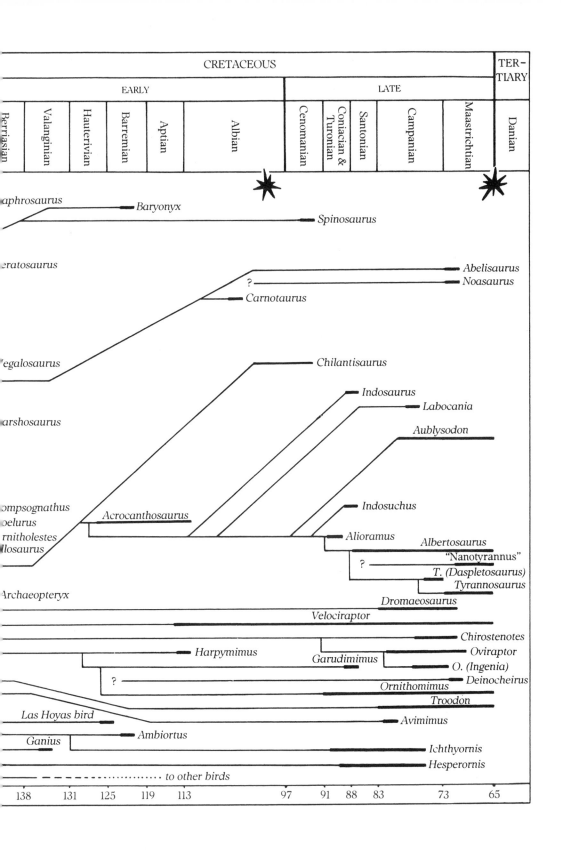

CRETACEOUS

TER-TIARY

EARLY

LATE

Berriasian | Valanginian | Hauterivian | Barremian | Aptian | Albian | Cenomanian | Coniacian & Turonian | Santonian | Campanian | Maastrichtian | Danian

...aphrosaurus
Baryonyx
Spinosaurus

...eratosaurus
Abelisaurus
? Noasaurus
Carnotaurus

...egalosaurus
Chilantisaurus

...arshosaurus
Indosaurus
Labocania
Aublysodon

...ompsognathus
...oelurus
...rnitholestes
...losaurus
Acrocanthosaurus
Indosuchus
Alioramus
Albertosaurus
? "Nanotyrannus"
T. (Daspletosaurus)
Tyrannosaurus

Archaeopteryx
Dromaeosaurus
Velociraptor
Chirostenotes
Harpymimus
Oviraptor
Garudimimus
O. (Ingenia)
? Deinocheirus
Ornithomimus
Troodon
Avimimus

Las Hoyas bird
Ganius
Ambiortus
Ichthyornis
Hesperornis
·········· to other birds

138   131   125   119   113   97   91   88   83   73   65

As you may notice, all forty of the skeletal drawings in Part II, representing thirty-four species, are drawn in the same pose, running full tilt with their mouths open and the left hind limb pushing off. The neck is shown in "neutral posture," with the vertebrae following the curvature in which they naturally articulated. The head is gently flexed on the curved neck. The left arm is shown partly tucked up, with the bones in the same direct side view as the hind-limb elements, making it possible to contrast the size and shape of the finger and toe claws. I also show them this way—even though the arm and leg bones really faced a little outwards because the elbows and knees were bowed out—both to simplify the execution and to make the comparisons between the species easier. The same advantages of simplification of execution and comparability are gained by drawing all the skeletons in a uniform pose—although some modest differences that do exist among the species are reflected in the restorations. I have found this uniform system to be very valuable in understanding these creatures, and my thoughts about a dinosaur have often changed after preparing a detailed skeletal restoration and contrasting it to others.

Too often the reader is presented with skeletal and skull restorations in side view only, which leaves him or her in the dark as to the full form of the three-dimensional creatures. Hence, I have drawn the skull and/or skeleton of a representative species or more of each group in multiple views.[1] It is often not possible to get good top and other views of particular specimens, so in some cases the multiple views were based in part on specimens different from those used for the side views. In the front and back views of the skeletons the head, neck, and tail are omitted, for they are unduly complex to render from these perspectives and obscure the trunk and hips. Although many of the protobirds could tightly fold their arms, I show them tucked in like other theropods for easier comparison, and to make them visible in the front views.

The limb's outward bowing can be seen in the front and back skeletal views. In the top views the vertebral column gently undulates, with the right side of the hip swinging forward along with its limb as the left leg pushes off, and the base of the tail swinging to the left as its caudofemoralis muscle helps pull back on the femur. The vertebral undulations are not shown in the front and back views.

Skeletal Muscle and Life Restorations

In making my restorations I have usually avoided taking someone else's skeletal or skull drawings and reposing them, for I have found that they are not always reliable. Instead, detailed figures and photographs of the individual bones, or a photograph of a good specimen are used to build up original restorations. I try to draw a skull and skeleton, from the species type, since it is these remains that are used to characterize the species. But sometimes the type remains are too inferior relative to other specimens to make this worthwhile, or they have not been published yet and I have not been able to see them. Remember that virtually no fossil skeleton is 100 percent complete; parts were either lost before preservation or by weathering before the specimen was found. Except for a few very good skulls, some restoration is almost always necessary. In some cases, the restored skull or skeleton is made up of two or more specimens, with the elements adjusted as much as possible to a common size.[2] Elements that do not ossify and are just about never preserved, such as sternal elements and ribs, are also restored. On the other hand, the many little joints within each abdominal rib are deliberately left out. Care was taken to reproduce the profile of each bone as accurately as possible—something I have noted is not done in many skeletal drawings. Of course, this was less feasible when the quality of a specimen was inferior, and the restorations based on them show it: they look less real.

The muscles, and the keratin horn coverings of the hornlets, horns, bosses, beaks, and claws are profiled in solid black around all the views of the skeletons (a suggestion of Robert Bakker's). Profiling bones in black has the advantage of being truer to their shape than outlining. This is because the edge of an inked area marks the exact outer boundary of a bone, as opposed to a single ink line which straddles the bone's boundary and makes it appear slightly larger than it actually is.

In the skull drawings, missing parts are indicated by lined areas—except teeth, which are outlined when absent. Whenever possible I included the skull's interior bones, the braincase, and the mouth roof elements, but these are often not available. Note that a part of the mouth roof sometimes projects below the level of the upper jaw, beneath the eye sockets—this is not part of the side of the skull. The bony eye rings are indicated in those that had them. In doing the skeletons and skulls, both naturally articulated and mounted remains were used to better understand how the animals went together. This is important, but it must be done cautiously because postdeath distortion of the bones and incorrect mountings can mislead the illustrator.

The thirty-seven skull drawings, representing thirty-three species, are always presented to the same upper-jaw length. Within each group the skeletons are presented to the same femur length. This set of skeletal and skull drawings is not complete, as new discoveries are being made so fast these days that a good many have not been published yet. Among these new, quality finds are a crested *Coelophysis,* a brow-horned *Carnotaurus,* a crested allosaur head, fin-backed *Acrocanthosaurus atokensis,* and the early ostrich-mimic *Harpymimus.* We hope more complete examples will turn up of these poorly known theropods: fin-backed *Spinosaurus,* sickle-clawed *Noasaurus,* the tyrannosaurs *Aublysodon* and *Albertosaurus megagracilis,* the ostrich-mimics *Chirostenotes* and *Deinocheirus,* and the rest of the head and tail of birdlike *Avimimus,* among others. It is always exciting to sit down with some good remains and do a new skeletal restoration. It is a way of recreating the past, and you are never quite sure what you will come up with.

For many of the skeletons that have been drawn in multiple views, I have also done shaded muscle studies. Some of the muscle studies are overlays of the skeletal drawings, except that the head and neck are usually pulled back up more. For variety some of the muscle restorations are posed in assorted typical activities —a simple task because once the skeleton has been drawn it is easy to repose it for a muscle restoration.

With only two exceptions (in Figures 5-2 and 7-3 center) all the life restorations—drawings of dinosaurs as they may have looked when alive—in this volume are those for which the shoulder or skull has been drawn. I do not do life restorations of species known only from teeth or a few bones because the potential for misleading is obvious. Some of the older life drawings in this book were done before I did the species' final skeletal restoration, and I have modified such illustrations to bring them as close to current standards as possible. Having thoroughly worked over the theropods, I do not expect the current restorations of the better known species' basic forms to need much reworking in the future. However, new skin or insulation impressions may alter their superficial appearance substantially, and send me back to the drawing board again!

For those who like to know these things, the skeletal restorations are done in ink, the shaded drawings are soft—oil- or water-based—pencil, sometimes smoothed with medium-soft lead pencil, and ink on coquille board. All were corrected with typewriter white-out and, less often, gesso.

Explanation of the Data Synopses

The catalog of predatory dinosaurs that follows in Chapter 11 is organized so that it goes from the general—classes and orders—down to the particular—families, genera, and finally species. In this way we follow the phylogenetic order, as far as I can determine, of these dinosaurs. For each species there is a synopsis of basic data followed by a discussion; the synopses are explained here.

CLASS NAMES THROUGH FAMILY NAMES: These, the taxonomic names for each ranking, are never italicized. Every letter is capitalized only when the name is used as a heading. Otherwise, only the first letter is capitalized. Family names are usually derived from the genus name of one of its members, and even if the name of the genus later proves invalid, the original family name is usually retained. Note that if the placement of a subfamily is tentative, then its name is preceded by an asterisk (*). For the reader's convenience, all the family's species are listed under the family name when more than one species is present.

GENUS AND SPECIES NAME: This, the proper binomial scientific name, is always italicized. Every letter is capitalized only when the name is used as a heading; otherwise only the first letter of the generic title is capitalized, and the species name is *invariably* not capitalized. Example: *Allosaurus fragilis,* or *A. fragilis* for short. Note that if the placement of a species within a certain family is tentative, then its name is preceded by an asterisk (*). If the name of a genus or species is for various reasons more uncertain than usual, then it is followed by a question mark. If a specimen's species status is really uncertain, then the species is left unnamed, such as *Elaphrosaurus* sp.

AUTHOR AND YEAR: This appears immediately after the scientific name, either in the heading or, if the name is used only in the text, the first time it appears in these sections. It cites the person who named the species, genus, or higher taxa, and the date of its publication. Example: *Tyrannosaurus rex* Osborn, 1904. If the generic title of the species has since been changed, then the citation appears in parentheses. For example, *Megalosaurus bradleyi* Woodward, 1910 became *Proceratosaurus bradleyi* (Woodward, 1910), via *Proceratosaurus* Huene, 1926. Likewise, if an already-named higher taxonomic title is modified to another rank, such as a family name into a subfamily, the original namer's name appears in parentheses. In a few cases I have found it necessary to come up with new names; the term *new* appears immediately after these. The first reference for each genus and species name is in the bibliography, but the same is not true for all higher rank names.

SYNONYMS: Many dinosaur names later prove to belong to genera or species that have already been named. In such cases the rules of zoological nomenclature demand that the first valid name nearly always be used, because this helps cut down on the confusion. Often the secondary names are well known, so the major synonyms are listed in order that the reader will not think that they have been forgotten or ignored. For example, the current title of the big tyrannosaur *Albertosaurus* was hardly used until recently; it used to be known by the more widely recognized *Gorgosaurus.* In other cases, a generic name that is appropriate for some species has been incorrectly used for others—*Megalosaurus,* for instance. No attempt is made to list all the minor synonyms.

TYPE, BEST AND DISPLAY SPECIMENS: The type is the specimen that the species is based upon. More properly called the holotype, it can vary widely in quality. Paratypes are secondary specimens that are used to bolster the identity of the species, especially when the holotype specimen is not very good. Paratypes are not specifically indicated. The best specimen or specimens aside from the types are also listed, as are institutions in which skeletons are displayed for public view.

MUSEUM ABBREVIATIONS:
AMNH AMERICAN MUSEUM OF NATURAL HISTORY, NEW YORK
ANSP ACADEMY OF NATURAL SCIENCES OF PHILADELPHIA
BMNH BRITISH MUSEUM (NATURAL HISTORY), LONDON
BSP BAYERISCHE STAATSSAMMLUNG FÜR PALÄONTOLOGIE, MUNICH
BYU BRIGHAM YOUNG UNIVERSITY, PROVO
CM CARNEGIE MUSEUM OF NATURAL HISTORY, PITTSBURGH
CV MUNICIPAL MUSEUM OF CHUNGKING, PEOPLE'S REPUBLIC OF CHINA
CMNH CLEVELAND MUSEUM OF NATURAL HISTORY
FMNH FIELD MUSEUM OF NATURAL HISTORY, CHICAGO
GI GEOLOGICAL INSTITUTE, ULAN BATOR, MONGOLIA
GSI GEOLOGICAL SURVEY OF INDIA, CALCUTTA

HMN	Humboldt Museum für Naturkunde, East Berlin
ISI	Indian Statistical Institute, Calcutta
IVPP	Institute of Vertebrate Paleontology, Beijing
JM	Jura Museum, Eichsätt
LACM	Los Angeles County Museum
MACN	Museo Argentino de Ciencias Naturales, Buenos Aires
MC	Museo de Cipolleti
MCZ	Museum of Comparative Zoology, Cambridge
MLP	Museo de La Plata
MNA	Museum of Northern Arizona, Flagstaff
MNHN	Musée National d'Histoire Naturelle, Paris
MUO	Museum of the University of Oklahoma, Norman
NMC	National Museum of Canada, Ottawa
NMW	Naturhistorisches Museum Wien, Vienna
OUM	Oxford University Museum, Oxford
PIN	Palaeontological Institute, Moscow
PVL	Paleontologia Vertebrados Instituto Miguel Lillo, Tucumán
QG	Queen Victoria Museum, Salisbury
ROM	Royal Ontario Museum, Toronto
SAM	South Australian Museum, Adelaide
SDSM	South Dakota Schoool of Mines and Technology, Rapid City
SMNS	Staatliches Museum für Naturkunde, Stuttgart
TMP	Tyrrell Museum of Paleontology, Drumheller, Alberta
TTU	Texas Tech University, Lubbock
UCMP	University of California Museum of Paleontology, Berkeley
UNSJ	Universidad Nacional de San Juan
USNM	United States National Museum, Washington, D.C.
UUVP	University of Utah Vertebrate Paleontology Collection, Salt Lake City
YPM	Yale Peabody Museum, New Haven
ZPAL	Palaeozoological Institute, Warsaw

TIME: This is indicated, when possible, by the time stage (always ends in -*ian*) the subject lived in. This in turn is in an epoch (Early, Middle, Late) of one of the three Mesozoic periods. These are all formal, capitalized names. However, it is sometimes helpful to note from what part, early or late, of a stage an animal is known. Note that in geology, upper equals late, lower equals early. A particular problem is presented by the Cretaceous period which, despite being the longest in the Mesozoic, is split into only two epochs. So which level of the epoch the stage comes from is also noted. See the time chart in Figure 10-1 (pages 224-25) for the relative and actual ages of each time unit.[3] However, take them with a grain of salt.

The age of a species depends on the age of the formation it is found in. This, more often than not, is not as certain as we would like. There are two complementary ways of aging a formation. Briefly, if the formation has the proper material in it, usually one or more layers of volcanic ash, then it can be directly aged. This is done by measuring the relative proportions of certain radioactive isotopes in the ash. Radioactive materials "decay" at very precise rates, but sampling problems and the like still leave us with a plus or minus error of up to 5 percent, and as we go back in time a 5 percent error means an increasing error in absolute time. Other problems may bias the sample even more. Also—and contrary to common images—the age of dinosaurs was not especially volcanic compared to today, so many formations cannot be aged directly. When that is the case, then a second method is used: the fauna and flora of the formation— especially microfossils, but dinosaurs also—are compared to those of formations whose ages are known. This is best done with marine organisms, so terrestrial dinosaur formations that merge with marine formations are the most readily dateable by this method. Of course, not all dinosaur formations do this, and those that do not pose particular problems. Recently, the reversals of the magnetic poles as recorded in certain rocks have become important in aging. It is all very complicated, with many methods used on a given formation.

There are some dates that are pretty well pinned down. In particular, we know that the dinosaur extinction occurred sixty-three to sixty-five million years ago. But in most cases there is a fair amount of error. The actual and relative ages of the Late Triassic and/or Early Jurassic formations that bear coelophysians and dilophosaurs are a headache; for instance, the Kayenta was once Late Triassic, then earliest Jurassic, now late Early Jurassic. The sickle-claw and tyrannosaur beds of Mongolia are especially difficult to date. If a taxa's time stage is more uncertain than usual, this is indicated with a question mark.

HORIZON AND DISTRIBUTION: The horizon is the unified complex of sedimentary beds, usually called a formation, that the species' remains are found in. Sometimes the species is found only in the lower and upper beds of a formation. Or the species may be found in more than one formation, usually of similar age but differing locations. The distribution is essentially where the formation or formations containing the species are. However, the species may be known from only one locale in a formation. The important thing to remember is that the actual distribution of the species was almost always wider than the formation we happen to find it in. Also remember that formations only form where sediments were being deposited, in lowlands and intermountain basins. We cannot find the faunas that lived on the eroding Mesozoic highlands.

MAIN ANATOMICAL STUDY: The best source or sources for detailed information on the skeletal remains of each species is listed here, if the original source for the species' name does not already fulfill this task. In a number of cases a good anatomical study has not yet been done, even for animals known since the 1800s, so none can be listed.

SPECIMEN MEASUREMENTS: If a skeleton has been reconstructed, then the measurements are given. The species' largest specimen may also be included, as may be a small youngster. If no skeleton has been restored, the type or largest specimen's measurements are cited.

If the measurement is preceded by the symbol for approximate (~), this is because the specimen is incomplete. Such approximate measurements may be taken from a reconstructed specimen, or may be estimated from another of the species' specimens. If the measurement is also followed by a question mark, then the best specimen of a species is far too incomplete for measurement. Instead, the value is estimated from related species.

SKULL LENGTH: From the tip of the snout to the tip of the wing of the braincase; this is often but not always the greatest length of the skull. Always in millimeters (10 mm = 1 cm or 0.3937 in). All the skull restorations were drawn to a common upper-jaw length of 175 mm.

TOTAL LENGTH: From the tip of the snout to the tip of the tail, measured along the main bodies of the vertebrae. Always in meters (1 m = 1000 mm, 3.281 ft, or 1.094 yd). Virtually no specimen is complete enough for this to be measured with total accuracy, and some reconstruction is usually involved. Only when whole skulls or sections of the vertebral column are missing is the approximate sign used. Lengths for species lacking a skeletal restoration are estimated from related species. Remember that when a dinosaur is said to be like a certain living animal in size, I am referring to its weight. Long tails make these bipeds relatively longer than most mammals and birds of similar mass.

FEMUR LENGTH: The length between perpendiculars of the articular joints of the thighbone. I include this because it is a key measurement of a major bone, around which I calculate the other measurements of the skeleton—specifically, all the skeletal restorations were drawn to a common femur length of 105 mm. In addition, the femur lengths of some species have not been published elsewhere, and others have had to be estimated.

HIP HEIGHT: This gives an idea of the vertical height of the animal when standing still in a normal, horizontal pose. The measurement is always approximate because it depends on the exact stance of the hind limbs. If there is no skeletal restoration, hip height is estimated only if a good hind limb is known for the species. Always in meters.

WEIGHT: Tonnage is used when the subject is above 1 metric tonne (1 mt = 1000 kg or 1.025 U.S. tons), kilogrammage is used when the subject is below that value, and grammage when it is below a kilogram (1 kg = 1000 g or 2.205 lb). Because the shape of predatory dinosaurs is unlike that of anything alive today, the only way to estimate their weights is from models. The restored skeletons were carefully sculpted as muscle models in nondrying plasticine. The predators' bellies were always sculpted as hollow; otherwise, their latest victim would be counted as part of their weight. The bellies of the herbivorous ornithomimids and oviraptors always contained plant material so their bellies were fuller. The model was then cut into smaller sections, and care was taken to seal up all holes. The volume of the model was measured by dropping the sections into a graduated cylinder and reading off the displacement of water. This is accurate to within about 3 percent. From this, the estimated volume of the actual dinosaur is calculated. Weight is a simple function of the volume and the density, or specific gravity. For example, the specific gravity of water is 1.0 (1 kilogram of water equals 1 liter). Animals are mostly water. Bones are denser, but most animals float because of their air-filled lungs. So the specific gravity of paleodinosaurs and early theropods was about 0.9. However, the extensive air sacs of birds make them less dense, at about 0.8. The avetheropods probably had better developed air sacs than early theropods, but less than birds, so they are given intermediate specific gravities of 0.85. Since I believe small dinosaurs were feathered, and since both flying and land birds' feathers usually make up about 6 percent of their total mass, this value is added to those animals below 100 kg. The bigger ornithomimids may have been feathered, but probably only partly so, like ostriches, so their possible feathers are ignored. Multiply the volume by the specific gravity and you have the weight of the dinosaur.

Weights based on multiview skeletal restorations have a plus or minus error value of about 15 percent. This is quite acceptable since individuals can vary this much in their weight as their conditions change. Indeed, I model the dinosaurs in "lean" condition, without the seasonal deposits of fat that could have regularly boosted their weight by 15 percent or more. For those skeletons drawn in side view only, care was taken to follow what is known about the widths of their body parts, and the accuracy of their weight estimates is only a little less. Species for which a good skeleton is not available are estimated from species of similar form. Of course, such weights are more approximate.

Note that the weights are those of specific specimens, not averages for the species as a whole. I try to give weights for more than one specimen to give an idea of its range. The great bulk of a species' population will be near the population's average weight, and since such typical-sized skeletons are what we can expect to find in the fossil record, many of the weights given here are close to average, or under it if only one or a few juveniles are known. A small but substantial portion of a population will exceed the average by 30 to 50 percent, so it takes very large numbers of remains, such as those known for *Coelophysis bauri* or *Allosaurus atrox,* to have much chance of catching these. Exceptional "world record" specimens often bulk twice the population's average weight, but they are so rare that their chances of being recorded in fossil dinosaur populations is virtually nil.

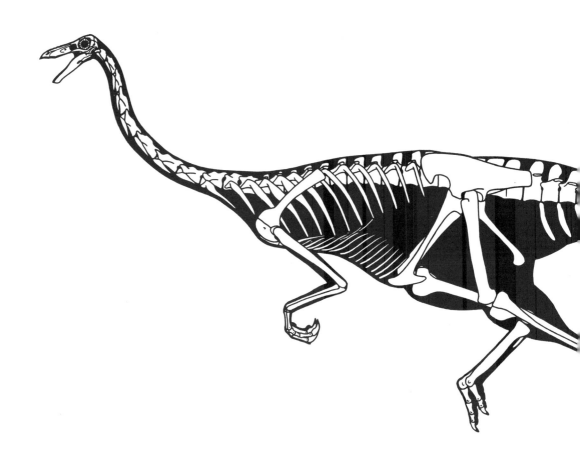

CLASS ARCHOSAURIA (Cope, 1869)
SUBCLASS OR INFRACLASS DINOSAURIA (Owen, 1841)

What is a predatory dinosaur? After all, not all theropods were predators.[1] Simply put, predatory dinosaurs are those that lack herbivorous teeth, or ancestors who had them. This excludes all prosauropods, brontosaurs, and ornithischians. It includes the primitive paleodinosaurs, the more specialized herreravians, and the classic dinosaurian killers, the bird-footed theropods.

It is an interesting coincidence that *Lagosuchus talampay-ensis* and *Tyrannosaurus rex* were among the very first and very last predatory dinosaurs, and were the smallest and largest too. There was a sixty-thousandfold size difference between them. Which were the largest monsters? Of course *T. Rex*, at six to twelve tonnes, still holds the record. *Deinocheirus mirificus,* which is known only from forelimb bones, may have been as heavy. *Spinosaurus aegyptiacus* was lighter, but it was perhaps the longest theropod at around fifty feet. A number of species, *Tyrannosaurus bataar, Allosaurus amplexus, Acrocanthosaurus atokensis, Ceratosaurus ingens, Metriacanthosaurus shan-gyouensis,* and some others cluster around four to five tons. Quite common are megalosaurs, allosaurs, tyrannosaurs, and even a very early herrerasaur in the two-to-three-tonne area. But just wait, it is most unlikely that the biggest has been turned up yet!

Some Things That Were Not Predatory Dinosaurs

This is a good place to mention some fossils that have been thought to be predatory dinosaurs, but probably are not. Most are fragmentary to greater or lesser degrees. Among the more notorious of these are the alleged "predatory prosauropods" of the Late Triassic, of which *Teratosaurus* Meyer, 1861 is the best known. They are sometimes believed to combine blade-toothed jaws with stocky prosauropod-like bodies, the prosauropods having been the most primitive of the herbivorous dinosaurs. But closer investigation invariably shows that these *are* the skeletons of herbivorous prosauropod dinosaurs, mixed in with the teeth and skull parts of predatory thecodonts or dinosaurs. What often happened is that predatory thecodonts or dinosaurs shed some of their teeth while they were killing or feeding on a herbivore. Or, in the case of *Teratosaurus,* the skull bones turned out to be those of a big rauisuchid thecodont.[2] Never has a predatory skull

actually been found attached to a prosauropod neck, nor will one ever be since a bulky herbivore's body is wholly unsuitable for a hunter. The worst of these mix-ups are claims that some of the early giant brontosaurs had predatory heads. The supposed "predatory prosauropods" were often called paleopods, but since they never really existed the title is best dropped. In a related case, Late Triassic *Lukousaurus* Young, 1948 is often considered a theropod, but the snout is more likely that of a thecodont or early crocodilian. It is too poorly preserved and incomplete to tell for sure.

It was recently contended that the new and strange segnosaurian dinosaurs from Late Cretaceous Mongolia were aberrant herbivorous theropods. Their four-toed feet alone show that this cannot be correct. The finds also included an excellent skull, and when I saw it I knew immediately that these were not predatory dinosaurs at all. Instead, they were late-surviving ornithischian-like prosauropods.[3] The story might not end here. A big arm with incredibly long claws from Late Cretaceous Mongolia is named *Therizinosaurus* Maleev, 1954. Believed to be theropodian, the shoulder girdle and humerus are similar to segnosaurs' and may be segnosaurian. Some other segnosaur-like humeri assigned to theropods, such as that of *Alectrosaurus,* are more likely to be segnosaurs too.

At the small end of the size scale is little *Avipes* Huene, 1932 of Middle Triassic Europe. Based on three cannon bones, it is sometimes considered the first theropod. But it is too fragmentary for us to tell.[4]

Then there is *Palaeornis* Emmons, 1857 from the Late Triassic of North Carolina. For over a hundred years it has been cited as a dubious set of bird or theropod hip vertebrae. It turns out that it is really a piece from the snout of a crocodile-like thecodont called a phytosaur.

Primitive Paleodinosaurs

SUPERORDER PALEODINOSAURIA new

Paleodinosaurs are the first predatory dinosaurs, found over much of the world in the Middle and Late Triassic (about 235 to 220 million years before present). Already rather birdlike, and in some cases fully bipedal, they still lack the long avian ilium in the hip and the tripodal foot of true theropods. They also have fewer neck and more trunk vertebrae than the latter. Both the theropods and the herbivorous dinosaurs are descendants of early predators of this kind. The earliest herbivorous dinosaurs, the prosauropods, are not all that different from paleodinosaurs in general form, the main differences being that prosauropods are spade-toothed, quadrupedal, and much heavier in construction.

Frustratingly, no good paleodinosaur skull or hand has been published yet. Paleodinosaurs probably did have the divergent thumb weapon since the even more primitive ornithosuchids had it. They probably had five fingers too, like their herbivorous dinosaur relatives.

Paleodinosaurs were not spectacularly successful, and they did not last long; only ten or so million years. Perhaps their herreravian and theropod descendants proved to be too much for them. They were less diverse than theropods, and some were smaller than any theropod. On the other hand, in their brief sojourn they did achieve some evolutionary advances—for instance, staurikosaurs developed the deep hips so characteristic of later dinosaurs—and laid the groundwork for the success of their descendants the theropods and birds, and the herbivorous dinosaurs.

The Protodinosaur Lagosuchians

The members of this order of paleodinosaurs are not only the very first predatory dinosaurs, they are the very first of any dinosaurs. Often considered thecodonts—which is why their names commonly end with the -*suchus* usually reserved for thecodonts—their S-curved neck, highly erect gait, completely mesotarsal ankle, and digitigrade foot make them truly dinosaurian. Along with the even more primitive thecodont ornithosuchians, lagosuchians can be regarded as protodinosaurs, the base of the great radiation to come. Discovered only recently, they have told us a lot about the beginnings of dinosaurs. So far, good remains are known only from 235-million-year-old Argentina, but they probably lived elsewhere too.

Lagosuchians are small predators, in fact, downright tiny. They, and their small ornithosuchid relatives also, went through much the same size squeeze that accompanied the evolution of birds and mammals. This size squeeze probably marked the evolution of a fully avian-mammalian physiology. Lagosuchians were the first erect-gait, high-endurance runners of earth history, since high metabolic rates would have allowed the latter. Because the forelimbs were still long enough and suitable for locomotion, they may have run with a bounding gallop as well as a birdlike run. Their small size, partial quadrupediality, and rabbit-like hind limbs are responsible for their names, which usually began with a derivation of Classic Greek for rabbit, *lago*.

Not surprisingly, lagosuchians were very, very primitive dinosaurs. Their archaic nature can best be seen in their still thecodont-like hips, which had a short pubis quite different from other predatory dinosaurs. Because the ischium was short, it supported limb muscles almost down to its lower end. The neck was also short, despite the small skull. Yet they were already diversifying in form, showing a good deal of variation in skull and foot proportions. They were quickly replaced by more derived paleodinosaurs.

ORDER LAGOSUCHIA new

FAMILY LAGOSUCHIDAE Bonaparte, 1975

Lagosuchus talampayensis

*Lewisuchus admixtus

This family lacks the peculiar foot of *Lagerpeton* (pages 243-44) and could be the group ancestral to all the rest of the dinosaurs. The bladed, serrated teeth suggest they hunted fairly large prey for animals of their size.

SUBFAMILY LAGOSUCHINAE (Bonaparte, 1975)

GENUS *LAGOSUCHUS* Romer, 1971

LAGOSUCHUS TALAMPAYENSIS Romer, 1971

SYNONYM—*Lagosuchus lilloensis*
TYPE—MLP 64-XI-14-11
BEST SPECIMEN—PVL 3870
TIME—Ladinian of the Middle Triassic
HORIZON AND DISTRIBUTION—Ischichuca Formation of Argentina
MAIN ANATOMICAL STUDY—Bonaparte, 1975

	PVL 3870	PVL 3871
SKULL LENGTH—	~33 mm	
TOTAL LENGTH—	.41 mm	~.51
FEMUR LENGTH—	44 mm	55
HIP HEIGHT—	.12 m	~.15
GRAMMAGE—	91	~180

The first protodinosaurs—as exemplified by bounding, ferret-sized Lagosuchus talampayensis—appeared about the same time as the first protomammals, in the late Middle Triassic. Both groups started out small-bodied, the protomammals even more so than the protodinosaurs. Giants of each type would come later.

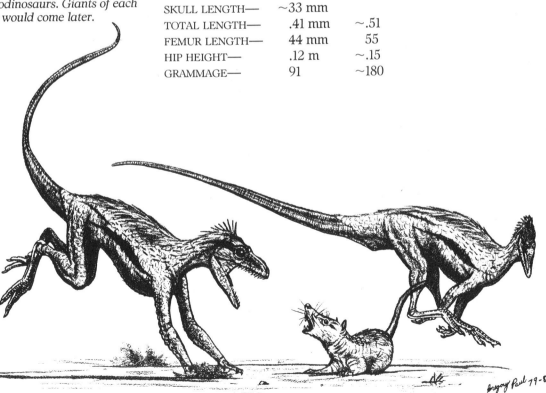

Gregory Paul 79-87

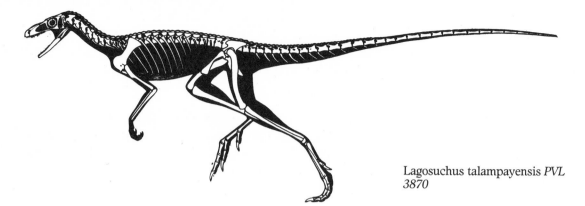

Lagosuchus talampayensis *PVL 3870*

At a sixth of a kilogram, this ferret-sized predator is both the smallest and most primitive of all dinosaurs. Along with *Lewisuchus,* it is also the earliest. That a number of specimens are known, all from one site, indicates but does not prove that they were adults. What little is known of the skull shows that it was small for the skeleton; in the restoration most of the skull is patterned after other protodinosaurs. Most of the skeleton is known, except for the hands and much of the tail. Alfred Romer made the largest specimen the basis of the species *L. lilloensis,* but it is not really different. Originally it was thought that supposed specializations in the hip made this species unsuitable as a general dinosaur ancestor, but better remains showed that these peculiarities do not really exist.

The Ischichuca Formation saw the high point of basal paleo-dinosaur evolution, for it also includes *Lagosuchus's* larger relatives, *Lewisuchus* and *Lagerpeton.* Assorted medium-sized to large thecodonts were also around, and all hunted *Lagosuchus.* Its prey, in turn, consisted of insects, small reptiles, juveniles of other archosaurs, and small protomammals.

SUBFAMILY LEWISUCHINAE new

GENUS *LEWISUCHUS* Romer, 1972

LEWISUCHUS ADMIXTUS Romer, 1972
TYPE—MLP 64-XI-14-14
TIME—Ladinian of the Middle Triassic
HORIZON AND DISTRIBUTION—Ischichuca Formation of Argentina

	Type
SKULL LENGTH—	~140 mm
TOTAL LENGTH—	~1.15 mm

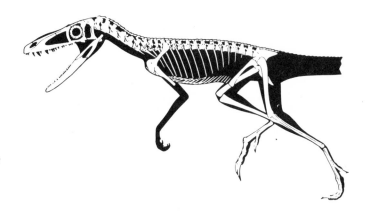

Lewisuchus admixtus *type MLP*
64-XI-14-14

FEMUR LENGTH—	105 mm
HIP HEIGHT—	.27 m
KILOGRAMMAGE—	1.3

A set of upper and lower jaws, the teeth, the back of the skull and much of the skeleton are believed to come from one individual. If so, it is a strikingly big-headed animal; note how large the neck vertebrae are to support the head. It is also a bigger animal than *Lagosuchus;* about the size of a large mink. The second toe is unusually long and robust (the opposite of *Lagerpeton*); it was probably a defensive weapon. *Lewisuchus* is endowed with small armor scutes, a primitive thecodont character that it is presumed all lagosuchians had. The hips are missing, and as a result I cannot be *sure* this is a lagosuchid, but the general similarity to its Ischichuca neighbor *Lagosuchus* suggests that it is. *Lewisuchus* probably hunted much the same prey as *Lagosuchus,* but larger victims and the odd *Lagosuchus* and *Lagerpeton* were included in its diet.

FAMILY LAGERPETONIDAE Arcucci, 1986

GENUS *LAGERPETON* Romer, 1971

LAGERPETON CANARENSIS Romer, 1971
TYPE—MLP 64-XI-14-10
TIME—Ladinian of the Middle Triassic
HORIZON AND DISTRIBUTION—Ischichuca Formation of Argentina

	Type
HIP HEIGHT—	~.21 m
FEMUR LENGTH—	75 mm
GRAMMAGE—	~450

Only the hind limb, hips, and some vertebrae are well preserved in this protodinosaur, including in some new specimens just described by Andrea Arcucci. The foot is odd, and unique, because the fourth cannon bone and toe are longer than the others. Why it is this way is an unanswered question, but it means that *L. canarensis* deserves a family of its own, and that it and any relatives were an evolutionarily dead end, a side show. *Lagerpeton* was apparently intermediate in size to its Ischichuca relatives; not enough is known about it to tell us much about its habits.

Staurikosaurs

As early predatory dinosaurs evolved, they quickly acquired more birdlike attributes, such as the long pubes in the hips and the full bipedalism of the staurikosaurians, another order of paleodinosaurs. Like lagosuchids, staurikosaurs did not last long as a group. They were larger, though, and more powerful, making them the first dinosaurian big-game killers. There looks to be a staurikosaur present in the Arizonian Chinlo Formation;[1] it is neither a herbivore nor the world's oldest dinosaur as originally proposed.

ORDER STAURIKOSAURIA new

FAMILY STAURIKOSAURIDAE Galton, 1977

Pseudolagosuchus major
Staurikosaurus pricei
Ischisaurus cattoi

GENUS PSEUDOLAGOSUCHUS Arcucci, 1987

PSEUDOLAGOSUCHUS MAJOR Arcucci, 1987
TYPE—PVL 4629
TIME—Ladinian of the Middle Triassic
HORIZON AND DISTRIBUTION—Los Chanares Formation of
    Argentina

	Type
FEMUR LENGTH—	115 mm
KILOGRAMMAGE—	~2?

Andrea Arcucci thinks this is a close relative of *Lagosuchus,* but the pubes are too long for that. Overall its femur and tibia look rather like a staurikosaur's, one more primitive than *Staurikosaurus* itself. If so then this is the earliest of the group. But this too could be wrong, and *Pseudolagosuchus* could even be a theropod. Not a whole lot is known of this little beast, its most distinctive feature is the modest elongation of the spines of the tail vertebrae.

GENUS *STAURIKOSAURUS* Colbert, 1970
SYNONYM—*Herrerasaurus*

STAURIKOSAURUS PRICEI Colbert, 1970
SYNONYM—*Herrerasaurus ischigualastensis*
TYPE—MCZ 1669
TIME—early Carnian of the Late Triassic
HORIZON AND DISTRIBUTION—middle Santa Maria Formation of
    southernmost Brazil
MAIN ANATOMICAL STUDIES—Colbert, 1970; Galton, 1977

	Type
SKULL LENGTH—	~220 mm
TOTAL LENGTH—	2.08 m
FEMUR LENGTH—	229 mm
HIP HEIGHT—	.61 m
KILOGRAMMAGE—	19

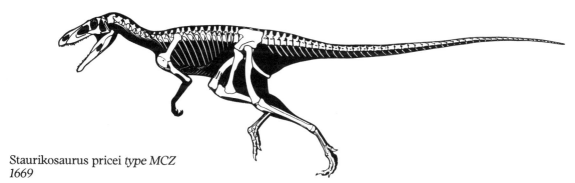

Staurikosaurus pricei *type MCZ 1669*

The only specimen is just about the best late paleodinosaur skeleton we have. The skull is missing, and the teeth are missing from the lower jaw, but the lower jaw's length shows that this was a big-skulled and probably big-toothed predator. The lower jaws are very distorted, yet I think the end of the lower jaw is a little downcurved, like in the herbivorous prosauropod dinosaurs. Most of the vertebral column, part of the shoulder blade, and the hips and hind limbs (excepting the foot) are also known. Some other details in the skeletal restoration, especially the skull

and humerus, have been taken from other four-toed predatory dinosaurs such as *Frenguellisaurus* (page 248).

Although not a large animal, the big head suggests this dinosaur tackled fairly large prey. Big thecodont predators were its main competition and source of danger.

A pair of Staurikosaurus pricei *at sunset. Except for the lower jaw, the skull of the specimen is missing—so the heads shown here are based upon those of a related species.*

GENUS *ISCHISAURUS* Reig, 1963

ISCHISAURUS CATTOI Reig, 1963
TYPE—MACN 18.060
TIME—late Carnian of the Late Triassic
HORIZON AND DISTRIBUTION—lower Ischigualasto Formation of
    Argentina

	MLP 61-VIII-2-3
FEMUR LENGTH—	340 mm
KILOGRAMMAGE—	~60

More of this species is known than has been published. The short humerus confirms that staurikosaurs were bipedal. (Also in line with bipedalism are the staurikosaur-herrerasaur's short backs.) A leopard- or wolf-sized predator, *I. cattoi* was in danger from larger *Herrerasaurus,* and *Frenguellisaurus,* and also from the giant thecodonts of the Ischigualasto Formation.

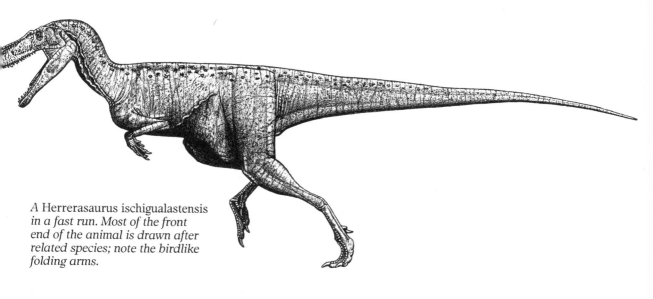

*A Herrerasaurus ischigualastensis
in a fast run. Most of the front
end of the animal is drawn after
related species; note the birdlike
folding arms.*

Bird-Mimicking Herrerasaurs

SUPERORDER HERRERAVIA new

At first glance these are very like staurikosaurs, including their four-toed feet. Yet some unexpectedly avian-like features appear in these dinosaurs, including a long-strap scapular blade, a birdlike hip joint, and a backward-pointing pubis. The humerus of *Frenguellisaurus* also has bird-style shoulder and elbow joints (shown in Figure 4-11, page 108). This implies that the arm could fold more tightly than in most dinosaurs, although not as well as in protobird theropods and birds. Even early theropods lack these features. And if the "Protoavis" remains (see page 251) belong in this group as I believe, then they are either confirmation that the herrerasaurs were remarkable imitators of birds, or evidence that birds evolved from these early dinosaurs.

Hefty size was another thing this group developed, especially in great *Aliwalia*. It is not known whether herrerasaurs had light armor or not; either is possible. Part of a herrerasaur femur came from the middle Stubensandstein of Germany.[1] Also found in the middle Stubensandstein was a snout that looks like an advanced staurikosaur or herrerasaur femur. (The snout has often been assigned to *Procompsognathus,* but in 1981 John Ostrom showed that it does not belong to that taxa.) Since these German herrerasaur remains are middle Norian in age, they may represent the last known paleodinosaurs. Although like all four-toed predatory dinosaurs a short-lived bunch that lasted only five to ten million years, the herrerasaurs conducted some intriguing evolutionary experiments.

FAMILY HERRERASAURIDAE Benedetto, 1973

Frenguellisaurus ischigualastensis

Herrerasaurus ischigualastensis

Aliwalia rex

**Walkeria maleriensis*

*GENUS *FRENGUELLISAURUS* Novas, 1987

**FRENGUELLISAURUS ISCHIGUALASTENSIS* Novas, 1987
TYPE—UNSJ 53
TIME—late Carnian of the Late Triassic
HORIZON AND DISTRIBUTION—lower Ichigualasto Formation of
    Argentina

	Type
SKULL LENGTH—	560 mm
KILOGRAMMAGE—	~350?

This species provides the first good skulls, two to be precise, of a primitive predatory dinosaur. The type includes a head with jaws that is missing most of the roof pieces, plus some tail bones. Another specimen with a complete but crushed skull has been languishing in the MCZ for years, the skeletal parts—including the bird-style shoulder blade and humerus mentioned above—were described by Donald Brinkman and Hans-Dieter Sues.[2] The long, low skulls of these individuals look similar and may be the same species. The most interesting item is the size of the tooth at the middle of the upper jaw; it was a good-sized fang that probably poked out from under the lips. Otherwise the head was strongly built, especially in the snout and jaws. In terms of evolutionary development, *Frenguellisaurus* was clearly intermediate to staurikosaurs and herrerasaurs. Fernando Novas noted its similarity to the latter, while Brinkman and Sues emphasize the similarity of its hip's ischium to the former. I think it is a primitive herrerasaur because the MCZ vertebrae have their kind of distinctive hour-glass shape. Since I do not think herrerasaurs are theropods, this is not considered to be the first known theropod—contrary to the suggestion by Novas that it was. *Frenguellisaurus* shared its Ischigualasto habitat with its close relatives *Ischisaurus* and *Herrerasaurus*.

GENUS *HERRERASAURUS* Reig, 1963

HERRERASAURUS ISCHIGUALASTENSIS Reig, 1963
TYPE AND BEST SPECIMEN—PVL 2566
TIME—late Carnian of the Late Triassic
HORIZON AND DISTRIBUTION—lower Ischigualasto Formation of
  Argentina

	Type
TOTAL LENGTH—	~3.9 m
FEMUR LENGTH—	473 mm
HIP HEIGHT—	1.1 m
KILOGRAMMAGE—	~210

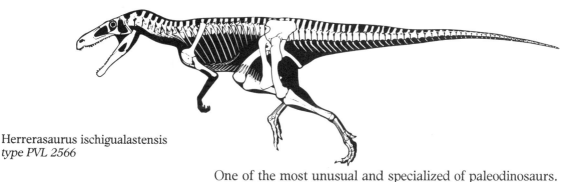

Herrerasaurus ischigualastensis
type *PVL 2566*

One of the most unusual and specialized of paleodinosaurs. A big-toothed jawbone Reig referred to this species may not really belong, so we know nothing for certain of its head. The one shown on the skeletal restoration is drawn after *Frenguellisaurus,* as are the humerus and some of the forward vertebrae. The slender shoulder blade is taken from a newly identified relative, and it parallels those of advanced theropods and birds. The back-swept pubis and well-developed antitrochanter joint surface in the hip socket each match the similar structures found in both ornithischians and protobirds. The pubes also have a big boot, otherwise known only in the advanced theropods. The vertebral bodies are hourglass-shaped, like those of the allosaurs. All in all, a remarkable suite of advanced features. It has been suggested that *Staurikosaurus pricei* was a juvenile of *Herrerasaurus,* but the discovery of juvenile *Herrerasaurus* hips and other differences show that this was not so. It has even been offered that herrerasaurs were early brontosaurs, far as it may be from reality.

Herrerasaurus was the prey and possible competitor of giant thecodonts. The Ischigualasto Formation marked the heyday of four-toed predatory dinosaur evolution, for bigger *Frenguellisaurus* and smaller *Ischisaurus* were also present (note that the species names of both *Herrerasaurus* and *Frenguellisaurus ischigualastensis,* are after the formation). Most of the herbivores *Herrerasaurus* dined upon were rather slow and bizarre reptiles and mammal-like reptiles, as only a few small plant-eating dinosaurs were yet around.

GENUS *ALIWALIA* Galton, 1985

ALIWALIA REX Galton, 1985
TYPE—NMW 1889
TIME—late Carnian or early Norian of the Late Triassic
HORIZON AND DISTRIBUTION—lower Elliot Formation of South
    Africa

	Type
TONNAGE—	~1.5?

There is not much to this animal—just the ends of a femur, plus a maxilla that may or may not belong to it. But it is important because it shows that herrerasaurs got really big, as large as a typical *Allosaurus*. And this only ten or so million years after the first dinosaur skeletons are known! *A. rex* seems to be more advanced in some details than *Herrerasaurus,* so I accept its being a separate genus at this time. Its prey included big prosauropods, and similar-sized thecodonts were the likely competition.

GENUS *WALKERIA* Chatterjee, 1987

*WALKERIA MALERIENSIS Chatterjee, 1987
TYPE—ISI R306 (juvenile)
TIME—late Carnian of the Late Triassic
HORIZON AND DISTRIBUTION—Maleri Formation of east-central
    India

	Type
FEMUR LENGTH—	~120 mm
KILOGRAMMAGE—	~3?

Sankar Chatterjee identified the snout tip, vertebrae, broken femora, and ankle bones of this dinosaur as those of a coelophysid. I disagree because the design of the femur is definitely herrerasaur-like, and the snout does not have the deep kink near its tip that coelophysids have. It appears to be a relative of *Herrerasaurus*, although not enough is known to be sure it is in the same family. What is most intriguing is that this dinosaur also shares some distinctive features with "Protoavis." More cannot be said at this time, but I believe that this supports the idea that "Protoavis" came from the herrerasaur group. Although the teeth are fairly large blades, it is odd that they are unserrated. That the upper arches of the vertebrae are not fused to the main spools suggests the type specimen was a youngster when it died.

FAMILY UNNAMED

GENUS "PROTOAVIS" Chatterjee, unofficial
MAIN SPECIMENS—TTU
TYPE—late Carnian of the Late Triassic
HORIZON AND DISTRIBUTION—Dockum Group of Texas
GRAMMAGE— ~350

These recently discovered remains have thrown an interesting twist into what is becoming the reasonably well-running turbine of bird origins. Only informal information is available at this time, so the name given these remains should not be italicized yet. At least two individuals and maybe more, skull and skeletal parts have been found,[3] some much smaller than the others. The rich confusion may be the result of many types of animals having been mixed in together—including perhaps some flying pterosaurs, which also imitate birds. It is also possible that two related species are involved.

The "Protoavis" remains seem more birdlike in some details than *Archaeopteryx* or other protobird theropods, with the exception of *Avimimus*. Yet, as discussed in Chapter 8, the "Protoavis" complex also retains some primitive characters that indicate it was not as close to birds as it first seemed. Among these could be a four-toed foot (the fossil evidence is ambiguous) and an archaic ankle. The combination of these archaic features with the absence of bird remains from the Jurassic suggests, but does not prove, that "Protoavis" is an imitator of birds, rather than a true ancestor. It could be an early theropod bird-mimic, and, since *Herrerasaurus* already shows surprisingly birdlike adaptations, it may be that "Protoavis" is a further, extreme development of that group. If so, then this little "herrerasaur-bird" was a failed experiment, one that would be repeated with more success by advanced theropods and true birds. But if "Protoavis" turns out to be a real protobird, then it is the first avetheropod. It is difficult to say more because the fossils are incomplete and jumbled, need more work, and await publication.

The few small teeth crowded in the front of the jaws indicate that little "Protoavis" was picking up even smaller animals and insects. Maybe it fished, too. It may well have had wing-feathered arms. However, the small, slightly keeled sternum, relatively short forelimbs, and broad hand imply that flight was at best crude. These are, all in all, rather odd and most perplexing remains.

PALEODINOSAUR, HERRERAVIAN, OR EARLY THEROPOD?

GENUS *SALTOPUS* Huene, 1910

SALTOPUS ELGINENSIS Huene, 1910
TYPE—BMNH R3915 (juvenile?)
TIME—late Carnian of the Triassic
HORIZON AND DISTRIBUTION—Lossiemouth Sandstone of Scotland

	Type
TOTAL LENGTH—	~.9 m
FEMUR LENGTH—	48 mm
HIP HEIGHT—	~.15 m
GRAMMAGE—	~200

Frequently mentioned as a very early dinosaur, the one small skeleton is badly preserved and lacks the head, neck, pubes, and much of the feet. Nor can it be said how many hip vertebrae there are, how long or short the hip's ilium is. Hence, it cannot be told if *Saltopus* is a paleodinosaur, herreravian, theropod, or maybe even something else altogether. Similar in proportions to slender *Procompsognathus* and *Coelophysis,* it could be one of those, perhaps a juvenile. If it is a theropod, it is among the earliest. Its main competitor was a somewhat larger ornithosuchid protodinosaur.

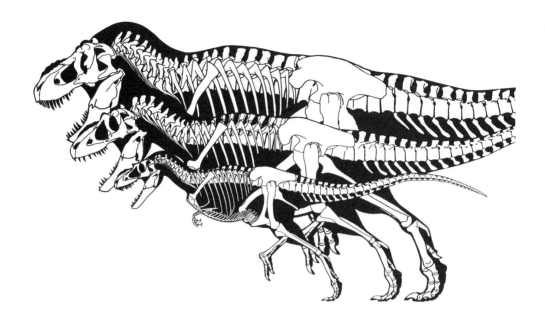

Theropod Multitudes

SUPERORDER THEROPODA (Marsh, 1881)

This is the main body of predatory dinosaurs, the wildly successful, very birdlike dinosaurs that dominated the bigger meat-eating roles worldwide for some 160 million years. Two preavian adaptations—an elongated ilium in the upper pelvis and a bird foot—mark all the classic theropods from *Coelophysis* to *Tyrannosaurus*. Although the long ilium is also found in some other dinosaurs, including "Protoavis," the bird foot—in which the inner cannon bone does not reach the ankle—is especially distinctive. It is not proven to appear anywhere else, and may have evolved only once, so it is a good minimum definition of the Theropoda. (In this regard, the name Theropoda, which means beast-footed, is most inappropriate. Avepoda would be much better, but it is too late for that.) The usually consistent count of 10, 13, 5, neck, trunk, and hip vertebrae is also distinctive.

Theropods were much more diverse than paleodinosaurs and herreravians. Some were small, some gargantuan; some were even herbivorous. It seems that in the middle of their evolution, a few theropods decided to take flight lessons. Their bird descendants are with us today, so in that sense theropods can be said to have been in existence for 225 million years.

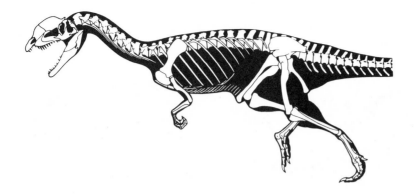

ORDER PALEOTHEROPODA new

The theropods are divided into two great groups: the paleotheropods and the avetheropods. Paleotheropods were less advanced and birdlike than avetheropods, but still sophisticated predators of the bird mold. Although replaced by the avetheropods as the dominant terrestrial predators in most parts of the world by the time of the Late Jurassic, paleotheropods were more successful in one regard: they survived just as late as avetheropods, to the end of the Cretaceous, and since they had started out earlier, they were around longer. Paleotheropods even managed to remain the top predators in Cretaceous South America right to the end.

Paleotheropods, which means primitive theropods, are distinguished from avetheropods in four main ways. Their lower jaws are not double-jointed, their rib cages are not yet birdlike, their ankles lack a tall astragular process, and the central cannon bone is robust. Many other skull and skeletal details are also less derived. There are two main paleotheropod groups: the gracile coelophysids and relatives on the one hand, and the generally later, usually more robust forms such as the metriacanthosaurs on the other.

The earliest theropods were—judging from what we know of the procompsognathids and coelophysids—slender, gracile forms. Their long necks set them apart from the paleodinosaurs on the one hand, and the more advanced ceratosaurs and intertheropods on the other. The detailed design of early paleotheropods, including the forward-sloping pubis and very robust central cannon bone, shows that they were the most primitive of theropods. They did quite well at dominating the Late Triassic and Early Jurassic, and were still around as late as the Cretaceous. In that regard, these theropods are "early" only in a loose sense; there was extensive temporal overlap with other theropods.

SUBORDER CERATOSAURIA (Marsh, 1884)

FAMILY PROCOMPSOGNATHIDAE Huene, 1929

This is not much of a group, having only one known species. The name unfortunately implies a close relationship with *Compsognathus,* which was a much later and more advanced theropod. Although by no means the earliest, *Procompsognathus* is the most primitive predatory dinosaur with a well-preserved theropod-type foot. The most primitive thing about it are the broad pubes—almost all other theropods had much narrower hips. For this reason, *Procompsognathus* stands alone, and the more advanced coelophysids and other theropods should not be put in its family as has been recently suggested. Besides, the skull appears to lack the coelophysian's kinked snout.

GENUS *PROCOMPSOGNATHUS* Fraas, 1913

PROCOMPSOGNATHUS TRIASSICUS Fraas, 1913
TYPE—SMNS 12591
TIME—middle Norian of the Late Triassic
HORIZON AND DISTRIBUTION—middle Stubensandstein of Bavaria
MAIN ANATOMICAL STUDY—Ostrom, 1981

	Type
SKULL LENGTH—	~70 mm
TOTAL LENGTH—	~1.1 m
FEMUR LENGTH—	93 mm
HIP HEIGHT—	~.26 m
KILOGRAMMAGE—	1

Most of the one specimen is badly crushed and much of the neck, tail, arms, and hips are missing. Fortunately, the birdlike feet and broad, long pubes are in good shape. Although about half the size, the long slender skull and skeleton are shaped very much like *Coelophysis* (page 262). Also like *Coelophysis* are the large bladed teeth that indicate this was a big-game hunter. Living alongside this theropod were much larger herrerasaurs.

The Early Coelophysians and Dilophosaurs, and the Incredible Spinosaurs

First appearing something over 225 million years ago in the Triassic, the small coelophysians and their larger dilophosaur relatives are the earliest theropods for which really good remains are known. Multitudes of beautiful skeletons are available, many from the famous Ghost Ranch quarry of Arizona. This abundance is making these among the best understood of predatory dinosaurs. The elaphrosaurs may be coelophysids, and strange *Baryonyx* and *Spinosaurus* may be their descendants too. If so, then the group survived all the way into the Cretaceous.

Coelophysians include some of the first theropods, but even these already have some sophisticated features. Among them is a kinked articulation between the premaxilla and maxilla, in the front of the upper jaw. This kink may have been mobile, and it got larger as these theropods evolved. The joint seems to have weakened the snout—not an obvious benefit to a predator. But

The muscles of Coelophysis rho- *desiensis holotype QG 1.*

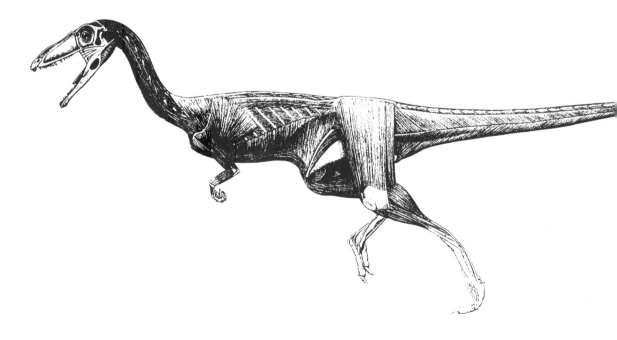

things were not really that bad. Vomers, the paired rodlike bones in the front of the roof of the mouth, acted as tension braces and bolstered the snout. The frontmost teeth were always fairly conical, and those on the expanded tip of the lower jaw radiated from one another like the spokes of a wheel. These supple, expanded jaw tips with their conical teeth look like special tools for picking up small prey.

There is no evidence that coelophysians retained any sort of primitive armor. Yet, despite all these advanced features, they are still primitive due to, among other things, their fourth—albeit weak—finger, reptilian-type rib cage, and thick central cannon bone. As explained in Chapter 8, pages 190-91, these early, independently evolving theropods developed the specializations on their own, some in parallel with other theropods, some not. Among them was the reversal from 13 trunk and 5 hip vertebrae in coelophysians to 14 and 4 in dilophosaurs, and perhaps in spinosaurs. In sum, coelophysians-dilophosaurs-spinosaurs were an evolutionary side group that did their own thing with kinked snouts, double head crests, and reduced hips. Certainly they were not especially close relatives of birds, as was suggested by Michael Raath in 1984. On the other hand, as the first of the birdlike theropods for which good remains are known, coelophysids are critical to understanding bird origins. Gerhard Heilmann postulated "Proaves," a hypothetical bird ancestor that he thought would be a quadrupedal climber descended directly from thecodonts, but he was wrong. Small terrestrial bipeds such as *Coelophysis* were the real proavians.

In the old system of classifying theropods, the light coelophysians and elaphrosaurs were once considered coelurosaurs, the heavy dilophosaurs and spinosaurs, carnosaurs. It now seems dilophosaurs and spinosaurs may be the direct descendants of early species of *Coelophysis*. This would be interesting, since *Dilophosaurus* lived at the same time as later species of *Coelophysis*. The coelophysians and dilophosaurs are now placed in the same family, and are easily different enough from the spinosaurs for the latter to be placed in a separate family.

All these predators are always lightly built and long in the head, neck, trunk, tail, and hind limbs. They look very speedy.

FAMILY COELOPHYSIDAE new

Coelophysis bauri
C. rhodesiensis

*Elaphrosaurus bambergi

Liliensternus liliensterni

Dilophosaurus wetherilli

The coelophysid snout is sharp and narrow, and the teeth often differ substantially from one another (they are heterodont) because the premaxillas are more conical and less serrated—sometimes wholly unserrated—than the cheek teeth. While the frontmost teeth seem built for holding small creatures, the large blades on the rest of the jaws are superb slashers. It therefore appears that coelophysids were exceptionally well equipped to pursue both small and large prey.

Coelophysids show a tendency to develop large yet delicate double crests on the head. First noted in big *Dilophosaurus,* a small *Coelophysis* has them too. These crests are expansions of the normal, sharp-rimmed nasal horn ridges and preorbital horns found in crestless *Coelophysis.* They are made up of a few vertical struts of fairly thick bone, between which are sheets of bone so thin that they are translucent. Being so thin and lacking the intensive blood-vessel channels needed to support horn sheaths, they were covered only with skin. Their fragility shows that they were display structures, and never used in combat.

The common co-ossification of various neck, pelvic, and hind-limb bones in *Coelophysis* and *Elaphrosaurus* is quite bird-like. As we get to know enough remains, we see that coelophysids persistently come in two markedly distinct forms in each locale, a "robust" and a "gracile" type as explained below. Since the variation tends to be present when the individuals are of similar size one might think we were looking at twin species. However, because all three *Coelophysis* species, and *Dilophosaurus* too, show this dual nature, it is more likely to represent a sexual difference.

Usually *Coelophysis* is placed in the family Podokesauridae. However, the only *Podokesaurus holyokensis* Talbot, 1911 specimen, which was never good to begin with, was destroyed in a fire, and only bad casts remain. Some consider *Podokesaurus,* which came from the Early Jurassic of Connecticut, to be the same as *Coelophysis;* others think that it may be very different. I think people will always be disagreeing about *Podokesaurus,* and this is just too much ambiguity to put up with. Another name for the family, Halticosauridae, is also based on some hopelessly fragmentary remains. So I offer Coelophysidae as the new name for the family. *Dilophosaurus* and *Liliensternus* are just super versions of *Coelophysis,* so they are a subfamily of this family.

SUBFAMILY COELOPHYSINAE new

GENUS *COELOPHYSIS* Cope, 1887
SYNONYMS—*Longosaurus, Syntarsus*

Although discovered in the 1880s, this genus was not well known to scientists and the public until the opening of the Ghost Ranch quarry in the 1940s and the Zimbabwean finds in the sixties. The genus is usually considered to consist of only *C. bauri.* But it takes careful work to show that it is a separate species from *Syntarsus rhodesiensis,* since the more that is known about them the more alike they appear. So, I see no justification for keeping them as separate genera.[1]

The case for placing *C. bauri* and *C. rhodesiensis* in one genus is strengthened by the substantial yet similar variation found *within* their respective populations. Each has a "gracile" form in which the skull and hind limb are long yet lightly built, and the forelimb is short relative to the rest of the animal. The heavier bodied "robust" form is the opposite in these regards. There are also detailed differences, especially the presence of a better developed outer ridge below the femur's head in "robust" variants. If one looks at only one form of one of the species, and at the opposite form of the other, they look fairly different. but the equivalent "robust" and "gracile" forms of each species look quite like one another.

Coelophysis is small, about 10 to 20 kg, about as heavy as coyotes and jackals. There is little exceptional about its design, but it is graceful and elegant. Skulls are long, low, triangular, and sharp-snouted. The neck is quite long and slender, the body is shallow, and the tail is large. The arms are quite small. *Coelophysis* is perceived as the archetypical small theropod—too much so, in fact, because most small theropods have longer and more birdlike forelimbs. Its small size might lead one to expect *Coelo-*

physis to be a small-game hunter, and as explained above their jaw tips were well suited for this. But *Coelophysis* has a larger head than *Ornitholestes* and *Ornithomimus,* it bears long rows of serrated blade teeth, and the long snout contained large jaw-closing muscles. The gregarious accumulations of many coelophysid skeletons suggests they hunted in packs. So it appears they hunted fairly large prey too.

A new Kayenta Formation species that looks to me to belong to *Coelophysis* is being studied by Timothy Rowe at Austin. Most similar to *C. rhodesiensis,* it has broken off *Dilophosaurus*-like double crests adorning its head. Its late appearance also implies that *Coelophysis* lasted a long time, some twenty-five million years of the Late Triassic and Early Jurassic.

COELOPHYSIS BAURI Cope, 1887

SYNONYMS—Coelurus bauri, Longosaurus longicollis
TYPE—AMNH 2722
BEST AND DISPLAY SPECIMENS—Many GRQ specimens in a
    number of institutions
TIME—late Carnian? to early Norian of the Late Triassic
HORIZON AND DISTRIBUTION—Chinle Formation of Arizona

	AMNH 7223	AMNH 7224	AMNH 7242
SKULL LENGTH—	268 mm	216	~80
TOTAL LENGTH—	2.68 m	2.86	
FEMUR LENGTH—	210 mm	210	
HIP HEIGHT—	.55 m	.56	
MASS—	15.3 kg	19.9 kg	~700 g

This theropod has become very well known because of all the skeletons found in the small Ghost Ranch quarry, discovered in 1947. This quarry comes from the same strata as the famous Petrified Forest. *C. bauri* makes up most of the quarry specimens, with thecodonts and a few other animals also mixed in. Although the area of the quarry is not that great, the number of *Coelophysis* skeletons packed into it is remarkable, perhaps well over five hundred. These include many juveniles, some one third the size and a small fraction of the weight of the adults, but no hatchlings. Some of the adult skeletons (including the two figured here) contain the remains of youngsters they must have eaten. Although the skeletons are often nearly complete and articulated, they are somewhat crushed. How the quarry came to be is not

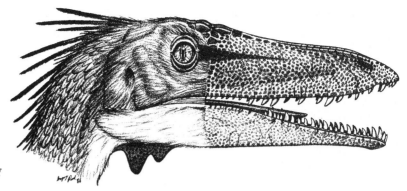

The head of Coelophysis bauri. *The tip of the snout is kinked, and paired horn ridges run along the nasals.*

fully understood, but a study is due out soon. I do not think this was a single pack, for even migrating predators do not go about in groups this size.

I have restored the often-reproduced pair of skeletons that lie side by side on the same Ghost Ranch block, for these complete specimens represent the two forms of the species—7223 is "gracile," and 7224 "robust." Only the top of the skull of 7223 can be seen, so I used a similar MCZ skull for the side view. *Coelophysis* is often considered a small-skulled predator, but 7223 shows this is not always so. As you can see, 7223 is especially like *C. rhodesiensis*. When I first drew up 7224, I did some of the details after *C. rhodesiensis*. When I sent the drawing to a preparator who was working on uncovering the skeletons on one of the Ghost Ranch blocks, he called back to ask how I knew *C. bauri* looked the way it does. This species' snout appears to be shallower yet more solidly built, and overall it is longer and lower than the African species. In fact, most restorations miss how very long and low this species was. *C. bauri* did not co-ossify its hip and other bones as much as its African cousin either. There are potentially serious problems in identifying this species, since the type is very poor, and not from near the Ghost Ranch specimens.[2] I have not listed all the synonyms of this species because most are not important. An exception is *Longosaurus longicollis* Welles, 1984, most fragmentary remains of which appear to fall within the variation of *C. bauri*.

C. bauri was the main predator in the Chinle; rarer staurikosaurs and flesh-eating thecodonts were its competition. The most numerous big herbivores in the Chinle were large-bodied, tusked mammal-like reptiles and armored aetosaur thecodonts.

Neither was especially fast, and they were vulnerable to pack attacks by *Coelophysis.* Some small herbivorous dinosaurs were also present, but rather rare.

COELOPHYSIS RHODESIENSIS (Raath, 1969)
SYNONYM—*Syntarsus rhodesiensis*
TYPE—QG 1
BEST SPECIMENS—type and a number of CQ specimens
TIME—Hettangian of the Early Jurassic
HORIZON AND DISTRIBUTION—Forest Sandstone and Stormberg
     Formations of southern Africa
MAIN ANATOMICAL STUDIES—Raath, 1977, 1984

	Type
SKULL LENGTH—	~210 mm
TOTAL LENGTH—	2.15 m
FEMUR LENGTH—	208 mm
HIP HEIGHT—	.53 m
KILOGRAMMAGE—	13.0

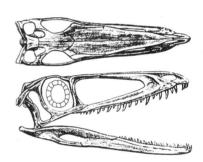

It is coincidence that like *C. bauri,* this species is found in a quarry that contains an intense, albeit much smaller, concentration of skeletons. The Chitake quarry is only ten feet across and holds a little over two dozen specimens. This could be a single pack, perhaps driven to an oasis waterhole during a drought only to succumb when it finally dried up. These Chitake quarry skeletons are not as complete or well articulated as the Ghost Ranch

Coelophysis bauri *MCZ 4327 and AMNH 7223 gracile*

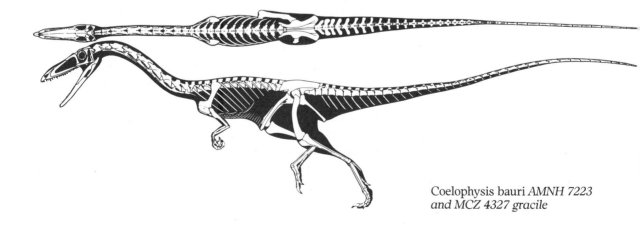

Coelophysis bauri *AMNH 7223 and MCZ 4327 gracile*

Coelophysis bauri *AMNH 7224*
robust

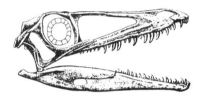

Coelophysis rhodesiensis *type*
QG-1

Coelophysis rhodesiensis
type QC 1

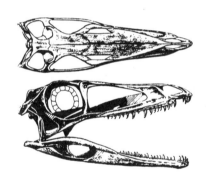

263

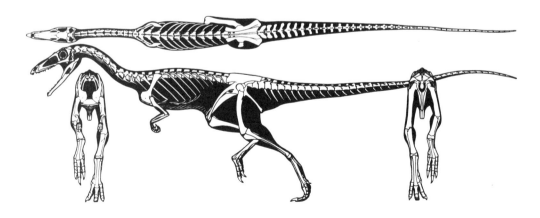

specimens, but the bones are exquisitely preserved. Unlike in the Ghost Ranch quarry, no really small youngsters are present. Virtually nothing else is found in the quarry itself, but prosauropods are abundant in the immediate vicinity.

Gracile Coelophysis rhodesiensis *in a fast run.*

The skeletal restoration is based mainly on the "robust" type specimen, but the skull and neck are from other specimens and there may be proportional errors. In particular, the head may represent the "gracile" type. Michael Raath believes the "robust" forms are females because they are a little more numerous than the "gracile" ones, and it is true that female birds of prey are usually bigger than the males. But the sample size is too small to be certain, and males are stouter than females in most predator species. Like *Elaphrosaurs,* the neck ribs tend to ossify to their vertebrae in mature individuals, as do the pelvic bones. Raath's skeletal and life restorations make the species much too kangaroo-like, with an oddly downkinked tail. The ribs are not right either, the front ones being too long, and the shoulder girdle is set way too far back, making the neck too long.

C. rhodesiensis was a true desert animal, living among dunes and oases. However, it may have been—like many predators—nondiscriminating in the habitats it preferred, and more widespread than we realize. It mainly hunted juvenile and adult prosauropods. This was no picnic, since prosauropods could bounce kangaroo-style on their stout tails and lash out at attackers with

big recurved hand and foot claws. But *C. rhodesiensis,* being a small, lean animal that could take a few tumbles, may have dashed in repeatedly to slash the victim until it was crippled. Among its smaller prey may have been gliding early lizards.[3]

*GENUS *ELAPHROSAURUS* Janensch, 1920

Lately, there has been much ado about this being an early ostrich-mimic ornithomimid because of its light build and slender, straight humerus.[4] It has even been placed in the family Ornithomimidae. This is a mistake. The humerus is really more like that of *Coelophysis,* just less strongly built. The forelimb and some upper hand bones that may belong to the genus are rather short, and the skeleton's lightness of build is of coelophysid proportions, not ostrich-mimic. The low ankle process and a very robust central cannon bone are too. Much too primitive to be closely related to the very advanced ostrich-mimics, *Elaphrosaurus* instead seems to be a fairly large, late-surviving coelophysid. Because it still has five hip vertebrae I do not consider it a dilophosaur, but the hip is unusually short so it may be close to that group. One caution is that if the now unknown head proves to lack a kinked snout, then its coelophysid status becomes questionable. Also questionable are past claims that this genus lived in mid-Cretaceous times of north Africa; these claims are based on such scrappy remains that they are probably wrong.

Galton in 1982 identified as *Elaphrosaurus* sp. a well-preserved humerus that came from the same Morrison Formation

Elaphrosaurus bambergi *in hot pursuit of the ornithischian* Dryosaurus lettowvorbecki. *The theropod's head and crests are restored after other coelophysians.* Elaphrosaurus *was at that intermediate size which may have borne both feathers and scales. Note that it is the plant eater that has fierce looking "eagle" eyes, not the theropod.*

Garden Park quarry that also produced the type skeletons of *Ceratosaurus* and *Allosaurus*. The bone is a little more *Coelophysis*-like than that of *E. bambergi,* for it still has a rectangular deltoid crest.

ELAPHROSAURUS BAMBERGI Janensch, 1920

TYPE—HMN dd
TIME—Tithonian of the Late Jurassic
HORIZON AND DISTRIBUTION—Tendaguru Formation of East
 Africa
MAIN ANATOMICAL STUDY—Janensch, 1925

	Type
TOTAL LENGTH—	6.2 m
FEMUR LENGTH—	529 mm
HIP HEIGHT—	1.46 m
KILOGRAMMAGE—	210

This is the only good theropod skeleton from the Tendaguru, a formation famous for its super-gigantic brachiosaurian sauropods. The missing head has led those arguing for ostrich-mimic affinities to speculate that it had a toothless beak. The skull must have been a long, low-toothed one, probably like those of *Coelophysis* and the dilophosaurs. There are small, bladed, *Coelophysis*-like teeth in the Tendaguru Formation that are right for it. It *may* even have been crested. The shoulder girdle, lower arm, and most of the hand are not preserved. This appears to be the longest-trunked and shallowest-chested theropod I have come across, and the base of the tail has an unusual downward bend in it. *Z. bambergi* was too small and light-bodied to take on the stegosaurs and sauropods of its habitat. Instead, it concentrated on the small, fast ornithopod herbivores.

Elaphrosaurus bambergi *type HMN dd*

SUBFAMILY HALTICOSAURINAE (Huene, 1948)

Dilophosaurs, the more familiar name we will informally use for this group, retain both the basic slender design and many skeletal details of coelophysians. In addition, they were more advanced in a number of fine points, such as an avetheropod-like ankle and foot. Yet they are more "primitive" in their failure to co-ossify many bones, and even more so in having *shorter* hips and less hip vertebrae. Why dilophosaurs did such a peculiar thing with their hips is a complete mystery.

GENUS *LILIENSTERNUS* Welles, 1984
SYNONYM—*Halticosaurus*

In 1984, Michael Parrish and Kenneth Carpenter described a new partial skeleton that may well belong to this genus. Over a third heavier than the *L. liliensternus* skeleton described below, and from the Dockum deposits of New Mexico, it may be of the late Carnian or early Norian Age. If so, it is the earliest theropod of such size we know about.

LILIENSTERNUS LILIENSTERNI (Huene, 1934)
SYNONYM—*Halticosaurus liliensterni*
TYPE—HMN R1291
TIME—late Norian of the Late Triassic
HORIZON AND DISTRIBUTION—Upper Keuper Formation of
　　　　Germany

	Type
SKULL LENGTH—	~395 mm
TOTAL LENGTH—	5.15 m
FEMUR LENGTH—	440 mm
HIP HEIGHT—	1.09 m
KILOGRAMMAGE—	127

When I saw the skeleton of this jaguar-sized dinosaur in East Berlin, I thought it was a large species of *Coelophysis*.[5] Samuel Welles, however, realized that it was a new dilophosaur genus. In fact, it is an almost perfect intermediate to *Coelophysis* and *Dilophosaurus* (see below). It is more advanced than the former, and is like the latter in many details such as the humerus and foot. Yet it remains more primitive and *Coelophysis*-like in other aspects. Even its size is intermediate. One of the most important points is that the ilium of the hip is unusually short, as in *Dilo-*

phosaurus. This suggests that *Liliensternus* also had only four hip vertebrae.

Since the skeleton is only fairly complete, a number of details are from other members of the group. The skull is especially incomplete. Because both a species of *Coelophysis* and one of *Dilophosaurus* have paired crests, I gave *Liliensternus* some too.

GENUS *DILOPHOSAURUS* (Welles, 1970)
SYNONYM—*Megalosaurus*

DILOPHOSAURUS WETHERILLI (Welles, 1954)
SYNONYM—*Megalosaurus wetherilli*
TYPE AND BEST SPECIMEN—UCMP 37302
TIME—late Sinemurian to Pliensbachian of the Early Jurassic
HORIZON AND DISTRIBUTION—Kayenta Formation of Arizona
MAIN ANATOMICAL STUDY—Welles, 1984

	Type	UCMP 77270
SKULL LENGTH—	523 mm	590
TOTAL LENGTH—	6.03 m	
FEMUR LENGTH—	550 mm	
HIP HEIGHT—	1.36 m	
KILOGRAMMAGE—	283	~400

The type specimen of this wonderful dinosaur was found in 1942, and consists of a very good skull and skeleton recently described by Samuel Welles. It was first thought to be a species of *Megalosaurus* (see page 280), but Welles later realized it is very different. The crests were incomplete and unrecognized in the first skull, but the discovery of a second larger skull revealed their presence. Whether this second skull is the same species as the first is not certain; the few specimens known seem to show the kind of sexual or species differences seen in *Coelophysis*. The type specimen is a "gracile" example. A brown-bear-sized predator, *Dilophosaurus* could be a direct descendant of *Coelophysis* and *Liliensternus*. It parallels advanced theropods in such things as having a narrow central metatarsal in the foot. It also has a very unusual articulation between the cheek's suspensorium bones, which help support the lower jaw. The upper part of the shoulder blade has a rather peculiar shape. A few years ago sculptor Rodger Walshlager of Richard Rush Studios built a full-scale sculpture of this theropod to my specifications.

It is odd how extreme the kink between the premaxilla and maxilla is, and that the nostrils are placed further back than in

The double-crested head of Dilophosaurus wetherilli *in two views.*

Dilophosaurus wetherilli *in a fast run.*

other theropods. These features are taken even further in *Baryonyx.* Some believe the snout was too weak for attacking prey, which has been taken to mean that *Dilophosaurus* either used its feet to kill, or scavenged for food. But as I explained above, the tip of the snout is better braced than previously thought, and in any case, true terrestrial scavenging animals are a myth (see Chapter 2). Besides, *Dilophosaurus* has exceptionally large, although slender, bladed maxillary teeth that were much more lethal than its claws, so *Dilophosaurus* probably hunted big game like other slashing theropod. Most of this big game consisted of fair-sized prosauropods. That the snout was so highly mobile

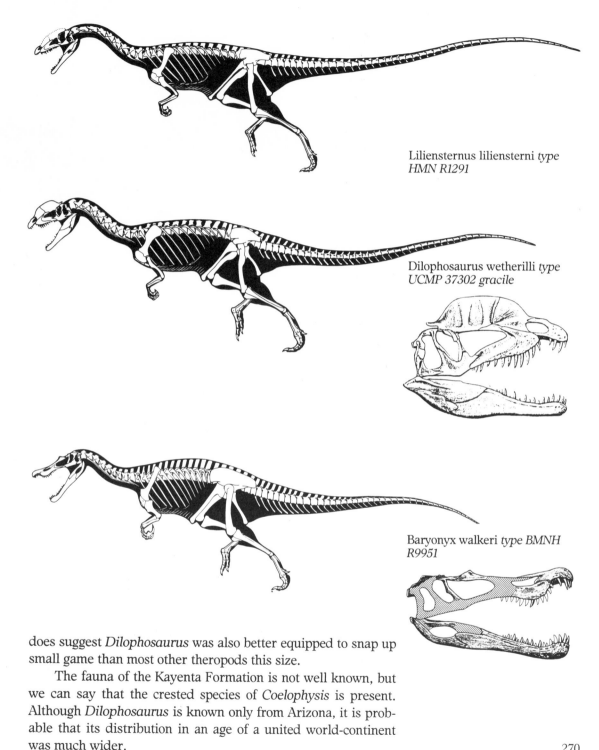

Liliensternus liliensterni *type HMN R1291*

Dilophosaurus wetherilli *type UCMP 37302 gracile*

Baryonyx walkeri *type BMNH R9951*

does suggest *Dilophosaurus* was also better equipped to snap up small game than most other theropods this size.

The fauna of the Kayenta Formation is not well known, but we can say that the crested species of *Coelophysis* is present. Although *Dilophosaurus* is known only from Arizona, it is probable that its distribution in an age of a united world-continent was much wider.

270

FAMILY SPINOSAURIDAE Stromer, 1915

Baryonyx walkeri

Spinosaurus aegyptiacus

The spinosaurs are so bizarre that their very dinosaurian status has been challenged. I once thought them to be overgrown crocodilians. *Spinosaurus* has also been considered a close relative of fin-backed *Acrocanthosaurus,* and restored as a tyrannosaur, both of which it was certainly not. In addition, Alan Charig and Angela Milner doubt whether *Baryonyx* and *Spinosaurus* are close relatives. However, I agree with Philippe Taquet that the slender, semiconical, crocodile-like teeth with microscopically fine serrations, plus the crocodile-like lower jaw with expanded tips, are very alike in the two species.[6] So is the seeming lack of the typical theropod S-curve in the neck. As for whether they are theropods, and just what kind, the loose, deeply kinked articulation near the tip of the snout, the posteriorly postioned nostrils, and slender teeth of *Baryonyx* are surprisingly similar to those of eighty-million-year-older *Dilophosaurus,* and appear to be extreme developments of the latter's snout. Likewise, the long, primitive main bodies of the neck and trunk vertebrae and the shallow rib cages in *Baryonyx* and *Spinosaurus* are rather dilophosaurian. So my best guess, hinted at by Charig and Milner, is that spinosaurs are specialized, late-surviving dilophosaurs. We need more remains to be sure.

Spinosaurs may have hung on so long because of their strange specializations, ones that seemingly emphasized the coelophysian-dilophosaur adaptations for hunting small game. The long slender snout and teeth with ultra-fine serrations suggest such habits. The lower jaws of *Baryonyx* are reported to be wafer-thin, and the mobile snout seems good for manipulating small prey. Fishing is a very plausible activity, and the expanded crocodile-like tips of the upper and lower jaws are in line with this idea. Partly digested fish scales have even been found inside the rib cage of *Baryonyx*. But no living land animal as gigantic as spinosaurs survive on fresh-water fish alone. Even brown bears do so only during the brief and intense salmon runs through narrow mountain streams, a far cry from the spinosaur's low-lying floodplain waters where fish were usually not as numerous and easily scooped up. So terrestrial small game and scavenging must have been important too. The large teeth and massive, big-clawed arms would have allowed them to bring down even fairly

Fishing Baryonyx walkeri *catches a* Lepidotes. *Observe that—as the texture and vessel openings of the jaw bones show—this species had the same kind of lips found in other theropods, so the teeth are not bare as in crocodilians.*

big game. I have no answer, however, for why spinosaur necks may lack the strong S-curve that is normal in theropods.

GENUS *BARYONYX* Charig and Milner, 1986

BARYONYX WALKERI Charig and Milner, 1986
TYPE—BMNH R9951
TIME—Barremian of the late Early Cretaceous
HORIZON AND DISTRIBUTION—Wealden Formation of England

	Type
SKULL LENGTH—	~1100 mm
TOTAL LENGTH—	~9.5 m
FEMUR LENGTH—	~1000 mm
HIP HEIGHT—	~2.5 m
TONNAGE—	~1.7

This beast was published just as I was finishing this book. Its discoverer was a London plumber and amateur fossil hunter, William Walker. Much, but by no means all, of the skull and skeleton are known.[7] My skeletal drawing is a preliminary one that will need replacing when the full description comes out. Taquet has also found very similar upper jaws' tips that might belong to *Baryonyx* from Aptian time of Niger, Africa.[8] This spinosaur has an unusually large number of teeth for a theropod, many more than its relative does. *Baryonyx* also has a small midline crest atop the skull; this could be a unified form of the double crest of dilophosaurs. More likely is that the side crests were lost in favor of the central one; much the same happened as tyrannosaurs evolved from allosaurs. Tall vertebral spines like those of *Spinosaurus* have not been found. Missing parts of the skeleton, including a lot of the tail, have been filled in from other members of this clade. The long, robust forelimbs have been cited as evidence of a partially quadrupedal gait. However, the arm is not really that long, and the long, slender fingers tend to argue against regular walking. The arms and the big claw were robust probably because they were defensive weapons—an interesting thing since iguanodonts, the herbivorous ornithischians that lived alongside *Baryonyx,* also had robust arms equipped with a big thumb spike for stabbing predators.

GENUS *SPINOSAURUS* Stromer, 1915

SPINOSAURUS AEGYPTIACUS Stromer, 1915
TYPE—destroyed in WW II
TIME—Cenomanian of the early Late Cretaceous
HORIZON AND DISTRIBUTION—Baharija beds of Egypt

	Type
TOTAL LENGTH—	~15 m?
TONNAGE—	~4.0?

This fantastic beast combined tremendous length with a nearly-six-foot-tall (1.6 m) fin over the back. At a possible fifty feet (an extrapolation from the type's incomplete set of vertebrae), this may be the longest known theropod, but claims that this theropod was the biggest of all and massed up to six tonnes are probably overstated.[9] Although the spinal column is a good deal longer than it is in the AMNH *Tyrannosaurus rex,* spinosaurs are much more lightly built, dilophosaur-like animals. So *Spinosaurus* probably weighed closer to 4 tonnes. But the lack of fusion between the upper and lower sections of the vertebrae indicate that this particular individual was not mature, and still had some growing to do. Aside from a number of tall spined neck, trunk, and tail vertebrae, only the front half of the lower jaw was ever found, and all are now lost. The lower jaw is deeper, more expanded at the tip, and more crocodile-like than in *Baryonyx.* The teeth are more conical and like those of crocs too, but, unlike *Baryonyx,* they are no more numerous than in most theropods. So, just which of the two species is the more advanced is not clear.

The vertebral spines were somewhat elongated over the neck. Exactly how much is not known, but they must have been only a fraction of the trunk spine's height. Likewise, the tail's neural spines were only a little elongated. The size of the fin back was unmatched by other known theropods; the fin of the allosaur *Acrocanthosaurus atokensis* was probably much lower. Strangely enough, two big herbivorous dinosaurs from mid-Cretaceous North Africa—the "duckbill" dinosaur *Ouranosaurus* and the brontosaur *Rebbachisaurus*—also have tall fins, although the locales and ages of these dinosaurs differ somewhat. Likewise, a number of spectacular fin-backed amphibians and early mammal-like reptiles such as *Dimetrodon* lived together way back in the Permian Period. Why the evolution of big sails in unrelated animals seems to cluster together is a mystery.

Despite its great size, *Spinosaurus* would have been vulnerable to attacks from the big allosaurs that shared its habitat.

Ceratosaurs

Most things about ceratosaurs—their lightly built jaw-support bones and roof of the mouth, four-fingered hand, and robust central metatarsal—are of coelophysian grade. And like *Coelophysis,* the bones of these primitive theropods show a surprising birdlike tendency to ossify and fuse within the pelvis and foot. But ceratosaurs lack such coelophysian specializations as the kinked snout, so they are not actually within that group. Also, the robust body and limbs, and the big, deep head are unlike coelophysians. The last mentioned features have led many to consider both ceratosaur species as carnosaurs, while those in the first two sentences caused others to think of them as coelurosaurs. A few advanced details, such as the head of the femur and the ankle, indicate that ceratosaurs were really the first of the post-coelophysid theropods. One thing I would really like to know is whether or not they had a pubic boot. The forward-sloping coelophysian design of the pubis suggests it did not, but Othniel Marsh said that an imprint of the boot was found in the sediments that the original *Ceratosaurus nasicornis* pubis lay in. If so, then ceratosaurs developed their own pubic boot in parallel with the more advanced theropods.

FAMILY CERATOSAURIDAE Marsh, 1884

Sarcosaurus? woodi

Ceratosaurus nasicornis
C. ? ingens

GENUS *SARCOSAURUS?* Andrews, 1921

SARCOSAURUS? WOODI Andrews, 1921
TYPE—BMNH R4840/1
TIME—Sinemurian of the Early Jurassic
HORIZON AND DISTRIBUTION—Lower Lias of England

	Type
FEMUR LENGTH—	315 mm
KILOGRAMMAGE—	~70

This is another theropod that was usually tossed into the Megalosauridae (page 280), but when I saw the type pelvis and femur at the BMNH, my mind immediately flashed ceratosaur. The pelvic bones figured in 1932 by Huene are ossified and fused, but more importantly they are nearly identical in shape to those of later *Ceratosaurus nasicornis* (see below). The strong ossification also implies the small specimen was adult. Since this lived some fifty-five million years before *C. nasicornis,* I presume this is a distinct species, if not genus, though not enough is known to be sure. That a ceratosaur was present this early is surprising, but not wholly unexpected since these were very archaic theropods. In spite of its much earlier age, the more dorsal placement of the otherwise similar femoral outer ridges imply that this may be a slightly more advanced species than *C. nasicornis.*

GENUS *CERATOSAURUS* Marsh, 1884
SYNONYM—*Megalosaurus*

CERATOSAURUS NASICORNIS Marsh, 1884
TYPE, BEST AND DISPLAY SPECIMEN—USNM 4735
TIME—Tithonian of the Late Jurassic
HORIZON AND DISTRIBUTION—Morrison Formation of the Rocky Mountain states
MAIN ANATOMICAL STUDY—Gilmore, 1924

	Type	UUVP 56
SKULL LENGTH—	625 mm	765
TOTAL LENGTH—	5.69 m	
FEMUR LENGTH—	620 mm	

The nasal-horned and big-toothed head of Ceratosaurus nasicornis.

HIP HEIGHT—   1.51 m
KILOGRAMMAGE—   524   ~980

    Despite living amongst much more advanced allosaurs, *Ceratosaurus nasicornis* was an old-style theropod. It was a bit like the thycaline, the wolf-like marsupial predator that cohabits with the Australian dingo.

    There is only one good specimen. It is from the same Garden Park quarry as the types of *Elaphrosaurus* sp. and *Allosaurus fragilis,* and is missing a fair number of pieces, including the humerus. New specimens fill in some of the gaps. Whether all these remains are one species is not known. The high ossification of the type specimen implies, but does not prove, that it is an adult, yet a large fragmentary specimen is larger still. Gilmore's very good USNM skeletal mount, with the back horizontal and the legs in a bent-knee run, was ahead of its time. At one time it was suggested that this species was so similar to *Allosaurus* that it might be the horned male of that form. But actually this is a very different animal. The most noticeable feature, the nasal horn, is rather like the ornitholestian's, but is set on a firmer base behind the nostrils. The horn is very narrow from side to side, and in life a horn sheath probably made it about half again as tall. By no means a killing weapon, the horn may have been a butting device for breeding or other disputes. Perhaps only one sex had it, though another specimen with a horn is known and none without have been found. The back of the skull is made up of remarkably light arches for such a large structure; no other big theropod's head is so very lightly built. Yet the snout is deep, and the teeth are enormous. The tooth blades are very flattened as well, unlike the stouter, smaller teeth of *Allosaurus*. *Ceratosaurus* seems to have been able to bring down relatively bigger prey than *Allosaurus*.

My look at the type convinces me that the surangular, from the back of the lower jaw, overlaps and braces the dentary from the front of the jaw like in other paleotheropods. So *Ceratosaurus* does not appear to have had the true double-jointed lower jaw that Robert Bakker draws it with.[10] But the surangular brace is shorter than in other paleotheropods, even the more advanced ones. This species, therefore, may have evolved its own kind of more flexible lower jaw to match the loose build of the rest of its skull.

This species also has an unusually straight neck for a theropod. The rib cage seems to be very flattened from side to side, quite unlike the barrel-chested allosaurs and tyrannosaurs. The trunk, hip, and tail vertebral spines are unusually tall and give this theropod a bit of a fin back, much as in *Metriacanthosaurus parkeri* and *M. shangyouensis*. The display potential of the tall spines was enhanced by something unique for a theropod—a single row of small, irregular armor scutes. This is a very primitive thecodont-like character, and whether it was inherited from

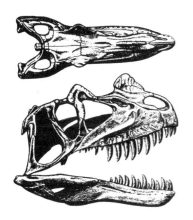

Ceratosaurus nasicornis type
USNM 4735

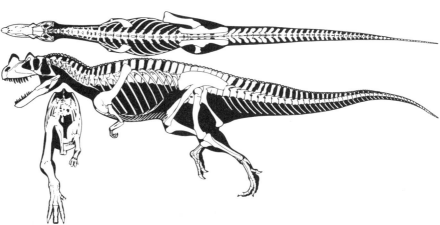

Two Ceratosaurus nasicornis have at it in a bruising yet non-lethal head-butting dispute.

those dinosaur ancestors or developed independently is not clear. The tail is both deep and broad, and unusually powerful, and may have been a sculling organ for swimming.[11] Like those of coelophysians, the hands are small and of little apparent use. Ratkevich made the bemusing claim that the co-ossified metatarsal bones of the foot made this a slow dinosaur; this in spite of the fact that fast ground birds and ungulates have co-ossified cannon bones too![12]

C. nasicornis was much less common than its neighbor *Allosaurus*. The adults of neither could safely attack the other, but big-toothed *Ceratosaurus* may have had an advantage in the fierce disputes over brontosaur carcasses.

CERATOSAURUS? INGENS (Janensch, 1920)
SYNONYM—*Megalosaurus ingens*
TYPE—HMN MB. R1050
TIME—Tithonian of the Late Jurassic
HORIZON AND DISTRIBUTION—Tendaguru Formation of East
    Africa
           Type
TONNAGE— ~5?

All that has been figured are some shed, flat-bladed ceratosaur teeth, but they are worth examining because they are quite big at nearly six inches long, and about the size of those of *Tyrannosaurus rex*. So there was a titanic killer, possibly a species of *Ceratosaurus,*[13] in the Tendaguru. This makes a lot of sense since the world's largest land animal, the brontosaur *Brachiosaurus brancai,* was abundant in the formation. A pact of big-toothed *C. ingens* would have been well able to bring down such 30-to-50-tonne prey.

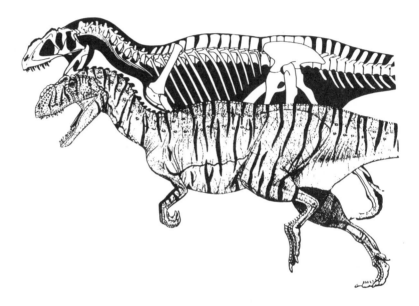

2

Late

Paleotheropods

279

Megalosaurs, eustreptospondyls, metriacanthosaurs, and other late paleotheropods always had big, deep skulls and stout necks, at least those known so far. More importantly, their hips and other details exhibit increasingly advanced features, including narrower central cannon bones. I call these intertheropods because they are intermediate to the early paleotheropods and avetheropods in design. These very successful theropods not only dominated the big predator niches in the Middle Jurassic, but did the same in South America until the very end of the Cretaceous. There they also developed sophisticated small forms.

SUBORDER INTERTHEROPODA new

The Peculiar Megalosaurs

The family Megalosauridae has wrongly included allosaurs, proceratosaurs, ceratosaurs, eustreptospondyls, dryptosaurs, and other odds and ends. True megalosaurs are most unusual theropods, and are best put in a group by themselves. What I know of the postcrania of the recently discovered abelisaurs of South America indicates that they are true, late-surviving megalosaurs—even if one of them, *Carnotaurus,* is incredibly aberrant. Even more amazing is that a *little* megalosaur with a sickle-toe claw seems to have been walking around the *latest* Cretaceous of South America. Among the megalosaurs' peculiarities is an extremely short forearm. More derived than coelophysians and *Ceratosaurus,* megalosaurs are still archaic in design, having fairly broad shoulder blades, unbooted pubes, ceratosaurlike ankles, and robust central cannon bones.

FAMILY MEGALOSAURIDAE Huxley, 1869

Megalosaurus bucklandi
M?. tanneri

Abelisaurus comahuensis

Carnotaurus sastrei

Noasaurus leali

SUBFAMILY MEGALOSAURINAE (Huxley, 1869)

GENUS *MEGALOSAURUS* Parkinson, 1822
SYNONYMS—*Poekilopleuron, Torvosaurus, Scrotum*

Much as the Megalosauridae is an often abused family, this is the most abused theropod genus. It has been used as a convenient grab bag, with more partial remains from more places and times tossed into it than any other. Long ago this practice got way out of hand, when the name was used even for Late Cretaceous theropods. Much of this supposed megalosaur material was inadequate for proper identification; some is very different and belongs to other taxa. On the other hand, a couple of differently named theropods appear to belong in this genus. The ilial blade and curved ischium of the *Torvosaurus* hip are very similar to those of the type of *M. bucklandi*. In turn, the arm of *Poekilopleuron* is like that of *Torvosaurus*. Since they all share the same exceptional design, I am tentatively uniting them in *Megalosaurus*.[1] If correct, true *Megalosaurus* ranged from Middle to Late Jurassic in age.

This is an unusually robust form, in the vertebrae, arm, and pelvis. The unbooted pubes are especially short and broad, very unlike any other post-procompsognathid theropod. As I explained in Chapter 8, this seems to be a secondary specialization, rather than truly primitive. What little is known of the skull shows that it is that of a normal big theropod.

MEGALOSAURUS BUCKLANDI Meyer, 1832
SYNONYMS—*Poekilopleuron bucklandi?, Poekilopleuron poikilopleuron?, Scrotum humanum?*
TYPE—OUM J13500 series
TIME—Bathonian of the Middle Jurassic
HORIZON AND DISTRIBUTION—Stonesfield Slate of England and Calcaire de Caen of France?
MAIN ANATOMICAL STUDIES—Parkinson, 1822; Eudes-Deslongchamps, 1838; Huene, 1926

OUM J13561

FEMUR LENGTH—	760 mm
TONNAGE—	~1.1?

This is the first named theropod dinosaur. Parkinson in 1822 was the earliest to publish it as *Megalosaurus,* and Buckland picked up the name when he described the type bones in 1824. But it did not get a species name until Meyer assigned it one in 1832. Actually, things may go back further than that, for in 1677 Plot described what looks like the lower end of a *Megalosaurus* femur.[2] He thought it belonged to a giant person. The fragment has since been lost, but Brookes refigured the bone and named it *Scrotum humanum* Brookes, 1783. Since the name was never used, it eventually became invalid. The proper type specimen is very fragmentary a dentary and its teeth, some vertebrae, an ilium, an ischium, and a femur being the main bones. Most or all of these bones may or may not belong to one individual. A number of other fragmentary remains from nearby localities may also belong to this species. Yet other remains from differing localities do not. It is all very complicated and confusing. Friedrich von Huene sorted out much of the mess in 1926, and a badly needed revision is underway. Neave Parker's restoration of *Megalosaurus*[3] is not at all satisfactory; the neck is too straight and short, the forearms too long, and the overall build too light.

Since French *Poekilopleuron buckandi* Eudes-Deslongchamps, 1838 lived at exactly the same time as *M. bucklandi* and appears to be a member of the genus, it is tentatively placed in the same species. Sad to say, the only specimen was destroyed in the last World War.

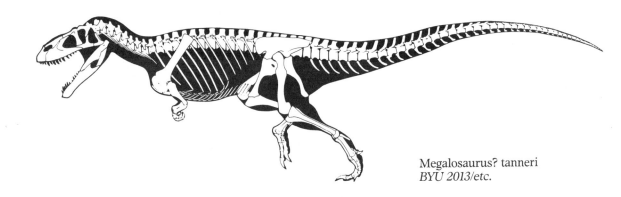

Megalosaurus? tanneri
BYU 2013/etc.

MEGALOSAURUS? TANNERI (Galton and Jensen, 1979)
SYNONYM—*Torvosaurus tanneri*
TYPE—BYU 2002
TIME—Tithonian of the Late Jurassic
HORIZON AND DISTRIBUTION—Morrison Formation of Colorado
                     BYU 2013
TOTAL LENGTH—   ~9.0 m
FEMUR LENGTH—   ~920? mm

HIP HEIGHT—   ~2.25 m
TONNAGE—   ~1.95

The remains of this species, like those of all Jurassic megalosaurs, are difficult to deal with because they are fragmentary and come scattered from various parts of a western Colorado quarry. The quarry appears to be in the uppermost Morrison; it is the same one that produced the unusually big "ultrasaur" and "supersaur" brontosaur remains. The biggest problem is that not all of the bones, which include both skull and skeletal pieces, necessarily belong to the species.[4] The skull parts are joined with those of *Abelisaurus* to render a tentative skull. The skeletal bones have been combined with other *Megalosaurus* specimens, including *Poekilopleuron*'s tail, to put together a composite restoration that might have a fair amount to do with reality.

These remains suggest that *Megalosaurus* competed with the also rare *Ceratosaurus* and common *Allosaurus* in the Morrison Formation. However, it is possible that new data will show this megalosaur's remains represent a distinct genus or genera of their own.

SUBFAMILY ABELISAURINAE (Bonaparte and Novas, 1985)

Jose Bonaparte and Fernando Novas created a new family for these recently discovered theropods, but the short forearm and megalosaurian skeleton of *Carnotaurus* indicate that they are megalosaurs. Apparently isolated on the southern supercontinent of Gondwanaland from northern competitors, these Cretaceous predators evolved in their own very, very strange ways. In one feature, a partly closed-off eye socket, they are like the allosaur *Acrocanthosaurus* and some tyrannosaurs. The front of the snout is also like those of tyrannosaurs in its shortness and depth. Yet the back of their skulls remained primitive in having slender jaw-supporting cheek bones.

Genyodectes serus Woodward, 1901 is almost certainly an abelisaur from the late Late Cretaceous of Argentina. Only the bones of the snout's tip were found. The teeth have the long length and slender build characteristic of abelisaurs, and since the front teeth do not have a D-shaped cross section, they are certainly not a tyrannosaur's, as Friedrich von Huene thought in 1923. It is possible that *Abelisaurus* is really the same thing as *Genyodectes*. But since it is no longer known which formation the latter comes from—the information was lost—it can no longer serve as a useful type and must be considered an invalid taxa. Another likely Argentinian abelisaur is *Xenotarsosaurus bonapartei* Martinez et al., 1986. Known mainly from some Late Cretaceous leg bones, it is possible that they too belong to one of the other species.

GENUS *ABELISAURUS* Bonaparte and Novas, 1985

ABELISAURUS COMAHUENSIS Bonaparte and Novas, 1985
TYPE—MC 11098
TIME—early Maastrichtian of the latest Late Cretaceous
HORIZON AND DISTRIBUTION—Allen Formation of Argentina

	Type
SKULL LENGTH—	856 mm
TONNAGE—	~1.5?

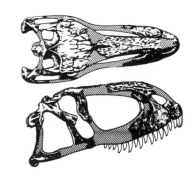

Abelisaurus comahuensis *type* MC 11098

The partial type skull is striking because of its combination of belonging to a very late age and having a primitive *Ceratosaurus* or *Yangchuanosaurus*-like appearance. Except for the partly closed-off eye socket and short snout, it probably provides the best idea of what a normal megalosaur skull looked like. Note that the skull is much less specialized than that of its earlier relative, *Carnotaurus*. The eye socket's orbital bar and simple lower cheekbones seem to link the two South American species, but this assessment may be wrong. If it is correct, then *A. comahuensis* suggests that the archaic megalosaurs survived to the end of the dinosaur era.

GENUS *CARNOTAURUS* Bonaparte, 1985

CARNOTAURUS SASTREI Bonaparte, 1985
TYPE—MACN CH894
TIME—Albian of the late Early Cretaceous
HORIZON AND DISTRIBUTION—Gorro Frigio Formation of
    Argentina

	Type
SKULL LENGTH—	570 mm
TONNAGE—	~1?

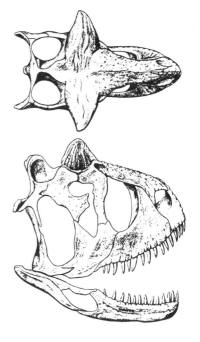

Carnotaurus sastrei *type MACN CH894*

This is easily one of the weirdest of dinosaurs. The type is a beautiful and nearly complete skull and skeleton with extensive skin impressions.[5] Found encased in a great hard, nodular concretion of rock, it has been difficult to remove from its encasement and we eagerly await illustrations of the skeleton. The most obvious skull oddities are the great orbital horns, far larger than those of any other theropod. It is easy to imagine these as butting weapons for combat with other members of its species. The whole skull is strange, in fact, being very tall for its length and strongly built. The transverse crest atop the back of the braincase is enlarged into a small frill to anchor bigger jaw and neck mus-

A close-up of newly found and incredible Carnotaurus sastrei, *showing its head and the skin that has been preserved as impressions in the sediment.*

cles. What makes it even harder to understand is that the lower jaw is quite slender and weakly put together. The teeth are rather slender, too. So while the robust skull implies great power, the mandibles and teeth indicate the opposite. Even the eyes are small for a theropod, for an orbital bar cuts off much of the eye socket. Perhaps this was to reduce the chance of eye damage during horn-butting fights. The deep snout may have contained enlarged nasal organs. Just what and how this predator hunted is not at all clear. As for the skin, by far and away the best yet found in a theropod, it includes rows of fairly large, nonbony semiconical scales, giving *Carnotaurus* a most interesting skin topography.

SUBFAMILY NOASAURINAE Bonaparte and Powell, 1980

GENUS *NOASAURUS* Bonaparte and Powell, 1980

NOASAURUS LEALI Bonaparte and Powell, 1980
TYPE—PL 4061
TIME—Maastrichtian? of the latest Late Cretaceous
HORIZON AND DISTRIBUTION—Lecho Formation of Argentina
Type
KILOGRAMMAGE— ~15?

The upper jaw's tall, simple maxilla is very like that of abelisaurs, especially *Abelisaurus* itself. It shows that the skull was fairly deep but lightly built. A better abelisaur-like character is the lack of top spines on the neck vertebrae, which instead have large upper side wings—this is mimicked in *Microvenator*. Unlike abelisaurs, the second toe is hyperextendable and has a large sickle claw, so it gets its own subfamily—indeed, if we come to know more of this theropod it may prove to warrant a separate family. Unlike true protobird sickle claws, this claw's retractor tendon anchored in a depression at the claw's base, instead of the usual kind of big, tuber-like heel process. Obviously a most unusual little beast, it would be good to know if it retained the hypershort forearm of other megalosaurs. If it did, then it could not have leaped on its victims' backs like the protobird sickle-clawed dinosaurs. Instead it might have lashed out with its claws in mid leap. Regardless, it seems that in the absence of competition megalosaurs evolved even into the small predator niches in Cretaceous South America. In doing so they became the counterparts of the northern protobird sickle-claws, long after the other archaic megalosaurs had bit the dust in the north. The evolution of such tiny forms from bulky ancestors is unusual, and helps shred up the old way of classifying theropods according to their size.

Eustreptospondylids and Metriacanthosaurs

These are the last of the paleotheropods. There also is, except for the tendency of some of the metriacanthosaurs to develop fairly tall vertebral spines, nothing fancy about the known remains. They are basic, big theropods. They show the beginnings of substantial pubic boots; the metriacanthosaurs are little more advanced on this point. *Yangchuanosaurus* also shows the initial stages of the evolution of the bird-type rib cage.

FAMILY EUSTREPTOSPONDYLIDAE new

Eustreptospondylus oxoniensis

Piatnitzkysaurus floresi

Gasosaurus constructus

Marshosaurus bicentesimus

Metriacanthosaurus? sp.
M.? shangyouensis
M. parkeri

SUBFAMILY EUSTREPTOSPONDYLINAE new

Usually, these have been considered megalosaurs or allosaurs, and they do have allosaur-like, flexible ball-and-socket neck articulations. But otherwise they are much too primitive to be allosaurs, and are quite different from the strange megalosaurs. *Eustreptospondylus* has the smallest boot at the end of its pubis so it is considered the most primitive. *Piatnitzkysaurus* and *Gasosaurus* are more like each other than either is like *Eustreptospondylus,* but enough differences exist to keep them separate genera.

GENUS *EUSTREPTOSPONDYLUS* Walker, 1964
SYNONYMS—*Megalosaurus, Streptospondylus*

EUSTREPTOSPONDYLUS OXONIENSIS Walker, 1964
SYNONYMS—*Megalosaurus cuvieri, Streptospondylus cuvieri*
TYPE AND DISPLAY SPECIMEN—OUM J13558 (juvenile)
TIME—late Callovian of the Middle Jurassic
HORIZON AND DISTRIBUTION—Middle Oxford Clay of England
MAIN ANATOMICAL STUDY—Huene, 1926

	Type
SKULL LENGTH—	~480 mm
TOTAL LENGTH—	4.63 m
FEMUR LENGTH—	520 mm
HIP HEIGHT—	1.33 m
KILOGRAMMAGE—	218

Eustreptospondylus oxoniensis type OUM J13558 juvenile

The type skeleton had long been the most complete known from England,[6] until the discovery of *Baryonyx*. The taxonomy of this specimen is very confused, and it is one of the many incorrectly placed in *Megalosaurus*. Though it has also mixed up with ambiguous *Streptospondylus*, Alick Walker finally recognized its unique status. The skull is little known, and many of the poorly ossified vertebrae are missing their upper halves. The last suggests that this lion-sized individual was not fully grown, so just how big this theropod got is not known.

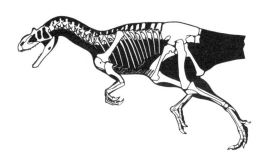

Piatnitzkysaurus floresi *type PVL 4073*

GENUS *PIATNITZKYSAURUS* Bonaparte, 1979

PIATNITZKYSAURUS FLORESI Bonaparte, 1979
TYPE, BEST AND DISPLAY SPECIMEN—PVL 4073
TIME—Callovian-Oxfordian of the Middle/Late Jurassic
HORIZON AND DISTRIBUTION—Cerro Condor Formation of
    Argentina
MAIN ANATOMICAL STUDY—Bonaparte, 1986

	Type
TOTAL LENGTH—	~4.3 m
FEMUR LENGTH—	550 mm
HIP HEIGHT—	1.4 m
KILOGRAMMAGE—	275

Little of the skull is known, but most of the skeleton is on display in Buenos Aires. This is a member of a recently discovered fauna, one that will help fill in the mid-Jurassic dinosaur gap. It is interesting that this Jurassic South American eustreptospondyl is more "advanced" than the South American megalosaurs of the Cretaceous. A medium-sized predator *P. floresi* probably made meals of juveniles and infirm adults of the large brontosaurs that shared its environment.

GENUS *GASOSAURUS* Dong and Tang, 1985

GASOSAURUS CONSTRUCTUS Dong and Tang, 1985
TYPE—IVPP V7265
TIME—Middle Jurassic
HORIZON AND DISTRIBUTION—Dashanpu of Sichuan, China

	Type
FEMUR LENGTH—	465 mm
KILOGRAMMAGE—	~160?

Not much is known of this species; a humerus, pelvis, and the femur are the most informative pieces. Like the other eustreptospondyls, it is not a very large theropod.

GENUS *MARSHOSAURUS* Madsen, 1976

MARSHOSAURUS BICENTESIMUS Madsen, 1976
TYPE—UUVP 2826
TIME—Tithonian of the Late Jurassic
HORIZON AND DISTRIBUTION—Morrison Formation of Utah

	UUVP 40-295
KILOGRAMMAGE—	~225?

Of this species we have little more than some snout bones and good pelvic elements. The pubic boot is larger than those of other members of the subfamily; in fact, it is tempting to put this theropod in the next subfamily. It does suggest that theropods of this general gestalt were present in North America.

SUBFAMILY METRIACANTHOSAURINAE new

GENUS *METRIACANTHOSAURUS* (Walker, 1964)
SYNONYMS—*Megalosaurus, Szechuanosaurus?, Yangchuanosaurus?*

Until now, all the Eustreptospondylid species discussed here have been placed in separate genera. However, the best skeletons of *M.* sp. and *M. shangyouensis* are not only from the same formation, but are alike in most details. The differences that do exist seem to be specific characters, especially the differing heights of the vertebral spines, which helped them recognize each other as members of different breeding populations. The sharing of a habitat by at least two species of the same genus is normal, as for instance the leopard *Panthera pardus* and the lion *P. leo* in Africa.

A continent away, contemporary and tall-spined *M. parkeri* appears to be even more like *M. shangyouensis* than is *M. carpenteri*. All three of these share similar hips with good pubic boots and strongly arched upper borders of the ilium, among other things. I do not like sinking *Yangchuanosaurus,* based as it is on superb skulls and skeletons, into the poorly known *Metriacanthosaurus,* but there is little choice unless new finds prove otherwise. The two tall-spined species appear to be a little more advanced than the other one, and deserve their own subgenus.

METRIACANTHOSAURUS? SP.

SYNONYM—*Szechuanosaurus campi*
DISPLAY SPECIMEN—CV 00214
TIME—Oxfordian of the Late Jurassic
HORIZON AND DISTRIBUTION—Shangshaximiao Formation of
    Sichuan, China
MAIN ANATOMICAL STUDY—Dong et al., 1983

	Type
TOTAL LENGTH—	3.8 m
FEMUR LENGTH—	420 mm
HIP HEIGHT—	1.0 m
KILOGRAMMAGE—	130

The fine jaguar-sized type skeleton is unfortunate enough to lack its skull. Originally, it was put in *S. campi,* but the type of that species consists of only a few teeth. There may be a few *S. campi*-like teeth associated with 00214, but these are rootless ones shed by another individual as it fed on the freshly deceased specimen. Although like *M. shangyouensis* (below) in many ways, this form is smaller, more slender, has shorter vertebral spines, and differs in some details. I do not think it is a juvenile of the latter, not only because it is different, but because it is better ossified than *M. shangyouensis* juveniles. Yet, there are so many uncertainties about this beast that I balk at giving it a new name.

METRIACANTHOSAURUS? SHANGYOUENSIS (Dong, Chang, Li, and Zhow, 1978)

SYNONYMS—*Yangchuanosaurus shangyouensis,*
    Yangchuanosaurus magnus
TYPE AND DISPLAY SPECIMEN—CV 00215 (juvenile)
BEST SPECIMENS—type, CV 00216

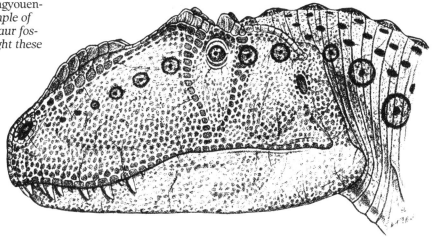

Metriacanthosaurus shangyouen-sis. *This head is an example of the wonderful new dinosaur fossils that are coming to light these days.*

TIME—Oxfordian of the Late Jurassic

HORIZON AND DISTRIBUTION—Shangshaximiao Formation of Sichuan, China

MAIN ANATOMICAL STUDY—Dong et al., 1983

	Type	CV 00216
SKULL LENGTH—	810 mm	1110
TOTAL LENGTH—	~7.9 m	~10.8
FEMUR LENGTH—	880 mm	~1200
HIP HEIGHT—	2.1 m	~2.9
TONNAGE—	1.33	~3.4

The magnificent type specimen is a product of the worldwide resurgence in dinosaur exploration that has unveiled unprecedented numbers of new forms. Only the forelimb, hind foot, and most of the tail are missing. Another species, *Y. magnus,* was based on the larger, less complete skull and skeleton 00216. But 00215's poorly ossified, and hence oddly shaped, ilium in the hip, tibia in the shank, and other bones show it is a juvenile of the former. Otherwise the two specimens are extremely similar, and the same species. This is a hefty, white-rhino-weight animal, approaching the larger allosaurs and tyrannosaurs in size.

The skull is very like that of *Ceratosaurus* and *Abelisaurus.* Still primitive, it has a single-unit lower jaw and a slender suspensorium. However the pubis is vertical and booted. Even more interesting is the well-preserved rib cage of CV 00215. It shows that the front ribs were becoming shorter and the posterior ones longer, the beginning of the birdlike rib cage and the sophisticated air-sac lung system it contains. At the same time the rib

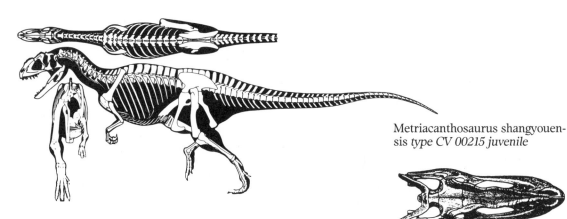

Metriacanthosaurus shangyouen-sis *type CV 00215 juvenile*

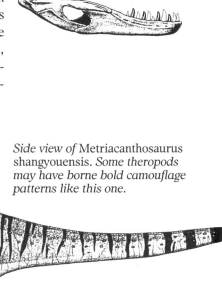

cage was rather slab-sided, like in *Ceratosaurus,* rather than broad-chested, as were allosaur's and tyrannosaur's.

The skull ornamentation resembles that of *Allosaurus,* with two parallel ridges astride the nasals and hornlets above and forward of the eye sockets. The unusually tall spines of the trunk, hip, and front tail vertebrae—though not nearly as tall as in *Altispinax* or *Acrocanthosaurus*—formed a low fin back that was highest at mid-trunk and tail base. Undoubtedly the fins were skin-covered display devices. Overall, a big, powerfully built, typically proportioned theropod with large teeth, this was a predator fully capable of taking on the adult sauropods and stegosaurs of its habitat.

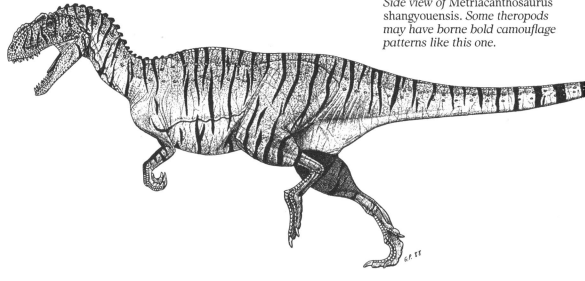

Side view of Metriacanthosaurus shangyouensis. *Some theropods may have borne bold camouflage patterns like this one.*

METRIACANTHOSAURUS PARKERI (Huene, 1926)
SYNONYM—*Megalosaurus parkeri*
TYPE—OUM J12144
TIME—early Oxfordian of the Late Jurassic
HORIZON AND DISTRIBUTION—Upper Oxford Clay of England

	Type
FEMUR LENGTH—	800 mm
TONNAGE—	~1.0

Yet again we come across a species that was long tossed into *Megalosaurus*. And again Alick Walker saved it from this unfortunate fate by recognizing this as a very different animal.[7] Not much is known of this species beyond its large size and the fact that the tall-spined vertebrae and femur are very similar to those of *M. shangyuensis*. The pubis and ilium are different enough to keep them as separate species.

Theropod Odds and Ends

These are theropods whose fragmentary remains are good enough to warrant notice, and indicate that they are either late paleotheropods or basal avetheropods, but too poor to tell which or of what kind. Such is Philippe Taquet's new small theropod of Jurassic Toarcian age from Morocco.[8] Then there is the perplexing front end of a lower jaw from the latest Jurassic Morrison Formation called *Labrosaurus ferox* Marsh, 1884. The jaw bone has an astonishingly contorted shape, and the toothless tip is deeply notched; it could come from anything from a peculiar and unknown theropod to a diseased *Allosaurus*.

ORDERS, SUBORDERS, AND FAMILIES UNCERTAIN

MEGALOSAURUS? NETHERCOMBENSIS Huene, 1923
TYPE—OUM J12143 (juvenile?)
TIME—early Bajocian of the Middle Jurassic
HORIZON AND DISTRIBUTION—Middle Inferior Oolite of England

	Type
KILOGRAMMAGE—	~175?

The skull and skeletal fragments of the rather small, possibly juvenile specimen are not enough to tell if this is *Megalosaurus* or something else.[9]

MEGALOSAURUS? HESPERIS Waldman, 1974
TYPE—BMNH R332
TIME—late Bajocian of the Middle Jurassic
HORIZON AND DISTRIBUTION—Upper Inferior Oolite of England
                         Type
KILOGRAMMAGE—   ~300?

The snout fragments and teeth of the medium-sized type specimen are, again, not sufficient to tell if this really is *Megalosaurus.*

GENUS *XUANHANOSAURUS* Dong, 1984

XUANHANOSAURUS QILIXIAENSIS Dong, 1984
TYPE—IVPP V6729
TIME—Middle Jurassic
HORIZON AND DISTRIBUTION—Lower Shaximiao Formation of
    Sichuan, China
                         Type
KILOGRAMMAGE—   ~250?

Suggestions that this is a megalosaur cannot be correct because the forearm bones are too long. However, the humerus and hand are of derived paleotheropod grade. There is a well-developed process on the shoulder blade that may have articulated with collarbones, and the paired, ossified breastplates are unusually large for a theropod, although not as large or birdlike as in some protobirds.

FAMILY ILIOSUCHIDAE? new

GENUS *ILIOSUCHUS* Huene, 1932

ILIOSUCHUS INCOGNITUS Huene, 1932
TYPE—BMNH R83
TIME—Bathonian of the Middle Jurassic
HORIZON AND DISTRIBUTION—Great Oolite of England
                         Type
KILOGRAMMAGE—   ~1.5?

Only some strikingly small ilia are available which, with their unusually prominent vertical ridge, are distinctive.

GENUS *STOKESOSAURUS* Madsen, 1974

STOKESOSAURUS CLEVELANDI Madsen, 1974

TYPE—UUVP 2938
TIME—Tithonian of the Late Jurassic
HORIZON AND DISTRIBUTION—Morrison Formation of Utah
                    UUVP 2320
KILOGRAMMAGE— ~80?

As with *Iliosuchus,* the hip's ilia are the main remains, although a premaxilla from the front of the snout may belong too. The ilia share a prominent ridge with *Iliosuchus,* and this led Peter Galton to synonymize the two genera.[10] This may be correct, but differences do exist and Galton and Powell revoked the unification in 1980. More likely, but still questionable, is that they belong to the same family. James Madsen suggested that *Stokesosaurus* may be a tyrannosaur, but the similarities are too few to make a good case for this.

PALEOTHEROPOD OR AVETHEROPOD?

FAMILY SEGISAURIDAE Camp, 1939

GENUS *SEGISAURUS* Camp, 1936

SEGISAURUS HALLI Camp, 1936

TYPE—UCMP 32101
TIME—Toarcian of the Early Jurassic
HORIZON AND DISTRIBUTION—Navajo Sandstone of Arizona
                    Type
KILOGRAMMAGE— ~5?

The one, badly beat-up skeleton of this species was found in the great and usually barren Navajo dune deposits. The head and many other elements are missing or badly damaged, so a skeletal restoration was not worth the effort. It appears to have a long, slender build of the *Coelophysis-Compsognathus* type. Usually *Segisaurus* is considered an archaic theropod, in part because it is from the Early Jurassic. Moreover, it has collarbones, unlike most theropods, and the pubes look short, broad, and unbooted. Some have even questioned whether *Segisaurus* is a theropod at all. But the foot is clearly theropodian, some advanced theropods are known to have collarbones, and the pubes may be broken— so these characters do not tell us much. As late as 1987, Gauthier cited certain other characters as supporting a primitive status.

Yet *Segisaurus* has a couple of derived theropod characters too. The shoulder blade is a thin strap, and what is preserved of the hand indicates that it was long and slender. Hence, I do not know if this species is a paleotheropod or an avetheropod; if the latter, then this is the earliest known example. A small prosauropod that is known in the Navajo was among this theropod's prey.

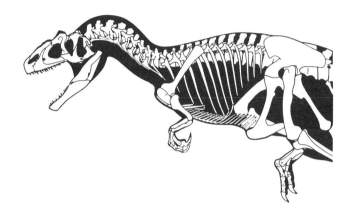

ORDER AVETHEROPODA new

The second of the two great theropod groups, this one includes both the classic tyrannosaurs and the ancestors of birds. Avetheropods are advanced dinosaurs that can be distinguished by their double-hinged lower jaws, details of the vertebrae, rib cages that contained avian-style air sac lung systems, half-moon-shaped or "lunate" wrist bones, three-fingered hands, big pubic boots, birdlike ankles, and narrow central cannon bones. If Richard Thulborn is right, then the collarbones of most avetheropods also have fused into "wishbone" furculas,[1] but this may be limited to protobirds.

Much more diverse than earlier theropods, avetheropods ranged in size from crows to giant mammoths; some flew, some browsed upon trees, and some killed with their feet. The group's first members may have appeared in the Early Jurassic, and they did well until the general collapse at the end of the Cretaceous. The birds that may have evolved from them continued through the extinction and are still happily flapping about.

B
Birdlike
Avetheropods

These are rather amorphous, primitive avetheropods; only *Compsognathus* is known from good remains. These theropods lack the characters that mark the allosaurs-tyrannosaurs and protobirds.

SUBORDER COMPSOGNATHIA new

FAMILY COMPSOGNATHIDAE Cope, 1875

GENUS *COMPSOGNATHUS* Wagner, 1861

COMPSOGNATHUS LONGIPES Wagner, 1861

SYNONYM—*C. corallestris*

TYPE—BSP 1563 (juvenile)

BEST SPECIMENS—type, MNHN CNJ 79

TIME—Tithonian of the Late Jurassic and Berriasian of the
     Early Cretaceous

HORIZON AND DISTRIBUTION—Solnhofen of Bavaria and the
     Canjuers lithographic limestone of France

MAIN ANATOMICAL STUDIES—Bidar et al., 1972; Ostrom, 1978

	Type	MNHN CNJ 79
SKULL LENGTH—	76 mm	105
TOTAL LENGTH—	.89 m	1.25
FEMUR LENGTH—	67 mm	110
HIP HEIGHT—	.21 m	.29
KILOGRAMMAGE—	.58	2.5

Little BSP 1563 was the first good dinosaur skeleton ever discovered. It did much to stimulate "Darwin's Bulldog," and caused Thomas Huxley to ally birds and dinosaurs—a great idea that unfortunately did not stick. There are continuing suggestions that *C. corallestris,* based on the bigger MNHN specimen, is a distinct species, but I agree with John Ostrom that it is an adult of the other one. The French specimen was first thought to be the same age as the type; it turns out to be a little younger, though not enough to challenge their being one species. The French specimen is important because it fills out many details of the skull and skeleton not clear in the first.

Actually, there is something downright spooky about the two German and French specimens. Both are preserved in coastal limestones in almost the same death pose.[2] The heads are thrown back over the trunk and the legs are half tucked up, which is not

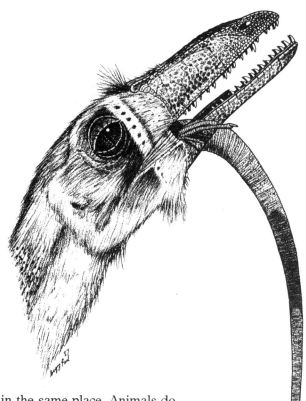

unusual, but the tails are broken in the same place. Animals do tend to assume consistent postures when dead, the tail break is a bit much though.

The slender shoulder blade, what may be a short first trunk rib, and the large half-moon-shaped carpal that seems to be in the wrist of the MNHN specimen indicate that this is an ave-theropod. Otherwise it would be considered an advanced inter-theropod. The overall form is rather *Coelophysis*-like, and the skull fairly large. But the teeth are rather small, widely spaced, and conical, with reduced serrations. The teeth are also a little heterodont, in that the front teeth are more conical than those behind, and lack any serrations. The front lower teeth radiate from one another like the spokes of a wheel, as in coelophysians. All this indicates that this house-cat-sized theropod was a full-time small-game hunter; the semiconical teeth could not do all that much damage to a big victim. This is not surprising since its home was a Jurassic European archipelago of small semiarid islands upon which only small vertebrates lived. In fact, a small, fast lizard was found in the belly of the type. *Compsognathus* may also have chased after smaller *Archaeopteryx* on occasion.

Its throat bulging, a Compsognathus longipes *swallows the long-tailed lizard* Bavarisaurus *that has been found in its belly.*

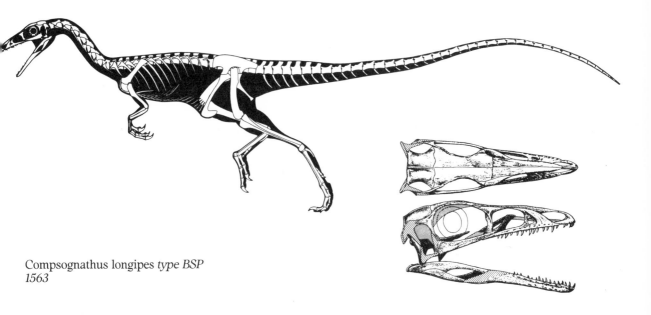

Compsognathus longipes *type BSP 1563*

The neck is moderately long, the tail exceptionally so. Ostrom suggests that the hands had only two fingers. This cannot be proven because the hand bones of the type are scattered to varying degrees over the slab of rock it lies upon, and in the other specimen the slab ends just at the hand. All in all, I doubt it. But this was a reasonable idea, quite unlike Alain Bidar and company's claim that the hand was encased in a fin, which they thought was used for swimming. The "fin" supposedly preserved in the slab is actually an artifact in the sediment. Earlier suggestions that armor is preserved with the type also proved to be sedimentary sports. Otherwise there is not much to say about the skull and skeleton except that it is gracile and typical for theropods of its size.

SUBORDER COELURIA new

In the now-outmoded system of dividing theropods into two main groups according to size, coelurosaurs were considered the smaller, lighter weight group, and contained a vast array of species. Here the group is restricted to only one or two species. Coelurosaurs are more advanced than *Compsognathus*: note the long pubic boots. These killers cannot be put in either the allosaur-tyrannosaur group or the protobirds.

FAMILY COELURIDAE Marsh, 1881

Coelurus fragilis

*Aristosuchus oweni

GENUS *COELURUS* Marsh, 1879

COELURUS FRAGILIS Marsh, 1879
SYNONYM—*C. agilis*
TYPE—YPM 1991-1993/2010
TIME—Tithonian of the Late Jurassic
HORIZON AND DISTRIBUTION—Morrison Formation of Wyoming
                    Type
KILOGRAMMAGE—   ~20?

John Ostrom is working on this species, and he concludes that a number of bones from the same place in the same quarry are a single individual, and from the type.[3] The neck is long, and the wrist has a well-developed lunate carpal. The somewhat more abundant *Ornitholestes* was its main competitor, but not knowing the skull of this one we cannot say much more about its habits.

*GENUS *ARISTOSUCHUS* Seeley, 1887

*ARISTOSUCHUS OWENI (Fox, 1866)
TYPE—BMNH R178
TIME—Barremian? of the late Early Cretaceous
HORIZON AND DISTRIBUTION—Wealden Formation of England
                    Type
KILOGRAMMAGE—   ~30?

This species' taxonomy is very convoluted.[4] The few bones known are rather like *Coelurus,* especially the pubes and neck vertebrae, so it is very tentatively put in the same family.

2

The

Allosaur-Tyrannosaur

Group

SUBORDER ALLOSAURIA new

Allosaur-tyrannosaurs are one of two main groups of avetheropods, the other being the protobirds. But instead of learning to fly, these became some of the biggest and most successful predators of all time. In fact, the forelimbs of aublysodonts' and tyrannosaurs' were almost lost, a far cry from the wings of some protobirds.

The membership of the small ornitholestians and aublysodonts in this group, in addition to the great allosaurs and tyrannosaurs, is a prime example of how the old system of sorting all small theropods into one group and all the big ones into another has fallen by the wayside. As ornitholestians, these theropods started out small 170 million years ago in the Middle Jurassic, and some members of the group were still small in the Late Cretaceous. Others soon reached the one-to-five-plus ton range, and stayed that way until the very end of the Cretaceous, some sixty-five million years ago. While allosaurs seem to be a sister group to, rather than the descendants of, ornitholestians, aublysodonts and tyrannosaurs probably were direct descendants of advanced allosaurs.

Ornitholestians and Allosaurs

It is not at all usual to put these theropods in the same group. Usually small *Ornitholestes,* somewhat larger *Proceratosaurus,* and giant *Allosaurus* are placed in various families. In fact, *Proceratosaurus* and *Allosaurus* have both been placed in the Megalosauridae. But these theropods all share unifying characters. For example, among the jaw-bearing bones at the back of the skull there is a contact between the squamosal and quadrate that is both broad, and slopes down and forward.[1] In most theropods these two bones touch each other only a little. The L-shaped upper end of the central cannon bone is also very alike and distinctive in *Ornitholestes* and *Allosaurus.*

Aside from these singularities, ornitholestians and allosaurs are fairly typical theropods, not only in overall form, but in being at about the halfway point in terms of advancement relative to other theropods. *Allosaurus,* for example, is much more derived than *Ceratosaurus,* and *Dilophosaurus,* but not as specialized as tyrannosaurs or birdlike as protobirds.

Small ornitholestians seem to have appeared first, in the Middle Jurassic, and a large species *may* have made it into the next period. The somewhat more advanced allosaurs were dominant in the Late Jurassic and early Cretaceous. If Late Cretaceous *Labocania* is an allosaur, then the group survived a surprisingly long time. As presented here the Allosauridae is also the largest theropod family, in both genera and species.

FAMILY ALLOSAURIDAE Marsh, 1878

Proceratosaurus bradleyi
P.? divesensis

Ornitholestes hermanni

*Rapator ornitholestoides

Allosaurus fragilis
A. atrox
A.? amplexus

Chiliantaisaurus? maortuensis
C. tashuikouensis

Acrocanthosaurus? altispinax new species
A. atokensis

Indosaurus matleyi

Labocania anomola

*Erectopus superbus

Carcharodontosaurus saharicus

Bahariasaurus ingens

SUBFAMILY ORNITHOLESTINAE Paul, 1988a

Proceratosaurus and *Ornitholestes* are distinguished from allosaurs proper by their nasal horns and conical piercing teeth, among other things. The horn's bony core was certainly enlarged by a horn covering. Rather like a chicken's comb in looks, it may have been used in butting fights with other members of the species. The horn differs from that of *Ceratosaurus* in being further forward on the skull, over the nostrils instead of behind them.

Another interesting thing about these dinosaurs is that the teeth are unusually heterodont—the front teeth differ substantially from the posterior ones. The front teeth are more conical, less serrated, and, in *Proceratosaurus,* smaller than those behind. This is interesting because heterodonty is usually thought of as something limited to mammals, in which the teeth are segregated into incisors, canines, and molars. The teeth at the front of the lower jaw radiate a little from each other like the spokes of a wheel. The teeth also have reduced keels and serrations. To greater and lesser extents, this is rather like *Compsognathus* and coelophysians, and *Ornitholestes* has an unusually small skull for its size. So ornitholestians were probably specialized small-game predators, and perhaps fishers too.

The neck vertebrae do not have as well developed ball-and-socket articulations as allosaurs, and the other vertebrae lack hourglass-shaped bodies. A broken, vaguely allosaur-like ankle bone from the Neocomian/Aptian age Strzelecki series of Australia was recently identified as belonging to *Allosaurus*.[2] This is probably not right; the bone is more likely to be from something like *Rapator.*

GENUS *PROCERATOSAURUS* Huene, 1926
SYNONYMS—*Megalosaurus, Piveteausaurus?*

PROCERATOSAURUS BRADLEYI (Woodward, 1910)
SYNONYM—*Megalosaurus bradleyi*
TYPE—BMNH R4860
TIME—Bathonian of the Middle Jurassic
HORIZON AND DISTRIBUTION—Great Oolite of England
                              Type
SKULL LENGTH—   275 mm
KILOGRAMMAGE—   ~100?

When first described this was yet another theropod confused with *Megalosaurus*. Friedrich von Huene later realized the error, but he thought it was a relative of *Ceratosaurus,* which inspired him to call it *Proceratosaurus*. Neither view is correct; instead this is the earliest known member of the allosaur-tyrannosaur group. It comes from deposits that bear one of those delightful Victorian titles, the Great Oolite near Minchinhampton. All that is known is a skull, and this lacks its upper third. Fortunately, a bit of the nasal horn is preserved, but its full shape is not known. The teeth in the tips of the jaws are much smaller and more conical than the rest, manifesting what is perhaps the greatest degree of heterodonty among theropods.

This is a much larger species than *Ornitholestes,* (see below) but whether *P. bradleyi* was as small-skulled relative to its body is uncertain. The skulls of these two theropods are so similar that they could be put in the same genus. However, their lower jaws differ too much to do this, since *Proceratosaurus* has a more slender, up-curved mandible. This fair-sized dinosaur was in danger from much larger *Megalosaurus*.

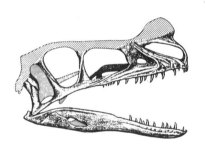

Proceratosaurus bradleyi *type*
BMNH R4860

PROCERATOSAURUS? DIVESENSIS (Walker, 1964)
SYNONYM—*Piveteausaurus divensis?*
TYPE—MNHN 1920-7
TIME—Upper Callovian of the Middle Jurassic
HORIZON AND DISTRIBUTION—Marnes de Dives Formation of
      France
MAIN ANATOMICAL STUDIES—Piveteau, 1923; Taquet and Welles,
      1977
                              Type
KILOGRAMMAGE—   ~50?

The few skeletal elements and a battered braincase indicate that this is an ornitholestian, instead of the megalosaur or allosaur it is often thought to be. Since it is so close in time and place, it may belong to the same genus as its fellow ornitholestian *Proceratosaurus.*

GENUS *ORNITHOLESTES* Osborn, 1903
SYNONYM—*Coelurus*

ORNITHOLESTES HERMANNI Osborn, 1903
SYNONYM—*Coelurus hermanni*
TYPE, BEST AND DISPLAY SPECIMEN—AMNH 619
TIME—Tithonian of the Late Jurassic
HORIZON AND DISTRIBUTION—Morrison Formation of the Rocky
    Mountain states
MAIN ANATOMICAL STUDIES—Osborn, 1903, 1916; Paul, 1987c

	Type
SKULL LENGTH—	138 mm
TOTAL LENGTH—	~2.08 m
FEMUR LENGTH—	207 mm
HIP HEIGHT—	.47 m
KILOGRAMMAGE—	12.6

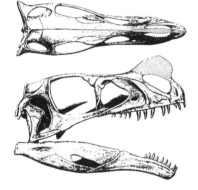

Ornitholestes hermanni *type
AMNH 619*

This is the only good small theropod known from the Morrison, a formation in which giants were the most common creatures. Fragments are scattered around the Morrison, but only one fairly complete skeleton with a complete skull has been found. This species has been mixed up with *Coelurus,* but by 1980 John Ostrom had shown that they are really quite different animals.

In my restorations I used allosaur parts to fill in gaps in the skeleton. My drawings differ much from Charles Knight's famous

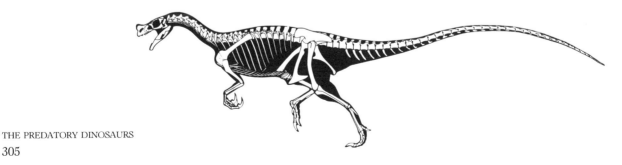

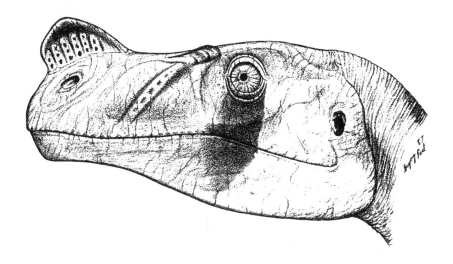

and beautiful sketch of *Ornitholestes* catching an early bird.[3] His restoration was based on Henry Osborn's first skeletal drawing, which Osborn later realized was much too long in the neck and trunk.

The head is unusually small for a predator—even this jackal-sized one—and so are the very short tooth rows, especially the lower set. Aside from fish, terrestrial prey consisted of larger insects, assorted lizards, rhynchocephalians (primitive lizard-like reptiles), hatchling dinosaurs snatched from under their parents' noses, and assorted small mammals. Why the lower jaw is so deep is unclear. The bar over the nostrils is very intriguing. Broken, it seems to flare upward at its two bases, so it probably supported a *Proceratosaurus*-like nasal horn.

The hand of AMNH 619 is very incomplete. The hand used in the restoration is an isolated specimen that appears to belong to this species, but this is hard to prove. The hip seems to be very like that of *Allosaurus*. *O. hermanni* is often put forth as an archtypical fast theropod. Actually, the lower limb elements are surprisingly short for an animal of this size. But as discussed in Chapter 6, this may not tell us much about its speed.

Surprisingly, it appears that little Ornitholestes hermanni *has a nasal horn. For a change of pace, I drew the head unfeathered and unscaled, like it is in some birds.*

*GENUS *RAPATOR* Huene, 1932

RAPATOR ORNITHOLESTOIDES Huene, 1932
TYPE—BMNH R3718
TIME—Albian of the late Early Cretaceous

HORIZON AND DISTRIBUTION—Griman Formation of New South Wales, Australia

Type

TONNAGE— ~1?

Based only on a thumb metacarpal with a peculiar inner process found elsewhere only in *Ornitholestes*, its placement in this group is hence *very* tentative. Some other large theropod bones from the Griman may belong to the species. Described as allosaur-like, they seem to fit the bill. However, Ralph Molnar has told me of his suspicions that *Rapator* is an abelisaur instead.

SUBFAMILY ALLOSAURINAE (Marsh, 1878)

A new and very nicely preserved skull from the Late Jurassic of China is very close to *Allosaurus*, except that the nasal ridges and orbital horn are combined into a prominent pair of long, low, rugose-surfaced crests. It has informally been titled "Jiangjun-miaosaurus," and other excellent bones may also belong to this taxon.[4]

GENUS *ALLOSAURUS* Marsh, 1877

SYNONYMS—*Antrodemus, Creosaurus, Epanterias?, Saurophagus*

Next to *Tyrannosaurus*, this is the theropod best known to the public. It is also the quintessential theropod, being a big-bodied, big-game predator that lacks most of the specializations of other species. Probably the best known *Allosaurus* illustrations are Charles Knight's two versions of *A. atrox* feeding on a dead brontosaur.[5] Interestingly, the sketchier of these drawings is the better, both in accuracy and feel. The more finished painting has overly large scales, and too simplistic a form. Stephen Czerkas has recently made a more up to date full size sculpture of this theropod.[6]

The skull is much stronger than a ceratosaur's, but still more open than in tyrannosaurs. On the other hand, Robert Bakker pointed out in 1986 that as in tyrannosaurs, the lower jaw's extra hinge joint was even more flexible than in most other avetheropods, to compensate for the skull's rigidity. The large snout and large cheek box contained an abundance of jaw-closing muscles, and the palate was strengthened to support an enlarged posterior pterygoideus muscle (these trends would be taken even further in tyrannosaurs). The serrated, blade teeth were rather stout, but surprisingly modest in size. Indeed, *Allosaurus* had a head that was not all that large for a theropod of its size. The head was marked by long horn ridges the edge of both nasals, and by a tall triangular hornlet in *front* of and above each orbit (not directly *above* the eye, as artists often show). These fairly sharp-rimmed ridges could have been used to deliver painful but noncutting head blows to other members of the species. This and other allosaurs are odd in that the quadrate and other jaw-supporting bones slope down and backward. Similar to *Ceratosaurus,* the backward-sloping quadrate is a return to the old archosaur condition.

Allosaurs are like tyrannosaurs in that they have an enlarged transverse crest at the back of the skull, atop the braincase. This supported a "bulldog" neck of powerful upper cervical muscles. This effect was enhanced by the unusually strong S curve of the neck. The neck was more flexible than in tyrannosaurs because of the vertebrae's forward-facing ball-and-socket joints. The trunk and front tail vertebrae are distinctive because the main bodies are pinched, hourglass-shaped spools, rather like those of the herrerasaurs.

The forelimbs were large and powerful, and bore three large claws, the inner being much the largest. Such well-developed arms must have been helpful in grappling with prey and dismembering carcasses. The moderately long hind limbs were not as specialized for speed as they were in tyrannosaurs. Although the tail was long and deep, it was rather narrow, and the toe claws were reduced and more hooflike than in earlier theropods.

Allosaurus was the most common predator in the Morrison fauna. In fact, *Allosaurus* is sort of symbolic of the Morrison, as are the great brontosaurs. Yet, there is something perplexing about the situation. The cow-to-rhino-sized camptosaurs and armored stegosaurs posed no special problem. But the Morrison herbivore fauna was dominated by 10-to-50-tonne colossi, the brontosaurs. Although not fast, brontosaurs were powerfully armed with clawed feet and long tails. One might expect the main Morrison predator to be a big-headed, big-toothed, 4-to-20-tonne brute capable of dispatching the brontosaurs on a regular basis, something like Chinese *Metriacanthosaurus shangyouensis.* Great *A. amplexus* was, at least in size, the kind of Morrison allosaur we are looking for, but it is apparently found only in the latest part of the formation. The main Morrison *Allosaurus* species was at best a two-tonner, and its head and teeth were rather small. Big-toothed *Ceratosaurus* appears to have been a better sauropod killer, except that it was yet smaller in size, and uncommon. But the situation in the Morrison may not have been all that bad. A pack of ten typical allosaurs would have weighed about fifteen tons, enough to take on brontosaurs of about that size.[7] Allosaurs could have also concentrated on the young, ill, and aged, using slash wounds to weaken and kill them. Oh, to see such a conflict! A pack of allosaurs splashing through the shallows of a stream, hoping to cull out a baby brontosaur from its herd. Some of the sauropods rear to swing out with their forefeet; others retreat to firmer ground, with the juveniles clustered among them. Brontosaur tails swish through the air.

The rather limited ability of most allosaurs to contend with adult brontosaurs may explain why their predator/prey ratios were about the lowest known in a dinosaur community (see Chapter 7, pages 164–69). *Allosaurus* was apparently much rarer in the contemporary, brontosaur-dominated Tendaguru Formation of East Africa.

ALLOSAURUS FRAGILIS Marsh, 1877
SYNONYMS—*Antrodemus valens, Antrodemus fragilis, Allosaurus atrox*
TYPE—YPM 1930

BEST AND DISPLAY SPECIMEN—USNM 4734
TIME—Tithonian of the Late Jurassic
HORIZON AND DISTRIBUTION—Morrison Formation of the Rocky Mountain states
MAIN ANATOMICAL STUDY—Gilmore, 1924

	Type	AMNH 600
SKULL LENGTH—	682 mm	810
TOTAL LENGTH—	7.4 m	
FEMUR LENGTH—	770 mm	
HIP HEIGHT—	1.8 m	
TONNAGE—	1.01	~1.7

Allosaurus fragilis is another taxonomic nightmare. It all started with part of a tail vertebra that Leidy in 1873 named *Antrodemus valens*. The vertebra is definitely allosaurid, and *Antrodemus* has been used by many authorities. But where the vertebra came from is uncertain (although the Morrison is probable), and it is hopelessly inadequate to determine the species.

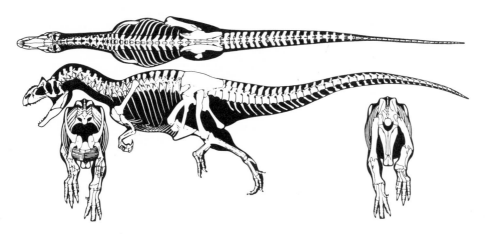

So, most dinosaurologists have abandoned the name *Antrode-mus*. Little better is the small assortment of YPM bones from the Garden Park quarry of Colorado that are the type of *Allosaurus fragilis*. These are not diagnostic to the species level either, but at least they definitely are Morrison. Better yet, the nearly complete skull and skeleton USNM 4734 comes from this quarry. Used as a "paratype," it can serve to define the species *A. fragilis*.

In looking at various *Allosaurus* restorations, you might wonder why some show a short, triangular-skulled creature, while others show a longer-snouted version. These unwittingly represent the two species of medium-sized allosaurs, *A. fragilis* and *A. atrox*. *A. fragilis* has taller, more pointed preorbital horns, and the only good skeleton is much more slenderly built than any *A. atrox,* especially in the neck and forelimb. One reason that these two types do not appear to represent the two sexes is that *A. fragilis* is much rarer than the other. And it is missing entirely from many quarries, including the Cleveland-Lloyd allosaur site. Robert Bakker believes that this species is found only in the Garden Park and other quarries of the lower Morrison formation,[8] but I think that the AMNH 600 skull, which comes from high up in the Morrison, is an *A. fragilis*.[9] Whether this species lasted until the very end of the Morrison, when giant *A. amplexus* reigned, is another question.

Although most of the skull bones of USNM are preserved, they are disarticulated and somewhat deformed. My restoration of the skull is somewhat different from Charles Gilmore's often-reproduced version, but it confirms that the skull was shorter in length and greater in height than most other theropods.

Allosaurus fragilis *USNM 4734*

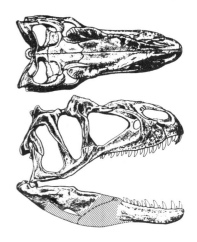

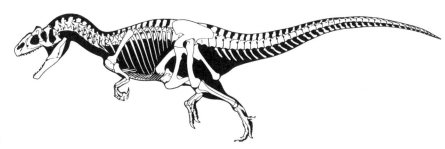

Allosaurus atrox *UUVP 6000*

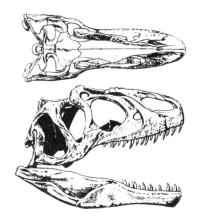

ALLOSAURUS ATROX (Marsh, 1878)

SYNONYMS—*Allosaurus fragilis, Antrodemus valens, Antrodemus fragilis, Creosaurus atrox*

TYPE—YPM 1890

BEST SPECIMEN—UUVP 6000

DISPLAY SPECIMENS—in many of the world's museums, most being casts of CLQ specimens

TIME—Tithonian of the Late Jurassic

HORIZON AND DISTRIBUTION—Morrison Formation of the Rocky Mountain states

MAIN ANATOMICAL STUDY—Madsen, 1976

	UUVP 6023	UUVP 6000	UUVP 3694
SKULL LENGTH—		845 mm	
TOTAL LENGTH—		7.9 m	
FEMUR LENGTH—	245 mm	860	905
HIP HEIGHT—		2 m	
KILOGRAMMAGE—	~30	1.32 tonnes	~1.55 tonnes

This has long been lumped in with *A. fragilis,* but Robert Bakker finds that this is a different species.[10] The type is not at all good, so I am not entirely sure *atrox* is the proper species title. Bakker also thinks it is a different genus, *Creosaurus,* a name invented by Marsh in 1878. This probably goes too far with the separation. The common Morrison theropod that shows up in almost all the quarries, it is in extreme abundance at the Cleveland-Lloyd quarry of Utah, where some four dozen individuals have been found. Juveniles down to almost one quarter adult size are common, but even these were well past the hatchling stage. This quarry also produced *Marshosaurus* and *Stokesosaurus*; it may have been a predator trap, rather like the Ice Age La Brea Tar Pits of Los Angeles. No tar was involved at the Cleveland-Lloyd, only mud, but as in the tar pits the bones are always found completely disarticulated and mixed together. Recent suggestions that a sudden flood created the quarry would not seem to explain why the herbivorous dinosaurs are so rare.

Compared to *A. fragilis, A. atrox* has a bigger, lower, more rectangular skull adorned with smaller, less triangular preorbital horns. The neck is shorter, and this and the forelimbs are more robustly built. I think it is a better proportioned and handsomer creature than *A. fragilis.* The skull of UUVP 6000 is one of the better preserved theropod skulls around. The tail and forelimb come from other specimens. No complete *Allosaurus* tail is known. James Madsen suggests there were fifty tail vertebrae, but this appears too high for such advanced theropods. Forty-five or less is more likely. Because abdominal "ribs," the gastralia, are so rare in the Cleveland-Lloyd quarry, Madsen believes that *Allosaurus* lacked them. This would be extraordinary for a theropod; their rarity is more probably due to the poor ossification of these flexible elements. The big specimen massed above is a Cleveland-Lloyd quarry femur; Edwin Colbert's 1962 2-tonne mass for an average specimen of this theropod is on the high side, even when they were carrying fat reserves.

A. atrox did not have much competition, for *A. fragilis* was uncommon and giant *A. amplexus* was apparently limited to only the upper Morrison. Indeed, it is possible that *A. atrox* did not make it into the upper Morrison; not enough is known to tell at this time. If *A. atrox* and *A. amplexus* did meet, then the first was the potential victim of the second.

ALLOSAURUS? AMPLEXUS (Osborn, 1878)
SYNONYMS—*Epanterias amplexus, Saurophagus maximus,*
    Allosaurus fragilis
TYPE—AMNH 5767
TIME—Tithonian of the Late Jurassic
HORIZON AND DISTRIBUTION—uppermost Morrison Formation of
    the Rocky Mountain states and Oklahoma
TONNAGE—   ~3–5

This is one of those dinosaurs you keep hearing about but know almost nothing about because so little has yet been published. The few original AMNH bones were first thought to belong to a brontosaur, but during 1921 Osborn and Mook showed that they were very much like *Allosaurus,* only much bigger. More complete remains were found in Oklahoma in 1934. These consist of two partial, very big skeletons, belonging to the MUO collections, from near the top of the Morrison Formation.[11] Such oversize allosaurs seem to show up only near the formation's top, so Robert Bakker notes that they cannot represent adults of the smaller *Allosaurus* species as others have implied. Alternately, if it turns out that the big allosaurs also lived in the earlier Morrison too, then they are too rare to be grown-ups of the smaller allosaurs. Instead, these specimens must be from at least one different species. It is always possible that more complete remains may yet prove that this is its own genus, *Epanterias*. The name *Saurophagus maximus* is probably redundant. This allosaur is about the same size as *Tyrannosaurus rex,* but more robust. On the other hand, this theropod was certainly less powerful than the great-skulled *T. rex.* Its stout bulk has caused some to think of it as a slow scavenger that specialized in taking over carcasses from more agile smaller allosaurs. This is an obsolete concept, and *A. maximus* was really a good runner and hunter, like all predaceous theropods.

It is not known whether *A. amplexus* evolved from one of the other two Morrison allosaurs, or moved in from someplace else. That *A. amplexus* may come from the last part of the Morrison is interesting because the formation's brontosaurs may have been becoming much bigger at this time. If so, then *A. amplexus* was the kind of theropod that had long been missing from the Morrison, one that may have come in to kill the formation's giant brontosaurs. Certainly a pack of these behemoths could bring down even a healthy adult sauropod. Dinosaurs remains above the Morrison Formation are rare, making it hard to tell if *A. amplexus* was ultimately successful at this life-style.

GENUS *CHILANTAISAURUS* Hu, 1964

Although it has been suggested that these species were ceratosaurs or megalosaurs, they are clearly allosaurs, with downswept back wings of the braincase and a medium-sized, L-shaped central cannon bone. Along with indosaurs and labocanians, these seem to be heavily built advanced allosaurs fairly close to the tyrannosaur's ancestry.

CHILANTAISAURUS? MAORTUENSIS Hu, 1964
TYPE—IVPP V. 2885
TIME—late Early? Cretaceous

HORIZON AND DISTRIBUTION—Maortu deposits of Inner Mongolia

Type

KILOGRAMMAGE— ~600?

This species is so poorly known that it is not possible to tell whether it really is in the same genus as *C. tashuikouensis* (below), or if on the other hand it is the same species. What is known suggests that they are similar animals.

CHILANTAISAURUS TASHUIKOUENSIS Hu, 1964

TYPE AND BEST SPECIMEN—IVPP V. 2884
TIME—early Late? Cretaceous
HORIZON AND DISTRIBUTION—Tashuikou deposits of Inner
    Mongolia

Type

FEMUR—   1190 mm
TONNAGE— ~4?

This is a very big allosaur, approaching the bigger tyrannosaurs in size. The arm is very massive and big-clawed, even for a big allosaur, and the humerus has a *very* prominent deltoid crest. In addition to a few skull and arm bones most of the hind limb is known, but not much else.

GENUS *ACROCANTHOSAURUS* Stovall and Langston, 1950
SYNONYMS—*Altispinax?*, *Megalosaurus?*

ACROCANTHOSAURUS? ALTISPINAX new species
SYNONYMS—*Megalosaurus bucklandi, Megalosaurus dunkeri,*
    Altispinax dunkeri
TYPE—BMNH R1828
TIME—Hauterivian? of the early Early Cretaceous
HORIZON AND DISTRIBUTION—Wealden Formation of England

Type

TONNAGE— ~1?

The type, which is just three tall-spined trunk vertebrae, was first placed in the much earlier *Megalosaurus bucklandi* by Sir Richard Owen in 1855. By 1926, Friedrich von Huene had associated them with another supposed megalosaur, *M. dunkeri,* from the Wealden, noting that neither could be *Megalosaurus* and proposing the new generic title *Altispinax*. But the type of *M. dunkeri* is only a tooth that may or may not go with the vertebrae, and a new species name has never been proposed, so von Huene's generic name has never been validated. Besides, the vertebrae are very similar to *Acrocanthosaurus atokensis,* and are best placed in that genus. Because this British acrocanthosaur is somewhat older than the American one, a new species is prudent, so I reemploy the name von Huene invented for it. If the one specimen is adult, and it may not be, then the species is smaller than *A. atokensis.* The spines' heights were moderate at about 350 mm.

ACROCANTHOSAURUS ATOKENSIS Stovall and Langston,
    1950
TYPE—MUO 8-0-S9
TIME—Aptian-Albian of the late Early Cretaceous
HORIZON AND DISTRIBUTION—Trinity Formation of Oklahoma

	Type	MUO 8-0-S8
TOTAL LENGTH—	~8 m?	
TONNAGE—	~2.3?	~3.1?

This is a special allosaur genus because the greatly elongated vertebral spines gave it a "fin" running atop the neck, back, and tail. Much of the rest of this large animal is rather straightforward allosaur, including the downswept braincase wings, flexible ball-and-socket neck vertebrae, long yet shallow pubic boot, and L-shaped central cannon bone. The preorbital horn was low, and it seems to have the same kind of projection of postorbital bone into the orbit seen in abelisaurs and some tyrannosaurs. The latter, among other things, has led to suggestions that this is in fact a tyrannosaur, but although it has a number of tyrannosaur features, it definitely is not one yet. Only two incomplete skeletons are published, but a newly found, bigger, and much better specimen will tell us a lot more.

Suggestions that this finback is a close relative of fin-backed *Spinosaurus* are falsified by the extreme differences in the rest of their morphology. Actually, even the fins differ. The acrocanthosaur fin starts just behind the skull and runs back to at least the front half of the tail. In the type specimen, it is some 200 to 300 mm tall over the neck and tail. The spines are incomplete over the back; if they were like those of *A. altispinax* then they were perhaps 500 mm tall. If so, then the *Acrocanthosaurus* sail was a very long but only moderately tall one; a better-developed copy of what is found in ceratosaurs and metriacanthosaurs, but quite unlike the short fore and aft length, ultra-tall fin of *Spinosaurus.*

GENUS *INDOSAURUS* Huene and Matley, 1933

INDOSAURUS MATLEYI Huene and Matley, 1933
TYPE—GSI K27/565
TIME—Coniacian-Santonian of the mid Late Cretaceous
HORIZON AND DISTRIBUTION—lower Lameta Group of central
    India

	Type
KILOGRAMMAGE—	~700?

Like the other late allosaurs, not much of this animal has been found. And also like most of the other late allosaurs, it was a heavily built, if small creature. It may have had big preorbital horns. This advanced Indian allosaur competed for armored ankylosaurs and brontosaurs with the early tyrannosaur *Indosuchus.*

GENUS *LABOCANIA* Molnar, 1974

LABOCANIA ANOMALA Molnar, 1974
TYPE—LACM 20877
TIME—Campanian of the late Late Cretaceous
HORIZON AND DISTRIBUTION—La Bocana Roja Formation of Baja
    California

	Type
TONNAGE—	~1.5?

The few known bones share similarities with chilantaisaurs and indosaurs on the one hand and tyrannosaurs on the other, and they have some peculiarities of their own. For instance, the hip's pubes and ischia are tyrannosaurian. Yet, the short backward-sloping, jaw-supporting quadrate is classic allosaur, and the front teeth are not yet D-cross-sectioned. So this is another specialized allosaur competing with tyrannosaur relatives. It is the last known allosaur, but allosaurs may well have survived right up to the final extinction. Although the skull seems rather small for the animal, it is very heavily built.

GENUS *ERECTOPUS* Huene, 1923
SYNONYM—*Megalosaurus*

ERECTOPUS SUPERBUS (Sauvage, 1882)
SYNONYMS—*Megalosaurus superbus, Erectopus sauvagi*

TIME—Albian of the late Early Cretaceous
HORIZON AND DISTRIBUTION—Sables du Gault of France

Type

FEMUR LENGTH—   470 mm
KILOGRAMMAGE—   ~200

By no means a megalosaur as first named, this little-known theropod *seems* to be another advanced allosaur approaching the tyrannosaur condition. I say so because even though it appears that there are still three fingers left on the hand, they and their claws are reduced, like those of the two-fingered tyrannosaurs. Other details, on the femur and the long foot, also suggest such a position, but we need more remains to be sure. In particular, the possibility that *Erectopus* is a primitive aublysodont cannot be dismissed. As with the following *Carcharodontosaurus saharicus,* I have not been able to pin down the location or number of the type specimen.

GENUS *CARCHARODONTOSAURUS* Stromer, 1931
SYNONYM—*Megalosaurus*

CARCHARODONTOSAURUS SAHARICUS (Deperet and
    Savornin, 1925)
SYNONYM—*Megalosaurus saharicus*
TIME—Albian-early Cenomanian of the Early-Late Cretaceous
HORIZON AND DISTRIBUTION—Baharija and other beds of north
    Africa
TONNAGE—   ~4?

Both *Carcharodontosaurus* and *Bahariasaurus,* (below) are based on such scrappy remains that I am not sure exactly what to make of them. The material does seem to show that two different, gigantic, and advanced tyrannosaur-like allosaurs lived together in the Baharija beds, alongside the much more archaic *Spinosaurus.* The type of *C. saharicus* is some distinctively straight-shafted teeth and some heavy-set advanced allosaurian skull bones bear such teeth. These vaguely sharklike teeth hint that *Carcharodontosaurus* had independently developed a unique way of cutting out wounds, rather than slicing the victim. Assorted skeletal elements have also been assigned to the species.

GENUS *BAHARIASAURUS* Stromer, 1934

BAHARIASAURUS INGENS Stromer, 1934
TYPE—destroyed in WW II
TIME—Albian-early Cenomanian of the Early-Late Cretaceous
HORIZON AND DISTRIBUTION—Baharija and other beds of north
    Africa
TONNAGE—   ~4?

Like *Carcharodontosaurus,* this theropod was tossed off as
a megalosaur. But a femur attributed to this species is classic
allosaur, the pubes are very narrow like tyrannosaur's, and in
the shank the fibula is of the tyrannosaur mold also. In fact, this
advanced allosaur's gracile build is the most tyrannosaur-like of
the group.

The Great Tyrannosaurs and Their Relatives

Although complete skeletons of *Allosaurus* were discovered
first, tyrannosaurs are the classic big theropods in the public's
eye, especially *Tyrannosaurus rex.* Some fragmentary theropods
rival the biggest tyrannosaurs in size, but no other theropod
group is as well-known anatomically, ranges so much in size, or
shows such a formidable combination of size, speed, and weaponry. These facts help make tyrannosaurs among my favorite
dinosaurs. Although the small aublysodonts are poorly known,
their combination of a very short arm, D-cross-sectioned front
teeth, and other details indicate that these are a very close sister
group to tyrannosaurs.

As for the tyrannosaurs proper, their basic characteristics
are known to most children: a very big heavy skull, powerful
bulldog neck, diminutive two-fingered forelimbs, and long powerful hind limbs. To this can be added a short, deep, and very
broad chest, a rather short, slender tail, and a deep but remarkably narrow hip. The big tyrannosaurs are anatomically quite
uniform; once you've seen one you have kind of seen them all.
But they are worth seeing; their form is exceptionally beautiful
and elegant, yet terrible and formidable.

The tyrannosaurs are very advanced theropods, birdlike in
some ways, but also their own in having a suite of distinctive
adaptations not found elsewhere. All these adaptations define

This sketch of the jaw-closing muscles of Tyrannosaurus torosus *shows the immense power behind the bites of tyrannosaurs. Notice the muscles supported by the crest atop the back of the skull, and the dashed line shows the path taken into the hollow lower jaw by some of the muscle fibers.*

how they hunted. In fact, one of the nice things about tyrannosaurs is that it is obvious what they were up to—unlike undersized *Allosaurus* or weird *Carnotaurus.* These were superpredators, built to tackle the biggest, most powerful game they could find.

To start with, no other known theropods had such large, stoutly constructed skulls and jaws. The broad snout, with its upcurved tooth row, is deep and heavily constructed. Both tyrannosaurs and aublysodonts had reduced preorbital openings; deepened maxillas and short premaxillas added strength to their snouts. Their premaxillas are deep, heavy, and support an exceptional and critical skull feature, D-cross-sectioned premaxillary teeth. The teeth increase rapidly in size going toward the mid jaw, so more of the teeth would cut into the flesh. Hence the "scoop bite" was further elongated and deepened. In tyrannosaurs the cheekbones are unusually massive, especially the greatly expanded squamosal and quadratojugal articulation that almost splits the cheek opening in two. Even the vomer bones in the front of the roof of the mouth have a unique, broad diamond shape that further strengthens the snout.[12] In two tyrannosaurs of very different size, *A. lancensis* and *T. rex,* many of the skull bones are tightly ossified together. All this bracing greatly reduced the skull's flexibility, to the point that it was probably no longer critical to the function of the skull. Sheer strength was the main criterion.

Tyrannosaur lower jaws are also exceptionally strong and deep, especially aft, where they may be almost as deep as the skull. Even the side of the back half of the lower jaw bulges outward to help accommodate more jaw muscles. The dentaries are rather short and stout. However, one head joint was made *more* flexible in order to compensate for the inflexible skull: the lower jaw's mid-length hinge joint.[13] These jaws must have been powered by massive muscles, and the cheek box *was* enormous, with an exceptionally large transverse crest at the top of the braincase expanded into a small frill that helped provide vast space for temporal muscles. The heavily built roof of the mouth and the deep rear section of the mandible show that the posterior pterygoideous muscle was more expanded than in other theropods. This gave tyrannosaurs an unusually and wickedly strong bite. The very large back surface of the skull, which included the transverse braincase crest, and the large neck vertebrae supported the most powerful "bulldog" set of neck muscles found in the theropods. The power of the neck directly enhanced the power of the skull.

Another striking feature of the tyrannosaur skull is the forward orientation of the eye sockets. Albertosaurs are broader behind the orbits than are allosaurs; *Albertosaurus lancensis* and *Tyrannosaurus* are even more so. The resulting binocular vision was somewhat less than a dog's, and much less than a human's, but it was quite good, especially in *T. rex*. It must have allowed them to deliver wounds more accurately than most other predacous dinosaurs. Some frontal bones from above the eye sockets may belong to aublysodonts, and they indicate that their binocular vision was limited.[14]

As detailed in Chapter 6, the tyrannosaur's unusually long, powerful, and gracile hind limbs (equaled only in some protobirds) made them among the fastest animals in earth's history. Their hips were not only very large, they are remarkably narrow from side to side. Certainly no known animal as big as *T. rex* was ever any faster.

The tyrannosaurs' and aublysodonts' very small forelimbs were useless for grappling with prey. Much speculation has been directed toward the use of these forelimbs, which, in tyrannosaurs at least, had only two fingers. This obsession is misplaced —the reduced size of the forelimbs shows they were not important to their owners, so they should not be important to us. In fact, in *Tyrannosaurus* and even more so in *Albertosaurus* the forelimbs became *ever smaller with time* and were on their way to complete loss. The shoulder blade did remain a strong rod,

The musculature of the tyrannosaur Albertosaurus libratus *AMNH 5458. The great power of the legs contrasts sharply with the atrophied forelimbs.*

but this was because it anchored powerful neck-skull muscles. Newman's suggestion of 1970 that tyrannosaurs used their arms to stabilize their bodies as they got up from the ground is unlikely. The forelimbs are so short that using them to help stand would require an awkward rear-end-up-first motion. It must have been easier to just stand straight up on the hind limbs alone, like a big bird does. That tyrannosaur humeri were often broken in life shows they were too unimportant to be strong enough for such functions. It is possible that at least the more slender-necked species used their fingers to pick their teeth, but even here the longer forelimbs of other theropods would have done a better job.

One often reads about the tyrannosaur's supposedly "eagle-like" feet and how they did nasty things to their prey with them. Nothing could be further from the truth. Tyrannosaur hind claws are greatly reduced, being short, broad, and rounded. Only ostrich-mimics have equally blunt, hooflike claws. Like some other avetheropods, tyrannosaurs could deliver a stun-mean kick with their powerful hind limbs. They probably fought intraspecific disputes like overgrown ostriches, balancing on one foot and pushing out with the other. But the claws were not important in dispatching prey.

A couple of Tyrannosaurus torosus *settle an argument by kicking at each other like overgrown ostriches. Although the kicks were immensely powerful, the blunt toe claws did not inflict much damage. The setting is a cattail marsh.*

Now we can get down to the real reason for the reduction of the arms, toe claws, and tail in aublysodont-tyrannosaurs. It was a way of directing a larger portion of their body mass to what was important to them—their head and legs.[15] Hence they were fast predators that dispatched prey with the head alone. Along with their binocular vision and D-shaped front teeth, these factors are clues to how tyrannosaurs hunted. It was an especially devilish variation of the big theropod tactic of avoiding a dangerous, extended grapple with the prey. They dashed in at speeds that may have rivaled those on the racetrack, then, as the tyrannosaur's binocular vision suggests, they accurately bit down and forward. Powering the tooth arc with their immense jaw and neck muscles, aublysodonts and tyrannosaurs could quickly cut out long, deep, cup-shaped wounds much worse than the slash marks made by other theropods. Considering that many or most of the Late Cretaceous prey animals were the great, fast-horned dinosaurs, the ability to cripple the target in one stroke was vital. Tyrannosaurs were especially adapted for this task.

Display devices in this group include a row of rugose irregularities atop the long, narrow nasal bones. This centerline ridge, which had replaced the twin nasal ridges of the ancestral allosaurs, supported a long, low, narrow horn boss. Whether this ridge boss was smooth, rough, or made of individual hornlets, is not certain. I suspect one of the latter two. Certainly this was not a tall horn as in ceratosaurs, because a prominent horn core is absent. There are also two paired horn bosses over the eyes. The aft set tends to be semicircular, and varies in size. The more ridgelike forward set varies a good deal more among the species. In albertosaurs the preorbital horn tends to be taller than the postorbitals. In *Tyrannosaurus* the aft set tends to become the taller one, while the preorbital horns flatten out and merge toward the skull roof midline, forming a broad plate. All of these may have been butting weapons, used like the short horns of giraffes to pummel the heads and sides of opponents of their own species. The boss on the cheek below the orbits is distinctive to tyrannosaurs, and I am sure it bore a little hornlet.

Aublysodonts and tyrannosaurs appear to have been the culmination of the ornitholestid-allosaur-tyrannosaur group. As such, they were protobird relatives. Appearing on the Mesozoic scene rather late, around the middle of the Cretaceous, they continued on until the final dinosaur extinction at 65 MYBP. These theropods are best known from western North America and Central Asia, where tyrannosaurs were spectacularly successful. In America, species of *Albertosaurus* were the first to appear and were common until they were partly displaced by species of *Tyrannosaurus*. There always seem to have been two, three, or even more tyrannosaur species living at the same time and place in western North America. Notably, the massive skulls and speed of the tyrannosaurs allowed them, and the smaller aublysodonts, to partly suppress both allosaurs and the big-brained sickle-clawed protobirds. Things were somewhat different in arid Mongolia. Here tyrannosaurs were small and not that common until near the end, when one giant *Tyrannosaurus* species became common and coexisted with the still abundant sickle-claws.

For many years the tyrannosaur family was named Deinodontidae. But because *Deinodon* itself was based on some hopelessly fragmentary remains, in 1970 Dale Russell resurrected Osborn's Tyrannosauridae. Actually, the Rules of Zoological Nomenclature favor the older name, but Tyrannosauridae has understandably become accepted. *Aublysodon* is different enough to deserve its own subfamily. A number of people are getting involved in taking a second look at tyrannosaurs. Robert Bakker has some new, interesting, and controversial ideas about them, Ken Carpenter is conducting research, and Philip Currie and I are engaged in a long-term study of the group. To arrive at a solid understanding of tyrannosaurs will take time. A lot of the genera and species are poorly defined, and many new and old specimens have to be prepared or reworked before we can figure out what is really going on.

Because they are the second largest theropod family, and particularly because more tyrannosaur species—six—are known by complete remains than in any other family, there are many tyrannosaur illustrations in this book. Besides, they are irresistible subjects. Tyrannosaurs were the final and greatest expression of big theropod evolution, and the best looking. Never before or since has the world seen anything like them.

FAMILY TYRANNOSAURIDAE Osborn, 1906

Aublysodon mirandis
A. huoyanshanensis
A. molnaris new species

Indosuchus raptorius?

Alioramus remotus

Albertosaurus? olseni
A. libratus
A. arctunguis
A. megagracilis new species
A. sarcophagus
A.? ("*Nanotyrannus*") *lancensis*

Tyrannosaurus (Daspletosaurus) torosus
T. (Tyrannosaurus) bataar
T. (T.) rex

SUBFAMILY AUBLYSODONTINAE Nopsca, 1928

These small, lightly built tyrannosaurids differ from more advanced tyrannosaurs in that the front teeth are unserrated. Their snouts are also distinctive, having low nasals and a sharp triangular profile. And their lower jaws are slender. But they were big-game hunters nonetheless—all, except perhaps for a tiny theropod from the Late Cretaceous of Mongolia whose snout Andrei Elzanowski is studying. It looks aublysodont to me, but it has conical piercing teeth for hunting insects and very small vertebrates. Another unanswered question is whether their very short forelimbs had only two fingers. Not quite enough is known about these theropods to do a skeletal restoration yet, but we can describe them as basically small, sharp-snouted tyrannosaurs with an upturned dentary tip.

GENUS *AUBLYSODON* Leidy, 1868
SYNONYM—*Shanshanosaurus*

AUBLYSODON MIRANDIS (Leidy, 1868)
TYPE—ANSP 9535
TIME—late Campanian of the late Late Cretaceous
HORIZON AND DISTRIBUTION—Judith River Formation of Alberta
    and Montana
NMC 343

KILOGRAMMAGE— ~80?

This species is based on an unserrated D-cross-sectioned premaxillary tooth from the Judith River. Philip Currie has some new Judith River bones that may belong to this primitive tyrannosaurid; I hope more complete remains will show up and tell us more.

AUBLYSODON HUOYANSHANENSIS (Dong, 1977)

SYNONYM—*Shanshanosaurus huoyanshanensis*
TYPE—IVPP V4878
TIME—Campanian? to Maastrichtian of the late Late Cretaceous
HORIZON AND DISTRIBUTION—*Subash Formation of China*

	Type
SKULL LENGTH—	~280 mm
FEMUR LENGTH—	275 mm
KILOGRAMMAGE—	~50?

The snout and premaxillary teeth of this again fragmentary form are very like those of the American remains above and can be put in the same genus.[16] Its tyrannosaurid skeletal elements prove that it was not a dromaeosaur.

AUBLYSODON MOLNARIS new species

TYPE—LACM 28741
TIME—Maastrichtian of the latest Late Cretaceous
HORIZON AND DISTRIBUTION—Hell Creek Formations of Montana
MAIN ANATOMICAL STUDY—Molnar, 1978

	Type
SKULL LENGTH—	~450 mm?
KILOGRAMMAGE—	~200?

The "Jordon theropod" type snout from Montana has the same shape and front teeth as the other aublysodonts, so it most likely belongs to the same genus. This specimen's bigger size, bigger teeth and more robust snout indicate it is a little closer to tyrannosaurs proper than the other two species are. I have named it after its describer.

SUBFAMILY TYRANNOSAURINAE (Osborn, 1906)

Allosaur-like *Indosuchus* and knobby-nosed *Alioramus* are rather odd, but the rest of the tyrannosaur genera and species are distinctly uniform. Still a few distinctive characters, including size, robustness, and features of the skull mark these genera and species. Generally, at 2500-to-10,000 + -kg *Tyrannosaurus* is bigger, more robust (even when similar in size), bigger-toothed, deeper-jawed, and shorter-snouted than 500-to-2500-kg *Alberto-saurus*. The two groups are further distinguished by the way they evolved. Big albertosaurs appear to have become increasingly more gracile, while remaining about the same size. *Tyrannosaurus* became ever larger and more robust with time. At the same time the two clades parallel one another. For example, both independently develop a bony process in the orbit, and both reduce their forelimbs with time.

Other tyrannosaur taxa have been described, but most are dubious. Philip Currie believes that some teeth and other bones suggest that a new, small gracile tyrannosaur was present in the Judith River Formation. There is also, from what I have seen of it, what appears to be a gracile late Late Cretaceous albertosaur newly found in Alabama.

GENUS *INDOSUCHUS* Huene, 1933

INDOSUCHUS RAPTORIUS Huene, 1933
TYPE—GSI K27/685
TIME—Coniacian-Santonian of the mid Late Cretaceous
HORIZON AND DISTRIBUTION—lower Lameta Group of central
    India
MAIN ANATOMICAL STUDIES—Huene, 1933; Chatterjee, 1978
                    Type
SKULL LENGTH—   ~750 mm
TONNAGE—   ~1?

Only well-preserved but isolated skull pieces have been found. I was skeptical about identifying them, but Sankar Chatterjee showed that they have D-cross-sectioned premaxillary teeth in the tip of the upper jaw, a tall, broad-tipped snout, a heavy dorsally convex maxilla, tyrannosaurian-type skull roof openings, and a narrowing of the skull bones above the orbits which suggests that binocular vision was already present. Because India was supposed to have been an isolated continent at this time, with its own unique fauna, there have been arguments that *Indosuchus* could not have been a tyrannosaur. But the bones say *Indosuchus* really was a small, heavily built, and very primitive tyrannosaur that in many ways was still like the advanced allosaurs it evolved from. Along with the allosaur *Indosaurus, Indosuchus* probably hunted the ankylosaurs and juvenile brontosaurs that shared its habitat.

GENUS *ALIORAMUS* Kurzanov, 1976

ALIORAMUS REMOTUS Kurzanov, 1976
TYPE—GI 3141/1
TIME—early Late Cretaceous
HORIZON AND DISTRIBUTION—Nogon-tsav Formation, Mongolia

	Type
SKULL LENGTH—	~700 mm
TOTAL LENGTH—	~6 m?
KILOGRAMMAGE—	~700?

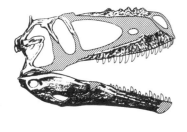

Alioramus remotus *type GI 3141/1*

This is the most recently discovered and unusual tyrannosaur. There is only one species, and since only an incomplete skull and skeleton is known, a skeletal restoration is not possible. One unusual point about this animal is the prominent, crinkly horn ridge on the nasals. However, such variation in horn morphology is just the kind expected between species, so this is not what makes this a seperate genus. What is really different about *Alioramus* is the lower jaw, which is much slimmer, straighter, longer in the dentary, and less advanced than the tyrannosaurs discussed below. The upper jaw's large maxillary bone is also lightly built, with a larger preorbital depression. In these respects this is one of the least advanced tyrannosaurs.

Otherwise, what is known of this genus and species is typical tyrannosaur in design, and looks rather like a small *Albertosaurus*. The unusual nasal ridge probably supported a much more prominent and irregular nasal horn than in other tyrannosaurs, but still not as tall a one as in *Ceratosaurus*.

GENUS *ALBERTOSAURUS* Osborn, 1905
SYNONYMS—*Alectrosaurus? Deinodon, Gorgosaurus*

For a long time, *Albertosaurus* was better known as *Gorgosaurus,* but in 1970 Dale Russell decided that the first name has priority. This may not have been the best thing. The problem is that the type skull of *Albertosaurus,* which is that of *A. sarcophagus,* is so badly preserved that much work will have to be done on it and other specimens in order to determine exactly what the genus encompasses. *Albertosaurus* appears to be restricted to North America, with the apparent exception of the Mongolian *A. olseni.* Perhaps it did not favor the drier habitats of Asia. Why this would be so is not obvious since big predators are often catholic in habitat choice.

This genus is generally less advanced than *Tyrannosaurus* in having a lower, longer-snouted, shallower-jawed, lighter skull with less interbracing in the skull roof. The adult's teeth are smaller, and point more backward than in *Tyrannosaurus*. There are fewer differences in the skeleton, though *Albertosaurus* never got larger than a white rhino. In a sense the species of *Albertosaurus* can be regarded as tyrannosaurian "foxes" relative to the more robust *Tyrannosaurus* "wolves and jackals." Russell made the pertinent observation that the slender albertosaurs may have tended to hunt the more easily dispatched duckbills, leaving the formidable horned dinosaurs for stouter *Tyrannosaurus*.

The members of this genus are very similar, except for *A. lancensis*, which is more *Tyrannosaurus*-like than the others, and at the least needs its own subgenus. *A. libratus*, *A. arctunguis* and *A. megagracilis* appear to form an increasingly advanced, shorter-armed, and gracile lineage.

ALBERTOSAURUS? (ALECTROSAURUS?) *OLSENI* (Gilmore, 1933)

SYNONYM—*Alectrosaurus olseni*

TYPE—AMNH 6554

TIME—early? Late Cretaceous

HORIZON AND DISTRIBUTION—Iren Dabasu Formation of Mongolia

	Type
SKULL LENGTH—	~600 mm
TOTAL LENGTH—	~5 m
KILOGRAMMAGE—	~500?

This poorly known species has a number of uncertainties about it. It is usually placed in its own genus because of the enormous forelimb bones found with the very incomplete type specimen. I am very skeptical about these forelimbs, however, because they look very like those of *Therizinosaurus* and segnosaurs, which are also in Mongolia. In fact, more recent finds assigned by Perle in 1977 to *A. olseni* show a typically slender tyrannosaur shoulder blade that could not support such a big arm. Perle drew a nearly complete skull reconstruction which, although too schematic to adapt for use here, is very like other albertosaurs, including the short teeth. It also lacks *Alioramus*'s peculiar nasal ridge. The hind limb is long and in most ways *Albertosaurus*-like. All in all, this looks like a small, primitive

Albertosaurus libratus *adult and youngster? Or two species? Drawn to the same scale, note that the smaller individual's teeth, which are partly covered by the lips, are absolutely larger than the bigger one's. On the side of the lower jaw, the bulge of the surangular bone typical of tyrannosaurs can clearly be seen.*

Asian albertosaur, primitive enough that it may be its own subgenus, or even genus, *Alectrosaurus*. It hunted the segnosaurs, protoceratopsids, and juvenile hadrosaurs in its area.

ALBERTOSAURUS LIBRATUS (Lambe, 1914)
SYNONYMS—*Gorgosaurus libratus, Albertosaurus sternbergi*
TYPE—NMC 2120
BEST SPECIMENS—type, TMP 85.62.1, AMNH 5458, FMNH
    PR308?, AMNH 5336?, USNM 12814? (juvenile?), AMNH
    5664? (juvenile?), ROM 1247? (juvenile?)
SPECIMENS ON DISPLAY AT—AMNH, FMNH, TMP, ROM, NMC,
    USNM
TIME—late Campanian of the late Late Cretaceous
HORIZON AND DISTRIBUTION—Judith River Formation, western
    North America
MAIN ANATOMICAL STUDY—Lambe, 1917

	AMNH 5664	AMNH 5458
SKULL LENGTH—	678 mm	1040
TOTAL LENGTH—	5.8 m	8.6
FEMUR LENGTH—	700 mm	1025
HIP HEIGHT—	1.9 m	2.8
MASS—	700 kg	2.5 tonnes

A running Albertosaurus libratus *youngster, or an adult* Albertosaurus sternbergi.

This is the best known of the tyrannosaurs in terms of known remains, which include a number of fine skulls and skeletons of varying ages. Many more are being found. First discovered in the Canadian section of the Judith River (formerly Oldman) Formation in the late 1800s, Lawrence Lambe named and described the type skeleton in the WW I years. Unfortuantely, he characterized it as a sluggish scavenger. Just to look at the form of the Lambe's skeleton as it was found in the ground belies this image.

It is interesting and important that two types of *A. "libratus"* heads have been found. In both the preorbital horn, which is much larger than the postorbital horn, is rather cylindrical. In the type and some others the cylinder points up and forward and forms a shorter triangle. In others the horn is more horizontal, rectangular, and longer; this second kind is seen in the FMNH skull. The suture patterns of the skull roof bones also differ, and the first form has bigger, and perhaps fewer, teeth. It may be that these types represent "gracile" and "robust" forms of the sort seen in the primitive coelophysians. But the skeletons of tyrannosaurs do not show as much dual divergence as the coelophysians do, and it has not yet been shown that theropod species in general are split into two such variants. Whether the differences indicate sexes or very similar species—à la lions and tigers—is not obvious at this time. Certainly the variation in *A. libratus* is more than within *T. rex* and some other theropod species. So those specimens that may, or may not, belong to the second type have been indicated with question marks. There are more of the second type than the first, yet most of the second group seem to be juveniles.

This brings us to another point. During 1970, Dale Russell noted that the much smaller *A. sternbergi,* based on skeleton 5664, is probably a juvenile. Also observe (see pages 334-35) that its orbital horns are of the FMNH skull type. One thing Russell did not notice is that the teeth of this two-thirds-sized albertosaur are literally larger than those of the big specimen. This may mean that they are different species after all. Yet, a few skulls of differing sizes do seem to show that the teeth get smaller as they approach full size, and this supports the possibilty that these skulls do represent a growth series. If so, such a dramatic tooth reduction is rare. That it can happen at all is because the teeth are continually replaced by new sets. If juveniles were abandoned by their parents at half size, their big teeth may have helped them get along in what was a very hard world. Or perhaps, like the needle-sharp teeth and claws of lion cubs, the youngsters' big teeth allowed them to protect themselves against nonrelations that wished them harm. Possibly it was just a genetic quirk of no particular meaning.

Other possible growth changes include a moderate decrease in relative limb length, especially the extremities, with increasing size. The transverse crest atop the braincase did not become large until adulthood, and the adult's skull was relatively bigger. There does not appear to be a consistent change in the length and depth of the snout relative to the rest of the head between different specimens.

Most *A. libratus* skulls have been flattened from side to side by the pressure of overlaying sediments, and this obscures the breadth of the back of the skull and the forward-facing of the eyes. This is shown by AMNH S336 and the new skull TMP

85.62.1. Somewhat crushed from top to bottom, they show the truly heavy build of the back of the head and the good binocular vision. Even worse is the oblique down and forward crushing a few skulls have experienced. Some artists have innocently failed to account for this, and drawn *A. libratus* with a weird, sort of pig-like snout. Like all big albertosaurs, it has smaller forelimbs than *Tyrannosaurus*. A few adult skulls show the beginnings of the kind of orbital process that becomes so well developed in later tyrannosaurs.

The adult skeleton is restored after the nearly complete New York specimen, whose skull horns are like the type's. FMNH PR308 is used to show the alternate skull form. The juvenile skeleton is one of the most complete dinosaur skeletons known, it lacks only a few tail tip vertebrae. I find this a particularly attractive dinosaur. With its big size, long limbs, long upturned skull, compact body, and long bulldog neck, it combines grace, speed, and power in an elegant hunting machine.

White-rhino-sized *Albertosaurus* was the dominant predator of the Judith River, making up about 75 percent of the big-predator fauna. The equally big *Tyrannosaurus torosus* was its main competitor, the smaller gracile albertosaur less so. The Judith River's most numerous inhabitants were rhino-sized duckbills, and they were probably the main prey of *A. libratus*. The duckbill's main defense was to run, perhaps into dense brush to try and lose the albertosaurs. However, the more powerful horned dinosaurs were by no means immune to the depredations of this tyrannosaur either.

ALBERTOSAURUS ARCTUNGUIS Parks, 1928a

TYPE—ROM 807

BEST SPECIMENS—type, TMP 81.10.1?

TIME—latest Campanian to early Maastrichtian of the late Late Cretaceous

HORIZON AND DISTRIBUTION—Horseshoe Canyon Formation of Alberta

	Type	TMP 81.10.1
SKULL LENGTH—		970 mm
TOTAL LENGTH—	~8.6 m	~8.0
FEMUR LENGTH—	1020 mm	950
HIP HEIGHT—	2.7 m	2.5
TONNAGE—	2.5	2.0

To be frank, I am not sure what to do with this species and the below *A. sarcophagus,* which are both from the Horseshoe Canyon Formation. This is because both species' old type remains leave a lot to be desired, and new specimens do not have enough comparable parts. This species' type, for example, is missing its head. There do appear to be two big, common tyrannosaurs in the Horseshoe Canyon. One is a robust species that may be *A. sarcophagus,* the other is gracile. The type of *A. arctunguis* is lightly built and long legged, and the same is true of the very nice new skull and partial skeleton, TMP 81.10.1 (both are missing their tails). So these *may* be the same gracile species. I have taken a bit of a risk and combined the two individuals to come up with a skeletal drawing that it is hoped represents *A. arctunguis.* If so then *A. arctunguis* had smaller arms and finger claws, and longer legs, than *A. libratus.* Also, the orbit is nearly cut in half by a postorbital bar like that of *Tyrannosaurus.* These characters imply that *A. arctunguis* was a direct descendant of *A. libratus,* and the direct ancestor of later *A. megagracilis.*

ALBERTOSAURUS SARCOPHAGUS Osborn, 1905
SYNONYMS—*Laelaps incrassatus, Dryptosaurus incrassatus*
TYPE—NMC 6500
TIME—latest Campanian to early Maastrichtian of the late Late
    Cretaceous
HORIZON AND DISTRIBUTION—Horseshoe Canyon Formation of
    Alberta

	Type
SKULL LENGTH—	~1000 mm
TONNAGE—	~2.4

As I said above, this and the other Horseshoe Canyon tyrannosaur *A. arctunguis* are real headaches. The type of this species is a partial, badly preserved skull, not enough to really tell us what kind of animal it is. Hopefully better remains will eventually help better define the species. Until then about all we can say is that it appears to be more heavily constructed than *A. arctunguis.* Just how closely related this species is to the other albertosaurs is not clear either.

ALBERTOSAURUS MEGAGRACILIS new species
TYPE AND BEST SPECIMEN—LACM 23845 (subadult?)
TIME—latest Maastrichtian of the latest Late Cretaceous

HORIZON AND DISTRIBUTION—Hell Creek Formation of Montana

MAIN ANATOMICAL STUDY—Molnar, 1978

	Type
SKULL LENGTH—	~900 mm
TOTAL LENGTH—	~7.5 m
TONNAGE—	~1.7

In describing the one partial skeleton, Ralph Molnar tentatively assigned it to the contemporary *A. lancensis*. While looking over the remains I became convinced that they are much too big and too immature—the poorly ossified elements and moderate sized transverse crest atop the braincase suggest it was not fully grown—to belong in the much smaller species. This animal is clearly not *Tyrannosaurus* either. The next question is whether it is *A. libratus* or *A. arctunguis*. The LACM animal's extremely atrophied forelimbs, down-bent nasals, very long snout, and long hind limbs strongly indicate that it is not. A new species is therefore named, one that describes its combination of large size and gracile build. In fact, this species probably got as big as *A. libratus*. Not enough is known to allow a skeletal restoration.

A. megagracilis is similar to and may be a direct descendant of the earlier *A. arctunguis,* which in turn may be a direct descendant of the yet earlier *A. libratus*. So these three species may represent a lineage in which size and basic design remained remarkably consistent, but the legs became increasingly long, the arms ever smaller, the snout longer, and the form overall more gracile.

Not only are the hand claws small, but their very small tubers for muscle insertion show that the arm was very weak. *A. megagracilis* is more advanced than even *Tyrannosaurus rex* in

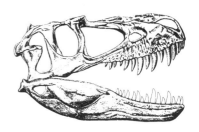

Albertosaurus libratus? *AMNH 5664 juvenile*

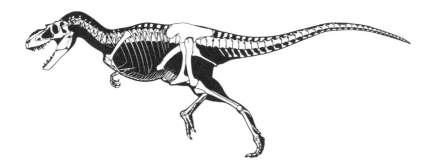

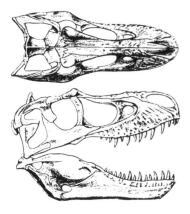

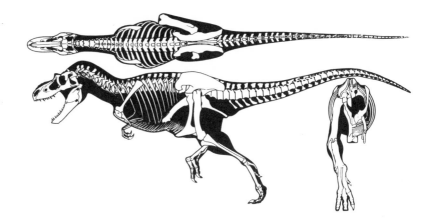

Albertosaurus libratus *AMNH 5458 and TMP 85.62.1*

Albertosaurus libratus *AMNH 5458*

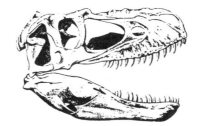

Albertosaurus libratus? *FMNH PR308*

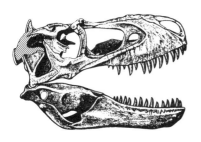

Albertosaurus arctunguis? *TMP 81.10.1*

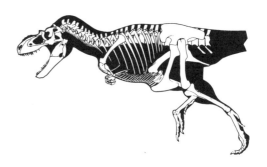

Albertosaurus arctunguis *ROM 807 and TMP 81.10.1*

forelimb reduction, and this indicates that given a little more time albertosaurs would have abandoned them altogether.

Time it did not have, for the rarity of *A. megagracilis* relative to *T. rex* suggests that, like many other latest Cretaceous dinosaurs, it was in trouble. If so, then the big albertosaur lineage may have been doomed even if the great extinction had not taken place. This lineage's decline seems to have been due to the lessening numbers of their preferred prey, duckbills, in Maastrichtian time, not because the genus was intrinsically inferior to *Tyrannosaurus*. Aside from *T. rex*, the competitor of *A. megagracilis* was the small and equally rare *A. lancensis*.

SUBGENUS *ALBERTOSAURUS* ("NANOTYRANNUS") (Bakker et al., unofficial)
SYNONYM—*Albertosaurus* ("Clevelanotyrannus")

ALBERTOSAURUS? ("NANOTYRANNUS") *LANCENSIS* (Gilmore, 1946)
SYNONYM—*Gorgosaurus lancensis*
TYPE—CMNH 5741
TIME—latest Maastrichtian of the latest Late Cretaceous
HORIZON AND DISTRIBUTION—Lance Formation of Montana

	Type
SKULL LENGTH—	602 mm
TOTAL LENGTH—	~5 m
KILOGRAMMAGE—	~500

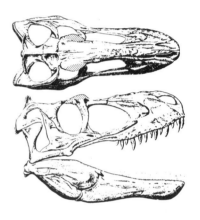

Albertosaurus *("Nanotyrannus")* lancensis *type CMNH 5741*

The only good specimen we have got of this one is a skull. Although small, it is not a young juvenile because of its combination of extremely good ossification, with some sutures obliterated by the bones' intergrowth, a large transverse braincase crest, and a big rugosity on the lower edge of the cheeks. Even big *Tyrannosaurus rex* skulls are no better ossified, so this individual was at least fairly close to being fully grown. *A. lancensis* was not necessarily faster than its giant relative, but this small animal could use its superior manueverablity to escape.

Note the smaller teeth of this adult tyrannosaur compared to similar-sized but big-toothed juveniles of *A. libratus*. The skull is oddly crushed, with the snout pinched narrower than it should be, and the back crushed down and backward so it is even broader than it really was. However, the truly greater breadth of the back of the skull, the more forward-facing eyes, and an advanced braincase make this the most *Tyrannosaurus*-like of the albertosaurs, despite its small size. Indeed, the smallness, *Tyrannosaurus*-like features, and the late appearance of this animal imply that it underwent a separate evolution from the big-bodied *A. libratus-A. arctunguis-A. megagracilis* lineage. It may also be more closely related to *Tyrannosaurus* than the other albertosaurs. Robert Bakker and associates intend to give this species the new generic title "Nanotyrannus" (which replaces the aborted "Clevelanotyrannus").[17] Alternately, it could be a subgenus of either *Albertosaurus* or *Tyrannosaurus*. The very long, low snout, big preorbital opening, shallow mandible, small teeth, and skull roof sutures cause me to keep it in *Albertosaurus*. An interesting and unanswered question is whether this species evolved from a big ancestor, or if they were always small like *Albertosaurus olseni*.

As with *A. megagracilis,* the rarity of this species suggests that it was in trouble. *T. rex* was a direct danger to *A. lancensis,* but was too big to be a direct rival. Its main competition came from the moderately larger *A. megagracilis,* and possibly from some of the larger, also rare sickle-claws. Certainly, small-bodied and small-toothed *A. lancensis* avoided the gigantic adult ceratopsids and duckbills in its habitat. It probably went after immature duckbills and other medium-sized herbivores such as dome-headed *Pachycephalosaurus.*

GENUS *TYRANNOSAURUS* Osborn, 1905
SYNONYMS—*Daspletosaurus, Dynamosaurus, Gorgosaurus, Tarbosaurus*

Traditionally, *Tyrannosaurus* is considered to consist of only one species, *T. rex*. However, tyrannosaurs are so like one another that all the usual genera cannot be justified; they are oversplit. In particular, *Daspletosaurus* and *Tarbosaurus* share most of the key characters that characterize *T. rex*: a stocky, heavy-boned build, relatively short lower hind limbs and large arms, a short snout, smaller preorbital horns, nasal bones that are tightly constricted between the preorbital bones, deep lower jaws, and long yet stout teeth that point a little more forward than they do in *Albertosaurus*. These three species form their own clade, and the amount of variation between them is less than that seen in some well-established modern or recent genera such as *Canis* (wolves and jackals) and even our own genus *Homo*. *Daspletosaurus* and *Tarbosaurus* are, therefore, junior synonyms of *Tyrannosaurus*. However, *Daspletosaurus* is different enough from the other two species to warrant its own subgenus.

To a fair extent the *Tyrannosaurus* species are the tyrannosaur's tyrannosaurs; they have taken to an extreme the development of skull size, strength, and power. This and the larger, more forward-pointing mid-upper-jaw teeth suggest a more potent wounding ability than the albertosaur's. The stoutness of *Tyrannosaurus* relative to albertosaurs is readily apparent in the skeletal restorations. They are not as graceful, but they have a well-proportioned, majestic attractiveness of their own.

Because *Tyrannosaurus* is shorter and stockier-limbed than *Albertosaurus,* it is tempting to ascribe slower speeds to it. However, the proportional differences are not great, while the morphology is almost identical. Perhaps *Tyrannosaurus* used the power of its stouter limbs to equal the running performance of *Albertosaurus.* Or perhaps the former were better sprinters and the latter better long distance runners. The very size of *T. rex* may have made it the fastest tyrannosaur; there is no way to be certain. Stout *Tyrannosaurus* was well built for ceratopsian killing. To safely and successfully hunt ceratopsians, tyrannosaurs probably had to surprise them, or panic them into a run in which they could be approached from the rear. Otherwise the powerful horned dinosaurs may have reared like enraged bears to try and intimidate the tyrannosaurs. If that failed, a running charge was the horned dinosaur's answer, and then the tyrannosaur often did the fleeing!

Unlike *Albertosaurus,* which remained pretty much the same size and became a little more gracile over ten or so million years, *Tyrannosaurus* became much larger and stouter during this same time. *Tyrannosaurus* may have evolved from unknown tyrannosaurs, but the fact that *T. torosus* and *A. libratus* were long confused suggests that a form of *Albertosaurus* may have been its ancestor. Because *T. bataar* and *T. rex* are so similar, they must have shared a recent, common ancestor, if they were not geographic subspecies of one another.

There is more variation in this genus than in *Albertosaurus,* and the lightly built skull of *T. torosus* makes it a subgenus separate from *T. bataar* and *T. rex*. In his 1970 study, Dale Russell reported a juvenile *T. torosus*-type skeleton from the Horseshoe Canyon Formation.

Oblique profile of a Tyrannosaurus torosus *head. Note the good degree of binocular vision, and the bulging jaw-closing muscles on what is in effect a little frill at the back-top of the head.*

SUBGENUS *TYRANNOSAURUS (DASPLETOSAURUS)*
    (Russell, 1970)

TYRANNOSAURUS (DASPLETOSAURUS) TOROSUS (Russell,
    1970)

SYNONYM—*Albertosaurus libratus*
TYPE, BEST AND DISPLAY SPECIMEN—NMC 8506
TIME—late Campanian of the late Late Cretaceous
HORIZON AND DISTRIBUTION—Judith River Formation of Alberta
                   Type/AMNH 5438

SKULL LENGTH—	1107 mm
TOTAL LENGTH—	9.0 m
FEMUR LENGTH—	1000 mm
HIP HEIGHT—	2.55 m
TONNAGE—	2.3

Until recently, this species' remains were lumped in with *A. libratus* of the same formation. But even as he dug up the first good skull and skeleton in 1921, Sternberg suggested that it was a new taxa, and Dale Russell made it the type of the evocatively titled *Daspletosaurus torosus.* However, as explained above, this species belongs in *Tyrannosaurus,* of which it is the earliest. No complete skeleton is known, but Russell combined the skull and

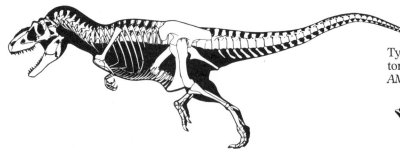

Tyrannosaurus (Daspletosaurus) torosus *type NMC 8506 and AMNH 5438*

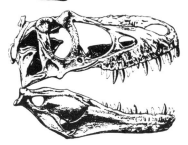

Tyrannosaurus (Daspletosaurus) torosus *type NMC 8506*

partial skeleton of the type with the hind limbs of equal-sized AMNH 5436 and restored a few parts to make a very good restoration, one that has been modified here. Philip Currie has a hefty new preorbital horn that may come from a somewhat larger example of this species.

As well as being smaller than those of the other genus members, the skull has bigger openings and lacks the bar that nearly cuts the orbit in two. On the other hand the skull is quite big for the body. The best skull of the species, ROM 8506, is crushed from side to side and obscures the fact that *T. torosus* had a good degree of binocular vision. The moderate-sized preorbital horn is triangular; the forelimbs are the biggest known in an advanced tyrannosaur. Russell has explained that since *T. torosus* is more robust than, and one fourth as numerous as similar-sized *A. libratus,* it probably went after the relatively less common and powerful horned dinosaurs more often than the albertosaur did.

SUBGENUS *TYRANNOSAURUS (TYRANNOSAURUS)* (Osborn, 1906)

TYRANNOSAURUS (TYRANNOSAURUS) BATAAR Maleev, 1955
Synonyms—*Tarbosaurus bataar, Tarbosaurus efremovi, Gorgosaurus lancinator, Gorgosaurus novojilovi*
TYPE—PIN 551-1
BEST SPECIMENS—type (skull), PIN 551-3, ZPAL MgD-1/3 (juvenile)
TIME—early to mid-Maastrichtian? of the late Late Cretaceous
HORIZON AND LOCALITY—Nemegt Formation of Mongolia
MAIN ANATOMICAL STUDY—Maleev 1974

	MgD-1/3	551-3	Type
SKULL LENGTH—	745 mm	1135	~1350

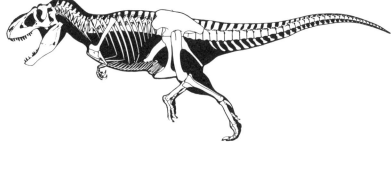

Tyrannosaurus (Tyrannosaurus)
bataar *PIN 551-3*

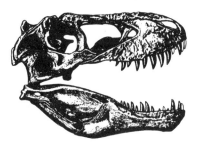

Tyrannosaurus (Tyrannosaurus)
bataar *type PIN 551-1 and PIN
551-3*

Tyrannosaurus (Tyrannosaurus)
bataar *ZPAL MgD-1/3 juvenile*

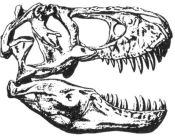

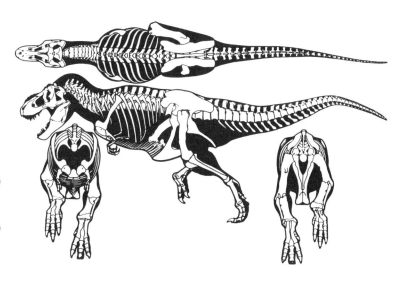

Tyrannosaurus (Tyrannosaurus)
rex *AMNH 5027*

Tyrannosaurus (Tyrannosaurus)
rex *type CM 9380 and AMNH
5027*

TOTAL LENGTH—	5.8 m	7.7	~10
FEMUR LENGTH—	700 mm	970	~1200
HIP HEIGHT—	1.9 m	2.4	~2.9
MASS—	760 kg	2.1 tonnes	~5

Discovered by the Soviet expedition of 1949, this taxa was at first correctly named *Tyrannosaurus bataar* by E. Maleev. But then he gave a smaller specimen the fine generic title, *Tarbosaurus,* and *T. bataar* is often sunk into the latter. But if the very big type skull had been found in North America it would have been assigned to *T. rex:* they are that alike! So much so that if they did overlap in time—the exact age of the Nemegt is hard to pin down —*T. bataar* may have even been an interbreeding, geographical subspecies of *T. rex,* much as the Eurasian brown bear and American grizzly are subspecies of *Ursus arctos. T. bataar's* somewhat smaller size might be due to its living in a harsher, more arid habitat. So Maleev was right the first time in making this *Tyrannosaurus.* The Mongolian predator does have smaller teeth, a shallower snout and mandible, and somewhat different skull roof bones than *T. rex.* Also, *T. bataar's* orbital horns, both before and behind the eye socket, appear to be the smallest among tyrannosaurs. The biggest complete *T. bataar* and *T. rex* skulls are the same length, so these individuals were about equal in size. Their skulls also share the same degree of binocular vision.

A more serious taxonomic problem is that the many good skulls and skeletons may represent more than one species.[18] Maleev and Osmolska believe in two or more, Rhozhdestvensky argues for one.[19] Initially, I inclined toward the former view. After all, three species of the big-cat genus *Panthera* are found in India (lion, tiger, and leopard), and there is always more than one tyrannosaur present in North American formations. That the Nemegt had only one seemed wrong. Yet, careful examination of published remains and those I saw in Warsaw leaves me pretty sure that Rhozhdestvensky is right. Whatever the specimen's size, the teeth of all the specimens are alike in size and design, the orbital horns are the same, and there just is no significant variation in morphology. One small, partial skull ("*Gorgosaurus novojilovi,*" Maleev, 1955[20]) has been restored as very long and low, quite different from the others. But the individual bones match other *T. bataar* skulls, and restored properly they form a normal skull. There have been suggestions that this specimen's foot bones are unique, but as far as I can tell they are not.

All Nemegt tyrannosaurs may therefore represent a growth

series of *T. bataar*. As the species grew up, the body became more robust, the shank and feet somewhat shorter, and the transverse braincase crest seems to have enlarged, rather like what appears to occur in *A. libratus*. Unlike the latter, *T. bataar* teeth show no dramatic alteration in size relative to the skull, but the snout did became longer as they matured.

Note that the larger skeletal restoration (see page 341) is of a fairly complete subadult skull and skeleton. Full adults were even more like *T. rex*, as shown by the big type skull. The juvenile skeleton is based on a superb individual that lacks only the tail.

Prior to the Nemegt deposition, Mongolia was too arid to support big herbivore populations large enough to feed big tyrannosaurs, so only a few big theropod teeth are known. Even the Nemegt was a dryer, more open, savanna-like habitat than were the heavily forested North American tyrannosaur environments. *T. bataar*'s prey consisted mainly of armored ankylosaurs, the big duckbill *Saurolophus,* and one or two of species of medium-sized brontosaurs. There is little doubt that 5-tonne *T. bataar* could bring down the 5-to-10-tonne brontosaurs in its neighborhood. So, although *T. rex* never met *Brontosaurus* itself, the comic books are correct in showing tyrannosaurs preying on its relative. These bulky herbivores may have provided most of *T. bataar*'s prey biomass. With the possible exception of the rare and possibly herbivorous *Deinocherius, T. bataar* had no competitors.

TYRANNOSAURUS (TYRANNOSAURUS) REX Osborn, 1905

SYNONYM—*Dynamosaurus imperiosus*

TYPE—CM 9380

BEST SPECIMENS—type, AMNH 5027, TMP 81.6.1

SPECIMENS ON DISPLAY AT—AMNH, CM, LACM (skull), SDSM (skull), ANSP (cast), TMP

TIME—late Maastrichtian of the latest Late Cretaceous

HORIZON AND DISTRIBUTION—Lance, Hell Creek, Scollard, Willow Creek, Frenchman, and upper Kirtland? Formations of western North America

MAIN ANATOMICAL STUDIES—Osborn, 1906, 1912, 1916

	AMNH 5027/type	UCMP 118742
SKULL LENGTH—	1355 mm	~1750
TOTAL LENGTH—	10.6 m	~13.6
FEMUR LENGTH—	1300 mm	~1675
HIP HEIGHT—	3.4 m	~4.4
TONNAGE—	5.7	~12

This is *the* theropod. Indeed, excepting perhaps *Brontosaurus,* this is the public's favorite dinosaur, having fought King Kong for the forced favor of Fay Wray and smashed Tokyo (with inferior special effects) in the guise of Godzilla. Even the formations it is found in have fantastic names like Hell Creek and Lance. Its place as the greatest of known land predators remains secure—no other giant consists of such complete skeletons, is bigger, or as powerful. Everything said about tyrannosaur strength goes furthest with this species, and no other theropod has such a large, thickly built, powerfully muscled skull, and such large teeth for its bulk. Only *Dilophosaurus* and juvenile *A. libratus* have teeth that are nearly as large in relative measure. Sickle-clawed *Velociraptor antirrhopus* may be as formidably armed for its weight, but it is a small animal. And along with its power, *T. rex* is the fastest known animal for its size!

A number of new finds are coming onto line, including the first combination of a skull with a fairly complete skeleton, at the TMP. The skeletal restoration is after the composite New York mount. Made from the first two known skeletons, these are identical in size. 5027 provides the skull, vertebral column, rib cage, and hips; 9380 the fore and hind limbs. The 5027 skull is crushed a little, giving it a falsely dished dorsal profile and little more breadth at its back end than it really had. Since this is the most complete and best known skull, these crushed features have misled many. On the other hand, Ralph Molnar has made the back of the skull too narrow and triangular.[21] The new skulls prove that this animal really was a *very* broad-cheeked animal. The roguse posterior orbital horn is larger than the reduced preorbital one, much as in *T. bataar.* The lower arm and hand are not known, but since the humerus is smaller than in other *Tyrannosaurus* species, it is likely that the arm as a whole was also. It was not until 1970 that Newman noted that the partial tail was restored with too many vertebrae. With a proper tyrannosaur tail count of thirty-seven to thirty-nine vertebrae, 5027 is thirty-four feet long, not forty-five as once claimed. Kenneth Carpenter has recently mounted a cast of this skeleton in a modern, accurate, and dynamic pose in Philadelphia. Estimates that 5027 massed close to 7 tonnes[22] are reasonable if they are presumed to include fat reserves, but these estimates are not really useful because they were based on unreliable museum models, and a commercial toy made by the BMNH. Substantial growth is possible even after the skull bones start to fuse together as in 5027. I note this because

PREDATORY DINOSAURS
OF THE WORLD

344

this and the other big *T. rex* specimens may or may not be sub-adults. This is possible because the biggest specimen is a tooth-bearing UCMP maxilla from the upper jaw that is 29 percent longer than 5027. It indicates a 12-tonne individual that could rear its head some twenty-three feet high, and could slide something the size of a whole human body down its gullet as if it were a raw oyster.[23] It is possible that this titan, known as it is from only one bone, represents a different species. If not, then 15-tonne individuals were probably fairly common, 20-tonne "record holders" were possible—though so rare that they may never be found. For comparison, most bull African elephants are 5-tonners and a fair number reach 7.5 tonnes; extremely rare are 10-tonners.

Suggestions that *T. rex* is really two species, or even two genera, have been circulating lately. Two genera is completely out of the question; at most it is a-lion-versus-a-tiger kind of species separation. But the type of *Dynamosaurus imperiosus* (a wonderful name) is a front lower jaw that is hardly distinguishable from the *T. rex* type. The somewhat distorted AMNH 5027 skull may be adding to the confusion because the upper jaw's left maxilla is too low. The right side is not so crushed and looks like other *T. rex* specimens. The hind limbs of some specimens do seem to be longer and more slender than those of the type, and they vary somewhat in the teeth. On the other hand, all the skulls are quite consistent in the preorbital horns and other skull details, more so than in *A. libratus*. So one species is most likely, perhaps one that came in "robust" and "gracile" versions, but the verdict is not in.[24]

Of course, *T. rex* is the most illustrated of theropods, and the most famous rendition is Charles Knight's FMNH painting of a confrontation with *Triceratops*.[25] The horizontal body pose is ahead of its time; on the debit side are such anatomical mistakes as the overly shallow back of the head and a small chest. Another well-known Knight *T. rex* effort[26] is much less satisfying, especially since the head is too small and lizard-like. Burian's often-reproduced *T. rex*[27] has a badly dwarfed head and lipless teeth —it is not at all good. Neither is Rudolph Zallinger's bloated and simplistic version in the YPM mural.[28] The rather uninspired commercial model put out by the BMNH is too small in the head and chest, too long-tailed, and has inappropriate plated skin.

The reason for the bulk and firepower of *T. rex* is apparent when one considers its main prey, *Triceratops*. Prior tyrannosaurs were going after rhino-sized duckbills and ceratopsids, but by the late Maastrichtian, elephant-sized *Triceratops* was far and away the most numerous herbivore. *Triceratops* was horrendously big, fast, and agile, and it was well-armed with beak and horns. Hunging it required an equally gigantic, faster, and even more formidably armed predator. Just how formidable only became clear to me as I did the illustration of *T. rex* biting *Triceratops* in Figure 2-6 (page 35). I had to measure things out, and was appalled to find that the tyrannosaur could bite out a wound a yard long, and well over a foot deep and wide. This would have wrecked the entire upper thigh of *Triceratops,* and cut down to the femur. Some "scavenger"! It is hard to conceive of such titanic battles, with elephant-sized predators sprinting alongside a thundering herd of horned dinosaurs.

Some remains indicate that *T. rex* lived in New Mexico's Kirtland Shale; if so, it hunted the brontosaurs there, while *Triceratops* was absent. As for competition, the smaller, more gracile and rare *Albertosaurus megagracilis* was about all, and it preferred the duckbills. *A. lancensis* was too small to be much more than its occasional prey, except when the albertosaur dared pick off a juvenile *T. rex* from under its parents' noses!

The culmination of tyrannosaur evolution, *T. rex* was one of the very last North American dinosaurs. Nothing else combined its size, speed, and power. Since its demise we have had to make do with lions and tigers and bears, and other "little" mammalian carnivores.

MYSTERIOUS *DRYPTOSAURUS*

SUBORDER UNCERTAIN

FAMILY DRYPTOSAURIDAE Marsh, 1890

GENUS *DRYPTOSAURUS* Marsh, 1877
SYNONYM—*Laelaps*

DRYPTOSAURUS AQUILUNGIS (Cope, 1866)
SYNONYM—*Laelaps aquilungis*
TYPE—ANSP 9995
TIME——Late Maastrichtian of the late Late Cretaceous
HORIZON AND DISTRIBUTION—New Egypt Formation of New
    Jersey
MAIN ANATOMICAL STUDY—Cope, 1870

	Type
FEMUR LENGTH—	890 mm
TONNAGE—	~1.5?

I discuss this species here for a lack of anywhere better to do it; it is being reexamined by Kenneth Carpenter and Dale Russell. This large, gracile, aberrant, and poorly known theropod has been considered everything from a megalosaur to a tyrannosaur, to even a dromaeosaur protobird. It is none of these. The ankle is advanced and looks avetheropodian, but it is also different from other theropods, so this taxa is a unique form. A number of other theropod remains in the United States have been placed in this genus; all are dubious at best. It seems that the forelimbs are large and have very big claws, and the teeth are fairly normal blades. Duckbills were among this big animal's prey.

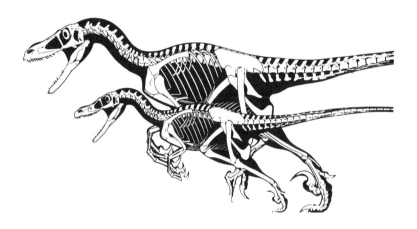

3
Protobirds:
Flying
and Nonflying

The members of this clade—the sister group to the allosaur-tyrannosaurs—did a fantastic and wonderful thing. They learned to fly (again, we assume that Triassic herrerasaurs and "Protoavis" are bird mimics that did not contribute to early bird evolution). Long-fingered, climbing small avetheropods of the Jurassic rather like *Compsognathus* and *Ornitholestes* may have been the beginnings of this group, which soon developed flying forms, the only known one of which is *Archaeopteryx*. What happened to the protobirds *after Archaeopteryx* is as interesting as what went on before. This is because most of the theropods closest to *Archaeopteryx* and birds lived after *Archaeopteryx*, and these Cretaceous protobirds—although nonflying—are in many important ways more birdlike than *Archaeopteryx* itself. It would seem that these were the secondarily flightless progeny of the

first flying protobirds. So, as true flying birds evolved, there may have been a parallel radiation of grounded protobirds. This is a new idea, and an unproven one. But as we shall see below, it is also logical. These long-forelimbed ground protobirds developed a number of peculiar adaptations, and seem to have displaced other theropods from the small-to-medium-predator roles. Others became herbivores, and one of the ostrich-mimics may have been gigantic.

Many features link protobirds and birds. For one example, in birds the snout is reduced. The maxilla, preorbital openings, jaw-closing muscles, and smell organs the snout contains are all reduced or lost. These things can be seen developing in protobirds; even the preorbital opening of *Velociraptor* is small compared to nonprotobird theropods. A common, but not strict, protobird trait is to have well-developed binocular vision. The way in which protobird eyes faced forward usually differed from that of tyrannosaurs (for an exception, see comments on *Dromaeosaurus,* pages 349–51). In protobirds the frontals that make

Velociraptor mongoliensis *and* Troodon mongoliensis *squabble over a* Protoceratops andrewsi *carcass. The first's greater fire-power matched the second's larger size.*

up the skull roof above the eye sockets are triangular and broader over the back of the eye socket; this is the bird way of binocular vision. But the purpose of stereo vision was the same in tyrannosaurs, protobirds, and birds: to improve the precision of head strikes.

Notice that unlike the hips of other theropods, here the long rod is missing from the end of the ischium bone. This means that the ischial-based limb muscles again anchored along most of the bones' length, as they had in the earliest dinosaurs. This is also an avian feature, and it probably had to do with the equally birdlike initial backward-swinging of the pubis. In 1969, Dale Russell suggested that the slender, bowed outermost digit of the hand of *Troodon* could rotate backward on the wrist bones and oppose the other fingers, somewhat the way our thumb does. If correct, then this would apply to *Archaeopteryx,* dromaeosaurs, and perhaps oviraptors too, because they have similar hands.

It is remarkable how ready for avian-style flight the Jurassic avetheropods were. All they had to do was elongate their forelimbs, modify them a little, and increase their power, and they could have flown.

SUBORDER PROTOAVIA new

ARCHAEOPTERYGIANS AND DROMAEOSAURS

Many theropods have been united into new groups in this book, but the placement of *Archaeopteryx* and the sickle-clawed dromaeosaurs in the same family is by far the most radical—yet it is also one of the most necessary. It used to be thought that the good-sized, sickle-clawed, ground-dwelling dromaeosaurs and troodonts were in the same theropod family, while little-winged *Archaeopteryx* was the first bird. But as Kenneth Carpenter and I worked on these animals, we were astonished at how alike, in detail after detail, dromaeosaurs and *Archaeopteryx* were. In some ways they were almost identical. *Troodon,* in contrast, is much different when one looks below its surface. If alive today, the dromaeosaurs and *Archaeopteryx* would very probably be in one family, so I have grouped them that way here. Small *Archaeopteryx* deserves its own subfamily, much as the small aublysodonts are in a distinct subfamily from the big tyrannosaurs.

Some will object that feathered flying *Archaeopteryx* must be a bird, while the ground-dwelling dromaeosaurs, for which feathers are not known, are theropods; hence they cannot be put

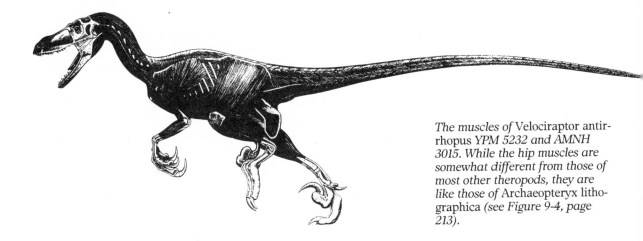

The muscles of Velociraptor antirrhopus *YPM 5232 and AMNH 3015. While the hip muscles are somewhat different from those of most other theropods, they are like those of* Archaeopteryx lithographica *(see Figure 9-4, page 213).*

in the same family. But, as explained in Chapter 4, small theropods may have been feathered, and the lack of feather preservation is not a valid taxonomic character. Nor is flight critical at the family level, since many living bird families have both flying and flightless members. The Rallidae and Anatidae—geese and ducks —are especially notorious for this. (The flightless Hawaiian goose, for instance, was eaten and killed off by the Polynesians.)

To list and explain all the minutiae that put archaeopterygians and dromaeosaurs in the same family would take a few pages, so I will just touch on the highlights. Being avetheropod protobirds, they already share the many characters that unite the members of this group. These include the shoulder girdle, forelimbs, wrist, hand, and the peculiar, slender protobird tail with its elongated processes. Additional features of this particular family's skull include the odd inverted-T shape of the quadratojugal, just above the jaw joint. At this stage, the upper process of the quadratojugal was moving forward and getting shorter; it was on its way to being lost and making this bone into the simple rod that it is in birds. Another skull detail is the pit on the top of the ectopterygoid, one of the mouth roof bones, in *Archaeopteryx*. The only other place this distinctive character is found is in the dromaeosaurs. And above the braincase's opening for the spinal cord is a bone that has a special diamond shape, the supraoccipital.

The most telling similarities are in the peculiar hips, which are virtually the same in tiny *Archaeopteryx* and big dromaeosaurs. The overall design of the long parallelogram-shaped ilia, with their big, back-swept bases for the pubis and simple circular hip sockets, is the same. So are the long backward-tilted pubes, whose aprons are triangular in cross section. The ischia seem the most different, because *Archaeopteryx* has some extra processes on its ischia, but they actually share the same short length and forward-pointing apron. The articulation between the ilium and pubis in both *Archaeopteryx* and dromaeosaurs has the same scalloped inverted-W shape. One will find that little item nowhere else. *Archaeopteryx* even has a hyperextendable second toe, as explained below. All in all, dromaeosaurs are larger, non-flying versions of earlier *Archaeopteryx*. Other protobirds are also very similar in some ways, such as the shoulder girdle and forelimbs of oviraptors. But they differ so much in other respects, such as the skull, that they cannot be put in the same family.

Why archaeopterygids had backward-pointing pubes is obvious. Actually they, and birds too, were doubly "retroverted" in that the coracoid below the shoulder joint is also tilted back. These parallel retroversions occurred because their tails were much more slender, and in the case of *Archaeopteryx* much shorter, than in other theropods. With less mass back aft, protobirds had to shift the belly, and the pubes that supported it, back under the hips to keep the overall center of gravity close to the hind limbs. As the belly was pulled back, the chest tended to go back along with it, causing the coracoid to swing backward too.

Since the big-booted pubes of these dinosaurs projected behind the ischium, some of the lower tail muscles probably attached directly to the ischium, which is avian. Another feature peculiar to this group and to troodonts as well, is the modification of the tail's first vertebrae so that the tail could bend 90 degrees upward at its base. This is proven by the articulated "fighting" *Velociraptor mongoliensis* specimen.

Archaeopterygians and dromaeosaurs were in many ways the most primitive of protobirds. And the longest lived, too, for they were successful from the Late Jurassic, over 145 million years ago, to the end of the Cretaceous, 65 million years ago.

FAMILY ARCHAEOPTERYGIDAE Huxley, 1872

Archaeopteryx lithographica

Dromaeosaurus albertensis
Adasaurus? mongoliensis

Archaeopteryx lithographica's head was a complex structure, with paired nasal horn ridges and preorbital hornlets.

Velociraptor antirrhopus
V. langstoni
V. mongoliensis

SUBFAMILY ARCHAEOPTERYGINAE (Huxley, 1872)

In 1984, Eugen Kessler reported that *Archaeopteryx*-like bones have been found in Berriasian age beds of Romania. Not enough has been published to be sure, but if this is true they are only a little younger than the German *Archaeopteryx* remains. It is notable that the Romanian finds also come from what were once islands.

GENUS *ARCHAEOPTERYX* Meyer, 1861
SYNONYM—*Archaeornis, Jurapteryx*

ARCHAEOPTERYX LITHOGRAPHICA Meyer, 1861
SYNONYMS—*Archaeornis siemensi, Jurapteryx recurva*
TYPE—BMNH 37001
BEST AND DISPLAY SPECIMENS—type, HMN MB. 1880/81
    (subadult) and JM SoS 2257 (juvenile)
TIME—Tithonian of the Late Jurassic
HORIZON AND DISTRIBUTION—Solnhofen of Bavaria
MAIN ANATOMICAL STUDIES—Beer, 1954; Wellnhofer, 1974;
        Ostrom, 1976a; Walker, 1984

	JM	HMN	Type
SKULL LENGTH—	39 mm	45	

TOTAL LENGTH—	.29 m	.405	.46
FEMUR LENGTH—	37 mm	52.5	60.5
HIP HEIGHT—	.12 m	.15	.17
GRAMMAGE—	69	260	370

It is a remarkable coincidence that this most famous of the protobirds was first discovered just two years after the publication of Darwin's *The Origin of Species.* Darwin's detractors had been using the lack of any known links between reptiles and birds to challenge his theory. Those deities of a fundamentalist sort must have been in a self-destructive frame of mind, because *Archaeopteryx* gave the aggressive Thomas Huxley just the ammunition he needed to blast away at those skeptical of evolution. A Solnhofen feather was found a year before, but whether it belongs to *Archaeopteryx* or something else is not knowable. In the decades since, five other skeletons have shown up, three at first misidentified as a pterosaur and a theropod. The ultrafine-grained Solnhofen limestones, laid down in a large lagoon in what was then the European island archipelago, were once coveted as high-quality lithographic stones. The *Archaeopteryx* we know from these limestones were therefore islanders. The quarries are still being worked, and a sixth headless skeleton has just come to light. New JM 2257 with its fine skull and further preparation of the type have revealed so much information that most of this animal's morphology is now known. All this has greatly refined the study of bird origins, and the combination of complete remains with well-preserved feathers makes *Archaeopteryx* among the most restorable of Mesozoic vertebrates. Yet some details remain obscure. HMN 1880 is the most complete and has superbly preserved wing, tail, and body feathers. The skull is crushed, though, and many of the skeletal bones are in bad shape after all these years. An old drawing of this specimen is supposed to show a small crest of head feathers that were removed during attempts to expose more of the skull bones. One good question is whether a flap of tissue stretched from the shoulder to the wrist in front of the arm, as in modern birds. One may have; but I cannot see a good impression of one among the specimens, so I leave it out of my restorations. There is no reason at all to believe that a membrane of skin was stretched between the fingers as Walter Bock implied in 1986. Instead, the fingers were free from one another and supple. The outermost wing feathers were sup-

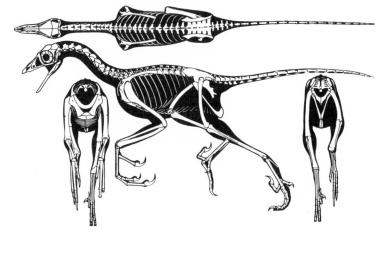

Archaeopteryx lithographica
HMN MB. 1880/81 subadult

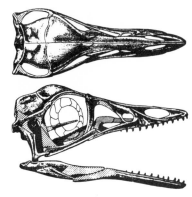

Archaeopteryx lithographica *JM
SoS 2257 juvenile*

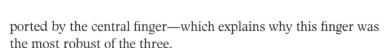

ported by the central finger—which explains why this finger was
the most robust of the three.

In size, *Archaeopteryx* is similar to a crow and, as shown in
Chapter 9, it was probably a good flier. Although there is no way
to be sure, the big wing-depressing pectoralis muscles are restored as making up 15 percent of the total mass in the two bigger
specimens, and 8 percent in the seemingly juvenile and smaller-
armed JM 2257. This brings us to the question of how early in
life *Archaeopteryx* flew. While a few birds like the mound-nesting
megapode fowl can fly very soon after they are hatched, most
cannot manage it until they are fully grown. Large wing feathers
are preserved with young JM 2257's forelimbs, but the arms are
a good deal shorter than in the bigger specimens, so flight must
have been limited at best.

There have been suggestions over the years that one or more of the various specimens are distinct species. HMN 1880 was sometimes thought to be a distinct species. HMN 1880 was sometimes thought to be a distinct genus from the type. The current issue is the claim that little JM 2257 is different enough in its teeth, proportions, and other details to be its own adult taxa, *Jurapteryx recurva* Howgate, 1984. Dispute over some of the specimen's features helps fuel these speculations. The most important centers around the orientation of the hip's pubis. It varies among the specimens, so people argue about which if any of these are broken at the base. I have inspected HMN 1880, and am perplexed as to why a break has been suggested. Although the area has been damaged by preparation, the pubis is normally attached to the ilium and the characteristic scalloped articulation can be made out. The other specimens are less well preserved and/or juvenile, so I have much less confidence in what they tell us. This is especially true of the JM example, whose ischium is as vertical as the pubis. No theropod, bird, or other *Archaeopteryx* specimen has so vertical an ischium; obviously, both it and the pubis were pushed forward from their true, backward-pointing poses. The skulls of HMN 1880 and JM 2257 seem to show more differences, since the first has a shorter lower jaw and a more forwardly sloping cheek region than the latter. I have restored HMN 1880's and JM 2257's skeletons so that you can compare them. To make them separate genera is too extreme, but it would be well within reason that more than one *Archaeopteryx* species patrolled the Solnhofen lagoons. Personally, I am not sure what to think, but I suspect that the differences have been exaggerated, and that those that can be proven real are the result of the specimen's differing ages.

Much more incredible claims have been made, among them that one of the outer finger joints is really a break. If true, then the hand would not be theropod-like after all. Every hand shows the joint, however, so a fantastic scenario was devised in which individuals broke their fingers as they crashed into the lagoon. This was little help since the articular surfaces of the joint are well preserved.[1] Just as bad were recent assertions that *Archaeopteryx* had a direct articulation between the furcula process of the shoulder blade and the vertebrae or ribs, and that the furcula articulated with the process of the coracoid in front of the shoulder joint instead.[2] Then there are the suggestions that the braincase articulated in a strange way with the jaw-supporting bones. Nothing alive or dead has heads or shoulders like these, and HMN 1880 and JM 2257 prove that *Archaeopteryx* did not either.[3] Instead, *Archaeopteryx* was a normal, if birdlike, theropod in every way. Alas, all these speculations have fed the notion that *Archaeopteryx* is well off the mainstream of early bird radiation. In reality, there is nothing in its design that prevents it from being the great-great-grandparent of all birds, although its remains appear a little too late for this to be literally true.

Something that *A. lithographica* did have was a fair degree of binocular vision, since the frontals were triangular like in most other protobirds.

One point about *Archaeopteryx* has been missed. Once, at a little gathering, I was looking over a high-quality cast of JM 2257. I was struck by something in the foot. Examination under a microscope confirmed that the roller joint surfaces on the middle joint of toe two are enlarged dorsally. Found elsewhere only in sickle-claws, this allowed the digit to hyperextend like a cat's claw. Not only that, but the three main toes have the same peculiar proportions seen in sickle-claws, with the hyperextendable toe shortened and the other two toes nearly the same in length to carry the load. This suggests, but does not prove, that *Archaeopteryx* walked with toe number two held clear of the ground. The claw of this toe is not exceptional in size or shape, but the sickle claw of *Adasaurus* is not very large either. Why *Archaeopteryx* had such an extra-supple toe is not clear. Perhaps it evolved as a hook-and-spike climbing aid in eary protobirds, and developed into a weapon in the sickle-claws. An unanswered question is whether *Archaeopteryx* drooped its toes when a foot swung forward for the next step, as I show it doing, or clenched them like perching birds do. The foot is preserved both ways in different specimens.

Although, as explored in Chapter 9 (page 209), *Archaeopteryx* was well adapted for climbing and leaping, it turns out that all the pictures showing *Archaeopteryx* high in the branches of trees are probably wrong. Paleogeographical and paleoecological work on the Solnhofen environment and plants shows that they were then in the northern tropical desert zone, and that the semi-arid islands supported only a low scrub of conifer bushes.[4]

So what was *Archaeopteryx* up to? We have already seen how the conical, unserrated, large-rooted teeth and hooked claws of *Archaeopteryx* were good for snatching aquatic life, and small land creatures and insects too. Chapter 9 also explains that *Ar-*

chaeopteryx was a seemingly good flyer and swimmer that lived on oceanic islands covered by low scrub and surrounded by lagoons. It is possible that *Archaeopteryx* was a crude "shorebird" that used its climbing and leaping heritage to live and nest like the South American hoatzin among the near-shore bushes.[5] It may have patrolled the shoreline for cast-up aquatic life. Or, it could have even flown slowly over the lagoons dropping down upon the disabled fish and squid-like creatures found near the surface, or pursuing them a short distance underwater. As it was a rather generalized animal, insects and small land animals may have made up part of its diet too. It could have flown from island to island if need be. *Archaeopteryx* was only modestly successful at this life-style, for its pterosaurian feeding competitors were far more numerous in the Solnhofen. On land, its known enemy and possible competitor was larger *Compsognathus,* from which it ran or flew toward safety.

Most restorations of *Archaeopteryx* give it a kind of "climbing bird" coloration, and this is quite possible. But if it was a "shorebird," then it may have been patterned more like gulls and terns, in greys, whites, and blacks. A serious mistake common to many *Archaeopteryx* illustrations is to show it with a short, thick, pigeon- or gull-like neck. Instead, its neck was long and slender, like in other small theropods.

The Wonderful and Spectacular Dromaeosaurian Sickle-Claws

This is one of the two sickle-clawed protobird groups—the much more advanced troodonts also have sickle claws. In addition to being hyperextendable, the second toe bears a deepened, transversely flattened, and strongly curved killing claw. The central bone of the second toe also has a large heel, the sickle claw an even bigger one. These increased the leverage and effective power of toe's retracting muscles. The dromaeosaurs' sickle-clawed toe differs from the troodonts' in that the central toe bone is about the same length as the first, not shorter.

The dromaeosaurs' short posterior ilium in the hip and small knee crest imply good leaping abilities, and along with the hyperextendable toe they may have inherited these features from archaeopterygians. That the modified toe may have evolved as a climbing aid in early protobirds and was *then* found suitable for alteration into a sickle-clawed weapon explains how some theropods could end up using their feet as primary weapons—this when most theropods reduced their foot firepower in favor of head power.

What all this means is that dromaeosaurs must have killed much differently than other theropods.[6] They probably ran alongside their prey and leaped onto their backs. Using their long, strong, big-clawed fingers to hold on, they could then wound the prey, leaping off before the latter could roll over and crush them. After this, it would have been a matter of waiting for the prey to weaken before the predator or the pack started eating. Quite big prey could be handled in this manner, although everything down to insects probably found its way into the bellies of sickle-claws—with the caution that small prey was caught in the jaws, not killed with the sickled claws as a few illustrations have shown.

As explained below, *Dromaeosaurus* and *Velociraptor* had different means for wounding their victims. The first used its jaws, the second its feet. That these two genera are still very close relatives is proven by the detailed design of many skull bones and the second toes. In particular, both have fully developed, inverted-T-shaped quadratojugals in the cheek, a classic dromaeosaur character. But each genus went on to develop its own distinctive way of killing.

It is likely that dromaeosaurs, and troodonts too, carried the sickle-clawed toe fully retracted so as to save it from wear on the ground. Indeed, the two other main toes, the third and fourth, were nearly equal in length—in most theropods the fourth toe is a good deal shorter than the third—and the entire locomotory load had passed onto them. While this is unusual for theropods, many other animals have only two running toes—or even one. To help strengthen the two running toes a modest flange of the fourth cannon bone backed the third. Such a flange appears to be present in *Archaeopteryx,* and as explained below *Troodon* has gone even further in this modification.

The sickle-claw's toes are fascinating enough in their own right, but the possibility that these creatures were the *descendants* of the archaeopterygians makes them even more fascinating. This possibility is based on the fact that dromaeosaurs have a number of avian features not found in *Archaeopteryx*. At first sight it seems to be the other way, since the latter is the one with the long wings and most modified shoulder girdle. But these are not general bird adaptations—they are specific to flying birds only. Flightless birds do not have them because they lost them when they lost flight. Dromaeosaurs may have done the same. The bird characters of dromaeosaurs are mostly subtle ones, yet they hint at past flight abilities. Most obvious is the great breastplate. A few nonprotobird theropods have fairly large sternals, but nothing as big or birdlike as the dromaeosaur breastplate. It is also birdlike in shape, and articulates with the coracoid bones in the avian manner. It is hard to imagine how such a breastplate could have evolved outside the needs of flight—flight more advanced than that of *Archaeopteryx,* which had not yet evolved such equipment. So, it appears that the dromaeosaurs had flying ancestors. They certainly are very similar to the flying archaeopterygians, and have a number of bird characters that the former lack. Dromaeosaurs even appear later. It therefore appears that dromaeosaurs are secondarily flightless Cretaceous descendants of the flying Jurassic archaeopterygians.

Other things that seem odd in a terrestrial animal start to make sense when a flying past is considered—the sickle-claw's well developed folding forelimbs for instance. Only flying pterosaurs, bats, and birds need to fold up their arms so tightly. Dromaeosaurs probably did not really need to, and may have inherited the ability instead. Likewise, the dromaeosaurs' interlocking, immobile shoulder girdles, which reduced the reach of the arms, make little sense in land predators. Instead, they look like a flight adaptation that they had not lost (see the comments on ornithomimid shoulders, page 380). The high-set shoulder joint, virtually unknown among nonflyers, is a typical feature of flying birds. Then there are the exceptionally upwardly bendable tail bases, and the peculiar kind of ossified tail rods. These are found elsewhere only in flying pterosaurs and *Archaeopteryx.* They probably evolved in archaeopterygians for flight control, and were retained for dynamic control on the ground—Rinchen Barsbold has vividly compared the dromaeosaur tail to a stiff riding crop. Even the bladed serrated teeth of dromaeosaurs can be explained in this scenario. The ancestral archaeopterygians had conical teeth, but after returning to a terrestrial existence and big-game hunting, dromaeosaurs needed slicing teeth, so they redeveloped them.

Dromaeosaurs may be just the first of an array of protobird theropods that lost the ability to fly. This "radical" idea is not really surprising. In fact, protobirds *should* have lost flight from time to time. After all, they would have been more susceptible to loss of flight than regular birds. Not only did they not fly as well in the first place, but they still had clawed fingers that they could use for predatory and other needs. Birds have lost working fingers, and they can do little with their forelimbs if flight is lost.

The reader should note that it is the similar designs, not their genealogical position vis-à-vis each other, that justifies placing the archaeopterygians and dromaeosaurs in one family. So the unification holds even if dromaeosaurs were the more primitive group. The earliest known dromaeosaurs are mid-Cretaceous, and they were already the dominant small predators. They remained common until close to if not actually to the final extinction, although they seem to have suffered somewhat from competition with aublysodonts and smaller tyrannosaurs. It may be that both *Dromaeosaurus* and *Velociraptor* were present in Asia and North America, although this has yet to be confirmed. *Hulsanpes perlei* Osmolska, 1982 was named on the basis of a clearly juvenile dromaeosaur foot from the Mongolian Barun Goyot Formation. It could belong to a species whose adults are already known, so it is not considered valid. *Phaedrolosaurus ilikensis* Dong, 1973, which is based on some seemingly dromaeosaurian but unassociated Chinese remains, remains too poor to make much of. [7]

SUBFAMILY DROMAEOSAURINAE Matthew and Brown, 1922

GENUS *DROMAEOSAURUS* Matthew and Brown, 1922
SYNONYM—*Adasaurus*?

This was never a common genus; its teeth suggest that it was present in the latest Cretaceous of the western United States, but not in the same formation as in Alberta.

DROMAEOSAURUS ALBERTENSIS Matthew and Brown, 1922
TYPE AND BEST SPECIMEN—AMNH 5356
TIME—late Campanian of the late Late Cretaceous
HORIZON AND DISTRIBUTION—Judith River Formation of Alberta
MAIN ANATOMICAL STUDY—Colbert and Russell, 1969

	Type
SKULL LENGTH—	230 mm
KILOGRAMMAGE—	~15?

This was the first described dromaeosaur, although at first its big teeth caused it to be confused with tyrannosaurs. That it had a sickle claw was not realized until John Ostrom's work revealed the true nature of these beasts. Only the type skull, which is not complete, and some of its foot bones are known. A large, long claw of the velociraptor-sickle type referred to this species could really belong to *Velociraptor langstoni*. Besides, *D. albertensis* has very robust second-toe bones quite like those of *Adasaurus mongoliensis* from Mongolia (described below), and much more robust than *Velociraptor's*. *Adasaurus* has a surprisingly short sickle claw, and *D. albertensis* may well have too.

If *D. albertensis* did have such a short sickle claw, this may explain its exceptionally robust skull, big teeth, and broad front tooth arcade. The skull certainly lacks the grace of *Velociraptor's*, and at first glance it looks rather primitive. But it is really a very specialized structure that has strayed far from the usual proto-bird path. The back of the head is astonishingly broad, much more so than in *Velociraptor*, because the braincase wings are greatly elongated. The frontals are not triangular like in *Velociraptor* or *Troodon,* something that can lead one to believe *Dromaeosaurus* did not have binocular vision. But the cheeks are much broader than the snout, so the eyes must have faced forward for stereoscopic vision. In all these features, *Dromaeosaurus* converged with and mimicked the tyrannosaurs.[8] This was because, like tyrannosaurs, its firepower was concentrated in its head. So, after leaping onto its prey *Dromaeosaurus* probably bit out wounds, rather than slicing with its claws velociraptor-style. The short sickle claws may have been more defensive weapons. Assuming *D. albertensis* did have a small sickle claw, it appears to be a rather primitive member of the subfamily, but one specialized in its heavy build. A small, coyote-sized animal, its main competitors were the more common aublysodonts, and other sickle claws such as similar-sized *Velociraptor langstoni* and somewhat larger *Troodon formosus*.

ADASAURUS? MONGOLIENSIS Barsbold, 1983
TYPE—GI 100/20
TIME—early Maastrichtian? of the late Late Cretaceous
HORIZON AND DISTRIBUTION—Nemegt Formation of Mongolia
KILOGRAMMAGE— Type ~15?

Since it is possible that this Asian species and *Dromaeosaurus albertensis* share similar small second-toe claws, they may be the same genus. Skull bones are known, as are more skeletal remains,[9] but not enough has been published for us to be certain of anything.

GENUS *VELOCIRAPTOR* Osborn, 1924
SYNONYMS—*Deinonychus, Saurornitholestes*

These are among my very favorite dinosaurs. Their long up-curved skulls, slender yet compact proportions, and great sickle claws make these elegant, attractive, yet demonic animals. There is nothing else like them.

Pound for pound, these are among the most powerful of known predators; certainly no other theropod had such a combination of foot, hand, and head weaponry. The jaws were well powered and bore long rows of bladed teeth. Hands were large and big-clawed. And of course there are the tremendous sickle claws, far larger than in any other known predator. Artists often understate the size of the claws. In some ways, they were the equivalent of the saber teeth of some extinct cats, weapons of power well beyond that normal for animals of their size. Especially so in dromaeosaurs, since the claws were worked by the most powerful set of muscles on the animal—the legs. Put a leopard and a *V. antirrhopus* together and the former would be

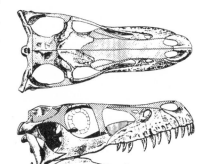

Dromaeosaurus albertensis *type* AMNH 5356

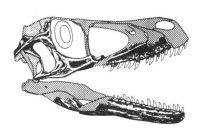

Velociraptor antirrhopus? *YPM 5210 robust*

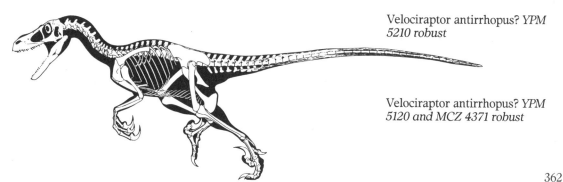

Velociraptor antirrhopus? *YPM 5120 and MCZ 4371 robust*

362

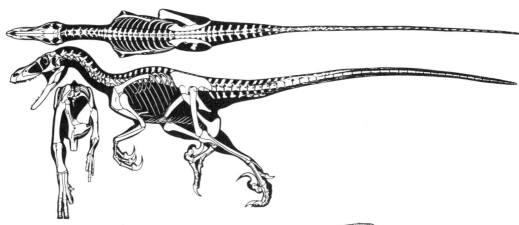

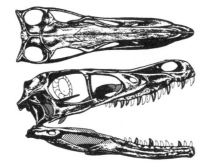

Velociraptor antirrhopus *YPM 5232 and AMNH 3015 gracile*

Velociraptor antirrhopus *YPM 5232 gracile*

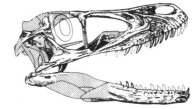

Velociraptor mongoliensis *GI 100/ 25*

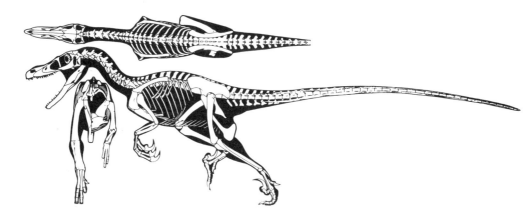

in trouble. Among theropods only *Tyrannosaurus,* with its extreme skull strength, equalled *Velociraptor* in total power relative to weight. These were big-game hunters, capable of bringing down animals much bigger than themselves. The jaws were secondary weapons; undoubtedly *Velociraptor* killed by deeply raking the prey's limbs or belly with its sickle claws, likely disemboweling the victim.[10] Both claws were probably used in tandem, to double the effect. Cassowaries, which have long saber claws on their second toes, do much the same to their enemies. As for speed, these powerful-limbed dinosaurs were certainly good runners. Perhaps not as good as the more gracile troodonts or tyrannosaurs, but then again, maybe so.

In a 1987 study of the big-horned dinosaurs, Dawn Adams noted that they were built in such a way that if the abdominal muscles were cut, then the whole animal would collapse. She suggested that the social sickle-claws were adept at leaping onto the sides of horned dinosaurs and reaching under with their feet to slice their belly muscles. This is a plausible idea. However, the horned dinosaurs, which lived in Late Cretaceous North America, were rhino-to-elephant-sized. At that time, most *Velociraptor* species were only jackal-sized, far, far too small to tackle such behemoths, and the bigger, wolf-sized *Velociraptor* species were too few to be important killers of horned dinosaur.

Usually the three species are placed in genera of their own. But bone for bone, and detail after detail, they are almost identical. The lightly built, upcurved skulls are quite distinctive and similar, the curvature due in part to the depressed nasals. The nasals are also L-shaped in cross section. At the front of the snout the lower edge of the premaxilla is stepped down from the rest of the tooth row. Preorbital bones, quadratojugals, and most everything else are carbon copies. The dentaries have unusually numerous small nerve and vessel openings, especially a distinctive one near the tip, and tend to be upcurved like the snout. The frontals are sharply triangular, so binocular vision was good. Braincase size seems modest relative to the skull, but the skull is strikingly large for the body and, as a consequence, the brain was large. The skulls show no more differences than those of modern jackals and wolves, which are in the same genus, and critical functional difference between the species' skulls and skeletons are lacking. They should therefore be regarded as one genus, one in which small gracile *V. mongoliensis* and *V. langstoni* are the "jackals" to the *V. antirrhopus* "wolf."[11]

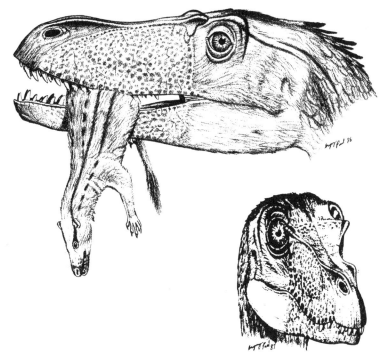

The heads of Velociraptor antirrhopus *YPM 5232 and* V. mongoliensis *are marked by their long upcurved snouts, with paired nasal horn ridges. Binocular vision was well developed, and protobeaks may have been present too.* V. antirrhopus *is shown holding on to the opossum-sized primitive mammal* Gobiconodon.

The numerous vessel and nerve openings on the nasals suggest that their sharp rims supported a well-developed horn ridge. The downstepped premaxilla may have supported a horn sheath contiguous with the nasal horn ridges, and the dentary's numerous foramina indicate it sported a long horn covering too. If true, then the nasal's and premaxilla's horn coverings may have formed a continuous protobeak, and the soft lips would have been displaced from the front of the mouth—in fact, it is possible that all protobirds had beaks of one sort or another. *Velociraptor*'s bladed teeth are modest in size, and very distinctive because the front keels' serrations are usually much finer than those on the rear. In most theropods the two sets are similar.

Birds have unique "saddle-shaped" neck articulations, and these are starting to develop in *Velociraptor*. Nonoverlapping neck ribs are bird adaptations, as are the hooked "uncinate" bones on the side of the rib cage. The last are obvious in the fighting *V. mongoliensis* skeleton, and can also be identified in the remains of *V. antirrhopus*.[12] The posterior trunk rib's shafts are bent ninety degrees near the top, so the rear half of the rib cage is square-topped in cross section, something also found in troofonts. The slender tail is marked by two bands of very long, ossified rods, one upper and one lower, which are forward extensions of the top and bottom tail bones along the last two thirds of its length. These made the latter section of the tail into a stiff whip-action balance for hard maneuvers; in contrast, the first few vertebrae just behind the hips could bend ninety degrees upward. Specimens of both *V. antirrhopus* and *V. mongoliensis* prove that the pubes pointed sharply backward, like in *Archaeopteryx* and *Adasaurus*. Unfortunately, we cannot compare *Velociraptor*'s skeleton to *Dromaeosaurus,* except to say that the former's foot is more slender.

Teeth and some slender second-toe bones indicate that a new, small species of *Velociraptor* was present in the very latest Cretaceous of western North America. Even more interesting is a tooth of the same age that Malcolm McKenna has at the AMNH; it indicates that a species as big or bigger than *V. antirrhopus* was alive then, although it seems much less common than the smaller form. Also at the AMNH is a hyper-extendable toe bone from the Late Cretaceous of Mongolia that looks like a *Velociraptor* somewhat bigger than *V. antirrhopus*. So *Velociraptor* was a very successful design that remained remarkably little changed in form for some fifty million years or more, a rare achievement. It was the arch medium-to-small-sized predator for this period, although competition from the smaller tyrannosaurs seems to have encouraged a partial trend toward smaller size as it evolved.

VELOCIRAPTOR ANTIRRHOPUS (Ostrom, 1969a)
SYNONYM—*Deinonychus antirrhopus*
TYPE—YPM 5205
BEST SPECIMENS—AMNH 3015, MCZ 4371, YPM 5232, YPM 5210
TIME—Aptian-Albian of the late Early Cretaceous
HORIZON AND DISTRIBUTION—Cloverly Formation of Montana
    and Wyoming
MAIN ANATOMICAL STUDIES—Ostrom, 1969a, 1976b; Paul, 1987c

	3015/5232	5210	4371
SKULL LENGTH—	332 mm	364	~410
TOTAL LENGTH—	3.06 m		3.43
FEMUR LENGTH—	284 mm		336
HIP HEIGHT—	.76 m		.87
KILOGRAMMAGE—	45	~52	73

This is my favorite velociraptor, and that is saying a lot. The long, low, streamlined skull 5232 is exceptionally attractive, and

Velociraptor antirrhopus *in a leaping attack against a herd of* Tenontosaurus tilleti. *The individual delivering the twin slashing strokes with its sickle claws is a solid black variant from the normal color pattern, a possibility inspired by the rare black leopard.*

along with the fantastic claw-armament array, makes it a far more interesting beast than any fantasy creature I know of. That this species is sunk into *Velociraptor* is rather unfortunate, because the name *Deinonychus* Ostrom, 1969a is a fine one. In this regard, note how similar the slender, upcurved dentary of skull 5232 is to that of *V. mongoliensis. V. antirrhopus* is usually considered a small dinosaur. But the largest individual was an eleven-foot-long animal whose head approached half a yard long, and was of male-timber-wolf mass. If alive today it would be considered a big predator.

Most of the skull elements are disarticulated, and the skull is usually drawn as rather allosaur-like. But the maxilla and nasals of 5232 are well preserved, and the latter show the same kind of depression seen in *V. mongoliensis*—albeit less strongly. The rest of the skull fits together in a long, low shape too. At one time the shoulder girdle's coracoid bone was mistaken for the hip's pubis, so initial restorations showed it with a shallow and most untheropodian belly. The finding of the real pubis of MCZ

4371 straightened this matter out. John Ostrom also seems to have switched the inner two fingers. He made the thumb the biggest clawed, and the second finger the divergent one. Instead, the hand was probably like *Archaeopteryx,* with the thumb divergent and bearing the second biggest claw.

The situation with Cloverly *V. antirrhopus* is complicated by the fact that two forms seem to be present. In the lower Cloverly Formation the very large MCZ skeleton has a fairly straight sickle claw. Higher in the Cloverly the smaller more gracile type foot and skeleton AMNH 3015 have much more curved claws. This is not a growth feature because the feet of the various specimens are about the same size. No skulls have been found attached to these skeletons. However, skull YPM 5232 may be from the same individual as the type foot. These have been combined with the same-sized skeleton 3015 into a skeletal restoration of one of the two forms. As for the other form, 5210 has a bigger and relatively deeper skull than 5232, and its lower jaw's dentary is straighter and stouter than the latter's. It is possible that the big 5210 skull goes with the big MCZ 4371 kind of skeleton, and I have made a restoration of this second form. So there may, and I repeat *may,* be a big robust-skulled and straighter-clawed *Velociraptor* in the whole of the Cloverly, and a smaller, lower skulled, more curved-clawed one in the upper part of the formation.[13]

What do these forms represent? If the curved-claw form is limited to the upper Cloverly, it is a species difference. And such extreme variation in claw curvature is not found in living carnivores, so I suspect this to be the case. As stressed before, it is not unusual for two similar species of a genus to cohabit the same territory. But the sample size is too small to prove temporal segregation at this time, and it is possible that the different forms represent the two sexes, perhaps of the "gracile" and "robust" sort that marks the earlier coelophysians (see pages 259-263). The question remains open.

Robert Bakker's *V. antirrhopus* rendition has become one of the most famous of dinosaur images.[14] It is, however, well out of date, with a head too short in length and too tall, and a much too shallow belly.

Velociraptor had no equivalent competition in the Cloverly. Its main prey was the abundant, half-tonne ornithischian *Tenontosaurus. Tenontosaurus* could bite with its beak and kick hard, and it was a fair runner, but it was no more powerful than a big horse and fair game for sickle-claws. Indeed, the main YPM *Velociraptor* quarry does include some pieces of a *Tenontosaurus* the velociraptors may have been feeding upon when they all died together.

VELOCIRAPTOR LANGSTONI (Sues, 1978)

SYNONYM—*Saurornitholestes langstoni*
TYPE—TMP P74.10.5
TIME—late Campanian of the late Late Cretaceous
HORIZON AND DISTRIBUTION—Judith River Formation of Alberta

	Type
KILOGRAMMAGE—	~5

There is not much known of this species, just bits and pieces of the skull and skeleton, yet it is an important one. Hans Dieter-Sues noted its close similarity to *V. antirrhopus,* so when I compared its skull-roof frontals to the type of *V. mongoliensis,* it was no big surprise to see they were virtually identical in shape and size. Sues assigned some dentaries from the Judith River to *Dromaeosaurus,*[15] but these are also of the *Velociraptor* mold, with numerous foramina and a pit in the tip.[16] Not only that, but they are robust like *V. antirrhopus,* and strongly curved like *V. mongoliensis.* They are also the right size to belong to *V. langstoni.* It is possible that further remains will show that this species differs more from its relatives than I think. But what is known indicates that a species of *Velociraptor,* one intermediate to the other two species, was alive in the Judith River. As such, this strengthens the case for bringing them all into the same genus. Teeth and skull-roof frontal bones indicate that *V. langstoni* was more common than *Dromaeosaurus albertensis* in the Judith River, and that something very like it lived in the later Horseshoe Canyon Formation.

VELOCIRAPTOR MONGOLIENSIS Osborn, 1924

TYPE—AMNH 6515
BEST SPECIMENS—type and GI 100/25
TIME—early-mid Campanian? of the late Late Cretaceous
HORIZON AND DISTRIBUTION—Djadokhta Formation of Mongolia
MAIN ANATOMICAL STUDIES—Sues, 1977b; Paul, 1987c

	Type	GI 100/25
SKULL LENGTH—	190 mm	249

TOTAL LENGTH—		2.07 m
FEMUR LENGTH—		~200 mm
HIP HEIGHT—		.5 m
KILOGRAMMAGE—	~6.7	15

This is the most advanced species of the genus, because of its greatly elongated snout with sharply depressed nasals. The rims of the L-cross-sectioned nasals are not as sharp as in *V. antirrhopus,* so the horn ridges may have been a little lower. The orbits are larger, but this is a simple function of the animal's quite small size, which is about that of a jackal or coyote.

It is common for a clade's members to increase in size with time. The velociraptor's seem to have done the opposite, but this is by no means unprecedented. For instance, the modern cheetah is smaller than the Ice Age species.

The type is an exquisitely preserved skull missing some of its back end. A large sickle claw was found, but the full nature of the species was not known until the discovery of the marvelous and famous "fighting" specimen GI 100/25.[17] Virtually complete, the skeleton is quite like that of *V. antirrhopus*. The few differences include a stouter lower arm, hand, and claws, and a smaller deltoid crest on the humerus. A key item preserved on the specimen is the very large, and very birdlike, sternal plates, quite similar to those of oviraptors. It is presumed that the other species of *Velociraptor* had them too. The sternum replaces the forward abdominal ribs, which have completely disappeared in birds. The reader should know that the proportions of the skeletal restoration are approximate.

Protoceratopids were the most common Djadokhta herbivores, and were the main prey of *V. mongoliensis*. These were no pushovers, having very big parrot-beaked skulls powered by enormous jaw muscles. Indeed, the remains of GI 100/25 are locked in mutually mortal combat with a small horned dinosaur, the velociraptor's hand still gripped in protoceratopsid's beak! *Oviraptor* was also its prey. This sickle-claw's main competitor was the somewhat less common *Saurornithoides mongoliensis,* which was larger but less formidably armed.

The Nonpredaceous and Bizarre Oviraptors

Although the name caenagnathids is more proper, I use oviraptors informally because it is more familiar and easier to say.

This animal really existed! Oviraptor philoceratops *in a fighting mode, and bouncing on its heavy tail.*

These are truly weird theropods, even more so than *Carnotaurus*. It is the convoluted shape of the skull, and the strange arrangement of the mouth roof and the jawbones that has us paleontologists scratching our heads, especially over *Oviraptor*. That they are beaked, however, is no more odd than it is for ostrich-mimics and birds. And the skeleton is fairly normal, if birdlike.

Certainly these were not true predators, for although the beak was somewhat parrot-like, it was not hooked as in predatory birds. It has been suggested that they were semiaquatic mollusk eaters, but the slender-boned skull seems too weak for this. On the other hand, the skull was too strongly built and specialized for picking up small mammals or stealing eggs, as has been thought, although such items may have made up part of their diet. Some sort of unusual herbivory was probable, but just what kind is not possible to tell. Adding to the confusion are the two conical teeth in the roof of the mouth of *Oviraptor*. Quite unheard of in other theropods, their function is a mystery. So is the mandible's portion of the jaw joint, for it is bulbous instead of being a grooved hinge. These jaw joints are most like those of the bizarre dicynodont mammal-like reptiles, and they indicate that *Oviraptor* fed with an odd back-and-forth motion of the jaws.[18]

The design of the palate and the intensely pneumatic skull bones indicate that these were somewhat closer to birds than archaeopterygids. However, some of the avian features must have been developed parallel to birds, for other, more advanced protobirds sometimes lack them.

FAMILY CAENAGNATHIDAE Sternberg, 1940

Microvenator celer

Chirostenotes pergracilis
C. rarus

Oviraptor (Oviraptor) philoceratops
O. (Ingenia) yanshini

SUBFAMILY CAENAGNATHINAE (Sternberg, 1940)

GENUS MICROVENATOR Ostrom, 1970

MICROVENATOR CELER Ostrom, 1970
TYPE—AMNH 3041 (juvenile?)
TIME—Aptian-Albian of the late Early Cretaceous
HORIZON AND DISTRIBUTION—Cloverly Formation of Montana

	Type
FEMUR LENGTH—	124 mm
KILOGRAMMAGE—	~3?

Only parts of the skeleton are known; its poorly ossified vertebrae indicate it was a young one. The hyperelongated upper ankle process is the sort advanced avetheropods had, while the lack of tall spines on the neck vertebrae mimic the same condition in the abelisaurian megalosaurs. These spineless neck bones, and the fact that the limb bones look very much like those of *Chirostenotes,* (see below) cause Philip Currie and Dale Russell to suspect that this is an early oviraptor. *Microvenator* lacks the back-swept pubes in the hips and coracoids in the shoulder seen in dromaeosaurs. *Microvenator* was always in danger from *Velociraptor antirrhopus.*

GENUS *CHIROSTENOTES* Gilmore, 1924
SYNONYMS—*Macrophalangia, Elmisaurus, Caenagnathus?*

At first, only a hand and foot from Alberta were known, but they came from different sites and were thought to be two different taxa, *Chirostenotes* and *Macrophalangia*.[19] Then a similar hand and foot were found together in Mongolia, showing that they were from the same kind of creature. Yet more recently, much of a skeleton has shown up in Alberta. The long thumb of this genus looks rather like that of a primitive ostrich-mimic, and is quite different from the short one of *Oviraptor*. Likewise, the feet are similar to the early ornithomimid *Garudimius*. So I was quite skeptical of Philip Currie's and Dale Russell's suggestion that this was really an oviraptor, but having seen the new skeleton, it is plain that they were right.[20] The finger claws have a little lip at the joint like *Oviraptor*'s, and the hip's ilium and ischium are clearly of the oviraptor type. This means that these primitive oviraptors either converge with the ostrich-mimics in the thumb and foot, or that they are closer relatives than we have realized. Gauthier pointed out in 1986 that the second toe of *Chirostenotes* may be hyperextendable. If so, it was less well developed than in *Archaeopteryx*, much less so than in the sickle-claws. Perhaps the toe was in the process of losing its hyperextendability; herbivores such as these would not have had much use for it.

The story does not end here. Primitive, oviraptor-like jaws have long been known from the same American sediments as *Chirostenotes*.[21] It is quite possible that these jaws, called *Caenagnathus* Sternberg, 1940, belong to *Chirostenotes,* and such is assumed here. Remains suggest that this genus was present in Alberta's Horseshoe Canyon Formation.

CHIROSTENOTES PERGRACILIS Gilmore, 1924
SYNONYMS—*Macrophalangia canadensis, Caenagnathus collinsi?, Caenagnathus sternbergi?*
TYPE—NMC 2367
BEST SPECIMEN—TMP 79.20.1
TIME—late Campanian of the late Late Cretaceous
HORIZON AND DISTRIBUTION—Judith River Formation of Alberta

	Type	NMC 8538
KILOGRAMMAGE—	~20?	~50?

Most of the limbs are known from the new TMP skeleton, but not enough of the skull and vertebrae have been found to fashion a skeletal restoration. The "*Caenagnathus*" lower jaws that may belong to this species have at various times been considered as belonging to a bird.[22] They are not especially odd in gross profile, but they have oviraptor features, including an unusually big opening in the lower jaw surrounded by slender interlocking bones, and an upwardly bulging jaw joint. Both the hand and legs are very long and gracile, and the central cannon bone is strongly pinched at its upper end, a characteristic of the genus.

There is a good amount of variation in the specimen's jaw and foot bones, enough to imply that either distinct sexes or two species may be involved. More remains are needed to see what is going on. The array of Alberta sickle-claws and tyrannosaurs were the nemesis of these more placid theropods.

CHIROSTENOTES RARUS (Osmolska, 1981)

SYNONYM—*Elmisaurus rarus*
TYPE—ZPAL MgD-1/172
TIME—early Maastrichtian? of the late Late Cretaceous
HORIZON AND DISTRIBUTION—Nemegt Formation of Mongolia
                        Type
KILOGRAMMAGE—   ~15?

The hand of this small, fragmentary species is virtually identical to that of *C. pergracilis,* and the feet of the two are also quite alike. So, unless new remains prove otherwise, this should definitely be put in *Chirostenotes*. The cannon bones show a tendency to fuse together, another feature common to the genus.

SUBFAMILY OVIRAPTORINAE (Barsbold, 1976)

Many skulls are known for the subfamily's two taxa. They are so alike that taken alone they would easily be the same genus, but the strong morphological and functional differences between the hands supports a subgeneric distinction.

The skull is very short in length and tall in height for a theropod. It looks something like a parrot's, and has slender cheekbones. Unlike other protobirds, binocular vision has been lost, a characteristic of herbivores that need to scan 360 degrees for predators. The braincase elements are bulbous, so the brain was quite large. The snout is especially short and deep, with a very reduced maxillary region. The roof of the mouth, instead of being vaulted like that of a proper theropod, is depressed below the upper jaw line. It is very unusual in detailed design, although avian-like in basic motif. The contorted lower jaws are also short and deep, especially at mid length. These features are truly out of the ordinary.

Somewhat more ordinary is the skeleton.[23] The shoulder girdle and forelimbs are very like those of *Archaeopteryx* and *Velociraptor*. They retain a big furcula, rather like *Archaeopteryx*'s but more wishbone-shaped, and the very large breastplate is similar to *Velociraptor*'s. The wrist's half-moon-shaped carpal block is co-ossified to the hand, a birdlike feature. The hand itself is surprisingly variable in the group, being ornithomimid-like in *Chirostenotes*, dromaeosaur-like in *O. philoceratops*, and quite unique in *O. yanshini*. The tail is said to lack the ossified rods of the sickle-claws—apparently the peaceful oviraptors did not need such accessories—and it is said that the tail is exceptionally deep. The parallelogram-shaped ilium and short triangualar-aproned ischium are in the protobird model. But—although it has been suggested otherwise—the pubes supposedly point a little forward as in normal theropods, not backward as in archaeopterygids.[24] The type skeleton of *O. philoceratops* seems to lack neural spines on the neck vertebrae. A close look leads me to think they are broken off, but I could be wrong.

So far, these two oviraptors are known only from Mongolia, including remains from the Nemegt Formation. *Velociraptor* and *Troodon* were constant dangers to them.

GENUS *OVIRAPTOR* Osborn, 1924

SUBGENUS *OVIRAPTOR (OVIRAPTOR)* (Osborn, 1924)

OVIRAPTOR (OVIRAPTOR) PHILOCERATOPS Osborn, 1924
TYPE—AMNH 6517
BEST SPECIMENS—type and GI 100/42
TIME—early to late Campanian? of the late Late Cretaceous
HORIZONS AND DISTRIBUTION—Djadokhta and Barun Goyot
    Formations of Mongolia
MAIN ANATOMICAL STUDY—Barsbold, 1983a

	Type	GI 100/42
SKULL LENGTH—	186 mm	210
TOTAL LENGTH—	~2.5 m	

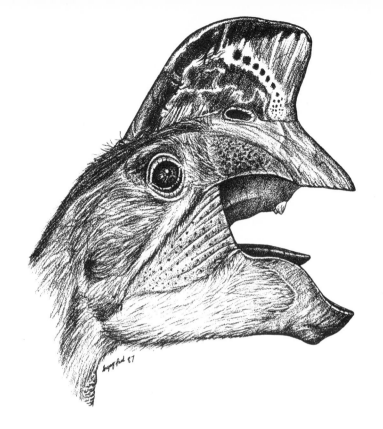

The unreal head of Oviraptor philoceratops. *Exactly what the crest was for is not clear. Observe the two little teeth astride the midline of the mouth's roof.*

FEMUR LENGTH—   ~262? mm
HIP HEIGHT—   ~.75 m
KILOGRAMMAGE—   33

The type skeleton was described in the same brief yet seminal paper as the two other Djadokhta protobirds, *Velociraptor mongoliensis* and *Troodon mongoliensis*. The toothless skull and skeleton had been only partly prepared, so the head's strangeness was obscured enough for Osborn to think it was an ostrich-mimic, which are also toothless. In fact, a few restorations have shown it as a low-headed, ornithomimid-like animal. This could not be further from the truth.

O. philoceratops was not satisfied, figuratively speaking, with the aberration of its skull, so it developed an intricately pneumatic, flattened premaxillary-nasal crest.[25] Presumably this crest developed as a visual display device. Structurally, it is very like the big head crest of the living cassowary, and it was probably enlarged by a light horn sheath. The shoulder and arm bones were remarkably large and strong, and the long, big-clawed fingers were very dromaeosaur-like. In fact, the thumb's short metacarpal may be a retained feature shared with dromaeosaurs.

Oriraptor (Oriraptor) philoceratops *type AMNH 6517 and GI 100/
42*

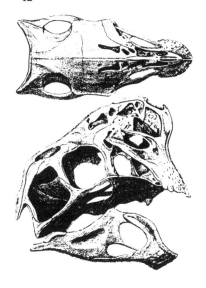

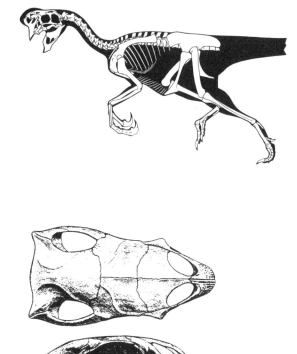

Oriraptor (Oriraptor) philoceratops *type AMNH 6517*

Oriraptor (Ingenia) yanshini?
ZPAL MgD-1/95

The skeletal drawing's front half is after the type, with the better preserved GI 100/42 head standing in. Most of the hind limbs are after other specimens, the lower hip bones are rather schematic, and the proportions are approximate. More complete oriraptor skeletons may be published soon.[26]

Peaceful *O. philoceratops* must have been the frequent victim of the sickle-claws. Speed was one of the oriraptor's defenses, but it may have stood its ground too, lashing out like a giant South American anteater with its powerful arms and biting like a parrot. Note that *O. yanshini* was a contemporary only later on, in the Barun Goyot Formation. It is likely that the two species preferred somewhat different kinds of vegetation, in order to avoid direct competition.

SUBGENUS *OVIRAPTOR (INGENIA)* (Barsbold, 1981)

OVIRAPTOR (INGENIA) YANSHINI (Barsbold, 1981)

TYPE—GI 100/30
BEST SPECIMENS—type and a number of others
TIME—mid-late Campanian? of the late Late Cretaceous
HORIZON AND DISTRIBUTION—Barun Goyot Formation of
    Mongolia
MAIN ANATOMICAL STUDY—Osmolska, 1976
                     ZPAL MgD-1/95
SKULL LENGTH—   105 mm
KILOGRAMMAGE— ~6?

Although the skull lacks the crest of *O. philoceratops, O. yanshini* is weirdly unique in having fingers that not only are very short, but become increasingly so going outward.[27] The fingers are also fairly stout, and the outer claws are reduced in size. Why the hand is this way is yet another oviraptorian mystery, though one suspects it has something to do with feeding habits. I do not agree with Barsbold's idea that they were webbed for swimming, because digits become longer to support webs, not shorter. Otherwise this species seems to be a somewhat smaller yet stouter version of *O. philoceratops.* It may have as many as seven hip vertebrae[28] and only eleven dorsals, which would be more and fewer respectively than known in any other theropod.

The Enigmatic Ostrich-Mimics

Along with oviraptors, the ostrich-mimics or ornithomimids are another theropod group that is not in tune with the predatory theme of this book. Toothless and small-skulled, the ostrich-mimics were ostrich-like herbivores, not arch predators. In fact, much else about these dinosaurs is also ostrich-like—the big eyes, long slender neck, compact body, and very long gracile limbs. However, unlike the big ground birds, the forelimbs are very long and have fingers, and of course there is a well-developed tail. I call them enigmatic because their feeding habits and relationships have long been perplexing to dinosaurologists.

The ostrich-like nature of these animals was recognized when the very first fragmentary remains, including a foot, were described by Marsh in 1890. Indeed, it is too bad that the family name is not Struthiomimidae (ostrich-mimic), instead of the less precise Ornithomimidae (bird-mimic). After all, all theropods are birdlike. Until recently the only good remains came from a handful of very similar and advanced species. In the last few years, new, more primitive species have been discovered, and these have been very helpful in eliminating some possible relationships of this group with others. The most primitive known species even has a few very small teeth near the tip of its jaws.

The combination of the unusual skull and the long, slender forelimbs bearing long, gently curved claws has long perplexed those trying to understand ornithomimid feeding habits. The key to understanding this problem is found in the small, beaked head and the long neck. Clearly, these creatures cannot be true predators. It has often been suggested that ostrich-mimics were omnivorous, picking up small animals and insects along with fruits and soft plants. Or that they were experts in stealing dinosaur and reptile eggs from their nests.

At this point we need to take a close look at the heads of big ground birds. The ostrich and emu are often thought of as omnivores that will eat any items they can swallow. But field observations indicate they are really grazers and browsers; they concentrate on picking up the higher quality plant parts that their rather simple digestive systems can cope with. Small animals and eggs are not on their menus, though emus do eat insects. Ostrich and emu heads are amazing because of how weakly they are built and muscled. Made of light struts and thin sheets of bone, their jaw muscles are small and have little leverage.

Quite different are the great birds that lived in New Zealand until recent centuries—the moas. Although their skulls are also small, they are much more strongly built. The skull and jaws are deep and heavily braced, and were operated by large muscles that gave them a powerful bite. The moas' big, broad bellies carried a more sophisticated digestive system for digesting plants, and the stomach contents of natural mummies show that they were biting off and eating more twigs than leaves.[29]

Ornithomimid skulls are alleged to have been frail. But they are really built more like those of moas than ostriches. The snouts and lower jaw were fairly deep. In advanced species the cheek opening is nearly closed off, and the quadrate sometimes braces the jugal in the cheek. All this helps strengthen the jaw joint. As for the muscles, the snout and strong roof of the mouth supported large jaw-closers. The temporal muscles at the back of the head are rather small, and ostrich-mimic skulls were not as powerful as those of predatory theropods. But they were much stronger than those of ostriches—an ornithomimid could probably bite your finger off, and could easily deal with twigs and other tough plant material. The slender neck and its muscles are again less so than in ostriches, so ornithomimids could peck and pull harder. All this tells us a lot of things. Such powerful jaws are not needed to eat eggs, nor are they necessary to grab and swallow small animals. Ostrich-mimic heads and necks can only be explained as an adaptation for browsing, probably on tougher grade plants than those consumed by ostriches. On the other hand, these theropods' relatively small bellies suggest they picked on less resistant plant parts more often than did moas.

But what about those peculiar forelimbs? Everything from grasping eggs to raking open animal and insect nests has been suggested for them. In 1985, Elizabeth Nicholls and Anthony Russell showed that, unlike those of other theropods, the thumb and fingers of *Ornithomimus* swing toward each other when they are flexed, so the hand works as a narrow hook rather than as a broad rake or grasping tool. When faced with a branch beyond the head's reach, ostrich-mimics may have hooked onto the branch's lower portion with a hand or two and pulled to bring the upper end within reach of the jaws. When not in use, the forelimbs could not be folded up as well as those of other protobirds, as the simplified elbow and wrist would not allow it.

Nicholls and Russell also believe that ornithomimid shoulder blades were mobile. This may well be correct, since the coracoid is fairly short, and both the furcula and large breastplate are missing so there is no interlocking between the bones. Perhaps ornithomimids lost these protobird flight adaptations as a way of freeing up the shoulder and increasing the reach of the arms.

Another idea about ostrich-mimics is that they were waders that fed on small aquatic vertebrates.[30] But we have already seen that their heads and forelimbs are not built for feeding on small animals. Besides, wading birds have long slender toes that provide good support on soft surfaces. Ostrich-mimics have much shorter and stouter running toes that are similar to those of rheas and emus.

An important thing is that ostrich-mimics' beaks, and oviraptors' too, were ensheathed with horn or keratin, just like in turtles and birds. Following the shape of the underlying bone, the horn covering lengthened the beak. Growing constantly as its edges were worn down, it kept its owner equipped with sharp cutting edges.

The smaller snout, relative to other theropods, suggests that their sense of smell was not as well developed as in predatory species. Confirmation comes from the brain's olfactory bulbs, which were smaller than in other theropods. Having only a so-so sense of smell, their big eyes served as the key food sensors and predator detectors. Ornithomimids might have bit and pecked at smaller theropods, and they could give a hefty "ostrich kick"—ostriches are known to kill lions with kicks—but their main defense was high-speed flight. Tyrannosaurs and sickle-claws were the main dangers to ostrich-mimics. In fact, being herbivores that had to forage for large amounts of fodder, ornithomimids and oviraptors must have slept much less than their predaceous relatives. Being a vegetarian can be tough.

Casts of brain cavities show that ostrich-mimic brains were about as large relative to their bodies as those of ostriches.[31] The braincases are very birdlike, with bulbous and pneumatic lower elements and the middle ear set in a circular depression.[32] A distinctive feature of ornithomimids is the thumb and its metacarpal, which are both long relative to the other fingers.

A big part of the ornithomimid enigma is their place relative to other theropods. They may have been members of the protobird group. This is indicated by their very birdlike braincases, middle ears and mouth roofs. As such, they may have descended from flying ancestors similar to *Archaeopteryx,* then greatly modified their form to meet the demands of a herbivorous, terrestrial life-style. The herbivory may have evolved in their flying ancestors, to be inherited by oviraptors, ostrich-mimics, and possibly the avimimids discussed on page 402. Indeed, ornithomimids may be close relatives of primitive oviraptors like *Chirostenotes* (see page 373). Or, the herbivory could have evolved independently. Ostrich-mimics are like the other advanced protobirds in that they have normal pubes, instead of the back-swept ones seen in basal protobirds and birds proper. As discussed elsewhere, this may or may not contradict their descent from protobirds. In any case, the first ornithomimids appear fairly early in the Cretaceous. These early remains include fairly advanced as well as primitive species, so they must have appeared even earlier in the Cretaceous. They spread to North America and became more common in the Late Cretaceous.

Most ostrich-mimics are small or medium-sized, but one possible member is gigantic. There has been a tendency to place each of the most primitive species in a family of its own. But there is as much or more variation in such single modern carnivore families as the Canidae. So I see no need for more than one ostrich-mimic family—the third largest among theropods—with a subfamily holding the primitive forms. Although the ostrich-mimics are extinct, it is nice to know that in ostriches one sees a modern evocation of their basic design. No other dinosaurs are so closely reproduced in the modern fauna.

FAMILY ORNITHOMIMIDAE Marsh, 1890

Harpymimus okladnikovi

Garudimimus brevipes

*Deinocheirus mirificus

Ornithomimus? affinis
O.? asiaticus
O. altus
O. edmontonicus
O. samueli
O. brevitertius
O. velox
O. bullatus

SUBFAMILY GARUDIMIMINAE (Barsbold, 1981)

GENUS *HARPYMIMUS* Barsbold and Perle, 1984

HARPYMIMUS OKLADNIKOVI Barsbold and Perle, 1984
TYPE—GI 100/29
TIME—Aptian-Albian? of the mid-Cretaceous
HORIZON AND DISTRIBUTION—Shinehuduk Formation of
    Mongolia

	Type
SKULL LENGTH—	~270 mm
KILOGRAMMAGE—	~125?

This is the second archaic ostrich-mimic to be known from good remains, and the most primitive. The type consists of an almost complete skull (albeit crushed) along with most of the skeleton. As only a preliminary note showing a few of the bones is out, I could not do a skeletal restoration of this very intriguing

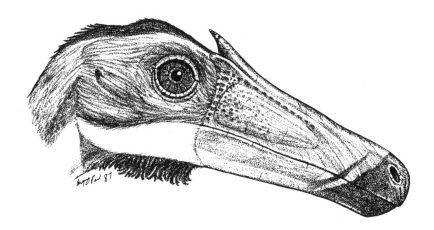

Garudimimus brevipes *had a straight-edged beak and a peculiar brow horn quite different from those of more advanced Or-nithomimus.*

theropod. The most interesting thing about it is that although the jaws are beaked, the tip of the lower jaw bears ten or eleven small conical teeth, making this the only ostrich-mimic that still has teeth. The mandible is down-curved, the hand is fairly un-modified with a moderate-length thumb, and the central cannon bone of the foot is only moderately compressed. Note that this very primitive ostrich-mimic lived at the same time as much more advanced species. *Harpymimus* was probably still eating small animals, as well as plants.

Garudimimus brevipes *type GI 100/13*

GARUDIMIMUS BREVIPES Barsbold, 1981
TYPE—GI 100/13
TIME—Coniacian-Santonian? of the late Late Cretaceous
HORIZON AND DISTRIBUTION—Baysheen-Shireh Formation of
    Mongolia

	Type
SKULL LENGTH—	260 mm
KILOGRAMMAGE—	~85?

This is the first primitive ostrich-mimic known from good remains, including an excellent skull. The long, low, toothless head is clearly ornithomimid, and the braincase includes the bulbous lower elements. The skull's primitive features include a normal theropodian cheek region and a straight, simple beak. The tip of the beak has a little notch. The skull's roof also has a rather strange little centerline horn in front of the eye socket. Primitive features of the foot include a less reduced central can-non bone, and a still present inner toe.

*SUBFAMILY DEINOCHEIRINAE (Osmolska and Roniewicz, 1969)

*GENUS *DEINOCHEIRUS* Osmolska and Roniewicz, 1969

**DEINOCHEIRUS MIRIFICUS* Osmolska and Roniewicz, 1969
TYPE—ZPAL MgD-1/6
TIME—early Maastrichtian? of the late Late Cretaceous
HORIZON AND DISTRIBUTION—Nemegt Formation of Mongolia
         Type
TONNAGE— 6–12

This is one of those enigmatic, poorly known dinosaurs that has us dinosaurologists all agog and drumming our fingers as we hope for more to show up. Only the arms and hands are known, and they are 2.4 m (almost 8 ft) long. Of course, some have not been able to resist comparing this set to the forelimbs of *Tyrannosaurus rex* and extrapolating fantastic sizes for the owner, but this is a false comparison because tyrannosaurs have unusually small arms for their size. Much more pertinent is John Ostrom's observation of 1972 that the *Deinocheirus* forelimbs are, bone for bone, much the same as those of ornithomimids. This includes the long thumb metacarpal, and the slenderness of all the long bones. However, the claws are more robust and strongly curved. if this is an ornithomimid, then the forelimbs should be relatively long relative to the body. But this still must have been an enormous animal. In the mass estimates, it is assumed this had about the same mass-to-scapula relationship as did small ostrich-mimics. What it looked like and what it did is anybody's guess, but its hands, which are more advanced looking than those of *Harpymimus,* suggest that it was a toothless ostrich-mimic. I place it as more primitive than *Ornithomimus* because its humerus has a bigger deltoid crest. The great claws may have evolved for nonpredatory feeding purposes, for they are too blunt for killing, but would have been effective defensive weapons. Whatever it was, *Deinocheirus* was a rare and bizarre member of the Mongolian fauna.

SUBFAMILY ORNITHOMIMINAE (Marsh, 1890)

GENUS *ORNITHOMIMUS* Marsh, 1890
SYNONYMS—*Archaeornithomimus?*, *Dromiceiomimus,*
   Gallimimus, Struthiomimus

This is the archtypical ostrich-mimic genus, well known for

decades from a number of skulls and skeletons. Usually it is split into several genera, based on supposed differences in the beaks and in the proportions of the skeleton. But while restoring their skulls, I noticed that things were not as they had been believed. Traditionally, the North American species were restored with straight-edged upper and lower beaks.[33] The new Mongolian *"Gallimimus"* was given a very different upturned beak tip.[34] Neither is right. Instead, the edge of the upper beak is fluted to greater or lesser degrees, often with an especially large flute on the maxilla, and the end of the lower jaw is kinked. Although the details differ, this means that all these advanced ostrich-mimics are much more similar than previously thought. Many a genus of living birds show more variation than this. The proportional differences in the body and limbs are also minor, often no greater than found in living species of ground birds. In fact, flipping through my skeletal restorations I often have trouble figuring out which is which. A good rule of thumb is that when *this* happens, you are dealing with species and not genera. Since there are no major functional differences between these species, this certainly is the way to go.

Other skull characters that typify this genus include the reduced cheek opening, bracing of the jaw-supporting quadrate by the cheek's jugal bone in at least some species, and a strongly forward-sloping quadrate. The eyes were bigger than those of ostrichs—although they are sometimes overblown in illustrations —yet their skulls were narrower. The eyeballs were therefore flattened, and could not move much in their sockets, meaning ostrich-mimics must have had to flick their heads to and fro to sight in on various objects. Because the eyes faced somewhat sideways, binocular vision was more limited than in some other protobirds, a typical adaptation for improving an animals ability to detect predators from behind.

An interesting feature is the tendency for the top of the nasals to be rugose. The rugosity probably supported a long, low nasal horn, similar to but lower than those of tyrannosaurs. This is surprising, and shows that these peaceful ostrich-mimics are not quite as ostrich-like as often supposed. In fact, this is a problem of many *Ornithomimus* restorations—they are *too* ostrich-like. After all, the skull is deeper and narrower than in ostriches, and the neck is shorter and less supple. The chest is shallow and not very broad. Abdominal ribs preserved in position show that the belly's lower contour is not as hollow as in hungry predatory theropods. This is so because ostrich-mimics always kept their bellies at least partly filled with digesting plant material in order to support the flora of microorganisms that do the actual breaking down of plant materials.

The humerus of this genus is odd in being very long and slender, with only a tiny deltoid crest. The hand is also out of the ordinary in that the thumb and its metacarpal are about as long as the other fingers, and the claws are often *very* long, slender, and only a little curved. All in all, quite peculiar.

Well-preserved hips show that the pelvic canal is unusually broad; it may have been that *Ornithomimus* laid big, ostrich-sized eggs. *Ornithomimus* tails are shorter than in most other theropods. This was probably a speed adaptation, a way of reducing weight. Ostrich-mimic hips are exceptionally big, and the hind limbs are extremely long, powerful, and gracile, with very long, slender cannons. Few other dinosaurs are built as much for speed, but ostrich-mimic limbs are closely matched by the remarkably similar limbs of the tyrannosaurs that hunted them. *Ornithomimus* is unusual among theropods and birds in having lost the inner toe: yet another speed adaptation.

I have to admit I was disappointed in the appearance of the skeletons as they turned out in restoration. They look rather unelegant; I had hoped for something more graceful. Dale Russell's 1972 restorations of these animals are more aesthetically pleasing, but this is because the backs are curved in the wrong direction and the knees are too straight. Then again, when one thinks about it, ostriches are not the most attractive of creatures either.

I also wish that the name *Struthiomimus* had priority, because it is much more appropriate. With its derived skull and highly modified limbs, this is easily the most advanced genus in the family. Because *O. affinis* lived some sixty million years before the last species of this genus, I include it somewhat reluctantly, even though it looks like it does belong. Otherwise, most of the species are so similar that it is difficult to sort out their relationships, so the order below is only approximate. In addition to the named species, John Ostrom points to some probable *Ornithomimus* remains from the mid-Cretaceous Cloverly Formation of Montana.[35] There are also a number of tenuous species based on poor material from the Late Cretaceous formations of the Rockies. Most of these probably belong to the better-known species.

ORNITHOMIMUS? (ARCHAEORNITHOMIMUS?) AFFINIS
Gilmore, 1920
SYNONYM—*Archaeornithomimus affinis?*
TYPE—assorted USNM specimens
TIME—Hauterivian or Barremian of the mid Early
Cretaceous
HORIZONS AND DISTRIBUTION—Arundel Formation of New Jersey
KILOGRAMMAGE—   ~125?

Primitive, curved toe claws led Dale Russell to place this in *Archaeornithomimus* Russell, 1972, which has similar feet (see next species). Although known only from scraps, it is an important species because it shows how early the first advanced ornithomimids appeared.

ORNITHOMIMUS? (ARCHAEORNITHOMIMUS?) ASIATICUS
Gilmore, 1933
SYNONYM—*Archaeornithomimus asiaticus?*
TYPE—AMNH 6569
TIME—early Late Cretaceous
HORIZON AND DISTRIBUTION—Iren Debasu Formation of
Mongolia
AMNH 6559
KILOGRAMMAGE—   ~20?

Because the fragmentary remains of this very small ostrich-mimic include cannon bones and curved toe claws that are more primitive than the later species of *Ornithomimus*, Russell gave it the new name *Archaeornithomimus*. This does not seem enough of a reason; for example, in the bear genus *Ursus* there is as much variation in claw shape. Actually, not enough is known to tell if this is a valid genus, or subgenus, or neither.

ORNITHOMIMUS ALTUS Lambe, 1902
SYNONYM—*Struthiomimus altus*
TYPE—NMC 930
BEST AND DISPLAY SPECIMEN—AMNH 5339
TIME—Late Campanian of the late Late Cretaceous
HORIZONS AND DISTRIBUTION—Judith River and Horseshoe
Canyon? Formations of Alberta
MAIN ANATOMICAL STUDIES—Osborn, 1916; Russell, 1972

Ornithomimus altus *browsing, using its arms to hold down a branch.*

AMNH 5339

SKULL LENGTH—	240 mm
TOTAL LENGTH—	4.3 m
FEMUR LENGTH—	480 mm
HIP HEIGHT—	1.4 m
KILOGRAMMAGE—	153

     The AMNH 5339 skeleton described by Fairfield Osborn was the first complete ornithomimid skeleton discovered. It remains the best. Unfortunately the back part of the skull is still unknown, and how square the beak's tip was is not clear. The fluting of the upper beak seems to be simpler than in other members of the genus, and the length of both the fore and hind limbs is moderate relative to the other species. In fact, the lack of any special features in this species makes it the most generalized member of the group. Although the specimen is complete, the length of the back is difficult to restore because the vertebrae are somewhat displaced, and still partly buried in the sediments.

O. altus appears to have been the most common ostrich-mimic in the Judith River, where *O. edmontonicus* and *O. samueli* were its companions. The modest differences in beak shape that exist between these forms probably indicate somewhat differing feeding habits, which helped them avoid direct competition with one another. Packs of small sickle-claws, and big and swift *Albertosaurus libratus,* were the main predators of *O. altus.* The species' presence in the Horseshoe Canyon Formation is not certain.

ORNITHOMIMUS EDMONTONICUS Sternberg, 1933
SYNONYM—*Struthiomimus curreli*
TYPE—NMC 8632
BEST AND DISPLAY SPECIMEN—ROM 851 (subadult?)
TIME—Late Campanian of the late Late Cretaceous
HORIZONS AND DISTRIBUTION—Judith River? and Horseshoe
Canyon Formations of Alberta

	ROM 851	NMC 12441?
SKULL LENGTH—	234 mm	
TOTAL LENGTH—	3.3 m	
FEMUR LENGTH—	435 mm	500 mm
HIP HEIGHT—	1.25 m	
KILOGRAMMAGE—	110	~165

This species is well known from the virtually complete ROM 851, which lacks only most of the tail. The skull is crushed, but it is fairly well preserved. Note that this is the only species of *Ornithomimus* for which the length of the trunk is certain. The tip of the beak is very square, the beak fluting is very well developed, and the nasals are more rugose than in other members of the genus. This is the sole theropod whose thumb metacarpal is actually longer than the others. The limbs are very long for the body, much as in *O. brevitertius. O. edmontonicus* was relatively uncommon in its two formations.

ORNITHOMIMUS SAMUELI (Parks, 1928b)
SYNONYMS—*Dromiceiomimus samueli, Struthiomimus samueli*
TYPE—ROM 840
TIME—Late Campanian of the late Late Cretaceous
HORIZON AND DISTRIBUTION—Judith River Formation of Alberta

	Type
SKULL LENGTH—	258 mm
KILOGRAMMAGE—	~150?

The only good remains of this species are a fine skull along with the front part of the animal. The upper arms are exceptionally long, and with details of the skull this suggests it is a close relative of, or perhaps ancestral to, the later *O. brevitertius*. The beak is straighter-edged with a sharper tip than in other members of the genus, and the nasal horn ridge is weakly developed.

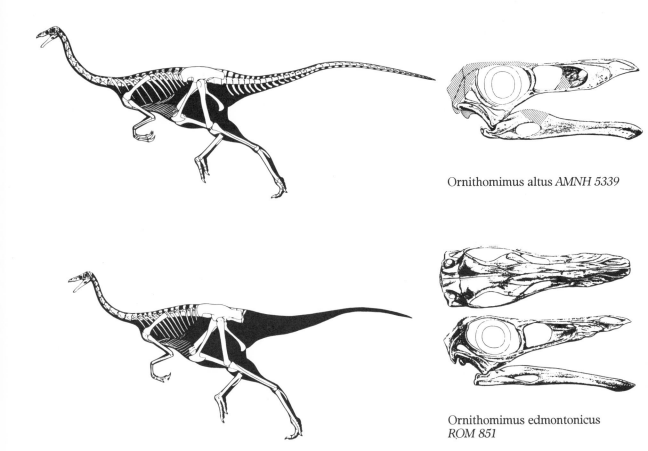

Ornithomimus altus *AMNH 5339*

Ornithomimus edmontonicus
ROM 851

Ornithomimus brevitertius *type ROM 867*

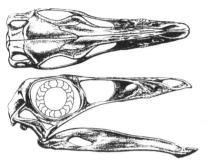

Ornithomimus samueli *type ROM 840*

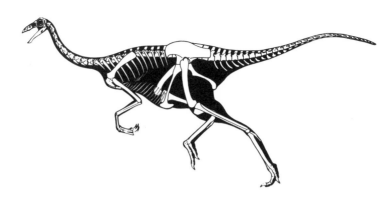

Ornithomimus bullatus *ZPAL MgD-1/94 and GI 100/10 juvenile*

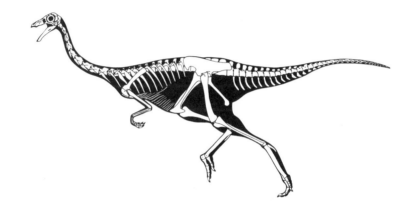

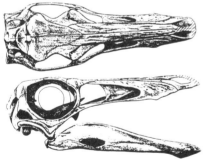

Ornithomimus bullatus *type GI 100/11*

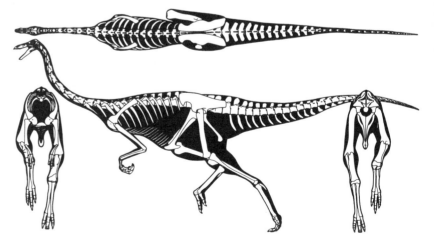

ORNITHOMIMUS BREVITERTIUS (Parks, 1926)

SYNONYMS—*Dromiceiomimus brevitertius, Struthiomimus brevitertius, Struthiomimus ingens*

TYPE—ROM 867

BEST SPECIMEN—NMC 12228

TIME—latest Campanian to early Maastrichtian of the late Late Cretaceous

HORIZON AND DISTRIBUTION—Horseshoe Canyon Formation of Alberta

MAIN ANATOMICAL STUDIES—Parks, 1926; Russell, 1972

	Type
SKULL LENGTH—	~240 mm
TOTAL LENGTH—	3.66 m
FEMUR LENGTH—	468 mm
HIP HEIGHT—	1.47 m
KILOGRAMMAGE—	144

As possible descendants of *O. samueli,* these two species were placed in a new genus *Dromiceiomimus* Russell, 1972. But as explained, all the advanced ostrich-mimics are too alike to be put in different genera. This is the hardest to restore of the *Ornithomimus* skeletons. A fair portion of the skull is preserved, but since it lacks the whole beak, I did not restore the head separately. The beak on the skeleton is after *O. samueli.* The skeleton is modified from Dale Russell's: I have made the neck and trunk a little longer and the forearm and hand a little shorter than he did, but I cannot prove all this since much of these parts are missing. What is known shows that this species is longer-armed and longer-legged than other ostrich-mimics. Its remains are abundant in the Horseshoe Canyon, much as *O. altus* was dominant in the Judith River. A contemporary of later populations of *O. edmontonicus,* these two risked ending up in the belly of the big tyrannosaur *Albertosaurus sarcophagus.*

ORNITHOMIMUS VELOX Marsh, 1890

TYPE—YPM 542/548

TIME—late Maastrichtian of the latest Late Cretaceous

HORIZONS AND DISTRIBUTION—Denver Formation of Colorado and Kaiparowits Formation of Utah

	MNA Pl 1762A
KILOGRAMMAGE—	~175?

Like all ornithomimids, Orni-thomimus bullatus had a fluted upper beak, distinctive from that of any living ground bird. Notice that there is a low rugose nasal ridge like in tyrannosaurs.

This is the first discovered of the ornithomimids, and still one of the least known despite a new yet very fragmentary specimen published by Frank DeCourten and Dale Russell in 1985.

ORNITHOMIMUS BULLATUS (Osmolska et al., 1972)
SYNONYM—*Gallimimus bullatus*
TYPE—GI 100/11
BEST SPECIMENS—type, GI 100/10 (juvenile), ZPAL MgD-1/1
    (juv.)
TIME—early Maastrichtian? of the late Late Cretaceous
HORIZON AND DISTRIBUTION—Nemegt Formation of Mongolia

	MgD-1/94	Type
SKULL LENGTH—	~170 mm	330
TOTAL LENGTH—	2.15 m	6.0
FEMUR LENGTH—	267 mm	660
HIP HEIGHT—	.79 m	1.9
KILOGRAMMAGE—	27	440

Discovered in the 1960s,[36] this is the largest species of *Orni-thomimus*—and, judging by the exceptional reduction of the cheek opening, the most advanced. On the other hand, the relatively short legs are not so advanced. The hands are especially small, and although it has been stated that the fingers could not move much, this is probably exaggerated. Notice that the snout is longer than in other species. Although the skull is attractive, this is otherwise the least graceful of the *Ornithomimus* species. GI 100/11 is not complete, so some of the neck and front trunk vertebrae and part of the hip are restored from other smaller specimens. Likewise, the restoration of baby MgD-1/94 includes the skull of 100/10.

Indeed, some of the more interesting things about this species are the juvenile skulls and skeletons, which give us a unique opportunity to examine growth in an ostrich-mimic. The skull is relatively larger and the snout is much shorter in the youngsters, while their eyes are very big. This is the normal pattern in growing animals. The forelimbs and tail get longer with age; the neck, trunk, and hind limbs seem to stay pretty much the same.

This was apparently the sole ornithomimid of the Nemegt. A primary enemy was the gigantic *Tyrannosaurus bataar,* and the sickle-claws gave it a hard time too.

More Sickle-Claws

Troodonts are the second radiation of fully predatory ground-dwelling protobirds. As such, these have sickle-clawed second toes and ossified-tendon tails, along with bladed teeth. They very possibly inherited the claw and tail from the archaeopterygians and dromaeosaurs, which despite many similarities are really much more primitive than troodonts. You can always tell a troodont's second toe from a dromaeosaur's, because the former's middle toe bone is much shorter than the inner toe bone. The lightweight troodonts can be thought of as the dinosaurian equivalent of the cheetah, compared to the velociraptors as heavier "leopards."

FAMILY TROODONTIDAE Gilmore, 1924

Troodon formosus
T. mongoliensis
T.? andrewsi

Bradycneme draculae

GENUS *TROODON* Leidy, 1856

SYNONYMS—*Saurornithoides, Stenonychosaurus, Pectinodon, Elopteryx?, Heptasteornis?*

Troodon's head differs from a dromaeosaur's in that it is rather ornithomimid-like in its long, slender proportions, and even more so in the braincase, middle ear, and roof of the mouth.[37] The parasphenoid, a frontward-pointing process of the braincase, is a bulbous structure, and the middle ear is set in a circular depression. As for the brain, it is quite large and well in the avian range.[38] Such similarities suggest that troodonts are advanced members of the protobird radiation. Other differences from dromaeosaurs include the tip of the snout and mandible, which are blunt and U-shaped in top view instead of narrow. The gracile snout has less room for jaw muscles and olfactory organs, and the olfactory bulbs of the brain are reduced, so troodonts smelled less adeptly than most other theropods. From what is known of the jaw-supporting quadrate and the mouth roof's pterygoid bone it articulated with, troodonts may have had the push-pull skull kinesis of birds. In this the snout can be lifted relative to the rest of the head. But it is hard to tell if *Troodon* was really like this without further remains.

There are many more teeth here than in most theropods. They have expanded roots like in *Archaeopteryx* and early birds, and are quite unusual in being short, small, semitriangular blades with a small number of large serrations. The serrations often do not reach the tip of the tooth. Leidy long ago described such a tooth, with serrations on the front and back keels, and named it *T. formosus*. Alas, things became increasingly confused after that. Among other things, the two additional genera *Saurornithoides* and *Stenonychosaurus* were named from Asia and North America. Their teeth often lack serrations on the front edge. The original *Troodon* tooth was itself thought to belong to one or another kind of herbivorous dinosaur, and even to a lizard. So were some other troodont jaws and teeth. But with John Horner's discovery of a jaw just outside the new Tyrrell Museum in the Horseshoe Canyon Formation,[39] *Troodon* was shown to have very variable teeth, representing all the various types. So there is only one basic kind of animal. Indeed, although future remains may prove otherwise the differences in the skulls known so far do not appear strong enough to establish a generic differentiation as far as Kenneth Carpenter and I are concerned,[40] although others disagree.

Troodon's frontals are sharply triangular, and its binocular vision was better developed than in any other dinosaur. Although the orbits were *very* large and circular along the upper rim, the size of the eye is exaggerated in many restorations.[41] These features led Dale Russell to speculate that this big-brained, small-toothed predator was a nocturnal mammal-hunter.[42] This is possible, and it certainly did pick up small animals when it could. The expanded crocodile-like tooth roots suggest it may have fished some, too, and the big tooth serrations were good for holding on to slippery things. But the bladed teeth were also good rippers, and the sickle claw a powerful weapon. So *Troodon* probably hunted large prey regularly, albeit prey that was smaller relative to what dromaeosaurs went after.[43] As to whether it was a nocturnal hunter, both day and night living animals have big eyes, so this does not tell us much. The real light-gathering differences are found in the relative proportions of color-sensitive cones and low-light-sensitive rods in the retina, and these are not the sorts of things we can measure in extinct animals.

The skeleton is much less well known, and the pelvis is a particular problem. A rather schematic drawing of a *T. mongoliensis* specimen is like archaeopterygids and oviraptors in the ilium.[44] The pubis seems to point forward, not backward. Ken Carpenter and I reexamined the poorly preserved pubis of the type *T. mongoliensis* and found its upper end to be a rather odd structure, unlike that of other theropods. *Troodon* is like dromaeosaurs in that the back half of its rib cage is squared off in top cross section. And the tail seems to have very much the same kind of elongated ossified rods found in dromaeosaurs.[45] Thulborn believes troodonts had an ossified furcula,[46] but this *may* be a co-ossified abdominal rib instead. The hand is similar to a dromaeosaur's, although much smaller. Yet the hand claws are larger than the hind foot's, the thumb claw being bigger than the sickle claw. It is not clear whether or not troodonts leapt onto their victims' backs and hung on like dromaeosaurs, though I doubt it.

Birdlike skeletal features are typified by the short, stout femur, and long, slender extremities, which are like but not as extreme as those in *Avimimus*. The ankle region is the most avian, being laterally narrow, and the lower fibula is either lost or very slender. The fourth cannon bone is a special oddity. This outermost of the three main foot bones is much the largest, and a large posterior flange of this bone backs the other two.[47] All this served to strengthen the functionally two-toed, sickle-clawed foot.

In 1982 Dale Russell and R. Sequin speculated on what might have happened to *Troodon* if it had not become extinct. Its big brain, binocular vision, bipedal stance, and grasping hands reminded them of protohumans, and they suggested that it could have developed into a very big-brained tool user, a dinosaurian version of humanity. The concept garnered much publicity, and for Russell much friendly abuse from other dinosaurologists. That tabloids cited Russell's work as confirmation that, among other things, dino-humans are reemerging from the ground in certain midwestern states has not helped! There *are* serious problems with the idea. Troodont brains were only about the size of ostrich brains, or a little bigger. They were not anywhere comparable to the much larger and more sophisticated brains of primates. Nor were theropod fingers the fine-tuned grasping organs of primates. Whether troodonts would ever become intellectual tool users is dubious, though not totally impossible. As for the postulated troodont "homonoid" itself, the model Russell and Sequin made looks suspiciously human with its lost tail and vertical body. One might expect a more theropod-like or birdlike horizontal posture, with a long tail sticking out behind. What bothers me is that the dino-homonoid speculation diverted public attention from what is really important about troodonts. These dinosaurs were more birdlike than *Archaeopteryx,* and were part of the initial bird radiation. They were not pseudo-human.

Teeth indicate that *Troodon* was present in a number of late Late Cretaceous formations of North America and Asia, including the Maastrichtian ones.

TROODON FORMOSUS Leidy, 1856
SYNONYMS—*Stenonychosaurus inequalis, Pectinodon bakkeri*
TYPE—ANSP 9259
TIME—late Campanian of the late Late Cretaceous
HORIZON AND DISTRIBUTION—Judith River Formation of Alberta
    and Montana
MAIN ANATOMICAL STUDIES—Russell, 1969; Currie, 1985, 1987
                    NMC 12340
SKULL LENGTH—   ~330 mm
KILOGRAMMAGE—   ~50

In their life sculpture of *T. formosus,* R. Sequin and Dale Russell give this species a much broader skull than *T. mongoliensis,*[48] but what bones are known are very like the latter's, so it *is* certain that *T. formosus* had a narrow skull too. I do not agree with the rest of Russell and Sequin's life sculpture either. It is overly scrawny, except for a too bulky trunk, and the leg muscles are much too light. *T. formosus* is usually considered a small species, but like *V. antirrhopus* it would be seen as a good-sized predator by modern standards. Aublysodonts and dromaeosaur sickle-claws were its prime rivals; small ornithischians, and perhaps juvenile duckbills, its main meals.

TROODON MONGOLIENSIS (Osborn, 1924)
SYNONYMS—*Saurornithoides mongoliensis, Saurornithoides junior?*
TYPE—AMNH 6516
BEST SPECIMENS—type, GI 100/1
TIME—early Campanian to early Maastrichtian? of the late Late Cretaceous
HORIZONS AND DISTRIBUTION—Djadokhta and Nemegt? Formations of Mongolia
MAIN ANATOMICAL STUDY—Barsbold, 1974

	Type	GI 100/1
SKULL LENGTH—	~215 mm	275
TOTAL LENGTH—	~2.0 m	
FEMUR LENGTH—	~200 mm	
HIP HEIGHT—	.6 m	
KILOGRAMMAGE—	~13	~27

This species is much better known than the above, especially via the new GI 100/1, which features a fine, nearly complete skull. A big question is whether this is one or two species. GI 100/1 is bigger and from a later formation than the type is. Rinchen Bars-

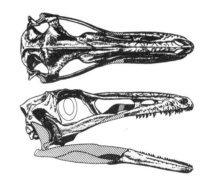

Troodon mongoliensis *GI 100/1*

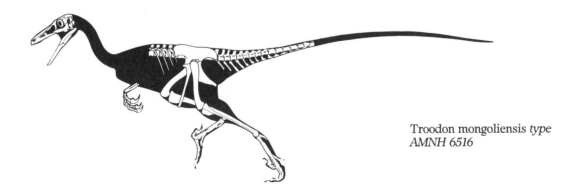

Troodon mongoliensis *type AMNH 6516*

This view shows to advantage the strong binocular vision of Troodon mongoliensis, *which mimics that of the cat. Also characteristic is the U-shaped tip of the lower jaw.*

bold considered it a separate species, and this could well be true. But the differences between the skulls are not great, and may be due to different stages of growth. And the time separation between the formations may not be great either. So, they are tentatively joined in one species as has been done elsewhere. Like *T. formosus,* this was a substantial-sized species that dwarfed the *Velociraptor* species they both lived with. On the other hand, the velociraptors were better armed, so the two genera were more balanced in total firepower than size alone would indicate. The skeletal restoration is of the type, with information from almost all the other *Troodon* specimens thrown in. Even then much is missing, especially the neck and chest.

TROODON? ANDREWSI (Harrison and Walker, 1975)
SYNONYMS—*Elopteryx nopscai?, Heptasteornis? andrewsi*
TYPE—BMNH A4359
TIME—Maastrichtian of the latest Late Cretaceous
HORIZON AND DISTRIBUTION—Sinpetru Formation of
    Transylvania
                            Type
KILOGRAMMAGE— ~3

This and its cohabiting Transylvanian relative *Bradycneme* are examples of how big mistakes can be made on fragmentary remains. The type *Elopteryx* femoral head and some ankles were thought to belong to birds, perhaps pelicans. More recently, it was thought they were owls, something no one now believes. Actually, some of the ankle elements, the ones assigned to *Heptasteornis,* are very like *Troodon,* which of course was birdlike. Likewise, the femoral head seems to be troodont, but it is not known which kind of ankle goes with the femoral head. So I consider *Elopteryx* indeterminate and invalid, and tentatively sink *Heptasteornis* into *Troodon.* This too could prove incorrect. But if right, this seems to be a small-sized example of *Troodon.*

*GENUS *BRADYCNEME* Harrison and Walker, 1975

BRADYCNEME DRACULAE Harrison and Walker, 1975
SYNONYM—*Elopteryx nopscai?*
TYPE—BMNH A1588
TIME—Maastrichtian of the latest Late Cretaceous
HORIZON AND DISTRIBUTION—Sinpetru Formation of
    Transylvania
                                    Type
KILOGRAMMAGE—   ~5?

The one good ankle is modeled after *Troodon,* but has a contorted shape unique to itself. So this may be a member of the family, or it may not.

Avimimids

In most respects, these are far and away the most birdlike of the protobirds. The fusion of *Avimimus*'s wrist and upper hand bones into one unit, the ulnar ridge that may have borne an array of "wing" feathers, and the very well developed arm-folding system certainly appear to have evolved under the impetus of advanced flight. At the same time, the forelimbs were much too short for any kind of flight, and it was impossible for *Avimimus* to manage even the "chicken flight" that some believe it could. So, avimimids must have been secondarily flightless.

A possible relative of *Avimimus* is Australian *Kakuru kujani* Molnar and Pledge, 1980. A small form from the middle of the Cretaceous, the only known bone is preserved as opal! Sold at an auction, its current whereabouts are unknown. This tibia is very slender, like *Avimimus*. The depression in the tibia for the ankle's ascending process is not only very tall, but is narrow like that of living ground birds. It looks exceptionally birdlike.

FAMILY AVIMIMIDAE Kurzanov, 1981

GENUS *AVIMIMUS* Kurzanov, 1981

AVIMIMUS PORTENTOSUS Kurzanov, 1981
TYPE—PIN 3907-1
BEST SPECIMENS—type, PIN 3907-1
TIME—early mid-Campanian? of the late Late Cretaceous
HORIZON AND DISTRIBUTION—Djadokhta Formation of Mongolia
MAIN ANATOMICAL STUDIES—Kurzanov, 1981, 1982, 1983, 1985

	Type	PIN 3907-3
SKULL LENGTH—		~70 mm
TOTAL LENGTH—	~1.6 m	
FEMUR LENGTH—	205 mm	
HIP HEIGHT—	.66 m	
KILOGRAMMAGE—	14	

Of the type's skull, only the braincase is present, and the rib cage and tail are missing.[49] Other specimens fill in some details, and confirm others. It is very doubtful that this animal was tail-less like birds, as Kurzanov believes. The broad posterior hips, the well-developed projection on the femur for tail-based muscles, and the forward-projecting pubes all mean that a well-de-

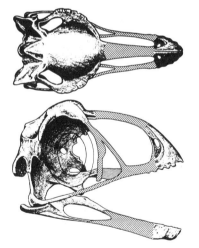

Avimimus portentosus *PIN 3907-3*

Avimimus portentosus *type PIN 3907-1 and 3907-3*

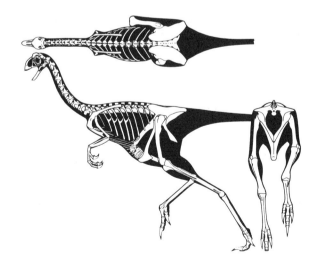

veloped tail was there. The breadth of the hips is remarkable; indeed, no other theropod has hips as wide as *Avimimus*. A nicely preserved and fairly complete second skull has been found; it appears to have been startlingly short and deep, not very large, and toothless. Instead, the upper beak had toothlike crenulations. Binocular vision was modest. The number of neck and trunk vertebrae is not certain, and the rib cage and breastplate are restored. Since even the early flying bird *Ambiortus* still had clawed fingers, it is assumed *Avimimus* did also. For some reason the fused wrist and hand elements were first misidentified as hind-limb bones. Like *Ornithomimus,* the inner toe is lost for speed and *Avimimus* is unique among theopods in having an outer cannon splint that is fused to the others. Small-headed, toothless *Avimimus* could not have been an archpredator. Herbivory is more likely, but just what role it played is not at all clear. Its velociraptor and troodont cousins were predators of this protobird.

The head is almost unbelieveably avian. Among many other details, the postorbital bar is lost, and the lower cheek elements

Avimimus portentosus was the most birdlike, longest-legged, and certainly among the swiftest of dinosaurs.

are reduced to a slender bar. Some sort of kinetic system must have been present, yet some parts of the head look like they have been secondarily refused together. The expanded braincase is bulbous, and the nostril's opening may reach back to the preorbital bar, a very birdlike feature. The upwards facing ilial plates of the hips are like birds. Then there are the bird-style lower hind limbs, which are extremely long for the body and femur, and very slender.

Avimimus is about as birdlike as "Protoavis" in the head "if not more," very much more so in the arm, hand, and leg, and less so in the pubis. It is heady and unsettling stuff—as early as the Triassic and as late as the Cretaceous there existed taxa that were so avian looking, yet so archaic and disparate in other ways.[50]

Assuming that dinosaurs were avian-mammalian-level endothermic homeotherms as argued in Chapter 7, and having a
calculator capable of handling exponents on hand, we can calculate various aspects of their energetics. Most important is the
metabolic rate, or calories burned over time. Standard metabolic
rate is the energy consumption when resting. But we are more
interested in the animals when they are active, and metabolic
rates are then usually about twice as high. The equation for calculating active metabolic rates in endotherms is:

$$M = 140(W)^{0.75}$$

Where M is kcal burned per day, and W is mass in kilograms.[1]
One thing you should be aware of is that the "calorie" you guide
a diet by is really a kilocalorie; the food industry thought it
sounded better to drop the thousand prefix. Note that the metabolic rate scales to mass to the 0.75 power, as discussed in Chapters 6 and 7. So we can calculate that an 8-tonne *Tyrannosaurus
rex* burns some 120,000 kcal/day, compared to about 3300 kcal/
day for a 70 kg *Velociraptor antirrhopus* or *Homo sapiens*. To get
estimates for ectotherms, just divide the value by from seven to
ten.[2]

Having the metabolic rate, we can easily figure out how
much our predators will need to eat for a given period of time.
Meat is rich in calories and easily digested; 90 percent of the
calories it contains are absorbed by the consumer. The equation
for calculating food consumption in endothermic predators is:

$$F = 0.11(W)^{0.75}$$

where F is kilograms of wet meat needed each day. Again, divide
the value by about ten to get an ectothermic estimate. Now we
can have some fun seeing what various theropods would have to
do to keep themselves going.

- A 12-kg *Ornitholestes hermanni* needs to eat 0.7 kg of flesh
  per day, so it would have to pick up fourteen 0.05-kg
  lizards and mammals daily.
- Ten 12-kg *Coelophysis rhodesiensis* kill a 20-kg prosauropod. Since, like other theropods, their irregular, bladed
  tooth rows were rather inefficient at taking flesh off the
  bones and could not crush bones, only 75 percent of the

animal can be eaten. The carcass would therefore supply the pack with about 1.8 days' worth of energy.

- Ten 70-kg *Velociraptor antirrhopus* kill a 400-kg tenontosaur. Predators can gorge themselves with about a quarter of their own body weight of flesh at a sitting, so they could eat most of the carcass the first time around. Waiting a day or so, they could finish it off. This will keep the theropods' energy needs satisfied for eleven days.
- A twelve-pack of 1.5-tonne *Allosaurus atrox* bring down a 20-tonne brontosaur. In theory, this would keep them going for forty-seven days, but the meat would rot well before they could eat it all. More probably other theropods joined in. The brontosaur could supply forty allosaurs with a full meal and two weeks' worth of energy. Note that because of their lower metabolic rates, the bigger theropods could go longer between meals.
- Now let's get down to real business. On average, an 8-tonne *Tyrannosaurus rex* must bolt down 93 kg of meat per day, or some 2000 tonnes in a sixty-year life, equal to the weight of a World War II destroyer! It is also the equivalent of nearly three thousand cattle, each of which could be eaten in a few bites. Since *T. rex* had a uniquely strong skull, it could consume more of a carcass than most theropods—perhaps 85 percent. So about four hundred 6-tonne *Triceratops* would feed a *T. rex* over its life. When *T. rex* killed a *Triceratops,* it took a few days to eat it, and then it had enough energy for fifty-five days. It is more likely that six tyrannosaurs organized to kill and eat the herbivore. Since each could take in *two tons* of meat at a sitting, they would leave the carcass a little hungry, but with some eight days' worth of calories on hand.

A final important value is the energy consumed per distance traveled. This is the same regardless of the metabolic rate of the animal. Though it might seem surprising, limb design, posture, and gait seem to have very little effect on the value—stumpy-limbed sprawling animals locomote about as efficiently as gracile erect ones (see pages 138-39 in Chapter 6). Also, energy cost per distance traveled is about the same regardless of speed—it costs much the same to walk as it does to run a kilometer. The main effect is that of size—bigger is relatively more energy-efficient. The equation for calculating locomotory energy consumption is:

$$L = 3.32(W)^{0.75}$$

where L is kcal burned per kilometer traveled.[3] Note that locomotory energy consumption and metabolic rates both scale close to the 0.75 power, so the ability to travel distances is in this respect independent of size. Big living predators generally travel ten or so kilometers each day, so locomotion takes up about 25 percent of their total active metabolic rate.

Knowing how to calculate feeding rates in predatory dinosaurs, we can now use the calculator to carry out some more straightforward calculations and estimate what their populations may have been like. One year's events in three of the best known big-theropod formations are looked at, plus a modern African community for comparison. In the last, hyenas and lions make up the bulk of the predator population. The titles Judith River and Lance are here used to indicate the large areas of similar floodplain deposits in their respective areas and times. The calculations are simplified, ballpark estimates, and are rounded off for clarity.

The primary factor in determining animal populations is the rainfall, for this determines the amount of plant growth. So, while even deserts can support surprisingly large-sized animals, they can support only a few of them for every square kilometer. We can only make rough estimates of past rainfalls, based on the fossil soils, stream and lake sizes, floral elements, and the like. The herbivore population in turn is dependent on the plant growth, and the predator population on the herbivore population. The Morrison appears to have been a seasonally wet-dry open forest, something like the Ngorongoro. The Judith River and Lance systems seem to have been even wetter forests.

Big herbivores eat only a small fraction of the available plant growth; insects and small animals get most of the rest. It is probable that the Morrison's great brontosaurs and shorter stegosaurs could reach more of the available plants than could the low-built duckbills and horned dinosaurs of the Judith River and Lance, or the grazing ungulates of the Ngorongoro.[1] Note that the average masses of both the herbivores and predators includes juveniles as well as adults. Knowing about how much each herbivore will eat, at 40 percent digestive efficiencies, it is simple to calculate their population densities and biomass. In general, the bigger the animals are, and the higher their metabolic rates, the lower their densities. Note that a theropod would usually have had to search a good deal of territory in order to find a victim, especially since dinosaurs tended to bunch together in big herds. This is quite unlike the situation if herbivorous dinosaurs had had low, ectothermic metabolic rates, in which case the herbivore populations would have been up to ten times as high per given area. Prey would have been just around the corner, much as some tropical islands are teeming with low-metabolic-rate giant tortoises.

The biggest problem in calculating the predator populations is to estimate how much of the herbivore population ended up in a theropod's belly each year. In living communities, predators can take up to a third of the prey animals each year. So it probably was in the Judith River, where the medium-sized tyrannosaurs were attacking duckbills of similar size. The Lance's giant *Tyrannosaurus rex* must have had a more difficult time with *Triceratops,* and the lower death rates of the big herbivores must have reduced the number of carcasses available for scavenging too. In the Morrison, the protective bulk and low death rates of the brontosaurs must have limited the amount of meat the allosaurs could get from them. Again, it is assumed that about 75 percent of each carcass was actually consumed, except for *T. rex,* who consumed 85 percent. With the proceeding estimates in hand, it is a simple matter to use the estimated values to come up with some density and biomass estimates. *T. rex* was probably rare, with only one individual for every few square kilometers, and its population over a good chunk of western North America was only in the low hundreds of thousands. The Judith River tryannosaurs, 75 percent of which were *Albertosaurus libratus,* were perhaps twice as common. The even smaller allosaurs, *Allosaurus atrox* mainly, must have been much more abundant per square kilometer, and the Morrison was a very big place, so this formation's theropod population may have been well over a million. In comparison, lions, hyenas, leopards, and Cape hunting dogs total some 7000 in the 25,000 sq km Serengeti ecosystem.[2] Because of heavy poaching, and because many of the one million big herbivores are migratory, the lion and hyena populations are only about a third that for every kilometer as they are in the nearby Ngorongoro Crater. And even the Ngorongoro does not seem to be supporting relatively as many predators as did some fossil mammal communities. The Alaskan wolf population is estimated to be only 25,000[3] over 1,500,000 sq km, but the extensive and harsh mountain and tundra environments, and modern hunters, are keeping this figure way down.

Note that since all the dinosaurs looked at here were big, it would not change things much if they had been bulk endotherms, instead of truly bird- or mammal-like in physiology. Things would, however, have been radically different in the unlikely event that theropods were bulk homeotherms with low, reptilian metabolic rates. The predators would then have been some fifty to a hundred times more populous, with perhaps fifty big thero-

ANNUAL	NGORONGORO CRATER	MORRISON	JUDITH RIVER	LANCE, ETC.
Rainfall (mm)	1000	1000	2000	2000
Plant growth (kg/km²)	1,500,000	1,500,000	2,500,000	2,500,000
Percent of growth eaten by herbivores	6.7	10	5	5
Herbivore's average mass (kg)	100	10,000	1000	2500
Each herbivore's plant consumption at 40% digestive efficiency (kg)	1000	23,000	5700	11,300
Number of herbivores/km²	100	6.5	21.9	11.1
Herbivore biomass/km²	10,000	65,000	21,900	27,750
Percent of herbivores eaten by predators	20	15	30	20
Above ×0.75 or . . . ×0.85	1500	7300	4900	4700
Predator's average mass (kg)	50	750	1000	2500
Each herbivore's meat consumption at 90% digestive efficiency (kg)	755	5750	7100	14,200
Number of predators/km²	2.3	1.27	0.68	0.33
Predator biomass/km²	115	950	680	825
Predator/prey biomass ratio	1.15	1.45	3.1	3.0
Total land area (km²)	250	1,000,000	200,000	200,000
Area's total predator population	570	1,270,000	135,000	60,000

pods packed into each square kilometer. Dale Russell commits an interesting contradiction in his work on this problem. He argues that big dinosaurs were bulk endotherms with high metabolic rates and low population densities like big mammals,[3] but elsewhere he suggests that dinosaurs had high population densities because they were reptiles with low metabolic rates.[4] Both cannot be true at the same time.

Notice that the predator/prey ratios of endothermic predators can be well above 1 percent; they do not have to be below this figure as has been argued (see Chapter 7). This means that the relatively high P/P ratios recorded in some fossil communities are in the endothermic range, despite the likelihood that the predator's numbers are inflated because their bones preserve more readily. Also important is the low ratio in the Morrison, where the small allosaurs could not easily cope with the giant brontosaurs, compared to the higher ratios in the Judith River and Morrison, where predator and prey were more equally matched. As you can see in Chapter 7 and the relevant references, the P/P ratios actually recorded in the sediments match these calculated ratios fairly well.

2. LIFE-STYLES OF THE BIG AND POWERFUL, AND THE SMALL AND FIERCE TOO

1. For studies of how some modern predators live, see Auffenburg, 1981; Craighead, 1979; Kruuk, 1972; Mech, 1970; Schaller, 1972.

2. Diamond, 1986; Bryant and Churcher, 1987. A big saber-toothed marsupial from the South American Tertiary and a number of saber-toothed mammal-like reptiles from before dinosaurian times were slashers too.

3. Bakker, 1986; Paul, 1987b.

4, 5. Paul, 1987b

6. Halstead and Halstead, 1981, take an extreme view in favor of big-theropod scavenging, and Barsbold, 1983a, does not think tyrannosaurs killed—see ref. 13 on page 420.

7. Houstan, 1979; Bartam, 1979.

8. Paul, 1987b.

9. Schaller, 1972; Bartam, 1979.

10. Marx, 1978.

11, 12. Farlow, 1976a, 1987. Philip Currie has told me about the possible new tyrannosaur bone beds.

13. Bird, 1985; Ostrom, 1972b, 1986a; Lockley, 1984, 1988; Lockley et al., 1986; Farlow, 1987.

14. Bird, 1985; Farlow, 1987; Lockley, 1988.

15. Farlow, 1987, is somewhat skeptical of these prints' meaning; Lockley, 1988, believes they show a pack going after the herd.

16. Leonardi, 1984; Lockley, 1988.

17. Diamond, 1986.

18. Kruuk, 1972; Auffenburg, 1981; Bryant and Churcher, 1987.

19. Paul, 1987b.

20. Information on the trackways is in Farlow, 1986, 1987; Kuban, 1986; Hastings, 1987; Thulburn and Wade, 1984; and see Chapter 5. In the film the herons were stalking doves, of all things.

21. When living predators are not on the hunt, their body language says so and herbivores will let them openly approach quite close. Likewise, normally walking theropods may not have spooked other dinosaurs.

22. Paul, 1987b.

23. There *is* one very good motion picture dinosaurian wrestling match, the classic match in the original *King Kong* between the main character and *T. rex*—not only because of the power and thrilling atmosphere of this cinematic tour de force, but because of its sense of humor. At one point Kong puts the tyrannosaur in a text book half-nelson.

24. In 1986, Bakker made the plausible suggestion that the broad-hipped brontosaurs dropped live calves.

25. As per Farlow, 1976b.

26. It is hard to be certain about predator/prey footprint ratios because of the difficulties in identifying prints (see Chapter 5), but the Triassic-Jurassic Newark-Supergroup print faunas of the eastern United States seem to have lots of small- to medium-sized theropod prints (Lull, 1953),

the Texas mid-Cretaceous sites an abundance of bigger ones (Farlow, 1987).

27. Bakker, 1971a.

28. Bakker, 1986.

29. Kruuk, 1972.

30. Coombs, 1980. However, it is possible that these toe-only prints are only merely poorly preserved "ghost" prints; see Chapter 5.

31. Not that these meat eaters were *always* archpredators. Like wild cats and dogs, even they must have eaten some vegetation on occasion, for nutrients, digestive problems, and the like.

3. A History of Predatory Dinosaur Success and Failure, and of Their Avian Descendants

1. Crompton, 1968; Hotton, 1980.

2, 3. Bakker, 1980, 1986.

4. Haubold, 1986, suggests that trackways from the Early Triassic were made by *Lagerpeton*-like protodinosaurs some ten million years before their skeletons appear, but it is difficult to tell without better evidence. Haubold also suggests that theropod trackways are known from the beginning of the Ladinian, about ten million years before their skeletons appear.

5. See Chapter 6 and ref. 14.

6. Olsen and Galton, 1977.

7. Paul, in prep.; Bower, 1986; Olsen and Sues, 1986; see the latter and other papers in the same volume for an in-depth survey of the dinosaurian world around the Triassic-Jurassic boundary.

8. Schmidt-Nielsen, 1972.

9. See Bakker, 1971a; Dodsen et al., 1980.

10. Jensen, 1981; none of the bones in this study are clearly those of birds, see Olson, 1985, and Thulborn, 1984, for critiques.

11. Bakker, 1986.

12. Olson, 1985.

13. Kessler, 1984, and a notice in the February 1987 *Society of Vertebrate Paleontology News Bulletin;* one should be skeptical about the ratites until more information is available.

14. Hou and Zhicheng, 1984.

15. See Olson, 1985, and references therein.

16. Paul, 1988b; and see Chapter 7.

17. Osmolska, 1980; Anderson 1987.

18. Russell, 1977 is an especially fine book on the Alberta dinosaur habitáts, although it is becoming somewhat dated. Lehman, 1987; Jerzykiewicz and Sweet, 1987, and Currie, 1987, are important recent papers. As for the wetness issue, the Horseshoe Canyon Formation is definitely wetter than the earlier Judith River in Alberta, but the relative conditions of other formations are less clear. Rigby, 1987, thinks that the last dinosaur-bearing formations of the western coastal floodplain were rather dry, a minority opinion.

19. Kielan-Jaworowska, 1974.

20. Paul, 1988a; it should be noted that some herbivorous dinosaurs do add support to this idea, including certain nonpredaceous theropods. Albertian *Chirostenotes pergracilis* and *C. rarus* look very alike, as do

the two continents' *Ornithomimus* species. Among nontheropods, the Mongolian and Albertian species of the duck-billed hadrosaur *Saurolophus* have long been known to be similar.

21. Chatterjee, 1984; however, Chatterjee ignores the possible late survival of armored stegosaur dinosaurs in Late Cretaceous India, which may support a faunal separation.

22. Bakker, 1977; Sloan et al., 1986.

23. Russell, 1971, 1984; Retallack and Leahy, 1986, and other letters in same volume; Sloan et al., 1986; Rigby, 1987; Leahy, 1987. Russell also argued that a nearby supernova may have caused the extinctions, an idea that no longer receives much attention from him, or elsewhere.

24. Paul, in prep.; data on abundances in Lehman, 1987.

25. The cheetah, which has a distressingly low breeding-success rate, seems to be the victim of a series of past genetic bottlenecks; see Lewin, 1987, and the references therein.

26. Alvarez et al., 1980; Alvarez, 1986.

27. Alvarez, 1986; Raup, 1986; Hsu, 1986; Crutzon, 1987.

28. Paul, 1988b.

29. Raup, 1986.

30. Davis et al., 1984.

31. The estimate that the terminal Cretaceous meteorite was 10 km across, and that it dug out a 100-km-or-so crater, is a rough one based on extrapolations from the amount of debris scattered over the globe. The crater made at the Triassic-Jurassic boundary was definitely made by an object of about this size; indeed, there is some evidence it was larger. This is a problem, for if the Cretaceous impact did have a much greater effect upon the world biota, then the meteorite and the crater (or multiple craters) that it made should been much larger than thought. Concerning the number of Mesozoic impacts, there are already three giant land craters known in the Triassic-Jurassic. Statistically, it is likely that the oceans received twice this number of impacts, some of which may be recorded in some new dust layers. More than half a dozen Mesozoic impacts as big as the last one are plausible; Paul, in press.

32. Officer et al., 1987; see Weisburd, 1987b, for a more informal discussion.

33. Sloan et al., 1986; much skepticism should be directed toward this report because isolated bones and teeth are often reworked from older deposits into newer ones. Not until a number of articulated dinosaur skeletons are found in post-Mesozoic deposits will I believe in such dinosaurian survivors.

34. For more information on these fossil birds, see Feduccia, 1980, and Olson, 1985.

4. The Nuts and Bolts of Predatory Dinosaur Anatomy and Action

1. Knight's classic artwork has been highlighted in Czerkas and Glut, 1982.

2. See Paul, 1987a; Bakker, 1987; and other papers in the two volumes of Czerkas and Olson, 1987, for the most extensive and up-to-date examination of dinosaur reconstruction; for basic instructions on restoring fossil vertebrates, see Paul and Chase, in press.

3. Barsbold, 1983a, discusses the possibility of this kind of skull flexibility.

4. Gingerich, 1973; Bakker, 1986.

5. McGowen, 1979, 1982, 1986.

6. For a better understanding of bird muscles, see McGowen's papers, and George and Berger, 1966.

7. Walker, 1964; Bakker, 1986.

8. Bakker, 1986.

9. Bakker, 1986, jacket illustration shows lips.

10. See Hopson, 1980; Raath 1977.

11. Spinar and Burian, 1972; Neave Parker in Swinton, 1970; Bakker, 1986.

12. Other dinosaurologists count nine neck and fourteen trunk vertebrae; it depends on which vertebra is considered to be the first in the trunk. I tag the first vertebra that bears a long rib that participates in the rib cage as the first trunk vertebra; this is the eleventh in the series. Note that, as shown in Fig. 6-6, the first neck vertebra is so small that it is easy to miss; the first big vertebra is the second.

13. Except, as I note in Paul, 1988b, that polar dinosaurs may have had heavy layers of fat in the winter for insulation like some pigs. This could have slowed down both predator and prey a bit.

14. See Schmidt-Nielsen, 1972.

15. Nicholls and Russell, 1985.

16. See Bakker, 1975, 1986; Bakker and Galton, 1974; Paul, 1987a.

17. Bakker, 1968, 1971b, 1986; Ostrom, 1969b; Paul, 1987a.

18. Bakker, 1986; Bakker and Galton, 1974; Paul, 1987a.

19. Tarsitano's 1983 paper is one of the odder analyses of theropod function. So is Jensen's 1981 study in which theropod knees are shown as not only straight but nearly unbendable, and their ankles as bending backward; no animal's legs work this way.

20. Spinar and Burian, 1972; Neave Parker in Swinton, 1970; Bakker, 1986.

21. Martin, 1984a.

22. See Muybridge, 1887, which remains a classic study of animal motion, and Cracraft, 1971b.

23. See pp. 362–363 in Chadwick, 1983; a superb film of a running ostrich was in the 1981 NOVA science series PBS broadcast "Animal Olympians."

24. Thulborn and Wade, 1984; also, some such prints may be poor-quality "ghost" tracks, see Chapter 5.

25. See Chapters 2 and 5.

26. Newman, 1970.

27, 28. Bakker, 1986, and his illustrations in Glut, 1982; Bakker was among the first to give theropods "drumsticks."

29. See Chapter 7 and its ref. 27 for more information on this.

30. Schaller, 1972.

31. Dale Russell personal comment.

32. See Weisburd, 1986; Morell, 1987; and *Carnotaurus* restoration on page 285.

33. In Paul, 1988b, I explain that even big dinosaurs *could* have borne a winter pelage over their scales. Not that there is any reason to think they did, it was just to point out that polar dinosaurs are not good indicators of their habitat's climate.

34. Ellenberger, 1974.

35. I am therefore perplexed why some, such as Ostrom, who believe that small theropods were endothermic object so strongly to insulating

them. It should be noted that a few modest-sized ground-dwelling endotherms are naked-skinned, like humans and some pigs, but smaller ones never are.

36. In Paul, 1988b, I note that the nonscaly, pitted-skin pattern found with one small herbivorous dinosaur specimen may have borne insulation.

37. See Feduccia, 1980; Olson, 1985.

38. Thulborn, 1985.

39. Bakker, 1986.

5. A Quick Look at Predatory Dinosaur Footprints

1. Lockley et al., 1986.

2. For a bemused account of how this creationist nonsense started in the 1930s, see Bird, 1985. For its solution, see Farlow 1986, 1987; Kuban, 1986; Hastings, 1987.

3. Hitchcock, 1848.

4. Lull, 1953, and Farlow, 1987.

5. Lockley et al., 1986; Bakker, 1986.

6. Predatory Dinosaur Speed

1. For recent advocations of relatively slow dinosaurs, see Coombs, 1978, and Thulborn, 1982.

2. Halstead and Halstead, 1981, for example.

3. Muybridge, 1887; note that Thulborn's 1982 claim that rhinos only trot is incorrect, as those of us who have seen the John Wayne African safari film *Hatari!* know.

4. McMahon, 1983, is a very good overview of animal locomotion.

5. Alexander, 1977; Garland, 1983.

6. Alexander, 1976; Bakker, 1987, has more information on trackway-speed formulas.

7. Bakker 1986, 1987.

8. Thulborn and Wade, 1984.

9. Welles, 1970.

10. The long-limbed theropod Welles, 1970, and Thulborn, 1982, believe made this trackway would have had a foot only a tenth the leg's length, impossible since even in ostriches this value is a fifth, in known theropods around a quarter give or take some.

11. Halstead and Halstead, 1981. See Bird's delightful 1985 account of hunting for dinosaur fossils for details on this trackway; however, Farlow, 1987, and I disagree with his picture of a theropod attacking the brontosaur's tail, for it certainly would have been knocked over.

12. For a very readable book on the subject, see Gordon, 1978.

13. Gregory, 1912; Howell, 1944; Coombs, 1978.

14. Although Fedak and Seeherman, 1979, assert that "clumsy" animals are less energy-efficient, this has never been established statistically, and there are efficient short-limbed animals as well as inefficient gracile ones, as indicated by Taylor et al., 1974. Data on stride frequencies and limb excursion arcs were taken from Muybridge, 1887.

15. McGowen, 1983.

16. Alexander, 1977; Garland, 1983.

17. Hotton, 1980.

18. Alexander, 1977.

19. Bakker, 1986, suggests such *T. rex* speeds, an extension of his long-standing advocacy of fast dinosaurs as per 1968, 1971b, 1975, 1980, 1987. Ostrom, 1987, calls the idea of such extreme speeds "preposterous," but the biomechanical evidence is more agreeable.

7. Warm or Cool Predatory Dinosaurs?

1. For the most extensive technical examination of the dinosaur physiology issue, see Bakker; Beland and Russell; Hopson; Hotton; Ricqles; and the other papers in the somewhat dated results of the 1980 AAAS Symposium. There is a need for a follow-up volume.

2. Spotilla et al., 1973.

3. Hotton, 1980.

4. Berman and Meltzer, 1978; Oliphant, 1983.

5. Ostrom, 1969b; Bakker, 1971b, 1975.

6. Seymour, 1976.

7. Hopson, 1980.

8. Ricqles, 1980; Reid, 1984; Ostrom, 1987, does not acknowledge these studies in his critical discussion of bone histology.

9. Laws et al., 1975; Eltringham, 1982.

10. Nelson and Bookhout, 1980.

11. Tropical mammals often have well-developed growth rings in the outer enamel, but not the dentine.

12. One possible test would be the bird *Hesperornis,* which had replaceable teeth. Currently there is dispute over whether some small teeth with growth rings belong to this bird, or to baby mososaur sea reptiles from the same deposits.

13. Laws et al., 1975; Eltringham, 1982; and the data in Laws et al., 1975.

14. Russell, 1973; Douglas and Williams, 1982; Duscheck, 1985; Davies, 1987; Parrish et al., 1987.

15, 16. See Axelrod, 1985.

17. Crowley et al., 1986, cite evidence for river and coastal ice, among other things. Parrish et al., 1987, believe that a sharp temperature decline in Campanian time led to chronic freezing weather in the arctic winter. Weisburd, 1987a, discusses some of the evidence for glaciers.

18 to 21. Paul, 1988b, explores these various points in more detail.

22. Hotton, 1980.

23. Reid, 1984.

24. See Schmidt-Nielsen, 1972.

25. Bakker, 1986, 1987.

26. Bakker, 1975, 1980.

27. Currie, 1987c; this contradicts Gauthier's 1986 suggestion that the theropod's hollow bones would have been less liable to be preserved and found.

28. Farlow, 1976b; Beland and Russell, 1980. One thing it would be helpful to know are the P/P ratios in the predatory ground bird and herbivorous mammal communities of the South American Tertiary.

29. For example, Desmond's 1976 book was very popular, but its arguments were flawed and did more harm than good to the endothermic hypothesis.

30. I was most startled to hear Russell say this over a dinner at the 1986 meeting of the Society of Vertebrate Paleontology. Something that Russell would be most interested in are the recent reports that atmospheric oxygen levels in the Late Cretaceous were nearly half again higher than today, which have been followed by arguments to the contrary. If oxygen levels were higher, the effects upon dinosaur physiology may, or may not, be profound.

8. The Genealogy and Nomenclature of Predatory Dinosaurs and Birds

1. See Gould, 1985, for a readable explanation of DNA-DNA hybridization; his endorsement of the procedure may be premature.

2. See Bonaparte, 1984; Parrish, 1986.

3. Paul, 1984a; Gauthier, 1986.

4. Paul, 1984a, 1984b; Sereno, 1984; Gauthier and Padian, 1984; Benton, 1984; Bakker, 1986; Gauthier, 1986.

5. Bakker, 1975, 1986.

6. Bakker, 1986; I was therefore perplexed to see Gauthier, 1986, try to maintain Saurischia as a formal monophyletic clade.

7. Paul, 1984a.

8. On the other hand, Gauthier, 1986, suggests that a particular outer shelf on the coelophysian's and ceratosaur's femoral heads make *them* a united clade. However, more advanced abelisaurs also have this shelf, and there are remnants of it even in protobirds such as *Velociraptor*.

9. Paul, 1984a.

10. Late in 1986, Bakker and Gauthier referred to advanced theropods of this general type as Dinoaves and Tetanurae, respectively. But Bakker clouds the issue by referring both they and ceratosaurs to the higher-ranking Neotheropoda, and neither of the workers' groups are assigned taxonomic ranks. Nor is it clear which has priority. This presented me, who had already pretty much finished this book, with something of a quandary. I decided to go ahead and start afresh with the order Avetheropoda.

11. Welles and Long, 1974, give a useful outline of theropod ankles, but there are errors. In particular, new *T. rex* ankles are like those of other tyrannosaurs.

12. Outlined in Paul, 1984a.

13. Chatterjee, 1982, 1985; in the latter, Chatterjee makes the rauisuchid *Postosuchus* look more theropod-like than it really was by drawing the trunk shorter than the vertebrae's measurements indicate it was.

14. Ostrom, 1974, 1976a.

15. Paul, 1984a; Gauthier and Padian, 1984; Gauthier, 1986. The last-named protobirds Maniraptora, but again no ranking was given, as per ref. 10, and his group differs somewhat from mine, so I put them in the new suborder Protoavia.

16. Milner, 1985.

17. Walker, 1984.

18. Tarsitano and Hecht, 1982; Martin, 1984a; however, these workers have not been vigorously defending their ideas of late.

19. Contrast Feduccia's 1980 and 1986 conclusions. Bock's 1986 assertion that there is not enough evidence yet available to decide which

archosaurs were ancestral to birds is just not so.

20. By Barsbold, 1983.

21. As explained by Kurten, 1976.

22. See Kurten, 1969 and 1976; the latter is an especially enjoyable explanation of how various aspects of paleontology are done.

23. Gauthier, 1986.

24. See Kurochkin, 1985; Marsh, 1880.

25. See Marsh, 1880.

26. Martin, 1984b.

9. The Beginnings of Bird Flight: From the Ground Up or the Trees Up?

1. For the most extensive technical examination of the beginnings of bird flight, see Yalden and the other results of the 1984 Eichstatt Symposium; Ostrom, 1986b, and the other papers in that volume; and Bock, 1986, and the other papers in that volume.

2. See Heilmann, 1926, for more details on the hoatzin.

3. Caple et al., 1983.

4. Bakker, 1986; Paul, 1987b, a semiaquatic role is also postulated by Thulborn and Hamley, 1984.

5. I completely disagree with Bock's idea that the ancestors of *Archaeopteryx* started out with arm and hand skin membranes that were later replaced by feathers. If an animal starts out with a membrane, it will end up with one like a bat or pterosaur. Also, his reconstruction of the proposed creature has no neck, but all theropods and birds have long necks.

6. See Rietschel, 1984.

7. Kurochkin, 1985.

PART TWO:

The Catalog of Predatory Dinosaurs

10. An Explanation of the Catalog

1, 2. For the methods of doing multiple views and cross-scaling, see Paul and Chase, in press.

3. Ages are from Harland et al., 1982.

11. The Predatory Dinosaurs

1. It had recently been suggested, erroneously it turns out, that one kind of ornithischian dinosaur was a meat eater.

2. Benton, 1984, 1986; Galton, 1985.

3. Paul, 1984b.

4. Benton, 1984.

PRIMITIVE PALEODINOSAURS

1. A photograph of the new staurikosaur skeleton is in Meyer, 1986.

BIRD-MIMICKING HERRERASAURS

1. This herrerasaur is in Galton, 1985.
2. Brinkman and Sues, 1987; the comments on the humerus joint are from my examination of the specimen.
3. See Beardsley, 1986.

1. EARLY PALEOTHEROPODS

1. Paul, 1984a.
2. A discussion of some of the problems with the nature of *C. bauri* is in Padian, 1986.
3. An illustration of *C. rhodesiensis* chasing a gliding lizard is in Bakker, 1975.
4. Russell, 1972; Galton, 1982.
5. A mistake I published in 1984a.
6. Taquet, 1984b; Taquet misidentified the snout tips as lower jaw tips.
7. See Bunney, 1986, for a photograph of the skull, and Milner and Croucher, 1987, for a schematic skeletal sketch.
8. Taquet, 1984b.
9. Mass estimates in Glut, 1982, and Huene, 1926.
10. Bakker, 1986.
11. Suggested by Marsh, 1884.
12. Ratkevich, 1976; easily one of the worst books on dinosaurs, it includes the absurd claim that dinosaurs could grow back a torn off limb or tail!
13. Janensch, 1925; Russell and Beland, 1980.

2. LATE PALEOTHEROPODS

1. Paul, 1984a.
2. See Halstead, 1970.
3. In Glut, 1982.
4. Jensen, 1985.
5. See Morell, 1987; and for a model of whole animal, see Volume I of Czerkas and Olson, 1987.
6. Photograph of skeleton on p. 138 of Glut, 1982.
7. Walker, 1964.
8. Taquet, 1984a.
9. Waldman, 1974.
10. Galton, 1976.

B. BIRDLIKE AVETHEROPODS

1. Thulborn, 1984.
2. Taquet, 1984a.

3. Ostrom, 1980.

4. See Ostrom, 1970, for much of the story; also, Galton, 1974, and Owen, 1876, for more remains.

2. THE ALLOSAUR-TYRANNOSAUR GROUP

1. Paul, 1984a, 1988a.

2. Molnar et al., 1981.

3. In Czerkas and Glut, 1982.

4. Dong Zhiming told me about this new allosaur; some information is in Anderson, 1987.

5. Fig. 47 in Czerkas and Glut, 1982, and Fig. 36 in Camp and Camp, 1968; the Camps' book, although now outdated, was one of the nicer dinosaur publications of the time.

6. Photograph of model in Weisburd, 1986, and in Volume I of Czerkas and Olson, 1987; this model's skin is based on *Carnotaurus* (see page 285).

7. According to Earle's 1987 observations on predator pack and prey size; see Chapter 2.

8. Bakker, in prep.

9. AMNH 600 is shown in Osborn, 1912.

10. Bakker, in prep.

11. Ray, 1941; the bones in the posed photos are actually casts and not necessarily of *A. amplexus*.

12. See Fig. 6 in Osborn, 1912.

13. Bakker, 1986; Barsbold, 1983a, says the lower jaw's extra hinge joint was too weak for biting live prey, but its depth at this joint provided the strength.

14. Currie, 1987b; this is an informative survey of this skull roof bone in Alberta's theropods.

15. Bakker, 1986; Breithaupt, 1987, is not convinced by such arguments on arm reduction, perhaps an example of the belief the reduction must have an intrinsic value.

16. Paul, 1987b.

17. This is a bit of a mess. "Clevelanotyrannus" appears in the bibliography of Currie, 1987b; perhaps the worst name given to a dinosaur of late; it has since been dropped in favor of "Nanotyrannus" in reports over the news service wires.

18. For a wonderful account of 1960's Polish-Mongolian Expeditions to dig up tarbosaurs and other Gobi dinosaurs, read Kielan-Jaworowska, 1969; the juvenile specimen on pp. 56 and 57 is ZPAL MgD-1/3.

19. Rhozhdestvensky, 1965; Maleev, 1974; Osmolska, 1980.

20. In Maleev, 1974.

21. Molnar, 1973.

22. Colbert, 1962; Alexander, 1985.

23. The frontispiece for this section is *T. rex* scaled to the size of UCMP 118742, and is to the same scale as Fig. 1-2. The human figure is 1626 mm (5'4") tall and 52 kg (115 lbs).

24. Another error is Welles and Long's 1974 belief that *T. rex* had a distinctive ankle that separated it from all other tyrannosaurs. The "ankle bone" has such a contorted shape that it is not an astragalus.

25. Fig. 105 in Czerkas and Glut, 1982, and Fig. 47 in Camp and Camp, 1968; also in Glut, 1982.

26. Fig. 48 in Czerkas and Glut, 1982; this illustration was the basis for the *T. rex* in the original film *King Kong,* and for many a plastic toy.

27. In Spinar and Burian, 1972.

28. The version often published, as in Barnett, 1955, is the preliminary sketch; the giant mural itself is a much more impressive piece of art.

3. PROTOBIRDS: FLYING AND NONFLYING

1. See Paul, 1984c, and references therein for discussion of this odd and rather amusing issue.

2. Martin, 1984a, 1984b; Whetstone, 1983.

3. See Chapter 4 for how protobird shoulder girdles really go together, and compare Walker's careful 1984 analysis to Whetstone's peculiar conclusions of 1983.

4. See Viohl, 1984.

5, 6. Paul, 1987b.

7. See comments by Sues, 1977b.

8. Paul, 1987b.

9. For hips, see Barsbold, 1979, 1983a, 1983b.

10. Paul, 1987b.

11. Paul, 1984a, 1987b, 1988a.

12. Fig. 52A in Ostrom, 1969a, is an uncinate process.

13. Paul, 1988a.

14. Can be seen in Weisburd, 1986; Desmond, 1976; Glut, 1982.

15. Sues, 1977a.

16. Philip Currie informs me that he has dentaries of this type with *V. langstoni* teeth.

17. Barsbold, 1983a; photographs in Hasegawa, 1986, and on p. 61 in Norman, 1985.

18. Cracraft, 1971a.

19. Gilmore, 1924; Sternberg, 1932.

20. Personal comment on the new TMP specimen.

21. Sternberg, 1940; Cracraft, 1971a.

22. Cracraft, 1971a.

23. Barsbold, 1976.

24. For hips, see Barsbold, 1979, 1983a.

25. Also see Barsbold, 1981, 1983b; Hasegawa, 1986.

26. These are described in print, but not illustrated, in Barsbold, 1976.

27, 28. See Barsbold, 1983a; also see ref. 50.

29. Trotter and McCulloch, 1984.

30. Osmolska, 1980.

31. Russell, 1972.

32. Osmolska et al., 1972; a number of people have questioned the inset middle ear, but I have seen a cast of *O. bullatus* that indicates its presence.

33. Parks, 1928b; Russell, 1972.

34. Osmolska et al., 1972.

35. Ostrom, 1970.

36. For the tale of the discovery of *O. bullatus,* see Kielan-Jaworowska, 1969.

37. Currie, 1985.

38. Russell, 1969.

39. Explained in Currie, 1987a.

40. Carpenter, 1982 (which is a survey of baby dinosaurs); Paul, 1984a; 1987b,c.

41. Such as in Russell, 1971, and Russell and Sequin, 1982.

42. Russell contradicts himself in 1969, and with Sequin in 1982, when he argues that the troodont's large eyes indicate night time habits, compared to 1973 when he suggested that the dinosaur's large eyes indicate daylight habits.

43. Paul, 1987b.

44. See Barsbold, 1979, 1983a.

45. Barsbold, 1974 and 1983a, says that *Troodon* does not have ossified rods, but most of the tail is missing. The design of the tail base and the elongation of the processes is similar to dromaeosaurs and indicates rods were present.

46. Thulborn, 1984.

47. Wilson and Currie, 1985.

48. Russell and Sequin, 1982.

49. Kurzanov, 1981–1987. Photograph on p. 52 in Norman, 1985.

50. Slow communications prevented full consideration of the following Mongolian protobirds. *Conchoraptor gracilis* Barsbold, 1986, is perhaps a small crestless species of *Oviraptor* from the Barun Goyot. Its status vis-à-vis *Ingenia* is unclear, and skull MgD-1/95 may belong to it. *Oviraptor mongoliensis* Barsbold, 1986, from the Nemegt has a taller, longer crest than *O. philoceratops*. No skeletons were figured. Barsbold et al., 1987, report on a foot of the oldest yet troodontid (unnamed) from the Early Cretaceous. *Borogovia gracilicrus* Osmolska, 1987, is another troodont foot from the Nemegt.

Appendix A: Predatory Dinosaur Energetics

1. Data from Gessamen, 1979.

2. Data from Bennett and Dawson, 1976.

3. Data from Fedak and Seeherman, 1979, with the exponent changed to $M^{0.75}$ in accordance with elastic similarity, as per McMahon, 1984.

Appendix B: Predatory Dinosaur Populations

1. Data from Schaller, 1972, and Farlow, 1976b.

2. Schaller, 1972.

3. Mech, 1970.

4, 5. Contrast Russell et al., 1980, with Beland and Russell, 1980, but note that Russell no longer supports ectothermic dinosaurs anyway.

BIBLIOGRAPHY

Adams, D. 1987. The bigger they are, the harder they fall: Implications of ischial curvature in ceratopsian dinosaurs. 1–6 in Currie, P. J., and Koster, E. (eds), Fourth Symposium on Mesozoic Terrestrial Ecosystems. Tyrrell Museum, Drumheller, Canada.

Alexander, R. M. 1976. Estimates of speeds of dinosaurs. Nature, 261, 129–130.

Alexander, R. M. 1977. Fast locomotion of some African ungulates. J. Zool., 183, 291–300.

Alexander, R. M. 1985. Mechanics of posture and gait of some large dinosaurs. Zool. J. Linnean Soc., 83, 1–25.

Alvarez, L. W., Alvarez, W., Asaro, F., and Michel, H. 1980. Extraterrestrial cause for the Cretaceous-Tertiary extinction. Science, 208, 1095–1108.

Alvarez, W. 1986. Toward a theory of impact crisis. Eos, 131, 248–250.

Anderson, I. 1987. Chinese unearth a dinosaurs' graveyard. New Scient., 116(1586), 28–29.

Andrews, C. W. 1921. On some remains of a theropodous dinosaur from the Lower Lias of Barrow-on-soar. Ann. Mag. Nat. Hist., 8(9), 570–576.

Arcucci, A. 1986. Nuevos materiales y reinterpretacion de *Lagerpeton chanarensis* Romer (Thecodontia, Lagerpetonidae nov.). Ameghiniana, 23(3–4), 233–242.

Arcucci, A. 1987. Un nuevo Lagosuchidae (Thecodontia-Pseudosuchia) de la fauna de los Chanares (edad Reptil Chanarense, Triasico medio), la Rioja, Argentina. Ameghiniana, 24, 89–94.

Arieli, A., Berman, A., and Meltzer, A. 1978. Indication for nonshivering thermogenesis in the adult fowl. J. Exp. Biochem. Physiol, 60C, 33–36.

Auffenburg, W. 1981. The Behavioral Ecology of the Komodo Monitor. Univ. of Florida Presses, Gainesville.

Axelrod, D. I. 1984. An interpretation of Cretaceous and Tertiary biota in polar regions. Palaeogeog., Paleoclimat., Palaeoecol., 45, 105–147.

Bakker, R. T. 1968. The superiority of dinosaurs. Discovery, 3, 11–22.

Bakker, R. T. 1971a. Ecology of the brontosaurs. Nature, 229, 172–174.

Bakker, R. T. 1971b. Dinosaur physiology and the origin of mammals. Evolution, 25, 636–658.

Bakker, R. T. 1975. Dinosaur Renaissance. Sci. Amer., 232, 58–78.

Bakker, R. T. 1977. Tetrapod mass extinctions. 339–468 in Hallem, A. (ed), Patterns of Evolution. Elsevier Sci. Publ. Co., Amsterdam.

Bakker, R. T. 1980. Dinosaur heresy—dinosaur renaissance: Why we need endothermic archosaurs for a comprehensive theory of bioenergetic evolution. 351–462 in Thomas, D. K., and Olson, E. C. (eds), A Cold Look at the Warm Blooded Dinosaurs. AAAS, Washington, D.C.

Bakker, R. T. 1986. The Dinosaur Heresies: New Theories Unlocking the Mystery of the Dinosaurs and Their Extinction. William Morrow & Co. Inc., New York.

Bakker, R. T. 1987. The return of the Dancing Dinosaurs. 38–69 in Czerkas, S. J., and Olson, E. C. (eds), Dinosaurs Past and Present, I. Natural History Museum of Los Angeles County, Los Angeles.

Bakker, R. T. (in prep.). Biochronology of the Morrison Formation.

In Proceedings of the 4th North American Paleontological Conference. NAPC, Boulder.

Bakker, R. T., and Galton, P. M. 1974. Dinosaur monophyly and a new class of vertebrates. Nature, 248, 168–172.

Barnett, L., et al. 1955. The World We Live In. Time Inc., New York.

Barsbold, R. 1974. Saurornithoididae, a new family of small theropod dinosaurs from Central Asia and North America. Palaeont. Polonica, 30, 5–22.

Barsbold, R. 1976. A new Late Cretaceous family of small theropods (Oviraptoridae n. fam.) in Mongolia. Doklady Akad. Nauk. SSSR, 226, 221–223.

Barsbold, R. 1979. Opisthopubic pelvis in the saurischian dinosaurs. Nature, 279, 792–793.

Barsbold, R. 1981. Toothless carnivorous dinosaurs of Mongolia (in Russian). Joint Soviet-Mongol. Palaeont. Exp., Trans., 15, 28–39.

Barsbold, R. 1983a. Carnivorous dinosaurs from the Cretaceous of Mongolia (in Russian). Joint Soviet-Mongol. Palaeont. Exp., Trans., 19, 1–120.

Barsbold, R. 1983b. On the "avian" features of the structure of carnivorous dinosaurs (in Russian). Joint Soviet-Mongol. Palaeont. Exp., Trans., 24, 96–103.

Barsbold, R., and Perle. A. 1984. The first record of a primitive ornithomimosaur from the Cretaceous of Mongolia. Paleont. J., 2, 118–120.

Barsbold, R. 1986. Carnivorous dinosaurs: Oviraptors (in Russian). 210–223 in Collected Scientific Transactions of the Institute of Evolutionary Morphology of the USSR Academy of Sciences.

Barsbold, R., Osmolska, H., and Kurzanov, S. M. 1987. On a new troodontid (Dinosauria, Theropoda) from the Early Cretaceous of Mongolia. Acta Paleont. Polonica, 32, 121–132.

Bartram, B. C. R. 1979. Serengeti predators and their social systems. 221–248 in Sinclair, A. R. E., and Norton-Griffiths, M. (eds), Serengeti: Dynamics of an Ecosystem. Univ. Chicago Press, Chicago.

Beardsley, T. 1986. Fossil bird shakes evolutionary hypothesis. Nature, 322, 677.

Beer, G. R. de. 1954. *Archaeopteryx lithographica,* a Study Based upon the British Museum Specimen. British Museum (Natural History), London.

Beland, P., and Russell, D. A. 1980. Dinosaur metabolism and predator/prey ratios in the fossil record. 85–102 in Thomas, D. K., and Olson, E. C. (eds), A Cold Look at the Warm Blooded Dinosaurs, AAAS, Washington, D.C.

Bennett, A. F., and Dawson, W. R. 1976. Metabolism. 127–223 in Gans, C., and Dawson, W. R. (eds), Biology of the Reptilia. Academic Press, New York.

Benton, M. J. 1983. Dinosaur success in the Triassic: A noncompetitive ecological model. Quart. Rev. Biol., 58, 29–55.

Benton, M. J. 1984. Fossil reptiles of the German Late Triassic and the origin of the dinosaurs. 13–18 in Reif, W. E., and Westphal, F. (eds), Third Symposium on Mesozoic Terrestrial Ecosystems. ATTEMPTO-Verlag, Tübingen.

Benton, M. J. 1986. The late Triassic reptile *Teratosaurus*—a rauisuchian, not a dinosaur. Palaeontology, 29, 293–301.

Bidar, A., Demay, L., and Thomel, G. 1972. *Compsognathus coral-*

lestris nouvelle espèce de dinosaurian theropode du Portlandien de Canjuers. Ext. Ann. Mus. d'Hist. Nat. Nice, 1, 1–34.

Bird, R. T. 1985. Bones for Barnum Brown; Adventures of a Dinosaur Hunter. Texas Christian Univ. Press, Fort Worth.

Bock, W. J. 1986. The arboreal origin of avian flight. Mem. Calif. Acad. Sci., 8, 57–72.

Bonaparte, J. F. 1975. Nuevos materiales de *Lagosuchus talampayensis* Romer (Thecodontia-Pseudosuchia) y su significado en el origin de los saurischia. Acta Geol. Lilloana, 13, 5–90.

Bonaparte, J. F. 1979. Dinosaurs, a Jurassic assemblage from Patagonia. Science, 205, 1377–1379.

Bonaparte, J. F. 1984. Locomotion in rauisuchid thecodonts. J. Vert. Paleont. 3(4), 210–218.

Bonaparte, J. F. 1985. A horned Cretaceous carnosaur from Patagonia. Natl. Geog. Res., 149–151.

Bonaparte, J. F. 1986. Les dinosaures (Carnosaures, Allosaurides, Sauropodes, Cetiosaurides) du Jurassique moyen de cerro condor (Chubut, Argentine). Ann. Paleont., 72, 247–289.

Bonaparte, J. F., and Novas, F. E. 1985. *Abelisaurus comahuensis*, n.g., n.sp., carnosauria del Cretacico Tardio de Patagonia. Ameghiniana, 21(2–4), 259–265.

Bonaparte, J.F., and Powell, J.E. 1980. A continental assemblage of tetrapods from the Upper Cretaceous beds of El Brete, northwest Argentina. Mem. Soc. Geol. Fr., 139, 19–28.

Bower, B. 1986. Nova Scotia fossils illuminate 200-million-year-old changes. Sci. News, 129, 86.

Breithaupt, B. 1987. Book review. Contr. Geology, 25, 71–72.

Brett-Surman, M. K., and Paul, G. S. 1985. A new family of birdlike dinosaurs linking Laurasia and Gondwanaland. J. Vert. Paleont., 5, 133–138.

Brinkman, D., and Sues, H.-D. 1987. A staurikosaurid dinosaur from the Ischigualasto Formation (Upper Triassic) of Argentina and the relationships of the Staurikosauridae. Palaeont., 30(3), 493–503.

Brooks, R. 1763. The Natural History of Waters, Earths, Stones, Fossils, and Minerals, with their Virtues, Properties, and Medicinal Uses; to which is Added, the Method in which Linnaeus has Treated these Subjects. V. London.

Bryant, H. N. 1987. All sabre-toothed carnivores aren't sharks. Nature, 325, 488.

Buckland, W. 1824. Notice on the Megalosaurus or great fossil lizard of Stonesfield. Trans. Geol. Soc. Lond., s. 2(1), 390–396.

Bunney, S. 1986. "Claws" makes its official debut. New Scient., 112(1536), 25.

Camp, C. L. 1936. A new type of small bipedal dinosaur from the Navajo sandstone of Arizona. Univ. Calif. Publ., Bull. Dept. Geol. Sci., 24, 36–56.

Camp, L. S. de, and Camp, L. S. de. 1968. The Day of the Dinosaur. Doubleday, New York.

Caple, G. R., Balda, R. P., and Willis, W. R. 1983. The physics of leaping animals and the evolution of preflight. Amer. Nat., 121, 455–476.

Carpenter, K. 1982. Baby dinosaurs from the Late Cretaceous Lance and Hell Creek Formations, and a description of a new species of theropod. Univ. Wyoming Contr. Geol., 20, 123–134.

Carrier, D. R. 1987. The evolution of locomotion stamina in tetrapods: Circumventing a mechanical constraint. Paleobiology, 13, 326–341.

Chadwick, D. H. 1983. Etosha, Namibia's kingdom of animals. Natl. Geog., 163, 344–385.

Charig, A. J. 1976. Dinosaur monophyly and a new class of vertebrates: A critical review. 65–104 in Bellairs, A., and Cox, C. B. (eds), Morphology and Biology of Reptiles, Linn. Soc. Symp. Ser. 3. Academic Press, New York.

Charig, A. J. , and Milner, A. J. 1986. *Baryonyx,* a remarkable new theropod dinosaur. Nature, 324, 359–361.

Chatterjee, S. 1978. *Indosuchus* and *Indosaurus,* Cretaceous carnosaurs from India. J. Paleont., 52, 570–580.

Chatterjee, S. 1982. Phylogeny and classification of thecodontian reptiles. Nature, 295, 317–320.

Chatterjee, S. 1984. The drift of India: A conflict in plate tectonics. Mem. Soc. Geol. France, 147, 43–48.

Chatterjee, S. 1985. *Postosuchus,* a new thecodontian reptile from the Triassic of Texas and the origin of tyrannosaurs. Phil. Trans. R. Soc. Lond. B, 309, 395–460.

Chatterjee, S. 1987. A new theropod dinosaur from India with remarks on the Gondwana-Laurasia connection in the Late Triassic. Geophysical Monograph Six, 183–189.

Colbert, E. H. 1962. The weight of dinosaurs. Amer. Mus. Novit., 2076, 1-16.

Colbert, E. H. 1970. A saurischian dinosaur from the Triassic of Brazil. Amer. Mus. Novitates, 2405, 1–39.

Colbert, E. H., and Russell, D. A. 1969. The small dinosaur *Dromaeosaurus.* Amer. Mus. Novit., 2380, 1–49.

Comte, A. 1835. Cours de Philosophie Positive. Paris.

Coombs, W. P. 1978. Theoretical aspects of cursorial adaptations in dinosaurs. Quart. Rev. Biol., 53, 393–418.

Coombs, W. P. 1980. Swimming ability of carnivorous dinosaurs. Science, 207, 1198–1200.

Cope, E. D. 1866. Remarks on dinosaur remains from New Jersey. Acad. Nat. Sci. Philadelphia Proc., 275–279.

Cope, E. D. 1870. Synopsis of the extinct Batrachia, Reptilia, and Aves of North America. Amer. Philosophical Soc. Trans. n. s., 14, 1–252.

Cope, E. D. 1878. A new opisthocoelous dinosaur. Amer. Nat., XII, 406.

Cope, E. D. 1887. A contribution to the history of the vertebrata of the Trias of North America. Proc. Amer. Philosophical Soc., XXIV, 209–228.

Cracraft, J. 1971a. Caenagnathiformes: Cretaceous birds convergent in jaw mechanism to dicynodont reptiles. J. Paleont., 45, 805–809.

Cracraft, J. 1971b. The functional morphology of the hind limb of the domestic pigeon, *Columba livia.* Bull. Amer. Mus. Nat. Hist., 144, 175–268.

Craighead, F. C. 1979. Track of the Grizzly. Sierra Club Books, San Francisco.

Crompton, A. W. 1968. The enigma of the evolution of mammals. Optima, 18, 137–151.

Crowley, T. J., et al. 1986. Role of seasonality in the evolution of climate during the last 100 million years. Science, 231, 579–584.

Crutzen, P. 1987. Acid rain at the K/T boundry. Nature, 330, 108–109.

Currie, P. J. 1985. Cranial anatomy of *Stenonychosaurus inequalis* (Saurischia, Theropoda) and its bearing on the origin of birds. Canadian J. Earth Sci., 22, 1643–1658.

Currie, P. J. 1987a. Bird-like characteristics of the jaws and teeth of troodontid theropods (Dinosauria, Saurischia). J. Vert. Paleont., 7, 72–81.

Currie, P. J. 1987b. Theropods of the Judith River Formation of Dinosaur Provincial Park, Alberta, Canada. 52–59 in Currie, P. J., and Koster, E. (eds), Fourth Symposium on Mesozoic Terrestrial Ecosystems. Tyrrell Museum, Drumheller, Canada.

Currie, P. J. 1987c. New approaches to studying dinosaurs in Dinosaur Provincial Park. 100–117 in Czerkas, S. J. , and Olson, E. C. (eds), Dinosaurs Past and Present, II. Natural History Museum of Los Angeles County, Los Angeles.

Czerkas, S. J., and Olson, E. C. (eds). 1987. Dinosaurs Past and Present, two volumes. Natural History Museum of Los Angeles County, Los Angeles.

Czerkas, S., and Glut, D. 1982. Dinosaurs, Mammoths and Cavemen: The Art of Charles Knight. E. P. Dutton Inc., New York.

Davies, K. L. 1987. Duckbill dinosaurs from the North Slope of Alaska. J. Paleont., 61, 198–200.

Davis, M., Hut, P., and Muller, R. A. 1984. Extinction by periodic comet showers. Nature, 308, 715–717.

DeCourten, F. L., and Russell, D. A. 1985. A specimen of *Ornithomimus velox* (Theropoda, Ornithomimidae) from the terminal Cretaceous Kaiparowits Formation of Southern Utah. J. Paleont., 59, 1091–1099.

Deperet, C., and Savorin, J. 1925, Sur la découverte d'une faune vertebrea à Timimoun (Sahara occidental). C.R. Acad. Sci. Paris, 181, 1108–1111.

Desmond, A. J. 1976. The Hot-Blooded Dinosaurs. The Dial Press, New York.

Diamond, J. M. 1986. How great white sharks, sabre-toothed cats and soldiers kill. Nature, 322, 773–774.

Dodson, P., Behrensmeyer, A. K., Bakker, R. T., and McIntosh, J. S. 1980. Taphonomy and paleoecology of the dinosaur beds of the Jurassic Morrison Formation. Paleobiol., 6, 208–232.

Dong, Z. 1973. Dinosaurs from Wuerho (in Chinese). Mem. Inst. Vert. Paleont. Paleoanthrop., Acad. Sinica, 11, 45–52.

Dong, Z. 1984. A new theropod dinosaur from the Middle Jurassic of Sichuan Basin (in Chinese). Vert. Palasiatica. XXII, 213–218.

Dong, Z., Chang, L., Li, X., and Zhou, S. 1978. Note on a new carnosaur (*Yangchuanosaurus shangyouensis* gen. et sp. nov.) from the Jurassic of Yangchuan district. Szechuan Province (in Chinese). Kexue Tongbao, 23(5), 302–304.

Dong, Z., and Tang, Z. 1985. A new mid-Jurassic theropod (*Gasosaurus constructus* gen. et sp. nov.) from Dashanpu, Zigong, Sichuan Province, China (in Chinese). Vert. Palasiatica, XXIII, 77–83.

Dong, Z., Zhou, S., and Zhang, Y. 1983. The dinosaurian remains from Sichuan Basin, China (in Chinese). Palaeont. Sinica, 162, 1–147.

Dusheck, J. 1985. Arctic dinosaurs raise questions. Sci. News, 128, 135.

Douglas, J. G., and Williams, G. W. 1982. Southern polar forests, the early Cretaceous floras of Victoria and their paleoclimatic significance. Palaeogeog., Palaeoclimat., Palaeoecol., 39, 171–185.

Earle, M. 1987. A flexible body mass in social carnivores. Amer. Nat., 129, 755–760.

Ellenberger, P. 1974. Le Stormberg superior—I le biome de la zone B/1. Palaeovert., Mem. extraord. Montpellier, 5, 1–141.

Eltringham, S. K. 1982. Elephants. Blanford Press, Dorset.

Eudes-Deslongchamps, J. A. 1838. Mémoire sur le *Poikilopleuron bucklandi,* grand saurien fossile, intermédiaire entre les crocodiles et les lezards. Mem. Soc. Linnéanne de Normandie, 6, 37–146.

Farlow, J. O. 1976a. Speculations about the diet and foraging behavior of large carnivorous dinosaurs. Amer. Midland Nat., 95, 186–191.

Farlow. J. O. 1976b. A consideration of the trophic dynamics of a Late Cretaceous large-dinosaur community (Oldman Formation). Ecology, 57, 841–857.

Farlow. J. O. 1981. Estimates of dinosaur speeds from a new trackway site in Texas. Nature, 294, 747–748.

Farlow. J.O. 1986. In the footsteps of dinosaurs? Nature, 323, 390.

Farlow. J. O. 1987. A Guide to Lower Cretaceous Dinosaur Footprints and Tracksites of the Paluxy River Valley, Somervell County, Texas. Baylor University, Waco.

Fedak, M. A., and Seeherman, H. J. 1979. Reappraisal of energetics of locomotion shows identical cost in bipeds and quadrupeds including ostrich and horse. Nature, 282, 713–716.

Feduccia, A. 1980. The Age of Birds. Harvard Univ. Press, Cambridge.

Feduccia, A. 1986. The scapulocoracoid of flightless birds: A primitive avian character similar to that of theropods. Ibis, 128, 128–131.

Fox. W. 1866. Another new Wealden reptile. Geol. Mag., 3, 383.

Fraas, E. 1913. Die neuesten Dinosaurierfunde in der schwabischen Trias. Naturwiss., 45, 1097–1100.

Galton, P. M. 1973. A femur of a small theropod dinosaur from the Lower Cretaceous of England. J. Paleont., 47, 996–1001.

Galton, P. M. 1974. *Iliosuchus,* a Jurassic dinosaur from Oxfordshire and Utah. Palaeontology, 19, 587–589.

Galton, P. M. 1977. On *Staurikosaurus pricei,* an early saurischian dinosaur from the Triassic of Brazil, with notes on the Herrerasauridae and Poposauridae. Palaeont. Z., 51, 234–245.

Galton, P. M. 1982. *Elaphrosaurus,* an ornithomimid dinosaur from the Upper Jurassic of North America and Africa. Palaeont. Z., 56, 265–275.

Galton, P. M. 1985. The poposaurid thecodontian *Teratosaurus suevicus* V. Meyer, plus referred specimens mostly based on prosauropod dinosaurs. Stuttgarter Beitrage zur Naturkunde, B, 116, 1–29.

Galton, P. M., and Jensen, J. A. 1979. A new large theropod dinosaur from the Upper Jurassic of Colorado. Brigham Young Univ. Geol. Stud., 26(2), 1–12.

Galton, P. M., and Powell, H.P. 1980. The ornithischian dinosaur *Camptosaurus prestwichii* from the Upper Jurassic of England. Palaeontology, 23, 411–443.

Garland, T. 1983. The relation between maximal running speed and body mass in terrestrial mammals. J. Zool, Lond., 199, 1557–1570.

Gauthier, J. 1987. Saurischian monophyly and the origin of birds. Mem. Calif. Acad. Sci., 8, 1–55.

Gauthier, J., and Padian, K. 1984. Phylogenetic, functional and aerodynamic analysis of the origin of birds. 185–198 in Hecht, M. K., Ostrom, J. H., Viohl, G., and Wellnhofer, P. (eds), The Beginnings of Birds. Fruende des Jura-Museums, Eichstatt.

George, J. C., and Berger, A. J. 1966. Avian Myology. Academic Press, New York.

Gessamen, J. A. 1979. Methods of estimating the energy cost of free existence. 3–31 in Gessamen, J. A. (ed), Ecological Energetics of Homeotherms. Utah State University Press, Logan.

Gilmore, C. W. 1920. Osteology of the carnivorous dinosauria in the United States National Museum. U. S. Nat. Mus. Bull., 110, 1–159.

Gilmore, C. W. 1924. A new coelurid dinosaur from the Belly River Cretaceous of Alberta. Bull. Can. Geol. Surv. Dept. Mines, 38, 1–12.

Gilmore, C. W. 1933. On the dinosaurian fauna of the Iren Dabasu Formation. Bull. Amer. Mus. Nat. Hist., 67, 23–78.

Gilmore, C. W. 1946. A new carnivorous dinosaur from the Lance Formation of Montana. Smith. Misc. Coll., 106, 1–19.

Gingerich, P. D. 1973. Skull of *Hesperornis* and early evolution of birds. Nature, 243, 70–73.

Glut, D. F. 1982. The New Dinosaur Dictionary. Citadel Press, Secaucus, New Jersey.

Gordon, J. E. 1978. Structures, or Why Things Don't Fall Down. Penguin Books, Middlesex.

Gould, S. J. 1985. A clock of evolution. Natural History, 94(4), 12–25.

Gregory, W. K. 1912. Notes on the principles of quadrupedal locomotion and the mechanisms of the limbs in hoofed animals. Ann. New York Acad. Sci., 22, 267–292.

Halstead, L. B. 1970. *Scrotum humanum* Brookes 1763—the first named dinosaur. J. Insignificant Res., 5, 14–15.

Halstead, L. B., and Halstead, J. 1981. Dinosaurs. Blanford Press, Dorset.

Harrison, C. J. O., and Walker, C. A. 1975. The Bradycnemidae, a new family of owls from the Upper Cretaceous of Romania. Palaeontology, 18, 563–570.

Harland, W. B., et al. 1982. A Geologic Time Scale. Cambridge University Press, Cambridge.

Hasegawa, Y. 1986. Gobi Desert Dinosaurs Exhibition. Japan Cultural Association.

Hastings. R. J. 1987. New observations on Paluxy tracks confirm their dinosaurian origin. J. Geol. Education, 35, 4–15.

Haubold, H. 1986. Archosaur footprints at the terrestrial Triassic-Jurassic transition. 189–201 in Padian, K., The Beginning of the Age of Dinosaurs. Cambridge Univ. Press, Cambridge.

Heilmann, G. 1926. Origin of the Birds. Witherby, London.

Hitchcock, E. 1848. An attempt to discriminate and describe the animals that made the fossil footmarks of the United States, and especially of New England. Mem. Amer. Acad. Arts Sci., 3, 129–256.

Hopson, J. A. 1980. Relative brainsize in dinosaurs: Implications for dinosaur endothermy. 287–310 in Thomas, D. K., and Olson, E. C. (eds), A Cold Look at the Warm Blooded Dinosaurs. AAAS, Washington, D. C.

Hotton, N. 1980. An alternative to dinosaur endothermy: The happy wanderers. 311–350 in Thomas, D. K., and Olson, E. C. (eds), A Cold Look at the Warm Blooded Dinosaurs. AAAS, Washington, D.C.

Hou, L., and Zhicheng, L. 1984. A new fossil bird from the Lower Cretaceous of Gansu, and the early evolution of birds. Sci. Sinica, B, XXVII, 1296–1302.

Houstan, D. C. 1979. The adaptations of scavengers. 263–286 in Sinclair, A. R. E., and Norton-Griffiths, M. (eds), Serengeti; Dynamics of an Ecosystem. Univ. Chicago Press, Chicago.

Howell, A. B. 1944. Speed in animals. Univ. Chicago Press, Chicago.

Howgate, M. E. 1984. Problems of the osteology of *Archaeopteryx*: Is the Eichstatt specimen a distinct genus? 105–112 in Hecht, M. K., Ostrom, J. H., Viohl, G., and Wellnhofer, P. (eds), The Beginnings of Birds. Fruende des Jura-Museums, Eichstatt.

Hsu, K. J. 1986. The Great Dying. Harcourt Brace Jovanovich, New York.

Hu, S.-Y. 1964. Carnosaurian remains from Alashan, Inner Mongolia. Vert. Palasiatica, 8(1), 56–63.

Huene, F. R. von. 1910. Ein primitiver Dinosaurier aus der mittleren Trias von Elgin. Geol. Pal. Abh. n. s., 8, 315–322.

Huene, F. R. von. 1923. Carnivorous Saurischia in Europe since the Triassic. Bull. Geol. Soc. Am., 34, 449–458.

Huene, F. R. von. 1926. The carnivorous saurischia in the Jura and Cretaceous formations principally in Europe. Rev. Mus. La Plata, 29, 35–167.

Huene, F. R. von. 1932. Die fossile reptil-ordung Saurischia, ihre Entwicklung und Geschichte. Mon. Geol. Palaeont., 1(4), 1–361.

Huene, F. R. von. 1934. Ein neuer Coelurosaurier in der thuringischen Trias. Palaeont. Zeit., 16, 149–170.

Huxley, T. H. 1868. On the animals which are most nearly intermediate between birds and reptiles. Geol. Mag., 5, 357–365.

Janensch, W. 1920. Uber *Elaphrosaurus bambergi* und die Megalosaurier aus den Tendaguru-Schichten Deutsch-Ostafrikas. Sitzber. Ges. Naturforsch. Freunde., 225–235.

Janensch, W. 1925. Die Coelurosauria und Theropoden der Tendaguru-Schichten Deutsch-Ostafrikas. Palaeontographica, Suppl. 7(1), 1–99.

Jensen, J. A. 1981. Another look at *Archaeopteryx* as the World's oldest bird. Encyclia, 58, 109–128.

Jensen, J. A. 1985. Uncompahgre dinosaur fauna: a preliminary report. Great Basin Nat., 45, 710–720.

Jerzykiewicz, T., and Sweet, A. R. 1987. Semiarid floodplain as a paleoenvironmental setting of the Upper Cretaceous dinosaurs: Sedimentological evidence from Mongolia and Alberta. 120–124 in Currie, P. J., and Koster, E. (eds), Fourth Symposium on Mesozoic Terrestrial Ecosystems. Tyrrell Museum, Drumheller, Canada.

Johnston, P. A. 1979. Growth rings in dinosaur teeth. Nature, 278, 635–636.

Kesler, E. 1984. Lower Cretaceous birds from Cornet (Roumania). 119–121 in Reif, W. E., and Westphal, F. (eds), Third Symposium on Mesozoic Terrestrial Ecosystems. ATTEMPTO-Verlag, Tübingen.

Kielan-Jaworowska, Z. 1969. Hunting for Dinosaurs. MIT Press, Cambridge.

Kielan-Jaworowska, Z. 1974. Migrations of the multituberculata and the Late Cretaceous connections between Asia and North America. Ann. South Afr. Mus., 64, 231–243.

Kitchner, A. 1987. Function of Claw's claws. Nature, 325, 114.

Kruuk, H. 1972. The Spotted Hyaena: A Study of Predation and Social Behaviour. Univ. Chicago Press, Chicago.

Kuban, G. J. 1986. A summary of the Taylor site evidence. Creation/Evolution, XVII, 6(1), 10–18.

Kurochkin, E. N. 1985. A true carinate bird from Lower Cretaceous deposits in Mongolia and other evidence of early Cretaceous birds in Asia. Cretaceous Res., 6, 271–278.

Kurten, B. 1969. Sexual dimorphism in fossil mammals. 226–227 in Westermann, G. E. G. (ed), Sexual Dimorphism in Fossil Metazoa and Taxonomic Implications. E. Schweizerbart'sche Verlagsbuchhandlung, Stuttgart.

Kurten, B. 1976. The Cave Bear Story. Columbia University Press, New York.

Kurzanov, S. M. 1976. New carnosaur from the Late Cretaceous Nogon-Tsav, Mongolia (in Russian). Joint Soviet-Mongolian Paleont. Exp., Trans., 3, 93–104.

Kurzanov, S. M. 1981. *Avimimus* and the problem of the origin of birds (in Russian). Joint Soviet-Mongolian Paleont. Exp., Trans., 24, 104–109.

Kurzanov, S. M. 1982. Structural characteristics of the fore limbs of *Avimimus*. Paleont. J., 16(3), 108–112.

Kurzanov, S. M. 1983. New data on the pelvic structure of *Avimimus*. Paleont. J., 17(4), 110–111.

Kurzanov, S. M. 1985. The skull structure of the dinosaur *Avimimus*. Paleont. J., 19(4), 92–99.

Kurzanov, S. M. 1987. Avimidae and the problem of the origin of birds (in Russian). Joint Soviet-Mongolian Paleont. Exp., Trans., 31, 1–95.

Lambe, L. M. 1902. New genera and species from the Belly River Series (mid-Cretaceous). Geol. Surv. Canada, Contrib. Canad. Palaeont., 3(2), 23–81.

Lambe, L. M. 1904. On *Dryptosaurus incrassatus* (Cope), from the Edmonton series of the North West Territory. Geol. Surv. Canada, Contrib. Canad. Palaeont., 3, 1–27.

Lambe, L. M. 1914. On a new genus and species of carnivorous dinosaur from the Belly River Formation of Alberta. Ottawa Nat., 28, 13–20.

Lambe, L. M. 1917. The Cretaceous theropodous dinosaur *Gorgosaurus*. Geol. Surv. Canada, Mem., 100, 1–84.

Laws, R. M., Parker, I. S. C., and Johnstone, R. C. B. 1975. Elephants and their habitats. Clarendon Press, Oxford.

Leahy, G. D. 1987. The gradual extinction of dinosaurs: Fact or artifact? 138–143 in Currie, P. J., and Koster, E. (eds), Fourth Symposium on Mesozoic Terrestrial Ecosystems. Tyrrell Museum, Drumheller, Canada.

Lehman, T. M. 1987. Late Maastrichtian paleoenvironments and dinosaur biogeography in the western interior of North America. Palaeogeog., Palaeoclimat., Palaeoecol., 60, 189–217.

Leidy, J. 1856. Notices of remains of extinct reptiles and fishes, discovered by Dr. F. V. Hayden in the badlands of the Judith River, Nebraska Territory. Proc. Nat. Acad. Sci., Philadel., 8, 72–73.

Leonardi, G. 1984. Le impronte fossili di dinosauri. 165–186 in Sulle orme dei Dinosauri. Paleont. Ricatore (C.N.P.Q) del Brasile.

Lewin, R. 1987. Bottlenecked Cheetahs. Science, 235, 1327.

Lockley, M. 1984. Dinosaur tracking. Sci. Teacher, 51, 18–24.

Lockley, M. G. 1988. Review (of Farlow, 1987). J. Vert. Paleont., 8, 110–112.

Lockley, M., Houck, K., and Prince, N. K. 1986. North America's largest dinosaur trackway site: Implications for Morrison Formation paleoecology. Geol. Soc. Amer. Bull. 97, 1163–1176.

Lull, R. S. 1953. Triassic life of the Connecticut Valley. Bull. Conn. Geol. Nat. Hist. Surv., 81, 1–331.

McGowen, C. 1979. The hindlimb musculature of the Brown Kiwi, *Apteryx australis mantelli*. J. Morph., 160, 33–74.

McGowen, C. 1982. The wing musculature of the Brown Kiwi *Apteryx australis mantelli* and its bearing on ratite affinities. J. Zool., 197, 179–219.

McGowen, C. 1983. The Successful Dragons. Samuel Stevens & Co., Toronto.

McGowen, C. 1984. Evolutionary relationships of ratites and carinates: Evidence from ontogeny of the tarsus. Nature, 307, 733–735.

McGowen, C. 1986. The wing musculature of the Weka (*Gallirallus australis*), a flightless rail endemic to New Zealand. J. Zool., 210, 305–346.

MacMahon, T. A. 1984. Muscles, Reflexes and Locomotion. Princeton Univ. Press, Princeton.

Madsen, J. H. 1974. A new theropod dinosaur from the Upper Jurassic of Utah. J. Paleont., 48, 27–31.

Madsen, J. H. 1976a. *Allosaurus fragilis*: A revised osteology. Bull. Utah Geol. Min. Surv., 109, 1–51.

Madsen, J. H. 1976b. A second new theropod dinosaur from the Upper Jurassic of Utah. Utah Geol., 3, 51–60.

Maleev, E. A. 1954. A new turtle-like saurian from Mongolia. Priroda, 3, 106–108.

Maleev, E. A. 1955. Gigantic carnivorous dinosaurs of Mongolia (in Russian). Dokladi Akad. Nauk. SSSR, 104, 634–637.

Maleev, E. A. 1974. Giant carnosaurs of the family Tyrannosauridae (in Russian). Joint Soviet-Mongolian Paleont. Exp., 1, 132–191.

Marsh, O.C. 1877. Notice of new dinosaurian reptiles. Amer. J. Sci., 14, 514–516.

Marsh, O. C. 1878. Notice of new dinosaurian reptiles. Amer. J. Sci., 15, 241–244.

Marsh, O. C. 1879. Notice of new Jurassic reptiles. Amer. J. Sci., 21, 501–505.

Marsh, O. C. 1880. Odontornithes: A monograph on the extinct toothed birds of North America. Prof. Paper, Engineering Dept., U.S. Army, 18, 1–201.

Marsh, O.C. 1884. Principal characters of American Jurassic dinosaurs, 8: The order of Theropoda. Amer. J. Sci., 27, 329–340.

Marsh, O. C. 1890. Description of new dinosaurian reptiles. Amer. J. Sci., 39, 81–86.

Martin, L. D. 1984a. The origin of birds and avian flight. 105–129 in Johnston, R. F. (ed), Current Ornithology. Plenum Press, London.

Martin, L. D. 1984b. The relationship of *Archaeopteryx* to other birds. 177–184 in Hecht. M. K., Ostrom, J. H., Viohl, G., and Wellnhofer, P. (eds), The Beginnings of Birds. Fruende des Jura-Museums, Eichstatt.

Martinez, R., Gimenez, O., Rodriguez, J., and Bochatey, G. 1986.

Xenotarsosaurus bonapartei nov. gen. et sp. (Carnosauria, Abelisauridae), un nuevo theropoda de la Formacion Bajo Barreal Chubut, Argentina. Actas IV Congreso Argent. Paleont. Biostratig, 2, 23–31.

Marx, J. L. 1978. Warm-blooded dinosaurs: Evidence pro and con. Science, 199, 1424–1426.

Matthew, W. D., and Brown, B. 1922. The family Deinodontidae with a notice of a new genus from the Cretaceous of Alberta. Bull. Amer. Mus. Nat. Hist., 46, 367–385.

Mech, L. D. 1970. The Wolf. Natural History Press, New York.

Meyer, H. von. 1832. Palaeologica zur Geschichte der Erde und ihrer Geschopfe. Frankfurt am Main.

Meyer, H. von. 1861. *Archaeopteryx lithographica* (Vogel-Feder) und *Pterodactylus* von Solnhofen. Neues Jb. Miner. Geol. Palaeont., 678–679.

Meyer, L. L. 1986. D-day on the painted desert. Arizona Highways, 62(7), 2–13.

Milner, A. R. 1985. *Cosesaurus*—the last proavian? Nature, 315, 544.

Milner, A., and Croucher, R. 1987. Claws. British Museum (Natural History), London.

Molnar, R. E. 1973. The cranial morphology and mechanics of *Tyrannosaurus rex* (Reptilia: Saurischia). Univ. Calif. at Los Angeles, PhD Thesis.

Molnar, R. E. 1974. A distinctive theropod dinosaur from the Upper Cretaceous of Baja California. J. Paleont., 48, 1009–1017.

Molnar, R. E. 1980. An albertosaur from the Hell Creek Formation of Montana. J. Paleont., 54, 102–108.

Molnar, R. E., and Pledge, N. S. 1980. A new theropod dinosaur from South Australia. Alcheringa, 4, 281–287.

Morell, V. 1987. The birth of a heresy. Discover, 8(3), 26–50.

Muybridge, E. 1887. Animals In Motion. Dover Books (1957), New York.

Nelson, R. C., and Bookhout, T. A. 1980. Counts of periosteal layers invalid for aging Canada Geese. J. Wildlife Manage., 44, 518–521.

Newman, B. H. 1970. Stance and gait in the flesh-eating dinosaur *Tyrannosaurus*. Biol. J. Linn. Soc., 2, 119–123.

Nicholls, E. L., and Russell, A. P. 1985. Structure and function of the pectoral girdle and forelimb of *Struthiomimus altus* (Theropoda: Ornithomimidae). Palaeontology, 28, 643–677.

Norberg, U. M. 1985. Evolution of vertebrate flight: An aerodynamic model for the transition from gliding to active flight. Amer. Nat., 126, 303–327.

Norman, D. 1985. The Illustrated Encyclopedia of Dinosaurs. Crescent Books, New York.

Novas, F. 1987. Un probable teropodo (Saurisquia) de la Formacion Ischigualasto (Triasico Superior), San Juan, Argentina. IV Congress Argentino de Paleontologia Biostratigraphica, 2, 1–6.

Officer, C. B., et al. 1987. Late Cretaceous and paroxysmal Cretaceous/Tertiary extinctions. Nature, 326, 143–149.

Oliphant, L. W. 1983. First observations of brown fat in birds. Condor, 85, 350–354.

Olsen, P. E., and Galton, P. M. 1977. Triassic-Jurassic tetrapod extinctions: Are they real? Science, 197, 983–986.

Olsen, P. E., and Sues, H.-D. 1986. Correlation of continental Late

Triassic and Early Jurassic sediments, and patterns of the Triassic-Jurassic transition. 321–351 in Padian, K., The Beginning of the Age of Dinosaurs. Cambridge Univ. Press, Cambridge.

Olson, S. L. 1985. The fossil record of birds. 80–238 in Farner, D. S., King, J. R., and Parkes, K. C. (eds), Avian Biology VIII. Academic Press, New York.

Olson, S. L., and Feduccia, A. 1979. Flight capability and the pectoral girdle of *Archaeopteryx*. Nature, 278, 247–248.

Osborn, H. F. 1903. *Ornitholestes hermanni*, a new compsognathoid dinosaur from the Upper Jurassic. Bull. Amer. Mus. Nat. Hist., 19, 459–464.

Osborn, H. F. 1905. *Tyrannosaurus* and other Cretaceous carnivorous dinosaurs. Bull. Amer. Mus. Nat. Hist., 21, 259–265.

Osborn, H. F. 1906. *Tyrannosaurus*, Upper Cretaceous carnivorous dinosaur (second communication). Bull. Amer. Mus. Nat. Hist., 22, 281–296.

Osborn, H. F. 1912. Crania of *Tyrannosaurus* and *Allosaurus*. Amer. Mus. Nat. Hist. Mem. (n.s.), 1, 1–30.

Osborn, H. F. 1916. Skeletal adaptations of *Ornitholestes, Struthiomimus, Tyrannosaurus*. Bull. Amer. Mus. Nat. Hist., 35, 733–771.

Osborn, H. F. 1924. Three new Theropoda, *Protoceratops* zone, Central Mongolia. Amer. Mus. Nov., 144, 1–12.

Osborn, H. F., and Mook, C. C. 1921. *Camarasaurus, Amphicoelias*, and other sauropods of Cope. Mem. Amer. Mus. Nat. Hist., n. s., 3, 249–387.

Osmolska, H. 1976. New light on the skull anatomy and systematic position of *Oviraptor*. Nature, 262, 683–684.

Osmolska, H. 1980. The Late Cretaceous vertebrate assemblages of the Gobi Desert, Mongolia. Mem. Soc. Geol. France, 139, 145–150.

Osmolska, H. 1981. Coossified tarsometatarsi in theropod dinosaurs and their bearing on the problem of bird origins. Palaeont. Polonica, 42, 79–95.

Osmolska, H. 1982. *Hulsanpes perlei* n.g. n.sp. (Deinonychosauria, Saurischia, Dinosauria) from the Upper Cretaceous Barun Goyot Formation of Mongolia. Neues Jb. Geol. Palaeont. Mh., 440–448.

Osmolska, H. 1987. *Borogovia gracilicrus* gen. et sp.n., a new troodontid dinosaur from the Late Cretaceous of Mongolia. Acta Paleont. Polonica, 32, 133–150.

Osmolska, H., and Roniewicz, E. 1969. Deinocheiridae, a new family of theropod dinosaurs. Palaeont. Polonica, 21, 6–19.

Osmolska, H., Roniewicz, E., and Barsbold, R. 1972. A new dinosaur, *Gallimimus bullatus* n. gen. n. sp. (Ornithomimidae) from the Upper Cretaceous of Mongolia. Palaeont. Polonica, 27, 103–143.

Ostrom, J. H. 1969a. Osteology of *Deinonychus antirrhopus*, an unusual theropod dinosaur from the Lower Cretaceous of Montana. Bull. Peabody Mus. Nat. Hist., 30, 1–165.

Ostrom, J. H. 1969b. Terrestrial vertebrates as indicators of Mesozoic climates. Proc. North Amer. Paleont. Conv., 347–376.

Ostrom, J. H. 1970. Stratigraphy and paleontology of the Cloverly Formation (Lower Cretaceous) of the Bighorn Basin area. Peabody Mus. Nat. Hist. Bull., 35, 1–234.

Ostrom, J. H. 1972a. Dinosaur. 176–179 in McGraw-Hill Yearbook, Science and Technology. New York.

Ostrom, J. H. 1972b. Were some dinosaurs gregarious? Palaeogeog., Palaeoclimat., Palaeoecol., 11, 287–301.

Ostrom, J. H. 1974. *Archaeopteryx* and the origin of flight. Quart. Rev. Biol., 49, 27–47.

Ostrom, J. H. 1976a. *Archaeopteryx* and the origin of birds. Biol. J. Linn. Soc., 8, 91–182.

Ostrom, J. H. 1976b. On a new specimen of the Lower Cretaceous theropod dinsaur *Deinonychus antirrhopus*. Breviora, 439, 1–21.

Ostrom, J. H. 1978. The osteology of *Compsognathus longipes* Wagner. Zitteliana, 4, 73–118.

Ostrom, J. H. 1980. *Coelurus* and *Ornitholestes*: Are they the same? 245–256 in Jacobs, L. L. (ed), Aspects of Vertebrate History. University of Northern Arizona Press, Flagstaff.

Ostrom, J. H. 1981. *Procompsognathus*—theropod or thecodont? Palaeontographica A, 175, 179–195.

Ostrom, J. H. 1986a. Social and unsocial behavior in dinosaurs. 41–61 in Evolution of Animal Behavior. Oxford University Press, Oxford.

Ostrom, J. H. 1986b. The cursorial origin of avian flight. 75–81 in Padian, K. (ed.), The Origin of Birds and the Evolution of Flight. California Academy of Sciences, San Francisco.

Ostrom, J. H. 1987. Romancing the dinosaurs. The Sciences, 27(3), 56–63.

Owen, R. 1841. Report on British fossil reptiles. Report Eleventh Meet. Brit. Assoc. Advanc. Sci., 66–204.

Owen, R. 1855. Monograph of the fossil Reptilia of the Wealden Formations II, Dinosauria. Palaeontogr. Soc., 1–54.

Owen, R. 1876. Monograph of the fossil Reptilia of the Wealden Formations VII, Crocodilia and Dinosauria? Palaeontogr. Soc., 2–7.

Padian, K. 1986. On the type material of *Coelophysis* Cope (Saurischia: Theropoda) and a new specimen from the Petrified Forest of Arizona (Late Triassic: Chinle Formation). 46–60 in Padian, K., The Beginning of the Age of Dinosaurs. Cambridge Univ. Press, Cambridge.

Parkinson, J. 1822. Outlines of Oryctology: An Introduction to the Study of Fossil Organic Remains. London.

Parks, W. A. 1926. *Struthiomimus brevitertius*—a new species of dinosaur from the Edmonton Formation of Alberta. Trans. Roy. Soc. Canada Ser. 3, 20(4), 65–70.

Parks, W. A. 1928a. *Albertosaurus arctunguis,* a new species of theropodous dinosaur from the Edmonton Formation of Alberta. Univ. Toronto Stud., Geol. Ser., 25, 1–42.

Parks, W. A. 1928b. *Struthiomimus samueli,* a new species of Ornithomimidae from the Belly River Formation of Alberta. Univ. Toronto Stud., 26, 1–24.

Parks, W. A. 1933. New species of dinosaurs and turtles from the Upper Cretaceous Formations of Alberta. Univ. Toronto Stud., Geol. Ser., 34, 1–19.

Parrish, J. M. 1986. Locomotor adaptations in the hindlimb and pelvis of the Thecodontia. Hunteria, 1(2), 2–35.

Parrish, J. M., and Carpenter, K. 1986. A new vertebrate fauna from the Dockum Formation (Late Triassic) of eastern New Mexico. 152–160 in Padian, K., The Beginning of the Age of Dinosaurs. Cambridge Univ. Press, Cambridge.

Parrish, J. T., et al. 1987. Cretaceous vertebrates from Alaska—

implications for dinosaur ecology. Abstracts, 40th Ann. Meet., Rocky Mt. Sect., Geol. Soc. Amer., 19(5), 326.

Paul, G. S. 1984a. The archosaurs: A phylogenetic study. 175–180 in Reif, W. E., and Westphal, F. (eds), Third Symposium on Mesozoic Terrestrial Ecosystems. ATTEMPTO-Verlag, Tübingen.

Paul, G. S. 1984b. The segnosaurian dinosaurs: Relics of the prosauropod-ornithischian transition? J. Vert. Paleont., 4, 507–515.

Paul, G. S. 1984c. The hand of *Archaeopteryx*. Nature, 310, 372.

Paul, G. S. 1987a. The science and art of restoring the life appearance of dinosaurs and their relatives. 4–49 in Czerkas, S. J., and Olson, E. C. (eds), Dinosaurs Past and Present, II. Natural History Museum of Los Angeles County, Los Angeles.

Paul, G. S. 1987b. Predation in the meat eating dinosaurs. 173–178 in Currie, P. J., and Koster, E. (eds), Fourth Symposium on Mesozoic Terrestrial Ecosystems. Tyrrell Museum, Drumheller, Canada.

Paul, G. S. 1988a. The horned theropods of the Morrison and Great Oolite, and the sickle-claw theropods of the Cloverly, Djadokhta and Judith River. Hunteria, 2(4),,1–9.

Paul, G. S. 1988b. Physiological, migratorial, climatological, geophysical, survival and evolutionary implications of polar dinosaurs. J. Paleont., 62, 640–652.

Paul, G. S. (in prep.). The giant meteoritic impacts and paroxysmal eruptions that did not kill off the dinosaurs.

Paul, G. S., and Chase, T. (in press). Reconstruction of fossil vertebrates. In Hodges, E. (ed), The Guild Handbook of Biological Illustration. Van Nostrand Reinhold, New York.

Perle, A. 1977. On the first discovery of *Alectrosaurus* (Tyrannosauridae, Theropoda) from the Late Cretaceous of Mongolia (in Russian). Problems Mongol. Geol., 1977(3), 104–113.

Perle, A. 1985. Comparative myology of the pelvic-femoral region in the bipedal dinosaurs. Paleont. J., 19, 105–109.

Piveteau, J. 1923. L'arrière-crane d'un dinosaurien carnivore de l' Oxfordien de Dives. Ann. Paleont., 12, 1–11.

Plot, R. 1677. The Natural History of Oxfordshire. Oxford.

Raath, M. A. 1969. A new coelurosaurian dinosaur from the Forest Sandstone of Rhodesia. Arnoldia, 4, 1–25.

Raath, M. A. 1977. The anatomy of the Triassic theropod *Syntarsus rhodesiensis* (Saurischia: Podokesauridae) and a consideration of its biology. PhD Thesis, Rhodes University, Salisbury.

Raath, M. A. 1984. The theropod *Syntarsus* and its bearing on the origin of birds. 219–228 in Hecht, M. K., Ostrom, J. H., Viohl, G., and Wellnhofer, P. (eds), The Beginnings of Birds. Fruende des Jura-Museums, Eichstatt.

Ratkevich, R. P. 1976. Dinosaurs of the Southwest. University of New Mexico Press, Albuquerque.

Raup, D. M. 1986. The Nemesis Affair. W. W. Norton & Co., New York.

Ray, G. E. 1941. Big for his day. Nat. Hist., 48, 36–39.

Reid, R. E. H. 1984. The histology of dinosaurian bone, and its possible bearing on dinosaurian physiology. Symp. Zool. Soc. Lond., 52, 629–663.

Reid, R. E. H. 1987. Claws' claws. Nature, 325, 487.

Reig, O. A. 1963. La presencia de dinosaurios en los "Estratos de

Ischigualastro" (Mesotriasico Superior) de las provincias de San Juan y la Rioja (Republic Argentina). Ameghiniana, 3, 1–20.

Retallack, G., and Leahy, G. D. 1986. Cretaceous-Tertiary dinosaur extinction. Science, 234, 1170–1171.

Ricqles, A. R. 1980. Tissue structures of dinosaur bone: Functional significance and possible relation to dinosaur physiology. 103–140 in Thomas, D. K., and Olson, E. C. (eds), A Cold Look at the Warm Blooded Dinosaurs. AAAS, Washington, D.C.

Rietschel, S. 1984. Feathers and wings of *Archaeopteryx,* and the question of her flight ability. 249–260 in Hecht, M. K., Ostrom, J. H., Viohl, G., and Wellnhofer, P. (eds), The Beginnings of Birds. Fruende des Jura-Museums, Eichstatt.

Rigby, J. K. 1987. The last of the North American dinosaurs. 119–135 in Czerkas, S. J., and Olson, E. C. (eds), Dinosaurs Past and Present, II. Natural History Museum of Los Angeles County, Los Angeles.

Romer, A. S. 1923. The pelvic musculature of saurischian dinosaurs. Bull. Amer. Mus. Nat. Hist., 48, 533–552.

Romer, A. S. 1971. Two new but incompletely known long-limbed pseudosuchians. Breviora, 378, 1–10.

Romer, A. S. 1972. *Lewisuchus admixtus,* gen. et. sp. nov., a further thecodont from the Chanares beds. Breviora, 390, 1–13.

Rozhdestvensky, A. K. 1965. Growth changes in Asian dinosaurs and some problems of their taxonomy. Paleont. J., 95–109.

Rozhdestvensky, A. K. 1974. A history of the dinosaur fauna from Asia and other continents and some problems of Paleogeography (in Russian). Trans. Joint Soviet-Mongol. Paleont. Exp., 1, 107–131.

Russell, D. A. 1969. A new specimen of *Stenonychosaurus* from the Oldman Formation (Cretaceous) of Alberta. Canadian J. Earth Sci., 6, 595–612.

Russell, D. A. 1970. Tyrannosaurs from the Late Cretaceous of western Canada. Nat. Mus. Nat. Sci., Publ. Paleont., 1, 1–34.

Russell, D. A. 1971. The disappearance of the dinosaurs. Canadian Geogr. J., 83(6), 204–215.

Russell, D. A. 1972. Ostrich dinosaurs from the Late Cretaceous of western Canada. Can. J. Earth Sci., 9, 375–402.

Russell, D. A. 1973. The environments of Canadian dinosaurs. Canadian Geogr. J., 87(1), 4–11.

Russell, D. A. 1977. A Vanished World: The Dinosaurs of Western Canada. National Museums of Canada, Ottawa.

Russell, D. A. 1984. The gradual decline of the dinosaurs—fact or fallacy? Nature, 307, 360–361.

Russell, D. A., Beland, P., and McIntosh, J. S. 1980. Paleoecology of the dinosaurs of Tendaguru (Tanzania). Mem. Soc. Geol. Fr., 59(139), 169–175.

Russell, D. A., and Sequin, R. 1982. Reconstruction of the small Cretaceous theropod *Stenonychosaurus inequalis* and a hypothetical dinosauroid. Syllogeous, 37, 1–43.

Sanz, J. L., Bonaparte, J. F., and Lacasa, A. 1988. Unusual Early Cretaceous birds from Spain. Nature, 331, 433–435.

Sauvage, M. H. E. 1882. Recherches sur les reptiles trouvés dans le gault de L'est du Bassin de Paris. Mem. Soc. Geol. Franc., 2, 1–41.

Schaller, G. B. 1972. The Serengeti Lion. Univ. of Chicago Press, Chicago.

Schmidt-Nielsen, K. 1972. How Animals Work. Cambridge Univ. Press, Cambridge.

Seeley, H. G. 1887. On *Aristosuchus pusillus* (Owen), being further notes on the fossils described by Sir. R. Owen as *Poikilopleuron pusillus,* Owen. Geol. Soc. Lond. Quart. J., 43, 221–228.

Sereno, P. C. 1984. The phylogeny of the Ornithischia, a reappraisal. 219–226 in Reif, W. E., and Westphal, F. (eds), Third Symposium on Mesozoic Terrestrial Ecosystems. ATTEMPTO-Verlag, Tübingen.

Seymour, R. S. 1976. Dinosaurs, endothermy and blood pressure. Nature, 262, 207–208.

Sloan, R. E., et al. 1986. Gradual dinosaur extinction and simultaneous ungulate radiation in the Hell Creek Formation. Science, 232, 629–633.

Spinar, Z. V., and Burian, Z. 1972. Life Before Man. American Heritage Press, New York.

Spotila, J. R., et al. 1973. A mathematical model for body temperatures of large reptiles: Implications for dinosaur ecology. Amer. Nat., 107, 391–404.

Sternberg, C. M. 1932. Two new theropod dinosaurs from the Belly River Formation of Alberta. Canadian Field-Nat., 46, 99–105.

Sternberg, C. M. 1933. A new *Ornithomimus* with complete abdominal cuirass. Canadian Field-Nat., 47, 79–83.

Sternberg, C. M. 1940. A toothless bird from the Cretaceous of Alberta. J. Paleont., 14, 81–85.

Stovall, J. W., and Langston, W. 1950. *Acrocanthosaurus atokensis,* a new genus and species of Lower Cretaceous Theropoda from Oklahoma. Amer. Midland Nat., 43(3), 696–728.

Stromer, E. 1915. Ergebnisse der forschungsreisen Prof. E. Stromers in den Westen Agyptens, Das original des Thero oden *Spinosaurus aegyptiacus* n. gen., n. sp. Abh. Bayer. Akad. Wissen.: Math.-natur. Abt., 13, 1–32.

Stromer, E. 1931. Ergebnisse der forschungsreisen Prof. E. Stromers in den Westen Agyptens, Ein Skelett-Rest von *Carcharodontosaurus* nov. gen. Abh. Bayer. Akad. Wissen.: Math.-natur. Abt., 9, 1–23.

Stromer, E. 1934. Ergebnisse der forschungsreisen Prof. E. Stromers in den Westen Agyptens, Dinosauria. Abh. Bayer. Akad. Wissen.: Math.-natur. Abt., 22, 1–79.

Sues, H.-D. 1977a. Dentaries of small theropods from the Judith River Formation (Campanian) of Alberta, Canada. Can. J. Earth Sci., 14, 587–592.

Sues, H.-D. 1977b. The skull of *Velociraptor mongoliensis,* a small theropod dinosaur from Mongolia. Palaeont. Z., 51, 173–184.

Sues, H.-D. 1978. A new small theropod dinosaur from the Judith River Formation (Campanian) of Alberta Canada. Zool. J. Linnean Soc., 62, 381–400.

Swinton, W. G. 1970. The Dinosaurs. George Allan & Unwin Ltd., London.

Talbot, M. 1911. *Podokesaurus holyokensis,* a new dinosaur of the Connecticut Valley. Amer. J. Sci., 31, 469–479.

Taquet, P. 1984a. Two new Jurassic specimens of coelurosaurs (Dinosauria). 229–232 in Hecht, M. K., Ostrom, J. H., Viohl, G., and Wellnhofer, P. (eds), The Beginnings of Birds. Fruende des Jura-Museums, Eichstatt.

Taquet, P. 1984b. A curious specialization of the skull of some Cretaceous carnivorous dinosaurs: The long and narrow snout of spinosaurids (in French). C. R. Acad. Sc. Paris II, 299(5), 217–222.

Taquet, P., and Welles, S. M. 1977. Redescription du crane de dinosaure theropode de dives (Normandie). Ann. Paleont. Vert., 63(2), 191–206.

Tarsitano, S. 1983. Stance and gait in theropod dinosaurs. Acta Palaeont. Polonica, 28, 251–264.

Tarsitano, S., and Hecht, M. K. 1982. A reconsideration of the reptilian relationships of Archaeopteryx. Zool. J. Linn. Soc., 69, 149–182.

Taylor, C. R., et al. 1979. Running in cheetahs, gazelles and goats: Energy cost and limb configuration. Amer. J. Physiol., 848–850.

Thulborn, R. A. 1975. Dinosaur polyphyly and the classification of archosaurs and birds. Aust. J. Zool., 23, 249–270.

Thulborn, R. A. 1982. Speeds and gaits of dinosaurs. Palaeogeog., Palaeoclimat., Palaeoecol., 38, 273–274.

Thulborn, R. A. 1984. The avian relationships of Archaeopteryx, and the origin of birds. Zool. J. Linnean Soc., 82, 119–158.

Thulborn, R. A. 1985. Birds as neotenous dinosaurs. Rec. New Zealand Geol. Surv., 9, 90–92.

Thulborn, R. A., and Hamley, T. L. 1984. A new paleoecological role in Archaeopteryx. 81–90 in Hecht, M. K., Ostrom, J. H., Viohl, G., and Wellnhofer, P. (eds), The Beginnings of Birds. Fruende des Jura-Museums, Eichstatt.

Thulborn, R. A., and Wade, M. 1984. Dinosaur trackways in the Winton Formation (Mid-Cretaceous) of Queensland. Mem. Queensland Mus., 21, 413–517.

Trotter, M. M., and McCulloch, B. 1984. Moas, Man and Middens. 708–740 in Martin, P. S., and Klein, R. G. (eds), Quaternary Extinctions. The University of Arizona Press, Tucson.

Viohl, G. 1984. Geology of the Solnhofen lithographic limestones and the habitat of Archaeopteryx. 31–44 in Hecht, M. K., Ostrom, J. H., Viohl, G., and Wellnhofer, P. (eds), The Beginnings of Birds. Fruende des Jura-Museums, Eichstatt.

Wagner, A. 1861. Neue beitrage zur kenntnis der urweltlichen fauna des lithographischen Schiefers; V Compsognathus longipes, Wagn. Abh. bayer Akad. Wiss., 9, 30–38.

Waldman, M. 1974. Megalosaurids from the Bajocian (Middle Jurassic) of Dorset. Palaeontology, 17, 325–339.

Walker, A. D. 1964. Triassic reptiles from the Elgin: Ornithosuchus and the origin of carnosaurs. Phil. Trans. R. Soc. (B), 248, 53–134.

Walker, A. D. 1972. New light on the origin of birds and crocodiles. Nature, 237, 257–263.

Walker, A. D. 1984. The braincase of Archaeopteryx. 123–134 in Hecht, M. K., Ostrom, J. H., Viohl, G., and Wellnhofer, P. (eds), The Beginnings of Birds. Fruende des Jura-Museums, Eichstatt.

Weems, R. 1987. A Late Triassic footprint fauna from the Culpepper Basin, Northern Virginia (USA). Trans. Amer. Phil. Soc., 77(1), 1–79.

Weisburd, S. 1986. Brushing up on dinosaurs. Sci. News, 130, 216–220.

Weisburd, S. 1987a. Sea cycle clock. Sci. News, 131, 154–155.

Weisburd, S. 1987b. Volcanoes and extinctions: Round two. Sci. News, 131, 248–250.

Wellnhofer, P. 1974. Das funfte Skelettexemplar von Archaeopteryx. Palaeontographica A, 147(4–6), 169–216.

Welles, S. P. 1954. New Jurassic dinosaur from the Kayenta Formation of Arizona. Bull. Geol. Soc. Amer., 65, 591–598.

Welles, S. P. 1970. *Dilophosaurus* (Reptilia: Saurischia), a new name for a dinosaur. J. Paleont., 44, 989.

Welles, S. P. 1971. Dinosaur footprints from the Kayenta Formation of northern Arizona. Plateau, 44, 27–38.

Welles, S. P. 1984. *Dilophosaurus wetherilli* (Dinosauria, Theropoda) osteology and comparisons. Palaeontographica A, 185, 85–180.

Welles, S. P., and Long, R. A. 1974. The tarsus of theropod dinosaurs. Ann. S. Afr. Mus. 44, 117–155.

Whetstone, K. N. 1983. Braincase of Mesozoic birds: I. New preparation of the "London" *Archaeopteryx*. J. Vert. Paleont. 2, 439–452.

Wilson, M. C., and Currie, P. J. 1985. *Stenonychosaurus inequalis* (Saurischia: Theropoda) from the Judith River (Oldman) Formation of Alberta: new findings on metatarsal structure. Canadian J. Earth Sci., 22, 1813–1817.

Witmer, L. M. 1987. The nature of the antorbital fossa of archosaurs: Shifting the null hypothesis. 230–235 in Currie, P. J., and Koster, E. (eds), Fourth Symposium on Mesozoic Terrestrial Ecosystems. Tyrrell Museum, Drumheller, Canada.

Woodward, A. S. 1901. On some extinct reptiles from Patagonia, of the genera *Miolania, Dinilysia,* and *Genyodectes*. Proc. Zool. Soc., Lond., 1, 169–184.

Woodward, A. S. 1910. On a skull of *Megalosaurus* from the Great Oolite of Minchinhampton (Gloucestershire). Quart. J. Geol. Soc., London, 66, 111–115.

Yalden, D. W. 1984. Forelimb function in *Archaeopteryx*. 91–98 in Hecht, M. K., Ostrom, J. H., Viohl, G., and Wellnhofer, P. (eds), The Beginnings of Birds. Fruende des Jura-Museums, Eichstatt.

Young, C. C. 1948. On two new saurischians from Lufeng, Yunnan. Bull. Geol. Soc., China, 28, 75–90.

INDEX

(Page numbers in boldface refer to main entries in catalog. Page numbers in *italics* refer to captions.)

443

445

447

Shanshanosaurus, 324–25
Shanshanosaurus
    huoyanshanensis, 325
shared-derived characters, 174
sharks, 38, 55, 63
shivering, in thermoregulation,
    151
shoulder girdle, 106–7, 107, 108,
    183
  beginnings of bird flight and,
    218, 359
shoulder joints, 184
shrews, 166
sickle-claws, 35, 195, 232, 323,
    374, 375, 377, 381
  bird origins and, 173
  claws of Noasaurus vs., 286
  hyperextendable second toes
    of, 195, 356, 357–58, 373
  see also dromaeosaurs;
    troodonts
Sinemurian Age, 60
sinuses, 90, 94, 99
sister clades or groups, 175
size:
  abundance related to, 74–75
  of dinosaurs vs. mammals, 54
  and gigantism in birds, 83–86
  locomotory energy
    consumption and, 405–6
  of mammals vs. predatory
    dinosaurs, 61–63
  metabolic rates and, 150, 154,
    157, 161–63, 168–69
  running speed and, 135–37,
    141–43, 142
  sexual variations in, 203–4
  speed of growth and, 155
  and survival of late
    Cretaceous cataclysm, 83
  temperature constancy and,
    54, 150, 162–63; see also
    bulk homeothermy
size squeezes, evolution and,
    163, 240
skeletal drawings, 226–27, 228–
    229
skin, 121–22
skull, 88–92, 90
  of Archaeopteryx, 350

of birds vs. predatory
    dinosaurs, 92
  braincase in, 101, 192, 193,
    194, 199
  diapsid openings in, 178–79,
    179
  drawings of, 227–28
  kineticism of, 88–92, 93
  length of, 233
  preorbital openings in, 88, 90,
    94, 98–99, 178–79
  see also head
sleep, 28–29, 29
smell, sense of, 98, 100, 381
snout, 124
  kinked, 191, 255, 256–57
Solnhofen Islands, 66, 66, 87,
    353, 355, 356, 357
songbirds (passerines), 86, 170
Sousa Formation, 130
South Pole, 159
species:
  as basic unit of taxonomy and
    systematics, 176
  formation rates of, 78–79
  genera with large number of,
    201–3
  identification of, 176–77
  names of, 229
specific gravity, 234
speed, 135–47
  anatomical design and, 138–
    143, 142
  calculated from trackways,
    137–38, 139
  elastic similarity and, 136–37,
    136, 143–45, 145, 146
  of flight, 216
  locomotory energy
    consumption and, 405
  measuring of, 145–46, 164
  of Ornithomimus, 386
  size and, 135–37, 141–43, 142
  of tyrannosaurs, 141–42, 142,
    144–45, 145, 146, 320, 364
sperm whales, 62–63
spinal column, 101–3, 110
  cantilevered over hind limbs,
    102–3
  cartilage discs in, 96, 101–2

of ceratosaurs, 103, 315
  fins on, 103
  musculature along, 103–4
Spinosauridae, 271–74
spinosaurs, 103, 257, 271–74
  in phylogenetic tree of
    predatory dinosaurs, 200
Spinosaurus, 67, 191, 228, 256,
    271, 273–74, 315, 317
Spinosaurus aegyptiacus, 237,
    273–74
splenial, 91
sprawling gait, 53
stallions, 35
Staurikosauria, 187, 244–46
Staurikosauridae, 244–46
staurikosaurs, 49, 187, 240,
    244–46, 247, 248, 261
  bipedalism in, 244, 246
  in phylogenetic tree of
    predatory dinosaurs, 185
Staurikosaurus, 245–46
Staurikosaurus pricei, 245–46,
    245, 246
  as juvenile of Herrerasaurus
    ischigualastensis, 249
stegosaurs, 63, 67, 266, 292,
    308, 407
Stegosaurus ungulatus, 65
Stenonychosaurus, 395
Stenonychosaurus inequalis, 397
sternal plate, 107, 107
Sternberg, C. M., 339
Stokesosaurus, 295, 311
Stokesosaurus clevelandi, 295
stomach, 106
storks, marabou, 85
Streptospondylus, 287, 288
Streptospondylus cuvieri, 287
stride length, 136, 137
Struthiomimidae, 378
Struthiomimus, 202, 384, 486
Struthiomimus altus, 387
Struthiomimus brevitertius, 392
Struthiomimus curreli, 389
Struthiomimus ingens, 392
Struthiomimus samueli, 390
Strzelecki, 303
Stubensandstein, herrerasaur
    remains in, 247–48